Workshop Proceedings:

Debating Multiculturalism 2

The Dialogue Society is a registered charity, established in London in 1999, with the aim of advancing social cohesion by connecting communities through dialogue. It operates nation-wide with regional branches across the UK. Through localised community projects, discussion forums, teaching programmes and capacity building publications it enable people to venture across boundaries of religion, culture and social class. It provides a platform where people can meet to share narratives and perspectives, discover the values they have in common and be at ease with their differences.

www.DialogueSociety.org

info@dialoguesociety.org

Tel: +44 (0)20 7619 0361

Dialogue Society

402 Holloway Road
London N7 6PZ

**DIALOGUE
SOCIETY**
LONDON 1999

Registered Charity No: 1117039

First published in Great Britain 2012

For citation please refer to this publication as *Draft Workshop Proceedings: Debating Multiculturalism 2*

© Dialogue Society 2012

ISBN 978-0-9569304-5-3

About the Workshop Editors

Steve Garner

Dr Steve Garner is senior lecturer in sociology at Aston University. He studied at Warwick before leaving education in Britain to go and live in Paris. There he did postgraduate work and taught in the University system. His PhD, on ethnicity, class, and gender in Guyana was completed in 1999. He has also worked outside academia, as a researcher at the Central Statistics Office, Ireland, and on EU projects for local government 1999-2001. He moved from Cork to take up a post in Sociology at the University of the West of England (UWE) in 2003, and came to Aston in October 2008. He is an internal associate of the InterLanD research centre. He is a member of the British Sociological Association; a Fellow of the Higher Education Authority, and External Examiner for the Department of Sociology and Politics, University of the West of Scotland, 2010-13.

Seref Kavak

Seref Kavak is a PhD candidate in Politics and International Relations at the Research Institute for Social Sciences at Keele University. He received his BA in Political Science and International Relations from Marmara University (Istanbul) and his MA in Modern Turkish History from Bogazici University (Istanbul). His MA thesis examined the transformation of a legal pro-Kurdish political party in Turkey with regard to the tension between ethnicity and national integrity. For one term he taught English and political history in Turkey. He currently researches diasporan associations in Britain focusing on their strategies and mechanisms for political mobilisation of the diasporan community and their political participation. His primary research interests are ethnicity, identity politics, cultural anthropology, social and transnational movements and political sociology. Seref's recent book titled *Kurdish Ethno-political Transformation in Turkey* has been publised by Lambert Academic Publishing (2012). He is also the author of a forthcoming book chapter in Turkish language titled "*Kürt Siyasetinin 2000'li Yılları: "Türkiyelileşme" ve Demokratik Toplum Partisi*" (Kurdish Ethno-politics in the 2000s: Turkey-fication and Democratic Society Party". Istanbul: Iletisim Yayinlari (forthcoming 2012). He enjoys ethnic and choral music and has sung in a number of polyphonic choirs.

Contents

About the Workshop Editors...3

Preface...9

Part 1: MULTICULTURALISM IN THEORY

Multiculturalism, 'Race', 'Post-Race': Implications for Pedagogy
Stephen Cowden and Gurnam Singh 11

Social Cohesion-a Benign Concept? Lived Experiences at the Borders
and Boundaries of 'Community'
Jackie Haq..25

Empowering Minority Communities While not Dismembering States:
Multiculturalism and the Model for Non-Territorial Autonomy
Ephraim Nimni..41

Multiculturalism: 'Spice' of Lives, 'Bane' of Legal Systems?
Esin Orucu 57

Dialogue and Multicultural Dynamics: Challenges to Hearing Cultures in
Conversation
Donal Carbaugh 71

Part 2: MULTICULTURALISM IN CONTINENTAL EUROPE

Was European Multiculturalism Destined to Fail?
Anya Topolski 85

Public Figures of Islam in Europe: Perspectives on Multicultural Public
Individuals
Cagla E. Aykac..99

Politics, Labour Markets, and the Feasibility of a Multicultural Spain
Francisco Beltran...111

Alevis' Struggle for Recognition in Turkey: an Analytical and Normative
Assessment
Devrim Kabasakal Badamchi...122

Diverse Feminisms in Turkey: Secular, Ethnic and Religious Women's
Movements
Omer Caha 137

Part 3: MULTICULTURALISM IN THE UK - I

Does Ethnic Diversity Lead to Community 'Inter-Ethnic Tensions'?
Reconciling the 'Contact' and 'Threat' Hypotheses: Ethnic Diversity
and the Moderating Effects of 'Inter-Ethnic Contact' and Community
Disadvantage Amongst White British Individuals in England and Wales
James Laurence 155

Rants Against Multiculturalism Caught on Camera in Britain: Racism
Without Races?
Fred Dervin 179

Faith in the Suburb: Discourses of Identity and Extremism in the Royal
Borough of Kingston upon Thames, UK
Rupa Huq...193

Black, Asian, and Minority Ethnic People (BAME) Political
Representation in the UK
Nader Fekri..207

Advancing Multiculturalism: Learning Lessons from Scholarly Advocacy
Karim Murji...235

Part 4: MULTICULTURALISM IN THE UK - II

Multiculturalism and the Impacts on Education Policy in England
Richard Race..243

Multi-Ethnic Schooling and the Future of Multiculturalism in the UK
Helen F. Wilson 259

Multiculturalism and Faith Traditions in the UK: Education,
Ethnography, Empiricism and Everyday Lives
Ian Williams..273

London: How Successful a Multicultural Model?
Jonathan Fryer 285

Unity and Diversity in a London Mosque
Judy Shuttleworth 295

Preface

The Dialogue Society has organised two academic workshops on the theme of 'Debating Multiculturalism' to take place in spring 2012. This publication comprises the papers accepted for 'Debating Multiculturalism 2', to take place in Istanbul at the beginning of May.

The Dialogue Society is organising this second workshop through its Birmingham Branch in partnership with Keele University and Fatih University, Istanbul. It is very grateful for the support of its two partners and to Fatih University for hosting the event. The first workshop, held in April, in Konya, was organised by the Dialogue Society's Leeds Branch in partnership with Leeds Metropolitan University and Mevlana University. While the first workshop focused primarily on the UK context this second workshop looks at multiculturalism across Europe as well as in the UK. Each workshop balances the perspectives of academics with those of practitioners concerned with intercultural relations.

The acute contemporary relevance of the topic of these workshops hardly requires introduction. Since the Second World War, European societies have increasingly experienced 'multiculturalism' in the sense of people of diverse cultural backgrounds living side by side. The 'state multiculturalism' publicly criticised last year in David Cameron's Munich Speech was a UK example of European government policies embodying a concern to ensure acceptance and respect for the cultural and religious identities of minorities. Cameron is one of a number of prominent voices in the European political mainstream, including also German Chancellor Angela Merkel and French President Nicolas Sarkozy, who claim that multiculturalism has failed to counteract fragmentation and extremism. Meanwhile, proponents of multiculturalism continue to stress its achievements in terms of reduced discrimination and progress towards inclusive, sustainable national identities. They urge that to abandon multiculturalism would be to abandon an achievable future of genuine equality, mutual respect and creative intercultural symbiosis. Whether multiculturalism should be jettisoned as a failure or defended as the path to a flourishing diversity is a crucial and pressing question for our time.

Istanbul, Turkey's largest city, is a stimulating location for discussions of multiculturalism in Europe. Turkey's recent record of combining political stability with economic growth and human rights reforms is concentrating minds on the capacity of the present European model of multiculturalism to cope with the eventual accession of Turkey to the EU. There is strong interest in the country in the so-called "Anglo-Saxon" practice of secularism as a framework for the ongoing evolution of multiculturalism. The city of Istanbul boasts a fascinating history of intercultural encounter, powerfully reflected in the Christian mosaics and Islamic calligraphy juxtaposed in the magnificent Hagia Sofia.

Naturally the views expressed in the papers are those of the authors and do not necessarily reflect the position and views of the Dialogue Society. The papers presented here are draft papers submitted and printed in advance of the workshop. A further volume of selected papers taken from the two workshops will be published in due course.

The Dialogue Society extends heartfelt thanks to the organising committee and especially our editors for the second workshop, Dr Steve Garner and Mr Seref Kavak.

Part I
MULTICULTURALISM IN THEORY

Multiculturalism, 'Race', 'Post-race': Implications for Pedagogy

Stephen Cowden[1] and Gurnam Singh

Introduction

"Racism is not a static phenomenon, but is constantly renewed and transformed." Frantz Fanon (1970 p.41)

In the above quote Frantz Fanon, the Martiniquan psychiatrist, philosopher and revolutionary reminds us that any attempts to theorise and talk about racism and therefore by association 'race'- and for that matter other aspects of human oppression and difference - are fraught with difficulties. This is not only because of the elusive and contested nature of the concepts involved, but, most critically, the subjectivity of those doing the theorising inevitably becomes part of the discussion (Singh and Cowden 2010). This is particularly so when one additionally invokes the discourses of 'post-race' alongside 'race'. In opening a discussion like this we recognise that there are some dangers; for example, are we simply engaging in ungrounded rhetorical speculation about 'how nice it would be if we could all be kinder to each other'? Or more significantly, as Tim Wise (2010) has recently outlined, is the term 'post-race' being used as a means of denying the on going significance and impact of racism, and thereby denying in repudiating the importance of anti-racist struggles? If the idea of 'post-race' potentially represents a conceptual turn or even

---

1 Dr Stephen Cowden is Senior Lecturer in Social Work Coventry University. He is originally from Melbourne Australia, but has lived in the UK since 1985. He did a BA at Melbourne University 1979 – 1983 and after leaving Australia and travelled throughout South Asia in 1984-5. After arriving in London he became involved in political campaigns in the areas of anti-racism, gay and lesbian rights and Irish solidarity. He worked in the NHS where he was an active trade unionist. He trained as a Social Worker in 1990-92 and then combined this work with further research in Australian studies (MA University of London 1992-94 and PhD University of Kent 1994 – 1999). He began work in the Social Work department at Coventry University in 2001 where his teaching and research interests concern Social Work and Social Theory, Critical Pedagogy and Ethics. Much of his work has been carried out collaboratively with Dr Gurnam Singh. He presently lives in Leamington Spa with his partner and three children.

more profoundly a paradigm shift, what is this toward? A useful starting point for our discussion comes from the work of W. E. B. Du Bois. The argument in his 1903 book *The Souls of Black Folk* about the 'colour line' represented one of the most influential and powerful framings of 'race' throughout most of the early 20th Century in the US and the post-colonial world. What is much less well known is Du Bois' later questioning of his own concept in the early 1950s following a series of visits to post war Poland. Reflecting on his experience in an essay for Jewish Life magazine entitled "The Negro and the Warsaw Ghetto," Du Bois outlines how the inhumanity of the Warsaw ghetto and the experience of the Jewish population invoked him to revise his idea about the contours of 'race';

> In the first place, the problem of slavery, emancipation and caste in the United States was no longer in my mind a separate and unique thing as I had so long conceived it. It was not even solely a matter of colour and physical and racial characteristics, which was particularly a hard thing for me to learn, since for a lifetime the colour line had been a real and efficient cause of misery. (Zuckerman 2004 p.45)

Coming out of the bitterness and brutality of the experience of racism in the US it was not just an intellectual and political challenge, but also a personal challenge to conceptualise the racialisation of 'white' people through Nazism and anti-semitism. The key point here is that the challenges in considering the idea of 'post-race' came from the starting point of anti-racism, of 'post-race' as an elaboration of anti-racism.

In that sense we have two broad aims in this discussion. In the first half we offer a contemporary reading of what we have called the discursive field of 'race – post-race', with a particular emphasis on the relationship between multiculturalism and 'race'. Firstly we discuss the way this field has been "renewed and transformed" by contemporary events; in particular the 'war on terror', the rise of religious authoritarianism, and the construction of Muslims as the other to the 'civilised world'. These events we argue have created an impasse for the state policy of multiculturalism whereby it has become trapped in the logic of assuming an equivalence between diversity on the one hand and social justice on the other. It is this concern that becomes the starting point for asserting a pedagogy of 'post-race'. While much of this paper is theoretical, in order to avoid remaining within an entirely abstract realm, we end the paper with a discussion of a short course we developed and delivered for the West Midlands Probation service staff on the "Preventing Violent Extremism" Agenda in which we sought to adopt a 'post –race' pedagogical perspective.

Multiculturalism and 'Race'

Whilst ideas about human difference arguably form a permanent feature of all human history, the idea of 'race' is a much more recent phenomena (Husband 1987). Broadly speaking, in terms of the systematic study of 'race' one can identify three pivotal points. The first can be understood as the emergence of scientific racism from the late eighteenth to the mid- twentieth century. The 'race' studied here was essentially a 'science' of physical differences, designed to explain and justify racist practices; in particular slavery and colonisation. The second key moment is represented by the emergence of political movements within European colonies and amongst oppressed so called 'racial' or 'national' groups in the colonial centre – the work of W.E.B. Du Bois is a classic statement of this position, and this lays the ground for modern anti-racism and anti-colonialism. It is also worth noting here that discourses of 'race' and 'nation' during this period and subsequently tend to become conflated (Anderson 1991). The third pivotal moment follows the revelation of the horrors of the Nazi racial state, resulting in the mass slaughter of Jews and other minorities on the ground of 'racial' impurity. It is through the impetus of these latter two moments that the international academic community rejected the 'scientific' basis of race and racial difference, and sociology of 'race' emerges for the first time (Hall 1980). This rejection of the notion of 'race' as a marker of human biological and/or moral superiority and inferiority has been crucial in allowing the concept to be understood through sociological categories such as ideology, social construction or as set of discourses. Seen in this way 'race' becomes 'racialisation', through which meanings become conferred on physical or cultural differences (Miles 2003).

The contemporary conception of Multiculturalism also becomes possible at this point, and what emerges is a kind of 'Enlightenment strategy' where the task becomes one of not ignoring 'race' but rather exposing and undermining the notion of superior or inferior 'races' by demonstrating the falsehood of these claims. While the prevailing attitudes and policies seeking to address the presence of racialised minorities had historically been accompanied by more exclusionary forms of nationalism, manifested at both state (in the form of immigration laws) and non-state (in the form of racist and far-right political movements) levels, this new approach to cultural diversity offered the prospect of an altogether positive view of cultural pluralism. Not withstanding the critiques of it by more radical black and anti-racist movements (see for example CCCS 1982; Sivanandan 1985; 1990), the concept of multiculturalism was hugely significant as an umbrella term for a broad progressive consensus around issues of 'race', hence its importance at the level of state policy.

Whilst this strategy of seeking to shift the social conception of 'race' to a benign marker of human difference, or in later variant, a celebration of human diversity, have been very significant there were some crucial weaknesses within this. Given that the idea of 'race' has historically been reliant on notions of superiority and inferiority, there was always a danger that supposedly 'benign' markers of difference could mutate into forms that are anything but benign. Nothing illustrates this more significantly than the shifting significance of "faith" as a marker of social difference within multiculturalist discourse. In the 1980s, concerns around 'faith' were present, but remained a minor issue as secular anti-racist ideas provided the backbone of these arguments. However as secular anti-racist movements went into decline, the definition of multiculturalism became increasingly dominated by religious and faith-based definitions of ethnicity. The situation today is one where the anti-racist element within Multiculturalism, concerned essentially with a critique of power, has been replaced by an orthodoxy within which the celebration of cultural and religious diversity is seen as an end in itself. As we have argued elsewhere (Singh and Cowden 2011) this has allowed new forms of community mobilisation around religious identification to become predominant within the cultural and political representation of ethnic minority communities, opening what we called a 'fault-line' within an earlier policy consensus around multiculturalism. These fault-lines were no more exposed than after the news that it was homegrown Islamist militants who had bombed London on 7/7. Politicians and commentators across the political spectrum not only blamed multiculturalism for this, but also reminded ethnic minority communities that they should stop living in the specificity of their cultural and religious ghettoes and start learning to be "British". Hence in the context of the "war on terror", the rise of global religious extremist movements, and the fracturing of the progressive consensus around multiculturalism, caused in part by its colonisation by religious movements, multiculturalist discourse found itself a hostage to arguments that it had at best legitimised segregation and at worst been complicit in terrorist bombings.

Post-race

It is in precisely the context of the crisis of consensus around Multiculturalism that we wish to examine whether a post-race paradigm offers a way forward. The appeal to this idea comes from the simple proposition, well made by Nayak, that 'there is no such thing as race' (2006 p.411). That is not to say that 'race' is absent from the individual and collective imaginary of society, which as Gilroy (2000) is at pains to remind us retains a powerful allure. However, it is also worth noting that the discursive field of 'race' is not in any what uniform or fixed. The starting point of 'post-race' thinking that we want to propose is that in addition to opposing racism one should also seek to assert a more positive conception of humanity. Following both Fine (2007) and Sen (2006) we would assert that such a conception needs to have a material and affective dimension; material in the sense that it needs to address the questions of political, economic and social discrimination and justice, and affective in that it requires the cultivation of a new consciousness. Fine (2007), using Arendt's notion of '*worldiness*' characterises this consciousness as one that 'refuses to rationalise the division of life of the mind into reified faculties or its separation from the life of work and politics' (2007 p.131). This is analogous to the rejection of the reification of 'race', on which racism and even some versions of anti-racism (See for example Gilroy 1990) rest, and the elective affinity between ideas of post-race and conceptualisations of cosmopolitanism.

In seeking to define our conception of 'post-race' we also need to distinguish our position from recent critiques, in particular Tim Wise (2010), who offers a trenchant critique of the discourse of "post-racial politics" in contemporary political and policy rhetoric in the US. He attacks Barack Obama's presidency for the way it combines a "rhetoric of racial transcendence" with a "public policy of colour blind universalism" (2010 p.16). In practice Wise argues that this has resulted in a failure to address the continuing problems of poverty, worklessness and incarceration amongst African-American communities in US cities, but also that this language of "colour-blindness" leaves the government without a narrative to counter the strident re-assertion of racist pathologisation, coming from groups like the "Tea Party". For us, 'post-race' must not mean a reversion to colour blind policies of previous decades, but needs to focus on processes of 'racialisation'. While "post-racial liberalism" undoubtedly entails a denial of the entrenched nature of the racialised class structure of neo-liberal capitalism in the US, we feel this analysis needs to be broadened out to incorporate the reconstruction of conceptions of 'race' around the narrative of "Islam versus the West", a crucial justification for the US and British government's invasions of Iraq and Afghanistan. As writers like Noam Chomsky and Edward Said have eloquently reminded us, racism always develops as a leading principle of thought and perception in the context of colonialism (Chomsky 2003; Said 1997). Hence while we strongly agree with the tenor of Wise's attack on "post-racial liberalism", we feel he focuses too narrowly on one area of "race-based injury", rather than looking at this in the context of the social, ideological, psychological and historical mechanisms that give meaning to racialised thought and practice across the body politic.

Implicit within our discussion so far is the idea that this conception 'post-race' is not necessarily new in itself, but rather a new synthesis of existing positions outlined below which we characterise as the field of 'race – post-race':

1. Liberal Multiculturalist – As noted above liberal multiculturalism began as an 'enlightenment' strategy which in its early stages appeals to universal ideals, which are important in the context of 'post-race'. However as its focus shifted toward the promotion of ethnic and 'cultural' particularity, it increasingly appealed to cultural relativism rather than universality. This appeal to relativism represents an impasse for multiculturalist discourse, leaving it on one hand unable to counter the charge of being an accomplice to religious extremism, but on the other, unable to provide the ground from which one might challenge contemporary reassertions of 'racialised' national identity.

2. Xenophobic Nationalism – This tradition has been present in the UK for most of the twentieth century, and despite the influence of multiculturalism at the level of policy, immigration law continues to be justified on the basis of arguments around 'race' and nation (Gilroy 1986). While the mainstream appeal of this was widely regarded as being defeated by political mobilisations, particularly by black communities and anti-racist activists, in the 1970s and 1980s (See Sivanandan 1990; CCCS 1982), the 'war on terror' has given these ideas new respectability, with a focus on Muslims as Europe's racial other. In the UK this is reflected in far-right origin and neo-fascist politics (such as the British National Party and English Defence League), but in northern Europe particularly key anti-Islamic arguments have come both from liberals (such as Pim Fortyn in the Netherlands) and from mainstream conservatives (such as Angela Merkel in Germany).

3. Critical Race Theory (CRT) – This begins in the work of US based legal theorist Derrick Bell who emerged as a critic of liberal gradualist approaches to persistent racial inequality. His key concern was understanding why the moral and political victories of the Civil Rights movement had had such marginal impact when it came to the implementation of real changes. CRT argues that a key reason for this is that key structures both in thought and institutional practice are constituted through 'race' and are therefore inherently resist conceptions of racial equality. In the UK this work has been developed by David Gilborn and Richard Delgado, who equally criticise the liberal multiculturalist view that 'race' can be transcended through appeals to reason, education and through gradualist shifts in state policy. CRT emphasises that the failure of these initiatives can only be accounted for through the pervasive nature of racism; which they argue must be given its due analytic primacy before we can move beyond it. The central problem for this position is its pessimistic view of social change, whereby 'race' becomes a kind 'black hole' from nothing can escape. We would argue that the weakness of this approach is firstly in the way it treats 'race' as a standalone category which can be analysed separately from a wider context, and secondly that its focus on the power and persistence of racism ignores the significance of past attempts at creating non-racial forms of social solidarity, and thereby closes this off this as an avenue which can be developed in the future.

4. Cosmopolitan-Humanist – This is a title we have given to a diverse body of work that is primarily identified with theorists like Paul Gilroy, Anthony Appiah, Jason Hill, Amartya Sen and Robert Fine. While all of these represent distinctive contributions in their own right rather than a conscious school of thought like CRT, we have grouped them together on the basis of an expressed concern with the way supposedly anti-racist initiatives, policies and political movements seeking racial equality end up re-inscribing 'race' in their very discourse. This is a critique levelled which has been levelled at both liberal multiculturalism and CRT. These writers are distinctive for the way they emphasise the importance of human sameness, and with an insistence that the rejection of the division of human beings according to arbitrary conceptions of 'race, religion, ethnicity must be undertaken *a priori*. This is exemplified in Paul Gilroy's argument for "Planetary Humanism" (2000) and Jason Hill's argument that becoming a "cosmopolitan" involves moving beyond "blood identities" (2009). While we regard this work, much of which takes the form of a philosophical rather than a properly sociological critique, as valuable for the way it places the possibility for transcending racial identities on the agenda, it's weakness lies in the gap between these utopian impulses and any discussion of a social practice through which these concepts might be articulated or realised – how, in other words, does one moves from the brutal reality of the racialised subject and inequalities, to this cosmopolitan 'state of grace'?

5. Marxist Race-Class Synthesis – Growing out the work of A. Sivanandan and the Institute of Race Relations, as well as the earlier work of Stuart Hall and Paul Gilroy, this perspective is essentially concerned with the relationship between 'race', class and the critique of capitalism. Hall exemplified this in his argument that 'race' needed to be understood essentially as 'modality' of class. While these thinkers saw that 'race' could be relatively autonomous at the levels of ideology for example, it always needs to be understood in the light of capitalist power structures and the politics of class. This position was eclipsed in the late 1980s with the decline of Marxism and concurrent rise of postmodernism, however it has been powerfully re-stated recently by Carter and Virdee who argue that if Sociology is to 'provide a more relevant account of the phenomena of racism and ethnicity' it needs to bring 'an emancipatory working class subject (one that is 'white' but also increasingly 'black' and 'brown' in the core of the capitalist world economy) back into their accounts of racism and anti-racism' (2008 pp.675-676)

With the obvious exception of Xenophobic nationalism, one would be able to extract to a lesser or greater degree, commitments towards post-race futures i.e. where racism, if not defeated becomes diminished. As Nayak points out, in recent times there has emerged 'a new cluster of ideas around performativity, identity and the body are crystallizing into an identifiable post-race lingua franca' (2006 p.414).

He argues that the impetus for 'post-race' comes from positions that combine the process of facing up to 'race' whilst at the same time rendering it mute. However, he is particularly critical of social constructionist accounts which, through their 'anti-foundational' ethos, far from hastening the death of 'race' have become completely reliant on 'the idea of race as some kind of ontological category, a real foundation for what one "is" (2006 p.415).

In order to avoid the problem identified by Nayak here, we would propose a new orientation towards Marxist 'race'/class arguments, that focus on the primacy a materialist account of 'race' in the context of global political economy, coupled with a moral imperative towards the transcendence and ultimate death of 'race' envisaged by Gilroy in his book *Against Race: Imagining political culture beyond the colour line (2000)*. Although requiring much more work, we argue that it is possible to bring together a properly sociological focus on analysing things as they really are in the life-world of the particular communities that we are working with (Habermas 1987) with a sense of immanence and utopian possibility. If these two sets of discourses appear to us as incompatible it may be that we need to be reminded that, as H.G. Wells put it, "the creation of utopias and their systematic critique is the proper object of Sociology" (cited in Levitas 2010).

Post- and Pedagogy Race

In spite of the fragmentation of discourses regarding the question of how 'race' is be outlined and conceptualised, the question remains as to the best way forward for those that are seeking to construct pedagogical strategies for undermining racism remains as important as ever. We now want to focus on how conceptions of 'post-race' might be developed at the level of pedagogy, giving a practical example of work we carried out with Probation Officers in the West Midlands.

At the centre of the expression of 'post-race' at the level of pedagogy is the creation of a context which enables racialised subjects to step through and beyond racially constructed subjectivity. However, anyone who has ever attempted this will know that this task is anything but simple or straightforward, and in seeking to understand this level of 'difficulty' we would return to the work Fanon in *Black Skin White Masks* (1986), particularly his discussion of the trauma caused by the imposition of racialised identities. It follows that the transcendence of these cannot take place without addressing that trauma. We also argue that this is the case for a both a white as well as a black person, or more broadly the dominant and the dominated 'other'. Paulo Freire, in his seminal text on critical pedagogy and emancipatory education *Pedagogy of the Oppressed* (1970) characterised the oppressed as having what he called a 'double consciousness':

...the oppressed suffer from the duality which has established itself in their innermost being. They discover that without freedom they cannot exist authentically. Yet although they desire authentic existence, they fear it. They are at one and the same time themselves and the oppressor whose consciousness they have internalized. (Freire 1970 p.30)

We argue that the desire to transcend 'race' evokes the same combination of yearning and resistance, and this understanding needs to be at the heart of pedagogical strategies whose objective is to allow people to, as Freire says, "regain their humanity" (1970 p.30). In this sense, we would use the idea of 'post race' as a heuristic tool, a basis for developing a pedagogy of 'hope' which offers an understanding of the construction of 'race' as essentially a misrecognition of material social relations, but at the same time, creates space for people to see themselves anew outside the real and symbolic violence of racialised categories within the space of the classroom. At the heart of such as pedagogy is the desire to promote critical dialogue, reflexivity and political awareness whereby learning becomes not a means to an end but an end in and of itself.

We contrast this with the dominant diversity based approaches, which are often expressed in terms of 'managing difference', 'cultural sensitivity' or a celebration of origins. For us these can be characterised with the pedagogical practice Freire calls the "Banking" method where students are told what to think – and in the context of the difficulty associated with classroom discussions of 'race' this often turns into an exercise in imposed "political correctness" where instead of learning about each other through dialogue, students learn what words not to use in class. Additionally, strategies based on the celebrations of origins can be regressive, not least for those people whose 'diversity' falls outside that which is being celebrated. And in this sense these strategies can act to reinscribe racialised subjectivity in their very process, in spite of being formally "anti-racist".

For us the pedagogical challenge is about the way one links diversity and sameness. Appiah in his book *Cosmopolitanism: Ethics in a World of Strangers (2006)* talks about the importance of conversation in transcending boundaries of identity, 'be they national, religious or something else'. For Apphia conversation is not only a 'literal' act but 'also a metaphor for engagement with the experience and the ideas of others' (2006 p.85). In this sense post-race pedagogical strategy needs to be orientated towards nurturing cosmopolitan identities which, as Sen notes do not have to be seen as "eliminating other loyalties" (2006 p.185) - there is nothing inherently wrong with people being able to identify with their particularities as they are manifested socially. But we would see the post-race element manifested through the way teachers should seek to give students permission, and thereby to develop the confidence, to move between and beyond those categories. Henry Giroux has characterised this process as "Border Crossing" (1993). A border in this sense is an inherited enclosed psychic space in which one resides; becoming a 'border-crosser' allows one to articulate a critical distance from aspects of one's inscribed identity/world view. As the metaphor suggests it implies stepping away from one's secure location but, as Giroux notes this allows students the opportunity to enter "new spaces in which dominant social relations, ideologies and practices are able to be questioned" (1993 p.178).

In offering a practical illustration of how this approach can be manifest in pedagogical practice we reflect on some training that we provided for the West Midlands Probation Service regarding the Home Office's "Preventing Violent Extremism" (PVE) Agenda. This came about as a result of an earlier session the group had received which they felt, far from throwing greater light onto the problem of violent extremism, ended up reinforcing a series of stereotypical representations of Muslims as dangerous, and therefore justifiably a "suspect community". The key issue here was the way the PVE Agenda was presented uncritically to the Probation Officers, as a set of prescriptions that the Government felt would enhance community and social cohesion. Again we would see the key problem here as the way the binary between Muslim/Non-Muslim was offered as common sense, and thereby fixed. The irony was that this training was supposed to be about "promoting diversity", and this exemplifies the very problem discussed earlier about the way and uncritical rendering of 'diversity' discourses can end up reinscribing racialised differences. In the attempt to address a legitimate and important contemporary issue, the training came to be experienced by the group, who were mixed group in terms of ethnicity, gender and religion, as contributing to a racialised binary amongst them.

In terms of our process we initiated, we began by situating the question of what constitutes "violent extremism" in history, pointing to the origins of terms like "extremism" and "fanaticism" in responses to the French Revolution. The became a backdrop to a discussion about political leaders and movements, such as Nelson Mandela, Martin McGuiness, Udam Singh, who were seen both as "terrorists" and "freedom fighters" respectively; the former two have interestingly enough gone on to become statesman. The approach we adopted was to use these figures to open up a discussion about who defines the distinction between moral and immoral ways of being and doing, and who defines the conceptualisation of the racialised other (Rattansi 1994).

Our role was not simply to say that these were "good" black or anti-colonial 'others', an approach that we see as the hallmark of "politically correct" diversity based, which simply invert otherness (Malik 1996). What we sought to do by contrast was to ask students to consider the circumstances which lead to political leaders such as those mentioned to advocate the use of violence as political weapon; in this way we sought to reintroduce questions of moral agency into the discussion. Alongside this we also asked participants to think about the ideas that these political movements were part of. Where did Nelson Mandela's ideas about a non-racial South Africa come from? Where did Martain McGuinesses' ideas about Northern Ireland being the "occupied six counties" of Ireland come from?

This allowed us to draw out the distinction between anti-colonial movements and their aims and aspirations, and the aims of religious fundamentalist movements, which were essentially concerned with the corrupted or *jihali* nature of modernity (Meek 2007) This allowed participants to understand, for example, the issue of gender not simply as being about the liberated West versus the backward East, but about women's struggles for justice and how ideas of honour (*"izzat"*) are often used to oppress. Our approach sought to avoid reducing the purveyors of violent extremist ideas as 'mad' people; we wanted rather to enable participants to consider, debate and critique these. One of the notable features of this discussion was the way it conferred agency on participants regardless of their faith background, 'race' or gender – it came to be space where the authoritarian discourse of Islamic fundamentalist movements was able to be problematised by the group, while at the same time allowing participants to be equally able to express concern with the way these issues were being dealt with by PVE agenda. We see this as an example of 'post-race' pedagogy in that it sought create a critical dialogue in which people were able to move out of their socially prescribed positions, and express their ideas as concerned citizens and professionals, rather than as "white", "Muslim" etc.

Henry Giroux has characterised teachers who uphold an emancipatory ideal of education as "transformative intellectuals" (1993). We see the question of intellectuality here linked to us taking our theoretical position very seriously, and using this as a mean toward us to take a critical stance toward our own practice, as well as the practice of others when engaging in debate and inquiry. Training and teaching concerned with issues of oppression, has historically relied on a discourse of the truth of "experience". Peter McClaren and Tomaz Da Silva have sought to problematise this by noting that:

> A major consideration for the development of contextual critical knowledge is affirming the experiences of students to the extent that their voices are acknowledged as an important part of the dialogue; but affirming students views does not mean that educators should take the meaning that students give to their experiences as face value, as if experience speaks romantically or even tragically for itself. The task of the critical educator is to provide the conditions for individuals to acquire a language that will enable them to reflect upon and shape their own experiences, and in certain instances transform such experiences in the interests of a wider project of social responsibility. (1993 p.49)

We see this as an important reminder for educators to themselves take responsibility, as much as they can, for the conditions under which students learn.

Conclusion

We began by discussing the current impasse of Multiculturalism, and it is this context that we see 'post-race' as a paradigm which offers trenchant opposition to racialised violence but also a vision around which progressive forces within disparate communities can coalesce. We see this coalescence as necessarily taking political struggles beyond identity politics toward a greater prize; that of universal social justice. There may be a moment emerging, associated with the Arab Spring and the more recent crisis of fundamentalist movements, which opens up new possibilities for the reinscription of a new Enlightenment, which would not be a reassertion of a European hegemonic Universalism, but something more profoundly inclusive. Our hope is that as a consequence of a series of crises associated with neo-liberalism and the attendant fragmentation of communities, coupled with democratic impulses across the world, new possibilities from below are emerging which offer novel ways of thinking about post-'race' collectivities.

Bibliography

Allman, P. (2001) *Critical Education Against Global Capitalism: Karl Marx and Revolutionary Critical Education*, Bergin & Garvey, Westport, Connecticut.

Baker, J. C. & Chase, C. (1993) *Josephine: The Hungry Heart*, New York: Random House.

Benedict R. O'G. (1991) *Imagined communities: reflections on the origin and spread of nationalism (Revised and extended. ed.*, London: Verso.

Bourdieu, P (1992) 'The Purpose of Reflexive Sociology', in *An Invitation to Reflexive Sociology* Polity Press: Cambridge.

Burbules, N. (1993) *Dialogue in Teaching. Theory and practice, Teachers* New York: College Press.

Carter, B. and Virdee, S. 2008. 'Racism and the Sociological Imagination', in *British Journal of Sociology* 59(4), pp.661-679.

CCCS (1982) *The Empire Strikes Back: Race and racism in 70's Britain*, London: Hutchinson.

Chomsky, N. (2003) *Hegemony of Survival: America's Quest for Global Dominance* London: Penguin/Hamish Hamilton.

Darder, A (2002) *Reinventing Paulo Freire: A Pedagogy of Love*, Cambridge: Westview Press.

Fanon, F. (1986) *Black Skin, White Masks*, London: Pluto Press.

Fanon, F. (1970) *Towards the African Revolution*, Harmondsworth: Penguin.

Ferguson, N. (2004) *Empire: How Britain Made the Modern World*, London: Penguin.

Ferguson, N. (2011) *Civilisation: The West and The Rest*, Allen Lane.

Freire, P. (1970) *Pedagogy of the Oppressed*, Harmondsworth: Penguin.

Gilroy, P. (1990) 'The End of Anti-Racism', in *New Community*, 17(1), pp.71-83.

Gilroy, P. (2000) *Between Camps: Nations, cultures and the Allure of Race*, London: Penguin/Allen Lane.

Gilroy, P. (2000) *Against Race: Imagining Political Culture Beyond the Color Line*, Cambridge Mass: The Belknap Press of Harvard University Press.

Giroux, H. (1993) *Border Crossings*, London: Routledge.

Goldberg, D. T. (2002) *The Racial State*, Oxford: Blackwell.

Habermas, J. (1987) *The Theory of Communicative Action: the Critique of Functionalist Reason (Vol II)*, Boston: MA, Beacon Press.

Hall, S. (1980) 'Race, Articulation, and Societies Structured in Dominance', in *Sociological Theories: Race and Colonialism*, Paris: UNESCO.

Hall, S. (1996) *Critical Dialogues in Cultural Studies, ed. David Morley and Kuan-Hsing Chen*, London: Routledge.

Hill, J. (2006) *Beyond Blood Identities Lanham*, Maryland: Rowan & Littlefield.

Hooks, B. (1990) *Yearnings: Race, Gender, and Cultural politics*, Boston MA: South End Press.

Husband, C. (1987) *Race in Britain: Continuity and Change,* Michigan: Hutchinson.

Kundnani, A. (2007) *The End of Tolerance: Racism in 21ˢᵗ Century Britain,* London: Routledge.

Lentin, A. and Titley, G. (2011) *The Crises of Multiculturalism: Racism in a neoliberal age,* London: Zed Books.

Levitas, R (2010) 'Back to the future: Wells, Sociology, Utopia and Method', in *The Sociological Review [Special Issue: Imagining the Political]*, 58(4), pp.530–547.

Malik, K. (1996) *The Meaning of Race: Race, History and Culture in Western Society,* Palgrave: New York University Press.

McClaren P. and Da Silva T. (1993) 'Critical Pedagogy and Counter Memory' in McClaren, P. and Leonard, P. *Paulo Freire: A Critical Encounter,* London: Routledge.

McLaren, P (2002) *Capitalists and Conquerours: A Critical Pedagogy Against Empire,* Oxford: Rowan and Littlefield.

Meek, J. (2007) 'The Original Targets: Review of *The Looming Tower: Al-Qaida's Road to 9/11* by Lawrence Wright', *London Review of Books,* 29(3).

Miles, R (2003) *Racism,* 2nd ed., London: Routledge.

Nayak, A (2006) 'After race: Ethnography, race and post-race theory', in *Ethnic and Racial Studies,* 29(3), pp.411–430.

Rattansi, A. (1994) 'Modern Racisms, Racialised Identities" in A. Rattansi and S. Westwood (editors) *Racism, Modernity and Identity,* Cambridge: Polity.

Said, E. (1997) *Covering Islam: How the Media and the Experts Determine How We See the Rest of the World,* 2ⁿᵈ ed., London: Vintage Books.

Sivanandan, A. (1985) 'RAT and the degradation of black struggle', in *Race & Class,* 26(4).

Sivanandan, A. (1990) *Communities of Resistance – Writings on Black Struggles for Socialism,* London: Verso.

Wise, T. (2010) *Color-Blind: The Rise of Post-Racial Politics and the Retreat from Racial Equality,* San Fracisco: City Lights Press.

Social Cohesion - a Benign Concept? Lived Experiences at the Borders and Boundaries of 'Community'

Jackie Haq[2]

Introduction

Despite the reoccurrence of major disturbances in urban towns and cities in the UK, as elsewhere, politicians, policymakers and commentators appear to be taken aback and, at times, affronted when such riotous behaviour and incivility emerges once again into the public domain. Historical and contemporary accounts of such violent episodes in the UK tend to be described as 'race riots', resulting in claims of a 'broken Britain', feral youths and the death of multiculturalism. Successive reports and inquiries are commissioned, conflicting analyses of the causes and responses to the violence are debated and new initiatives and policies follow in the wake of these violent outbreaks.

However, responding to public displays of collective violence when faced with the latest crisis neglects those daily forms of violence and abuse that are so common, they are 'hidden in plain sight' (Hill Collins 1998). This paper is a reflection on everyday conversations about two forms of persistent violence, namely domestic (gendered) violence and racial violence. The paper begins with an exploration of some relevant policy initiatives and theoretical understandings of community and cohesion. The paper then draws on community responses to both forms of violence, to illustrate the social construction and reconstruction of 'community' at the local, micro-level. In essence, this paper explores routine re-negotiations of community 'boundaries and border crossings': in doing so, it highlights implications for social cohesion.

---

2 Dr Jackie Haq MBE is Faithful Judgements Project Research Associate at PEALS (Policy, Ethics and Life Sciences) Research Centre, Newcastle University, exploring the role of religion in laypeople's ethical evaluations of new reproductive and genetic technologies. Her previous research on co-inquiry, co-production of knowledge and public engagement built on her longstanding commitment to achieving equality and social justice, working with marginalised, disadvantaged communities to attain positive, sustainable change. Jackie's doctoral thesis (2006) "The Border and Boundaries of Social Cohesion", critically examined the complexities of relationships within and between diverse communities through an ethnographic study of community responses to domestic and racial violence. Before university, Jackie was a community activist at local, regional and national levels, initiating, developing and implementing strategic, pragmatic and policy approaches to urban regeneration, through collective action. In 1992, Jackie was awarded the M.B.E. for 'services to the community' and the Jameson Award for 'combating urban poverty'.

Background to UK Social Cohesion Agenda in Aftermath of Riots and Disturbances

In the spring and early summer of 2001, social disturbances broke out in the UK on the streets of Bradford, Oldham and Burnley, resulting in damage to property, attacks on the police and violent confrontations between members of diverse communities. Locally, nationally and internationally, the events attracted wide media coverage, frequently being portrayed simplistically as 'race' riots.[3] As with other riots and disturbances elsewhere in the country, both recent and historical,[4] local and central Government reacted by setting up various inquiries and review panels to examine the circumstances underpinning and leading up to the conflict (Burnley Task Force 2002; Ritchie 2001; Cantle 2001)

In 2001, an inter-departmental Ministerial Group on Public Order and Community Cohesion, chaired by Home Office Minister John Denham, was established to "examine and consider how national policies might be used to promote better community cohesion, based upon shared values and a celebration of diversity", and a Community Cohesion Review Team, led by Ted Cantle, consulted local residents and community leaders across England on their views on community cohesion, with the aim of identifying good practice in addressing the issues locally, and building up to a national overview (Denham 2002).[5]

The Ministerial Group published its report *Building Cohesive Communities* (2001) alongside those of Cantle, Ritchie and Clarke. Many of the resulting recommendations from the gathered data were targeted at local authorities, which were seen to be of central importance in supporting initiatives aimed at developing more cohesive communities. The government continued to promote work on community cohesion: the Community Cohesion Unit nationally moved from gathering anecdotal evidence, after specific events, to developing guidelines based on monitoring and evaluation of existing and new programmes.

Yet, although 'community cohesion' as a concept was now firmly on the public policy agenda, few practitioners, policy makers or politicians claimed to know exactly what constituted 'cohesion':

---

3   For example, in Burnley, there was evidence of a turf war between rival drugs dealers; some property damage was committed when it was reported that far right extremists of the British National Party were meeting in a pub to plan attacks on Asian residents (Burnley Task Force 2002); in Oldham, some anger focused on policing (Denham 2002).

4   See for example Scarman 1981; Campbell 1993.

5   See report on http://www.homeoffice.gov.uk/docs2/comm-cohesion.html-chapter1 (accessed September 2004).

Community cohesion goes beyond the ideas of race equality and social inclusion with which we are all familiar. Community cohesion is about the dynamic relationships between and within communities. Ironically, it is easier to identify cases where community cohesion is not apparent…than it is to produce a detailed definition of the term (Beecham, Denham et al 2002 p.6).

Following the riots, the Local Government Association (LGA) published *Guidance on Community Cohesion* (2002) and the following definition was widely adopted, by the Home Office and others:[6]

> A cohesive community is one where:
> There is a common vision and a sense of belonging for all communities
> The diversity of people's different backgrounds and circumstances is appreciated and positively valued
> Those from different backgrounds have similar life opportunities
> Strong and positive relationships are being developed between people from different backgrounds in the workplace, in schools and within neighbourhoods.

Here, the government proposed similar (but not equal) life opportunities would available for all and peaceful co-existence would be the norm in public and personal interactions. Inherent in the political discussions, definitions or vision statements on community cohesion appeared to be the core premise that cohesion is positive and benign; lack of cohesion is negative and dangerous.

This definition had echoes of an earlier statement by then Prime Minister Blair (2001) laying out his related vision of neighbourhood renewal:

> My vision is of a nation where no-one is seriously disadvantaged by where they live, where power, wealth and opportunity are in the hands of the many not the few. This Action Plan is a crucial step in creating one nation, not separated by class, race or where people live.[7]

Both of these policy statements, while superficially positive, are problematic. On one level, they appear to promote a harmonious society, incorporating a respect for diversity; on another they disguise some of the persistent, underlying tensions in communal life and civil society. The pre-riot statement refers to inequalities

---

6 See Institute for Community Cohesion website for Guideline to Publications, available at http://www.cohesioninstitute.org.uk/Resources/AboutCommunityCohesion (accessed 24th March 2012).

7 See Foreword in Social Exclusion Unit (2001) A New Commitment to Neighbourhood Renewal, London: Social Renewal Unit.

of power, wealth and opportunity: the renewal strategy focused primarily on tangible and structural areas of regeneration, including economic, physical and environmental improvements. The post-riot statement, presents a more nebulous aim of attitudinal change, looking for 'appreciation' and 'being valued'. Critically, gender is not named: 'race' and class as sources of division become even more invisible; mentioned explicitly by the then Prime Minister in his vision statement in 2001, they were, at best, alluded to vaguely in the cohesion statement of 2004.

The absence of an overt gendered perspective to cohesion policy was not new. In 1998, Levitas noted that New Labour's policy on 'delivering inclusion' was premised on a masculine model of society, in which the women were further marginalised and disadvantaged:

> The problem of exclusion is, in the end, construed in terms of male unemployment, and social integration effected by paid work...unpaid work is invisible here. There is a failure to address caring, parenting and the interrupted employment careers – and lower pay – of women... [This] is a discourse about the interdependence of social cohesion and economic growth, in which paid employment...especially for men... is the central means of social integration and social control, and unemployment the overriding element in social exclusion. (Levitas 1998 pp.46-48)[8]

While 'race' and, to a lesser extent, class, were raised again later as sites of potential disadvantage or conflict within communities, the continued absence of a gendered perspective in the cohesion debate was a significant omission, given that the government had prioritised social cohesion following the riots in 2001, in which groups of mainly young men fought with each other and with the police.[9] Was the social cohesion agenda focused on counteracting the potential for young men to commit acts of violence in public, in communities, whether against the status quo or against the state? (See Burnett 2004; Kalra 2002). If so, then why was the gendered nature of the violence not overtly acknowledged? And why was the focus not widened to include the commonest form of gendered violence, domestic violence, as an equally valid threat to social cohesion, not least in respect of 'strong and positive relationships'? Why did policy on social cohesion abstain again from a women-orientated focus, signifying only 'partial gender-visibility'?

---

8   The emphasis on an economic, market-orientated driver for social cohesion was reiterated in the State of English Cities Report (2006), London: Office of the Deputy Prime Minister. In the section 'Real progress made on social cohesion', as in the rest of the report, there was no reference to racism or gender and scant reference to violence.

9   See Campbell 1993 for earlier accounts of the stand-off between police and young male rioters at the height of the 1991 riots, a phenomenon I witnessed personally.

The focus on so-called 'race' was more persistent, in policy and in political rhetoric. The reports on the disturbances in the north of England had purposefully concentrated on relationships between 'majority and minority' communities, with a particular spotlight on young Asian, working class men. Burnett (2004 p.9) claims that the cohesion agenda created a representation of 'white' violence as 'representative only of frustration and instability, whereas the violence of angry and desperate Asian youths is representative of inherent Asian criminality... Thus, the very concept of community cohesion became incorporated within a political circle of exclusion, segregation and control'.

This reflects the work of Alexander (2000; 2004) in which she notes the construction of the 'young Asian folk devil', an image that also signalled a gendered, as well as a religio-ethnicitised, conceptual shift.

[T]he term 'Asian' in relation to negative images and stereotypes has become synonymous with Muslim communities, again drawing on the notion of an emergent Pakistani and Bangladeshi underclass. Through the lens of the media... resistance has become increasingly synonymous with criminality and upheaval, with the breakdown of perceived traditional values and the growth of a pathologized culture of alienation and confusion. As part of this, representations of 'the Asian community' have moved from a concern with a uniformly victim status to that of perpetrator - a reinvention of passive recipient to active combatant which has simultaneously and significantly, transformed the gendered markers of imagined Asian identities. Concerns have thus increasingly focused on the public activities of young men - the youth in the streets (Keith 1995) - rather than the more domestic, 'private' concerns of young women. (Alexander 2000 p.7)

This shows that a focus on social order or economic inclusion alone is restrictive, leaving many questions about the substance, dynamics and enactment of 'cohesion' unexplored. The social divisions of 'race' and gender are heavily imbued with hierarchical power differentials that potentially sustain inequality and fuel injustice. Despite emerging in response to violent public confrontations, the cohesion agenda obscured the power conflicts inherent in the construction of communities. Specifically, it de-racialised 'race', and omitted to mention gender or a 'sense of injustice'.

Back et al (2002) see the disturbances in the north as a possible marker of a significant shift away from the previous emphasis on celebrating 'multicultural diversity', with the then Government spinning 'Janus-like', between 'multiculturalism' and 'assimilation'. Burnett and Whyte (2004) refer to the cohesion dichotomy as a 'double edged sword', which on one hand proposes an agenda for revitalising community and "improving socio-economic opportunities for all... [while]...

explicitly seeking to rid the country of difference", a project that they equate with a new expression of British Imperialism. Burnett (2004) point to the tensions between the state and media trying to create a common nationality while holding to a perception of self-segregating communities, referred to in the Cantle (2001) report.

Reflecting on this post-riot political discourse, Worley (2005) too notes a slippage in the language used, from 'community to 'national' cohesion. This signals a further tension in the cohesion framework: the New Labour government appeared undecided as to whether cohesion is cited within and between diverse yet similar communities, or is a project defining the one-nation state. This is echoed in the recent exhortations from Conservative Prime Minister Cameron and opposition leader Miliband, to communities facing severe economic and social hardships, to deliver the (presumably 'race' and gender neutral) Big Society" (Conservative Party 2010) or the "Good Society" (Miliband 2010).

Paradoxically, 'where Cantle indicated 'too much community' as a core problematic of the 2001 disturbances (in that he saw those communities as silos with their separate populations living 'parallel lives'), in 2011 it is the breakdown and loss of communities and community values - 'not enough community' - that is being mobilised as the core moral problematic' (Murji and Neal 2001 p.4.2).

What is Community?

The term 'community' is itself a problematic, malleable concept (Bauman 2001; Bell and Newby 1971). It has been variously defined as shared space in locally-based geographical locations, in neighbourhood studies including planning and environment (Stedman 2003; Talen 1999); as attachment to and interpretation of place (see Gieryn 2000); as people with common interests and lifestyles, whose links may transcend location; and as the more abstract 'sense of community' i.e. community spirit, often associated with locally based, collective action (Ahlbrandt 1984; Bell and Newby 1971; Crow and Allan 1994; Young and Willmott 1957). Cohen (1998) describes community as, '1) a group of people who have something in common with one another which 2) distinguishes them in a significant way from the members of other putative groups' (Cohen 1998 p.12).

Both internally and externally, nominal definitions of community, mostly posited as positive collectives, may actually mask more fragmented relationships:

> 2222: [community worker, Asian issues worker, Asian, female] I always challenge that notion of the community anyway…Just because there's people from a particular background or country or…religion, it doesn't necessarily make them a cohesive community…What you get is, quite often, a whole

set of individuals scattered here and there…There…might be some binding forces in terms of religion, but even then, people have such a wide range in perspective of what religion is…so it isn't cohesive.

In that sense, community is an arbitrary notion, open to negotiation and interpretation by the social actors involved. As such, it is a fragile concept, whose enactment depends on a consensus on the parameters of commonality, i.e. who is 'in' and who is 'out' and why this is so (Anderson 1983; Elias and Scotson 1994).

'Community' is also ingrained with hierarchal assumptions. The gender-blind approach to community, and cohesion, leaves unchallenged gendered and racialised assumptions about women's position in relation to the social construction and maintenance of community (Lewis 2005). Women, by default, are 'often constructed as symbolic border guards of ethnic and national collectivities' (Yuval-Davis, Anthias et al 2005 p.515). This latter position is evidenced by the political and media focus on women in Muslim communities, both as victims of violence and as guardians of the communities (Fenton 2002; Meer et al 2010). As Worley (2005 p.486) says, 'Talking about 'community' has particular implications in relation to lived experiences of race and gender'.

'Community' then, implies both similarity and difference, and may be a source of conflict, isolation and exclusion as well as unity. Community is much more than an attachment to place, a collectivity based on common bonds or a willingness to 'volunteer'. It is multifaceted and dynamic: "community" is as much a narrative product as an organic achievement' (Back 1996 p.133). It is those stories and accounts, which tell of the interactions at and across the socially constructed and embedded boundaries, not least those of 'race' and gender that are especially relevant to exploring social cohesion.

Method

The empirical data discussed in this paper were collected from an ethnographic study of community responses to domestic and racial violence, conducted in predominantly working-class areas in the North East of England. These neighbourhoods had experienced long-term physical and socio-economic decline despite successive regeneration initiatives. Latterly, rapid changes in the areas' ethnic diversity were perceived as significant indices of inter-communal tensions. In the first phase of the research, an in-depth analysis of academic literature, policy documents and wider sources of literature and media was conducted to give a context for the study. During 2001-02, fieldwork, comprising semi-structured interviews with groups and individuals, was augmented with participant and non-participant observations in local community groups and forums and at in public spaces at sub-neighbourhood levels: in addition, a reflexive fieldwork dairy was kept throughout this time, which was used to record further analyse the research process and findings. In total, thirty two semi-structured interviews, each lasting 1-2 hours, were conducted with 53 people from diverse ethnic minority and majority communities. Of these 34 were women and 19 were men, with ages ranging from 16 to 74 years.

In interviews, research participants were presented with two sets of vignettes, which had the central themes of a) domestic violence and b) racially motivated violence. When looking at both forms of violence, the scenarios were changed by one detail each time, creating a smooth progression from one situation to the next while highlighting specific variables such as age, gender or ethnicity. This method was a useful technique for determining the potential for and perceived existence of social cohesion across a range of specific, socially constructed boundaries, by soliciting the differing reactions to incidents of domestic or racial violence. The responses were contextualised by reference to and discussions on abstract concepts ranging from notions of public/ private space, to a 'sense of belonging' to a community (Jackson 2002; Mooney 2000). Because the scenarios given were in the form of stories in which the listener became an active participant, respondents offered anecdotes of their own, giving a deeper insight into the everyday conceptions, lived experiences and symbolic explanations of community (Denzin 1978; Geertz 2000; Hollway and Jefferson 2000).

My ethnographic study revealed complex, everyday imaginings and enactments of community as seen through the lens of 'race' and gender. Drawing on cross-community conversations, I briefly outline some community dynamics; perceptions of the frequency of both racial and domestic violence are then given and selected data used to illustrate gendered and racialised assumptions underpinning 'community'.

Constructing Community: Familiarity, Justice, and Reciprocity

At first many respondents talked of the breakdown of community, expressing a sense of loss for times past:

> 2228b: [resident, white, female]. Communication…Now you have lost a lot of that over the years. I think it's because a lot of people have separated themselves from different people. Instead of communicating all together, they have separated themselves.

> 2228a: [local shopkeeper, Asian, male]. We've had community here before… It used to be one big community. I have been here…for twenty-five years. And there was a community and a community spirit as well but

unfortunately that's died off over the years...what's happened is that people are staying here...say for 6 months, then they are going somewhere else, so there is no community here now for that reason. I think it's asylum seekers who are moving in to the area and other people are moving out now. [Laughs slightly]

The issue of segregated communities was a recurring theme. Throughout the research, the concept of familiarity, coupled with notions of justice (fairness) and reciprocity were highlighted. In the case of asylum seekers who arrived under the Government dispersal system, distinct boundaries of community defined by the settled communities were bolstered by a sense of injustice that existing long-term suffering remained unacknowledged by central government. The barriers towards newcomers were compounded by strong feelings of resentment at the expectation of welcome and support to be extended by existing residents. Many respondents, though not all, talked about asylum-seekers in terms of being racially and culturally different to long-standing communities.

Injustice was frequently underscored by the fault line of 'race' across longer-term communities too. Racialised divisions presented as resentment about perceived unequal allocation of resources; as a sense of injustice about perceived preferential treatment of groups other than the one with which they most identified; and as anger about a lack of reciprocity in community relationships.

Despite these tensions, many participants, including those above, spoke of day-to-day acts of support, common bonds and active community organisations that often transcended racialised boundaries. As the research progressed, it became apparent that understanding community cohesion was more complex than a reliance on evidence of social capital and social networks might suggest (see for example Hirschfield and Bowers 1997). Further exploration of community dynamics, solicited through responses to domestic and racial violence, indicated a process of distancing, sustained by an undercurrent of invisibility and hierarchical assumptions, brought into sharp focus when responding to moments of crisis.

Visibility of Racial Violence and Gendered (Domestic) Violence

Perceptions of the extent of racial and gendered violence varied among participants.[10] The majority of (though not all) white respondents did not identify racist abuse as a significant issue.

2216: [community activist, resident, white, female] I don't think there is

---

10 Racist and domestic violence includes verbal, economic, emotional and physical abuse.

racial violence round here to start with and I don't think you need to start that division; I've never really seen very much like that around here.

2218b: [resident, white, female] Well to be honest, I've never known of any racist violence here.

The 'invisibility' of racist abuse was not restricted to white residents' perceptions; some Asian respondents noted with frustration and disbelief that black/Asian colleagues and family members did not share their identification of persistent and endemic racism in all spheres of life – citing repeat incidents at work, during leisure time, when house hunting – even when visiting relatives in hospital.

1109: [community worker, Asian, male] If you can find me one Asian person [in this area] who would say they have never had any harassment because of race then I would have to say that they were lying…Whenever I go out…I know it is going to happen.

2222: [Asian issues worker, Asian, female] I've had members of my family, and…black colleagues too, who…say that they've never heard a racist remark and I think, have I been living somewhere else or have they? *How can they be disconnected from this* [my emphasis]?

In contrast to perceptions of racial violence, all participants acknowledged that domestic violence *per se* did occur, with only two respondents saying this violence was not seen in public spaces. However, domestic violence was made partially invisible through a selective process of both *denial* that domestic violence is present in all communities, and *relegation,* locating domestic violence in the 'private realm' of intimate partner relationships or as occurring in communities seen as different and outside that of the observer.

2217: [retired resident, Sikh, male] I tell you I never heard of violence to our woman, in our religion…I never heard of a man beating a woman in our religion. It is a very bad thing. You cannot dream it.

2216: [community activist, resident, white, female] I don't think communities themselves should [intervene] … it's interfering in that respect, cos …the community's not there as the police.[11]

2218a: [resident, white, male] To be honest I am not being racial but I think it is their culture; they [Muslims] don't like you to get involved.

---

11 Previously the respondent [2216] had discussed the need for collective involvement on other issues taking place in the community, including youth disorder. Her stance on community challenges to domestic violence is in direct contrast with those previously expressed views.

In comparing the responses to *both* forms of violence, it *broadly* appeared that more people claimed they would be likely to intervene when witnessing gendered violence, i.e. violence towards women by 'known men', compared to fewer people indicating that they would respond to racial violence, directed against males or females.

Empathy and Action

It has been suggested that bystander intervention is more likely if witnesses to incidents feel empathy with victims through shared personal characteristics and if they feel confident of a successful outcome for themselves and the victim (Laner and Benin 2001). Risk and potential repercussions were identified as deciding factors by participants in this study. However, when discussing domestic violence, responses indicated that racialised stereotypes and hierarchies underpinning perceptions of 'community' were significant.

> 2219: [community activist, resident, white, male] Now the [Asian] women, in their family, they have to do as they are told, basically it's their religion. So honestly...I cannot see any white couple getting involved. Because they [white people] know they [Asian women] have got to respect their husbands and do as their husbands say whether he's hitting them or not.

> JH: You are walking around and you see a young white couple. They are arguing. The man slaps the woman her on the face. You don't know who they are. What would you do?

> 2217: [retired resident, Sikh, male] If the things are so bad, if possible, I would go to the telephone box and tell the police. *You see being a coloured man, you know and I have no right to say something* [my emphasis].

For the first speaker [2219], non-intervention is premised on his assumption of culturally sanctioned gender violence. This has echoes of the notion of 'appropriate victims' - persons who are deemed to be 'un-worthy' or undeserving of intervention or support, and that lack of worthiness is, in part, premised on gendered assumptions of expected behaviour and stereotypes of those designated as 'Other' (Dobash and Dobash 1979).

The latter speaker [2217] identifies a hierarchical relationship premised on his ethnicity and that of the perpetrator and victim, in which he is not *entitled* to intervene. His voice is, publicly at least, silenced, although he does not discount the possibility that he would encourage a third party, the police, to intervene if the violence, in his judgment, reached an unacceptable level. This contrasts with his next response, to the same scenario, with different protagonists:

JH: And if you saw a young Muslim couple? [in domestic violence incident]

2217: [laughs] Well, I don't do anything, I just walk. You see, they are a different kind of religion. These people when the woman matter is come, they are very, very possessive!

The respondent [2217] now states that he would not intervene at all, on the basis that the perpetrator and victim were of a different faith group to his own, and further, as stated by respondent [2219] above, suggesting that gendered violence is culturally embedded in that group. Here, there is no reference to entitlement; rather there is a complete distancing, with no stated obligation to intervene, either directly or indirectly. Symbolically, these responses to domestic violence reflect a view of community where borders are permeated with gendered considerations linked to ethnicity, perceptions of culture and entitlement. Because of this, any potential 'border crossing' (in this case a response to a violent situation), is unlikely.

Borders and Boundaries of Community: Intersections of 'Race and Gender'

It has long been noted that the boundaries of community are brought into sharp focus at the borders, at points of potential interactions and crossings (Barth 1969). In the following account, a white mother of children of dual heritage is subjected to racial abuse.

2214a: [young resident, dual heritage, female] There was this woman – she's white but she wears the Asian clothes cos her husband is Asian and her kids are. So these lads started shouting at her and laughing at her for wearing the Asian clothes. So I stepped in because I thought well she is just like me because I am a bit of both[12], so I said, "Stop!...She's not done owt [anything] to you. It's nowt [nothing] to do with you what she's wearing!"

The superficial focus was on the woman's clothes (*shalwar* and *kameez*).[13] Her appearance placed her as 'other', as outside her ethnic and cultural community, especially in a predominantly white area, where she was very visible. The clothes were an outward marker of her relationship with an Asian man, and as a mother of children who are deemed to be 'non-white'. The stimulus and premise for the abuse was both her gender and her ethnicity *and her perceived transgression of racialised/gendered expectations*. The

---

12 Note here that the speaker identifies with woman she describes as white, while describing herself as 'a bit of both'.

13 In the current climate of Islamophobia, some form of 'Islamic' dress may be interpreted as 'un-British', even dangerous by association, because of the emphasis on the construction of the 'Muslim terrorist'.

assumed boundary violation here draws on a more biologically essentialist construction of 'race', and the persistence of miscegenation fears (Bland 2005 and Ferber 1998). This incident represents the power of 'race' and gender at the borders of community.

Conclusion

This paper presents some community perspectives on cohesion, based on lived experiences. It is offered with the caveat that it does not present a contextualised analysis of structural and economic disadvantage: rather it is a snapshot of day-to-day community boundary negotiations.

Community responses to domestic violence indicate that hierarchical assumptions and enactments of gender at the micro-level, particularly at the intersections of 'race' and gender, are central to the understandings of community and have practical implications for the inclusion and well being of women in society. This paper contends that, in the absence of a gendered perspective, political and policy debates on cohesion are flawed.

The boundaries of community are seen to be re/formed and frequently delineated along fault-lines of 'race' and ethnicity and mediated through notions of justice, entitlement and reciprocity. Paradoxically, the study found many examples of intercommunity co-operation, amicable social co-existence and everyday civility *despite co-existing perceptions of racialised differences and community segregation.*

Given these absences and contradictions, social cohesion is not a benign concept in that it is premised on partial-gender visibility and emerged from a post-riot, assimilationist agenda. Future research and action may benefit from further engagement with day-to-day, micro-level enactments and negotiations of community.

Bibliography

Ahlbrandt, R. (1984) *Neighborhoods, People and Community*, New York: Plenum Press.

Alexander, C. (2004) 'Imagining the Asian Gang: Ethnicity, Masculinity and Youth After the Riots', in *Critical Social Policy,* 24(4), pp.526-49.

Alexander, C. (2000) *The Asian Gang*, Oxford: Berg.

Anderson, B. (1983) *Imagined Communities: Reflections on the Origin and Spread of Nationalism*, London: Verso.

Back, L. (1996) *New Ethnicities and Urban Cultures*, London: Routledge.

Back, L, Keith, M, Khan, A, Shukra, K. and Solomos, J. (2002) 'The Return of Assimilation: Race, Multiculturalism and New Labour', in *Sociological Research Online,* 7(2), pp.1-14.

Barth, F. (ed) (1969) *Ethnic Groups and Boundaries*, Illinois: Waveland Press Ltd.

Bauman, Z. (2001) *Community: Seeking Security in an Insecure World*, Oxford: Polity.

Beecham, S, Denham, R, Raynsford, R, and Singh, G. (2002) *Draft Guidance on Community Cohesion*, unpublished.

Bell, C. and Newby, H. (1971) *Community Studies*, London: George Allen and Unwin Ltd.

Bland, L. (2005) 'White Women and Men of Colour: Miscegenation Fears in Britain after the Great War, in *Gender and History,* 17(1), pp.29-61.

Burnett, J. (2004) 'Community, Cohesion and the State', in *Race and Class,* 45(3), pp.1-18.

Burnett, J. and Whyte, D. (2004) *New Labour's New Racism*, Institute for Race Relations, available at: http://www.irr.org.uk/news/new-labours-new-racism/ (accessed 28th February 2011).

Campbell, B. (1983) *Goliath: Britain's Dangerous Places*, London: Methuen.

Cantle, T. (2001) *Community Cohesion: A Report by the Independent Review Team*, London: Home Office.

Clarke, Lord and Burnley Task Force (2002) *Report by the Burnley Task Force*, Chaired by Lord Clarke.

Cohen, A. (1998) *The Symbolic Construction of Community*, London: Routledge.

Conservative Party (2010) *Building a Big Society,* London: Conservative Party.

Crow, G and Allan, G. (1994) *Community Life: An Introduction to Local Social Relations*, Hemel Hempstead: Harvester Wheatsheaf.

Denham, J. (2002) *Building Cohesive Communities: A Report of the Ministerial Group on Public Order and Community Cohesion*, London: Home Office.

Denzin, N. (1978) *The Research Act: A Theoretical Introduction to Sociological Methods*, 2nd Edition, New York: McGraw-Hill Book Company.

Dobash, R. and Dobash, R. (1979) *Violence Against Wives: A Case Against the Patriarchy*, New York: Free Press.

Elias, N. and Scotson, J. (1994) *The Established and The Outsiders: A Sociological Enquiry into Community Problems*, London: Sage.

Fenton, Z. (2002) 'Silence Compounded: The Conjunction of Race and Gender Violence', in *Journal of Gender, Social Policy and the Law*, 11(2), pp.271-285.

Ferber, A. (1998) 'Constructing Whiteness: the Intersections of Race and Gender in US White Supremacist Discourse', in *Ethnic and Racial Studies*, 21(1), pp.48-63.

Geertz, C. (2000) *Local Knowledge: Further Essays in Interpretive Anthropology*, USA: Basic Books.

Gieryn, T. (2000) 'A Space for Place in Sociology', in *Annual Review of Sociology*, (26), pp.463-96.

Haq, J. (2006) *The Borders and Boundaries of Community: Responses to Domestic and Racial Violence*. PhD thesis. Newcastle University.

Hill Collins, P. (1991) *Black Feminist Thought: Knowledge, Consciousness, and The Politics of Empowerment*. London: Harper Collins Academic.

Hirschfield, A. and Bowers, K. (1997) 'The Effect of Social Cohesion on Levels of Recorded Crime in Disadvantaged Areas', in *Urban Studies*, 34(8), pp.1275-1295.

Hollway, W. and Jefferson, T. (2000) *Doing Qualitative Research Differently*, London: Sage.

Institute of Community Cohesion: A Guide to Publications [online] available at: http://www.cohesioninstitute.org.uk/Resources/AboutCommunityCohesion#2004 (accessed 24th March 2012).

Jackson, D. (2002) *Our Elders Lived It: American Indian Identity in the City*, DeKalb, Illinios: Northern Illinios University Press.

Kalra, V. (2002) 'Extended View: Riots, Race and Reports: Denham, Cantle, Oldham and Burnley Inquiries', in *Sage Race Relations Abstracts*, 27(4), pp.20-30.

Laner, M. and Benin, M. (2001) 'Bystander Attitudes Towards Victims of Violence: Who's Worth Helping?', in *Deviant Behaviour: An Interdisciplinary Journal*, (22), pp.23-42.

Levitas, R. (1998) *The Inclusive Society? Social Exclusion and New Labour*, Basingstoke, Hampshire: Palgrave.

Lewis, G. (2005) 'Welcome to the Margins: Diversity, Tolerance, and Policies of Exclusion', in *Ethnic and Racial Studies*, 28(3), pp.536-558.

Local Government Association (2002) *Guidance on Community Cohesion*, London: LGA Publications.

Meer, N, Dwyer, C and Modood, T. (2010) 'Embodying Nationhood? Conceptions of British National Identity, Citizenship, and Gender in the 'Veil Affair', in *The Sociological Review* 58(1), pp.84-111.

Miliband, E (2010) *Ed Miliband's Speech to Labour Party Conference* [Online] available at: http://www.guardian.co.uk/politics/2010/sep/28/ed-miliband-labour-conference-speech (accessed 3rd January 2012).

Mooney, J. (1993) 'The Hidden Figure of Domestic Violence in North London', in L. Morris and E. S. Lyon (eds.) *Gender Relations in Public and Private: New Research perspectives*, London: North Islington Council.

Murji, K and Neal, S. (2011); Riot: Race and Politics in the 2011 Disorders' in *Sociological Research Online*, 16 (4), available at: http://www.socresonline.org.uk/16/4/24.html (accessed 20th March 2012).

Office of the Deputy Prime Minister (2006) *State of the English Cities: Urban Research Summary 21*, London: Office of the Deputy Prime Minister.

Ritchie, David (2001) *Oldham Independent Review*, available at: http://www.oldhamir.org.uk/OIR%20Report.pdf (accessed 1st April 2012).

Scarman, L. (1981) 'The Brixton Disorders 10th-12th April 1981', London: H.M.S.O.

Social Exclusion Unit (2001) *A New Commitment to Neighbourhood Renewal*, London: Social Renewal Unit, available at: http://www.neighbourhood.statistics.gov.uk/HTMLDocs/images/NationalStrategyReport_tcm97-51090.pdf (accessed 26th February 2012).

Stedman, R. (2003) 'Is It Really Just a Social Construction? The Contribution of the Physical Environment to Sense of Place', in *Society and Natural Resources*, (16), pp.671-685.

Talen, E. (1999) 'Sense of Community and Neighbourhood Form: An Assessment of the Social Doctrine of New Urbanism', in *Urban Studies* 36(8), pp.1361-1379.

Worley, C. (2005) 'It's Not About Race. It's About the Community': New Labour and 'Community Cohesion', in *Critical Social Policy*, 25(4), pp.483-496.

Young, M. and Willmott, P. (1957) *Family and Kinship in East London*, London: Routledge and Kegan Paul.

Yuval-Davis, N, Anthias, F and Kofman, E. (2005) 'Secure Borders and Safe Haven and the Gendered Politics of Belonging: Beyond Social Cohesion', in *Ethnic and Racial Studies*, 28(3), pp.513-535.

Empowering Minority Communities While not Dismembering States: Multiculturalism and the Model for Non-Territorial Autonomy

Ephraim Nimni[14]

"The West and Europe must come to terms with the diversity of their past in order to master the necessary pluralism of their future." (Ramadan 2010 p.83)

The Problem of Minority Community Empowerment

It is widely accepted that human beings exist in different shapes and forms and that this fact does not undermine the attributes to our common humanity. In the medical sciences, even in genetics, the acceptance of human diversity is a cardinal point of departure for the study of the human genetic characteristics (Cavalli-Sforza 2005 pp.333-340). While the cultural domain is different and must not be reduced to biology or natural sciences, it is intriguing that, for reasons that will be discussed below, the political implications of cultural and religious diversity are often considered a problem in a world of nation states[15]. However, in the study of politics and society, cultural diversity and multilingualism are routine events (Joseph and Rahmani 2006 p.186). We do not loose or common human characteristics because we are constituted through the insertion to a community. On the contrary, to deny the importance and value of cultural diversity denies the very notion of human rights, as this means denying an important constitutive element of human beings. Recognition of difference is therefore a key part of the assertion of our

---

14 Ephraim Nimni is reader on Nationalism & Ethnic Conflict Resolution in School of Politics, International Studies & Philosophy at Queen's University Belfast. His teaching areas are comparative ethnic conflict, theories of ethnicity and nationalism, national cultural autonomy and minority rights, extra-territorial self-determination, multiculturalism, the Israeli Palestinian Conflict. His research interests follow two interrelated directions. He study comparative ethnic conflicts, theories of nationalism and minority rights, models of national self-determination that do not require separate nation states, multiculturalism and the applicability of the national cultural autonomy model to contemporary multination states. The second direction is the study of the Israeli Palestinian conflict from the perspective of conflict resolution. He is a member of the board of the journal Nations and Nationalism and Politikon.

15 Consider for example John Stuart Mill, the founding father of English liberalism, in his (in)famous assertion that "Free institutions are next to impossible in a country made up of different nationalities. Among a people without fellow feeling, especially if they read and speak different languages, the united public opinion, necessary to the working of representative government, cannot exist." (1861, republished 2008)

common humanity (Morris p.1), for human beings cannot be conceived outside their culturally and religiously diverse settings (Tibi 1994 pp.277). Even cultural and postcolonial hybridity is constitutive (Aizenberg 1999 pp.461-466).

Cultural and religious diversity is the norm in a world of nation states. A recurrent problem is how to organise multi-ethnic and multi-nation states so that majorities and minorities are able to coexist and effectively participate in the life of the state, bolstering allegiance without suffering cultural alienation and without resorting to territorial secession. Multicultural liberal democracies champion equality and individual human rights, but often misunderstand or misrecognize the identity cultural minorities, and thus have difficulties in accommodating culturally diverse minority communities. Here, regrettably, the Shadow of John Stuart Mill looms large. The republican and democratic nation-state has been an instrument of persistent policies of cultural homogenisation, problematising the relation between majoritarian democracy and diversity. The antagonistic relationship between majoritarian democracy and cultural diversity is often reflected in logic of 'diversity denial' and rejection of Multiculturalism (Conversi 2011 pp.3-4). The process of nation building has sadly been, simultaneously, a process of nation destroying (Nimni 2011 pp.55-66; Connor 1994 p.28).

Western Liberal theorists have assumed in many cases that the protection of individual human rights is sufficient to ensure justice between culturally diverse communities. Unfortunately, this is not the case. A state can permanently block the insertion or influence of a cultural minority without abandoning the individual civil and political rights of minority members. Consider the case of indigenous peoples. Those who have been conquered and destroyed by settler colonialism and those who have been made marginal minorities in their ancestral lands have a unique normative claim for self-governance, cultural recognition, and community rights. Yet, paradoxically, many colonial-settler societies are liberal democracies (US, Canada, Australia, and Argentina, to cite a few). Here, the principles of individual human rights are not sufficient to recognise the collective claims of indigenous peoples. To prevent these injustices, traditional human rights principles need to be supplemented with communal minority rights. Without these, and in a very paradoxical way, in the absence of community minority rights, the enforcement of abstract universal human rights principles may exacerbate ethno-cultural injustice (Kymlicka 1998 pp.214-224; Kymlicka 2001).

Consider the following: most contemporary nation states have a "*titular nation*". This term is taken from the study of nations in the former Soviet Union, but it is applicable to most contemporary nation states, whether they are liberal democracies or not. The term refers to a governing ethno-national community in the state, usually forming the majority of the population, typically after which the state is named (Prazauskas 1994 p.180). Now, liberal democracies are predicated on the principle of formal equality between citizens. However, this principle is often subverted by the linguistic and cultural privileges of the titular nation. Minorities of different kind and sorts are often invited to assimilate to the ways of the titular nation with equality as compensation. This is invitation is often couched in the language of integration and "Affirmative Action". These are measures designed to improve the standing of women and minorities. Such measures may seek to achieve equality as compensation to guarantee present and future equality (O'Brien 2007 p.19). However, in the case of minorities, and sometimes in the case of women (Pateman 1998), affirmative action is designed to erase constitutive differences in order to shape cultural minorities in the image of the titular nation. This procedure exacerbates ethno-cultural injustices and generates alienation, for in the eyes of many members of minority communities, the procedure violates the egalitarian ethos of liberal democracy. The standard accusation is 'we are only equals if we partake in the cultural behaviour of the majority'.

Minority Community Representation: Hopes and Difficulties

Without community representation, the "tyranny of the majority" becomes a danger for minority communities. Affirmative action humbles minorities or jeopardizes minority continuity. In an abstract sense, what is to stop majority communities from enforcing the majority's religion, or destroying the language or culture on the minority? Conversely, problems also occur from anxieties in the opposite direction. If minority communities have enshrined rights, is this a form a form of separation? Could enshrined minority rights be a divisive mechanism that leads to secession? The answer to both questions has to be simultaneous, and, can only be found in balance and proportionality in both directions, when majorities and minorities have sufficient motives and enticements to live together. For this very reason, it is crucially important to develop governmental modes that incorporate the material and symbolic needs of majorities and minorities, as well as offering recognition and institutional incorporation to minority communities. As Charles Taylor strikingly argues: *Misrecognition shows not just a lack of due respect. It can inflict a grievous wound, saddling its victims with a crippling self-hatred. Due recognition is not just a courtesy we owe people. It is a vital human need* (Taylor 1994 p.26). In addition, one can add, it is a crucial aspect of properly exercising human rights. It is argued here that models of non-territorial self-determination could significantly help in this task. Territorial representation is possible when minority communities inhabit a compact territorial space, yet in the majority of cases, minority communities do not reside compactly, making any territorial representation not feasible. This situation often causes intractable problems for the functioning of democratic polities, suggesting instead models of non-territorial autonomy (NTA) as a solution.

A moderate estimate puts the number of world nations to well above 3,000, while with the admission of South Sudan, there are 193 states represented in the UN. Less than 20 states are ethnically homogeneous (when cultural minorities account for less than 5% of the population)(Brown 1993 p.6). Nations with states are a small part of all nations, and it is not an exaggeration to say that the term 'nation state' — understood as one (cultural) nation in one state — is an unsuitable description (Govier 1997 p.269). While the overwhelming majority of states represented in the UN are not culturally homogeneous, the organisation of their political institutions often gives the impression they are, trapping cultural minorities into at best, ambiguity and at worst, alienation, subordination and it worst case scenario, ethnic cleansing.

In liberal democratic theories that attach a normative value to democracy — the ones that argue that democracy has more than an instrumental value to liberalism — expansive democracy refers to the effects of institutions in increasing individuals' control over self-governance, self-determination and self-development (Warren 1992 p.9). But here, either culture has no bearing in political representation, or, individuals are seen as culturally homologous (Kymlicka 1995; Kymlicka and Straehle 1999 pp.65-88). This renders invisible their community insertion, something that becomes seriously problematic when that kind of individual inclusion, the one that ignores community membership, is the source for the disadvantage that democratic theory wishes to remedy (Jovanovi 2012).

In view of the difficulties above, we are witnessing a slow transformation in modalities of Self Determination and the recognition of difference. This transformation is creating a convergence between multiculturalism and minority self-determination. The concept of national self-determination is in many cases, moving away for the rigid traditional interpretation in international law and liberal theory, towards a more flexible, non-territorial notion of community representation. Faced with the practical impossibility of building new states in areas where minorities and majorities residentially overlap, new forms of minority governance and representation began to emerge, spearheaded by the demands of indigenous peoples who have a strong case for self-determination coupled with a practical impossibility of building separate states.

We are experiencing a deflation of the nineteen-century nation state as a model for national liberation – not only because democratic nation states are internally and externally devolving power to regional forms of organisation, but crucially, because many democratic nation states have begun transferring jurisdictions to devolved regional governments that in many cases embody minority nations. Multi-level governance, understood as the exercise of authority across and within different jurisdictions, is slowly changing the way democratic representation is understood. Here the correlation of state, nation, and people is increasingly challenged by processes of migration and globalisation (Bauböck and Guiraudon 2009 p.439). For example, the increasing roles of transnational Diasporas are subverting nineteen-century notions of nationhood as linked to territoriality.

However, we are certainly not observing a reduction in minority demands. On the contrary, we are experiencing an important expansion of demands for cultural recognition. These demands come in many formats, including indigenous emancipatory movements, minority nationalisms, and multicultural demands for recognition of ethnic and religious minorities. This extraordinary expansion in the politicisation of minority communities signals, in Will Kymlicka's (2007 p.1) words, *a veritable revolution* in the relation between states and ethnic and religious minorities.

A momentous paradigm change over the last thirty years or so (Nimni 2010 pp.21-37) is giving birth to a new, more pluralist and multidimensional understanding of the relationship between nationalism and democratic governance (Moore 2001 p.7), particularly in settings that encourage multiple jurisdictions. A common element across the various versions of the new paradigm is that the dispersal of governance across multiple jurisdictions is considered both, more efficient than and normatively superior to a central state sovereign monopoly (Bache and Flinders 2005). These new theoretical insights emerged in the area of conflict resolution and multiculturalism. They advocate, in a vast display of empirical and comparative cases, a system of governance based on the participation of several democratically organised, ethno national communities with multiple jurisdictions. Here the governmental process is not of discrete, centralised, homogenous units, as in the old nation state model, but one in which governance is understood as a multilayered and multicultural mechanism, with regional and minority devolution and multiple jurisdictions (Kymlicka 1995; Gagnon and Tully 2001; Nootens 2004; Taylor 2004).

The growth of these new forms of democratic management emerged precisely because they come to terms with a difficulty that broke the back of old versions of national sovereignty and centralised government. This problem is *concurrently* at the centre of the move for a paradigm change. The shift responds to the crying need to break with the oppressive governance of cultural minorities to avoid the pain and wanton destruction that results from the estrangement of these minorities and their demands to build new states, and the need to find ways to provide national minorities with equal rights, governance, and political participation – *without dismembering existing states*.

The Modalities of Non-Territorial Autonomy

The term Non-Territorial Autonomy (NTA) is a generic term that refers to different practices of minority community autonomy that does not entail exclusive control over territory. Of course, in an abstract sense, all forms of community autonomy occur in a territory, but the specific difference of NTA is that it does not claim exclusive territorial control. In this way, the models and practices described here can take place while the autonomous communities reside in shared territorial spaces. These models challenge political prescriptions of exclusive territorial sovereignty while exercising this form of autonomy or self-determination. Non-Territorial autonomy takes variety of different forms such as Consociationalism and National Cultural Autonomy, but also forms of representation that de-territorialises self-determination, as in the case of indigenous communities, the juridical autonomy as with religious communities, or in the practice of many forms of religious and/or multicultural forms of representation. Models of non-territorial autonomy are a crucially important tool for the effective participation of minorities in public life, as advocated by the '*The Lund Recommendations on the Effective Participation of National Minorities in Public Life*'[16].

The National Cultural Autonomy Model

The NCA model has it is origins in the twilight of the Habsburg Empire and the attempt of Austrian socialists to convert the Empire from a conglomerate of squabbling cultural communities into a democratic federation of nationalities (Nimni 2001 p.xxii-xxiii). In contrast to most other forms of national autonomy, the NCA model rests on the idea that autonomous cultural communities could be organized as autonomous collectives whatever their residential location within a multinational state (Smith and Cordell 2008). In contemporary terms, the model was introduced in the Brussels-Capital Region (*Région de Bruxelles-Capitale, Brussels Hoofdstedelijk Gewest*) (van Parsij 2000 p.246) because of the impossibility to segregate the two communities in an urban environment (Dirk and Swyngedouw 2003 pp.127-139) and in a distorted version, in the Russian Duma. Paradoxically, the model applied in the Brussels Capital Territory has considerable similarities with the original Austrian socialist model, but this model is hardly mentioned. In contrast, the State Duma adopted the Russian federal law on National Cultural Autonomy in 1996, it has many references to the Renner-Bauer model, but in practical terms, the model implemented has little resemblance to it (Bowrin 2005 pp.191-206).

---

16 Organisation for Security and Cooperation in Europe (OSCE), High Commission for National Minorities (HCNM). http://www.osce.org/hcnm/32240. (Last accessed 8 April 2012). See also the 10 year commentary on the practice of the Lund Recommendations in: Marc Weller and Katherine Nobbs (eds.), Political Participation of Minorities: A Commentary on International Standards and Practice, Oxford University Press, 2010.

The model of national-cultural autonomy proposed by Karl Renner and Otto Bauer is based on the premise that ethnic and national communities can be organised as autonomous units in multinational states without considering residential location. In most conventional theories, national autonomy requires a territorial base for the autonomous national community, or at least the intention to build some kind of 'autonomous homeland'. In contrast, Bauer and Renner's theory rests on the idea of 'non-territorial national autonomy'. This means that autonomous communities are organised as self-governing collectives whatever their residential location within a multi-nation state (Anagnostou 2001 pp.94-124).

The NCA model acknowledges that national communities require recognition of their specificity and difference in the public domain and this is achieved through the existence of legally guaranteed autonomous corporations. Members of each national community, whatever their area of residence, form a single public body or association endowed with legal personality and collective rights. This model is based on the premise that the most controversial issues in the relationship between ethnic and national groups are issues concerning language, education and the recognition of cultural rights in the public domain. Networks of communication across cultural boundaries are crucial because the model recognises both, communities and individuals as legitimate interlocutors.

The Ottoman Millet System

There is in the NCA model a remarkable similarity with the Millet System in the Ottoman Empire, another NTA model. The important difference with the Millet System is that the latter was not organised according to democratic principles, as it vested all power and authority within the religious leader, the Chief Rabbi in the case of Jews (Hakham Bashi) and the Patriarch in the case of Christian communities. The Ottoman millet system has nevertheless shown remarkable tolerance and autonomy towards minority communities. Nuri Yurdusev argues that the Ottoman Empire granted more minority autonomy than many of the known empires (Yurdusev 2004 p.20). It recognised forms of institutional diversity and created a political and social environment for the reproduction of diverse cultures. It sustained both limited diversity and stability which are two notions rarely combined in the contemporary societies (Alptekin 2009 p.1). The leading scholar of contemporary theories of multiculturalism, Professor Bhikhu Parekh argues that despite its shortcomings, the Millet System had great virtues including *a remarkable record of religious toleration that puts Western Europe to shame* (Parekh 2009 p.205). The Ottoman Jewish community flourished under the Millet System. Sarah Abrevaya Stern argues that Ottoman Jewry in particular where protected in ways that minorities under Christian rule were not. Non-Muslims were allowed to maintain their own courts and institutions and evolved into corporate structures as a result. She further argues that as far as Jews were concerned, the success of the Millet System was reflected in the *virtual absence of anti-Semitism from the Ottoman landscape* (Stern 2005 p.55), something that cannot be said about Christian Europe. The noted political philosopher Professor Michael Walzer notes that the autonomous arrangements of the Millet System represents the most stable regime of toleration known in world history. Walzer claims that *the rulers recognised the value of group autonomy, and this recognition has worked effectively for group survival* (Walzer 2004 p.177). Will Kymlicka argues that while the Millet System was generally tolerant of group differences, it was not a liberal society for it did not tolerate individual dissent within its constituent communities (Kymlicka 1992 p.36).

Even in its illiberal and authoritarian form, it is very clear that the Ottoman Millet system afforded more tolerance and protection to minorities than current republican and majoritarian democracies, because the latter enshrines the rule of the titular nation and in many cases, alienate minorities. In this regard, it is intriguing why the Millet system is considered today an anachronism. The Millet system prevented ethnic identities from being put under pressure by a titular nation. Unlike the nation state, the logic of ethnic assimilation was not the dominant logic of Ottoman politics (Yegen 2009 p.557). Above all, the Millet system could certainly be reformed and organised democratically without losing its defining characteristics, as the Ottomanists (*Osmanlıcılık*) advocated. I could be transformed into a supranational political organisation that stresses patriotism of the multi-nation state and the group feeling of all citizens regardless of nation and ethnicity.

Consociationalism

Consociationalism is the better-known form of governance that requires collective (group) representation. It presents an alternative to the principles of majoritarian democracy and it is used to manage conflict in deeply divided societies. The term was popularised by Arend Lijphart (1997) and was further developed by John McGarry and Brendan O'Leary in a series of seminal works on Conflict Resolution and on Northern Ireland (Taylor 2009; O'Leary 2005; Mcgarry 2006 pp.249-277). It is more elite based than the NCA model, and it is based on the principles of a grand coalition across cultural divides, mutual veto on matters vital for the continuity of the minority communities, proportionality in representation and the segmental autonomy of each community. As with NCA, the aim is to make government more responsive to the concerns of minorities and offer alternative outcomes to territorial nationalism and secession. In this way, secessionist demands are neutralised and cultural minorities are encouraged to feel confident of representation and protection for their vital concerns (Lustick, Miodownik and Eidelson 2004 pp.210-11). The model has been applied with great success in Northern Ireland, leading to the pacification of the country and it has shown the way towards the resolution of what was an intractable the conflict.

Religious Autonomy for Minority Communities

Another form of NTA for minority communities is related to state legislation that partially empowers religious tribunals of minority communities to pass specific rulings for its congregations. These rulings have in some cases, the status of the law of the land. For lack of space, I will confine my examples to the United Kingdom, which is one of the few Western democracies that it is not a secular state. The lack of the militant secularism that characterises republican models (France for example) facilitates the acceptance of this limited autonomy on matters of religious importance to minority communities.

Divorce (Religious Marriages) Bill 2002

This legislation was petitioned by the Jewish community an enacted by the UK Parliament. It covers a human rights anomaly in Orthodox Jewish Law. For a divorce to be effective in the Orthodox Jewish community, a "get" must be obtained. A get is a consensual divorce in which mutual co-operation between the parties is required. The husband has to go before the *Beth Din* (Religious tribunal, akin to the Sharia Council in Islam) for a get and deliver it to his wife, and she is required to accept it. If he does not do so, the wife cannot remarry in Jewish law, although the husband may be able to do so (monogamy is not consensual in Judaism, some Jewish traditions accept polygamy in similar terms to those of Islam). This creates the problem that a get refusal has very different and very damaging implications for a woman. Without a get, a woman who has a child by her subsequent partner is defined as an adulteress under Jewish law. Her child becomes an illegitimate outcast, which is a stigma that carries on into future generations. A woman who is trapped in a marriage that she seeks to end is called in Hebrew, an "*agunah*", meaning one who is chained to a spouse against her will. If a wife refuses to accept her husband's get, he is known as an "agun". However, he does not suffer from the same disadvantages. As a result, a husband can effectively hold his wife to ransom, and can demand money, property or other rights concerning custody or child maintenance in return for a get. The Divorce (Religious marriages Bill) 2002 requires the dissolution of a religious marriage before granting a secular divorce, empowering the Beth Din to grant this divorce, and bringing in this way equality to the situation, for the husband will not be able to remarry in a civil court if he does not grant his wife a get. The husband can also be coerced by the civil tribunal (with alimony costs, damages, etc) to grant the religious divorce, something that the Bet din is unable to do. The Bill also empowers the Lord Chancellor to extend its provisions to other faiths, particularly in similar cases in the Islamic community. This implies the recognition not only of the Beth Din, but also of the Islamic Sharia Council, who are the ones that ultimately rule on the dissolution of the religious marriage.

While this is an example of limited autonomy for religious communities, it is nevertheless important for these issues are central to the lives of members of these communities, and by this kind of recognition of the authority of their religious law, these communities can feel better integrated into the wider society. This is also the opinion of the current Archbishop of Canterbury Dr Rowan Williams who has written an excellent and detailed article on the need for the incorporation of some aspects of Islamic Sharia Law into British Law (Williams 2008 pp.262-282).

The final example, is not of a form of NTA as such, but of an adaptation of Western Islamic communities to their status of minorities, a central condition for acquiring form of religious autonomy compatible with the values of human rights and the ethos of Western societies. *Fiqh al-Aqalliyyat* (the fiqh, or jurisprudence, of Muslim minorities) is a legal doctrine introduced by, Shaykh Dr. Taha Jabir al-Alwani, and Shaykh Dr. Yusuf al-Qara -Dawi of Qatar. This sustains that Muslim minorities, especially those residing in the West, need a special type of Jurisprudence to take care of their religious needs, which differ from those of Muslims residing in Islamic countries. It tries to resolve differences with the culture and values of the host societies from within the framework of Islamic jurisprudence. Its goal is to reinterpret some Islamic concepts, while at the same time, not being a religious reform movement that breaches orthodoxy (Fishman 2006). The expansion of this idea will allow Sharia Councils to develop jurisprudential roles that will not clash with the values of majority communities in the West. There are however, significant debates among Islamic scholars as to whether this is necessary. In particular, Hellyer and Ramadan remain somewhat sceptical, for they prefer a vision that sees Muslims in Europe, rather than Muslims as a minority in Europe (Hellyer 2009 pp.94-50). Such a debate is not uncommon among Western minorities, and it merits a wider discussion on status of minority communities in Europe.

The aim of this paper is to consider the difficulties of minority empowerment and participation in a world of nation states. Following the French Revolution, the European democratic state was predicated on the assimilation of minority cultures with democracy and individual civil rights as compensation. This form of minority coercion cannot be easily conceptualised in terms of dominant interpretations of human rights and require forms of minority protection and empowerment if those communities are reluctant to assimilate and also wish to participate in the democratic life of the state. Cultural diversity is the norm of the vast majority of nation states, and if integration and cohesion is a desired goal, some kind of community autonomy and representation is required. When minority communities are recognised and are given autonomy to organise their own affairs, they are more inclined to feel part of the common polity. The models of non-territorial autonomy discussed here, are designed to help in the goal of achieving greater integration and preventing the twin evils of secession and ghettoisation that often result from minority alienation and misrecognition.

Bibliography

Aizenberg, E. 1999 'I Walked with a Zombie: The Pleasures and Perils of Postcolonial Hybridity', in *World Literature Today*, 73(3).

Alptekin, H. (2009) 'Millet System Through the Prism of Multiculturalism', *Unpublished Conference Papers — Southern Political Science Association*, January Annual Meeting.

Anagnostou, D. (2001) 'Breaking the Cycle of Nationalism: The EU, Regional Policy and the Minority of Western Thrace, Greece', in *South European Society and Politics*, 6(1).

Anne Julie Semb, Anne J. (2005) 'Sami Self-Determination in the Making?', in *Nations and Nationalism*, 11 (4).

Bache, I. & Flinders, M. (2005) *Multi-level Governance*, Oxford University Press.

Bauböck R. and Guiraudin, V. (2009) 'Realignments of Citizenship: Reassessing Rights in the Age of Plural Memberships and Multi-Level Governance', in *Citizenship Studies*, 13(5).

Bauer, O. (2001) *The Question of Nationalities and Social Democracy*, Minneapolis: University of Minnesota Press.

Brown, Michael E. 1993 *Ethnic Conflict and International Security*, Princeton University Press.

Bowring, B. (2005) 'Burial and Resurrection, Karl Renner's Controversial Influence on the National Question in Russia', in: Ephraim Nimni, ed. (2005*). National Cultural Autonomy and its Contemporary Critics*, London: Routledge.

Cavalli-Sforza, L. (2005) 'The Human Genome Diversity, Project: past, present and future', in *Nature Reviews: Genetics*, 6(4), pp.333-40.

Connor, W. (1994) *Ethnonationalism, The Quest for Understanding*, Princeton: Princeton University Press.

Conversi D. (2011) 'Majoritarian democracy and globalization versus ethnic diversity?', in *Democratization*, forthcoming, pp.3-4, available at: http://www.tandfonline.com/doi/abs/10.1080/13510347.2011.626947.

Dirk, J. and Swyngedouw, M. (2001) 'Territorial and Non-Territorial Federalism: Reform of the Brussels Capital Region', in *Regional and Federal Studies*, 13(2).

Divorce (Religious Marriages) Bill 2002 United Kingdom Parliament Publications http://www.publications.parliament.uk/pa/cm200102/cmhansrd/vo011023/debtext/11023-05.htm (Accessed 8 April 2012)

Fishman S. (2006) 'Fiqh al-Aqalliyyat: A Legal Theory for Muslim Minorities', in *Research Monographs on the Muslim World*, Hudson Institute, Centre on Islam, Democracy, and the Future of the Muslim World.

Gagnon A. and Tully J. (eds.) (2001) *Multinational Democracies*, Cambridge University Press.

Govier, T. (1997) *Social Trust and Human Communities*, Montréal: McGill-Queen's University Press.

Hellyer, H.A. (2009) *Muslims of Europe, the "Other" Europeans,* Edinburgh University Press, pp.94-95.

Tariq, R. (2004) *Western Muslims and the future of Islam,* Oxford University Press.

Jahn, B. (2005) 'Barbarian thoughts: imperialism in the philosophy of John Stuart Mill', in *Review of International Studies,* 31, pp.599–618.

Joseph M. & Ramani, E. (2006) 'English in the World does not Mean English Everywhere: the case for multilingualism in the ELT/ESL profession', in Rani Rubdy, Mario Saraceni, (eds.) *English in the World: Global Rules, Global Roles,* London, New York: Continuum.

Jovanovi, Miodrag A. (2012) *Collective Rights, a Legal Theory,* Cambridge University Press.

Keating M. and McCarty J. (2001) (eds.) *Minority Nationalism and the Changing World Order,* Oxford University Press.

Kymlicka, W. (1998) 'Human Rights and Ethnocultural Justice', in *Review of Constitutional Studies,* 4(2).

Kymlicka, W. (2001) *Politics in the Vernacular,* Oxford University Press.

Kymlicka, W. (1992) 'Two Models of Pluralism and Tolerance', in *Analyse und Kritik,* (14).

Kymlicka, W. (1995) *Multicultural Citizenship,* Oxford University Press,

Kymlicka, W. and Straehle, C. (1999) 'Cosmopolitanism, Nation-States, and Minority Nationalism: A Critical Review of Recent Literature', in *European Journal of Philosophy,* 7(1).

Kymlicka, W. (2007) *Multicultural Odysseys, Navigating the New International Politics of Diversity,* Oxford University Press.

Kymlicka, W. (1995) *Multicultural Citizenship: A Liberal Theory of Minority Rights,* Oxford University Press.

Lijphart, A. (1997) 'Democracy in Plural Societies: A Comparative Exploration', in *New Haven,* CT: Yale University Press.

Lord Acton, L. *The History of Freedom and Other Essays, Section III: Sir Erskine May's Democracy in Europe.*

Lustick, I.S. and Miodownik, D. and Eidelson, Roy J. (2004) 'Secessionism in Multicultural States: Does Sharing Power Prevent or Encourage It?', in *The American Political Science Review,* 98(2), pp.210-211.

Mann, M. (2005) *The Dark Side of Democracy, Explaining · Ethnic Cleansing,* Cambridge University Press.

Morris, J. (2001) 'Impairment and Disability: Constructing an Ethics of Care That Promotes Human Rights', in *Hypatia,* 16(4).

Tibi, B. (1994) 'Islamic Law/Shari'a, Human Rights, Universal Morality and International Relations', in *Human Rights Quarterly,* 16.

McGarry J. and O'Leary B. (2006) 'Consociational theory, Northern Ireland's conflict, and its agreement: What critics of consociation can learn from Northern

Ireland', in *Government and Opposition*, 41(2), pp.249-277.

Mill, John S. (2008) *Representative Government, Ch 16, 'Of Nationality, as Connected with Representative Government'*, Forgotten Books.

Moore, M. (2001) 'Normative justifications for liberal nationalism: justice, democracy and national identity', in *Nations and Nationalism*.

Nimni, E. (2010) 'Nationalism, Ethnicity and Self-Determination: A Paradigm Shift?', in Keith Breen and Shane ONeill (eds.), *After the Nation? Critical Reflections on Post-Nationalism*, Palgrave MacMillan.

Nimni, E. (2011) 'Stateless Nations in a World of Nation States', in K. Cordell and S. Wolf (eds.) *Routledge Handbook of Ethnic Conflict*, London: Routledge.

Nimni, E. (1999) 'Nationalist multiculturalism in late imperial Austria as a critique of contemporary liberalism: The case of Bauer and Renner', in *Journal of Political Ideologies*.

Nootens, G. (2004) *Désenclaver la démocratie, Des huguenots a la paix des braves* Montréal, Editions Québec Amérique.

O'Brien, P. (2007) 'Gender Equality and the Constitutional Guarantee of Equality: A Comparative Study', in *Irish Student Law Review*, 15(9).

O'Leary, B. (2005) 'Debating Consociational politics: Normative and Explanatory arguments', in Noel, Sid (ed.). *From Power Sharing to Democracy: Post-Conflict Institutions in Ethnically Divided Societies*, Montreal: McGill-Queen's Press.

Parekh, B. (2000) *Rethinking Multiculturalism, Cultural diversity and Political Theory*, McMillan, Basingstoke: McMillian.

Prazauskas, A. (1994) 'The Influence of Ethnicity on the Foreign Policies of the Western Littoral States' in Roman Szporluk (ed.) *National Identity and Ethnicity in Russia and the New States of Eurasia*, London: M.E. Sharpe.

Pateman, C. (1988) *The Sexual Contract*, Stanford University Press.

Ramadan, T. (2010) *What I believe*, Oxford: Oxford University Press.

Roach, Steven C. (2005) *Cultural Autonomy, Minority Rights, and Globalization*, Ashgate Publishing Company.

Smith, D. and Cordell, K. (2008) (Eds.) *Cultural Autonomy in Contemporary Europe, Routledge*, London.

Stern, Sarah A. (2004) 'The Permeable Boundaries of Ottoman Jewry', in Joel Migdal (ed.) *Boundaries and Belonging: States and Societies in the Struggle to Shape Identities and Local Practices*, Cambridge University Press.

Taylor, C. (1994) *Multiculturalism: Examining the Politics of Recognition*, Princeton University Press.

Taylor, R. (2009) (ed.), *Consociational Theory, McGarry and O'Leary and the Northern Ireland Conflict*, London, Routledge.

van Parijs, P. (2000) 'Must Europe be Belgian? On Democratic Citizenship in Multilingual Polities', in Catriona McKinnon Iain Hampsher-Monk (eds.) *The Demands of Citizenship*, London and New York: Continuum.

Warren, M. (1992) 'Democratic Theory and Self-Transformation', in *The American Political Science Review*, 86(1).

Weller, M. and Nobbs, K. (eds.) (2010) *Political Participation of Minorities: A Commentary on International Standards and Practice,* Oxford University Press.

Williams, Dawn G. Andland, Roderic R. (2006) 'The Legitimation of Black Subordination: The Impact of Color-Blind Ideology on African American Education', in *The Journal of Negro Education*, 75(4).

Williams, R. (2008) 'Civil and Religious Law in England: A Religious Perspective', in *Ecclesiastical Law Journal*, pp.262–282.

Walzer, M. (2004) *Arguing About War*, Yale University Press.

Yegen, M. (2009) 'The Kurdish Question in Turkish State Discourse', in *Journal of Contemporary History*, 34(4), p.557.

Yurdusev, N. (2004) *Ottoman Diplomacy, Conventional or Unconventional,* Basingstoke: Palgrave MacMillan.

Multiculturalism: 'Spice' of Lives, 'Bane' of Legal Systems?

Esin Orucu[17]

Introduction

Nation states are still the predominant political units of our century. Indeed, in works looking at the legal cultures of Europe, or considering the European Union as a multi-level system of governance, or talking of Europe's legal pluralism, the nation states are the units of inquiry (Gibbon and Caldeira 1996 p.55). Offering a predominantly monolithic, centralised, territorial top-down model of law, the states provide the source of law and are the legitimiser of sources of law. When a state does not allow competing sources of law to exist, it is regarded as intolerant, undemocratic, even despotic and self-referential. When it does so however, in the western world, this only appears as a weak version of legal pluralism. Because here the top-down source of law is receptive to other sources, it is regarded as more tolerant, democratic, multicultural, and reflecting a more open society. In the western tradition, the stronger version of legal pluralism, in which levels of legalities of equal value co-exist in the same territorial or social space as overlapping orders, with the same status as state law and independent of it, is not favoured. Unitary nation states do not live comfortably with so many rivals. If the unitary state is still the rule, then cultural pluralism cannot be fully reflected in the legal system and becomes the exception.

'Inter-legality' is a complex problem and becomes a dilemma for the lawyers of the western world as they face multiculturalism, regional orders and the laws of indigenous peoples, displaced peoples and refugees, which challenge even the weak version of legal pluralism. Although the contemporary move seems to suggest a progression from monism to relativism and finally to pluralism, the question is whether the unitary nation state can cope with this progression? Can it accept the fact that all societies have diversity of legal orders, which overlap, interact and often conflict, and that 'official' state law is only one of these? What can it

---

17 Esin Orucu is Professor Emerita of Comparative Law and Honorary Senior Research Fellow, University of Glasgow; and Professor Emerita of Comparative Law, Erasmus University Rotterdam. She was born in 1940 in Istanbul. She graduated from Istanbul University, Law Faculty. She completed her PhD in Istanbul University. She is a member of the Istanbul Bar. She has been working and living in Britain since 1976. She also was part time Professor in the Netherlands (EUR) until 2005. She is retired but still teaches in Glasgow (Mixed legal systems). Her areas of teaching, research and interest include comparative law, mixed jurisdictions, Turkish law, language and culture and jurisprudence.

opt for: prohibition and assimilation, or integration by protecting diversity only as part of respect for cultural pluralism, or preserving and supporting diversity and pluralisation by enacting legislation to promote, maintain and develop diverse cultures and localisms?[18]

Anthropology (Gladwin 1964) and sociology may not have many problems in their approach to pluralism. But, how does law regard it? After all, the nation state was originally built on the idea of an identifiable culture, and though sub-cultural influence is of growing importance, 'it can in most cases still be treated as a cultural unit' (Gessner 1994 p.132). As culture is the product of historical influences and is not uniform but hybrid, what happens when official law meets diverse cultures? Can the state control the whole of the law? Can legislators provide a legal regime for each life-style? How is culture to be measured in the first place?[19] What should be the criteria of proof and who should carry the burden of proof? Who represents culture? And maybe more important, can cultural and social aspects of legal principles accept outside control?

Issues to Consider

Ethnic exclusionism versus universalism occupies much of today's discourse. Is it feasible to regard 'global' as 'a collection of diverse 'locals'? Does globalisation require us 'to recognise "the Other" and in doing so, to accommodate the "diversity" and "co-existence of cultures"' (Hannerz 1990 p.239)?[20] What of 'cultural relativism' and the 'limits of liberal toleration', or the impact of multicultural discourse on social cohesion? Globalised, universal human rights seen as integral to liberalism, democracy, individualism and progressive change, are presented against the pervasive dominance by the community or the state and claim inclusiveness (Howard 1993).

Legal pluralism refers to a social fact: the co-existence of different bodies of norms within the same social space.[21] State or official legal pluralism indicates a single national legal system in which state centralism still prevails, but with plural laws; the state recognising different rules for specific categories of persons such as was the case in colonial times, for instance. However, this is challenged today as being

---

18 For these views generally, see Örücü 2002 and Örücü 2010.

19 Culture and legal culture, which to a certain extent reflects general culture, are widely used terms that have no agreed definition. 'Legal culture, in its most general sense, should be seen as one way of describing relatively stable patterns of legally oriented social behaviour and attitudes. [...] Like culture itself, legal culture is about who we are, not just what we do'. [Emphasis added] See Nelken 2004 p.1-28.

20 Also see Santos 2002 p.268-289

21 For the ever-expanding catalogue of 'pluralist' approaches to law: classical, new, global, critical and post-modern, and the literature see Donlan 2011 p.30-33.

a narrow and weak version of legal pluralism by the demands of multiculturalism. Multiculturalism becomes a serious issue when it demands to be manifested in legal pluralism, since this appears to be a threat to the territorial integrity of a state, and to the monolithic values of the dominant culture within that state.

Legal development is a rational and natural response to existing social, economic, political, geographic and religious circumstances, and law can act as a harmonising agent. In fact, law can be a reactor to social change or its initiator. It can 'lead' and so change society rather than adjust a legal system to social change; it can 'follow' social change and reflect multi cultures; or, it can 'tinker' and seek to keep the existing system operating, while making adjustments to improve efficiency. There are significant consequences of these different approaches and their impact on the relationship between law and culture.

It can be claimed that there is an intimate connection between law and the culture of the society in which it operates. Some however, may regard law as a tool of social engineering, finding practical adjustments, and reconciling conflicting and overlapping interests. Can and should a legal system be used to change society, or is the law 'merely' a codification of existing social practices? Depending on ideological pre-dispositions and choice of illustrations, both questions can be answered in the positive.

Legal pluralism can be portrayed as an 'effective attack on the common sense of orthodox jurisprudence' by rejecting the 'oneness of state law as law or universality of western law'.[22] It may be that 'legal pluralism is the fact, legal centralism is a myth, an ideal, a claim, an illusion' (Griffiths p.1986). Since in the western world, the plural arrangement in a unitary legal system -the weaker version of legal pluralism- is the best on offer today, how is the paradox between cultural pluralism (or multiculturalism) and official law to be resolved? Can 'cultural and localised exceptionalism' and 'cultural relativism' trump 'globalising uniformity' and universal standards, or can 'globalising uniformity' always trump 'cultural exceptionalism'?

Within nation states, today's legal discourse concerning challenges of multiculturalism – linked to a sense of cultural identity - seem to focus on sporadic problems such as women's rights, forced marriages, intimate femicide, female circumcision or polygamy. Within the context of the European Union, cultural diversity or multiculturalism – linked to a sense of national identity - is mainly contained in Article 167, line 1 Treaty on the Foundation of the EU (TFEU):

---

22 A model of official law as always interacting with unofficial law and legal postulates, and never existing in isolation, has been offered with the state and its laws, society and its normative orders and religion and world-views, working together to achieve a balanced and sustainable legal order. See Chiba 1986 and Chiba 1989.

'The Union shall contribute to the flowering of the cultures of the Member States while respecting their national and regional diversity and at the same time bringing the common cultural heritage to the fore'. Here, multiculturalism signifies the linguistic and cultural -as understood broadly and not limited to legal culture alone- diversities characteristic of the Member States in the EU.[23] The question as to what extent cultural concerns should be accommodated beyond 'taking cultural aspects into account', especially in relation to the harmonisation process, is open to discussion. So is the question whether harmonisation is to be achieved at the cost of cultural diversity.

Illustrations of Some Ways of Coping:

Turkey

Turkish Republic is a centralist monolithic state in which the cultures and customs that the law meets are indigenous. However, by choice, desire and design, the legal system in Turkey was reconstructed after 1923 by borrowing from the Swiss, French, German and Italian legal systems. The legal system is secular and yet 98% of the people are Muslims. While the legal system has the aspiration to erase certain cultures and create a new one, whereby assimilating people into a chosen image, when law meets cultures that it does not cater for, the judges either try to eradicate and ignore them in keeping with the vision of the legislator, or accommodate them within the official framework.[24]

Our first example raises the issue of a claim based on an Islamic source unacceptable to the official law. In 1993 the name of a female trainee lawyer was removed from the Bar list because she came to court wearing a head cover and refused to remove it. According to the lower administrative court, as she was only a trainee and the matter solely a moral question, there was no violation of the respect due to the legal profession, which imposes certain conditions on appearance. The Turkish *Conseil d'Etat* (the *Danıştay*) however, saw no difference between a lawyer and a trainee and regarded the issue as outside 'the right to religious freedom', saying: 'The behaviour of the trainee is contrary to the principles of a *laic* state governed by the rule of law, is incompatible with the profession of a lawyer and is an obstacle to becoming and acting as a lawyer; the lower court's understanding of the law is incorrect.'[25] There are quite a number of cases of the Constitutional Court (*Anayasa Mahkemesi*) and the High Court (the *Yargıtay*) related to headscarf cases for university students

---

23 It is often claimed that 'what makes us European is our multiculturalism and yet it is this same multiculturalism that prevents us from becoming a unity'. Sefton-Green 2010 p.51 and see Harlow 2002.

24 See for analysis and examples, Örücü 2008.

25 92/3342, 93/2611, 5 July 1993.

along similar lines. The ECtHR has also given its support.[26] Here culture and belief can be sidestepped by the official law.

The second example shows how courts find themselves in a dilemma and use their discretion to appease localism. Prior to 2005, this happened when courts faced 'honour killings' among people from Eastern provinces, where the honour of a woman is in the control of the male members of her family. The courts always dealt with this problem within the framework of the then Penal Code (1926), received from the Italian one, but used the Code's facilities to reduce the penalty. Thus in a typical case, the killing was regarded as murder, but the accused benefited from article 52 of the Criminal Code, which said that if a crime is committed under aggravating circumstances and provocation, this can be taken into account in sentencing. However, academic debate in Turkey always regarded such killings as the ultimate violation of women's human rights, and the new Penal Code of 2005 followed suit.[27] Unfortunately, the issue has not gone away and has become a problem in countries such as Germany, Sweden and the Netherlands where many traditional Turkish families live and work. It has also spread to spousal relationships with husbands killing their wives who are either suing for divorce, have a relationship with another, or even after divorce. 'Intimate femicide' is usually presented in the form of a cultural defence, to be considered within the concept of 'provocation defence' putting 'belief' before 'gender'.[28] As Turkey is not officially a pluralistic society, the issue of cultural defence is not acceptable in the courts today, however, in the face of events, we could ask whether 'provocation' and 'belief' based illegal acts can trump rights of women. Does tradition and religion form the basis of such acts and how should the law and society deal with them?

The third is a telling example of an evolution: the *başlık*[29] (bride price) cases, once banned but now regarded as traditional gifts by the *Yargıtay*. The *Yargıtay* decisions up to the 1980's regarded moneys paid by the groom to the father of the girl to be against morality and therefore not to be returned upon the breaking up of the engagement. Then in 1986 the *Yargıtay* pronounced the banning by a local

---

26 The Grand Chamber of the ECtHR, following the Chamber decision, decided in the Leyla Şahin v. Turkey on 10.11.2005 that such a ban can be regarded as 'necessary in a democratic society' and that those who agree to undertake university education are to be deemed as having agreed to accept the principles of laicism, one of the fundamental principles of the state, since, 'in exercising his freedom to manifest his religion, an individual may need to take his specific situation into account.'

27 Now it seems the women are forced to commit suicide.

28 See for the Canadian examples, Dick 2011.

29 *Başlık* is money given by the man to the father of the girl to secure the engagement and thereby the marriage.

administration of the payment of dowry, to be illegal, saying that an administration could not ban a tradition or convert it into an offence. The court held that, 'This centuries old tradition is a fact which can only be banned by the legislator, if regarded as against public policy.'[30] The Court opined that this should be a matter of education and not of law. Today, when the engagement comes to an end, among the gifts to be returned – whether given to the parties or their families or those acting as such - are those whose value is beyond the ordinary, that is, things of great value. As moneys and goods, given under the name of *başlık*, are now consistently considered by the courts as gifts, their return can also be demanded. The practice of these payments continues, especially in rural areas, where it is considered a compensation for the loss of unpaid labour in fields, gardens and households for domestic chores. Here culture wins.

In fact, this tradition emanates from religion, and these institutions are reminiscent of *mahr*, an Islamic custom, interpreted by western courts according to varied legal constructs such as multiculturalism, fairness, public policy and gender equality. Thus the Turkish courts appear to have taken very similar attitudes to this one time banned practice in the name of 'politics of recognition', and are in fact accommodating an Islamic practice within the *laic* legal framework, by giving it a neutral name: *hediye* (gift).

Britain

In Britain the cultures met by the official laws are not indigenous, but mainly the result of a colonial heritage. Where in the past the legal system reflected the values of a homogeneous society,[31] now, the courts regard diverse cultures as custom, even when it is Islamic and therefore law for Muslims. The legal systems of Britain react to such new challenges 'in a basically defensive form', the official stance being assimilationist, though the legal treatment of diverse legal cultures seems inconsistent and confused (Menski 2000 p.xvii). Most 'other' culturally rooted values are ignored, dismissed or even penalised rather than being officially recognised. However, in courts, some groups such as Sikhs get more favourable treatment than others (ibid). Case law shows that there are certain unacceptable customs such as arranged, forced and child marriages (regarded as violating rights), female circumcision (described as cruel, inhuman or degrading treatment), polygamy (violating sexual equality in the formation of marriage), the religious way of slaughtering animals publicly (public policy), *talaq* (no judicial hearing and fair trial) and the wearing of beards and turbans (violating requirements of employment law).[32]

---

30 86/2-564, 299; 26.5.1986

31 People from a common European stock, white, Christian with a common language English, born in a particular territory, with allegiance to the Union and loyalty to the monarch.

32 Jones & Gnanapala 2000 p.100, for family law see p.106-137 and employment law see p.219-231.

If we pick up one example, an area of continued concern both in England and Scotland, it is that of arranged, forced and child marriages. The issue is seen as one of 'flawed' or 'not true or free' consent, and in British law bilateral consent is central to validity of marriage. When a person marries out of deference to parents' wishes, the marriage is not void, but any indication of pressure or threat is regarded as beyond the limits of parental influence, can constitute duress, and the courts can see this as a cause of nullity. Thus a marriage, even if consummated, can be declared null and void, if it can be shown that consent was obtained as a result of force or fear.[33] The pursuer may be of either sex. For instance, a case, in which a girl of nineteen succeeded in having her arranged marriage annulled at the Court of Session in April 2002, highlights the view that to be meaningful, freedoms and human rights must apply equally to all citizens. 'In a democracy, tolerance does not mean turning a blind eye to intolerable practices. Promoting diversity is not about accommodating unacceptable behaviour.'[34]

Scotland has gone even further and the Scottish Parliament passed the Forced Marriage etc. (Protection and Jurisdiction) (Scotland) Act 2011, whereby making provision for protecting persons from being forced, or who have been forced, into marriage without their free and full consent, and for amending the jurisdiction of the sheriff court in relation to actions for declarator of nullity of such marriage. This Act illustrates the stance the legal system takes against culture and tradition of mostly the Pakistani population.

A Specific Issue: Equality

One of the most important concepts of our times is equality, which suggests supremacy and finality, and absolute and total inclusiveness, being the ultimate expression of generality and homogeneity. On the whole, European official laws take a stance that can be called 'combating multiculture' and assert that equality demands that all citizens adhere only to 'the law of the land' (Jantera-Jareborg 2009 p.143). However, cultural context indicates open-endedness, at times incommensurable co-existence of cultures, values and viewpoints and diversity.[35] Have we now reached a stage where we can reject the terms of neutrality and consider the difference in the nature and composition of the community? Can one talk of a collision between the 'formal, universalistic' conception of equality and the

---

33 In Mahmud v.. Mahmud, 1994 SLT 599 the marriage was never consummated, but in Mahmood v. Mahmoud 1993 SLT 589 it was.

34 Editorial in the Newspaper The Herald (24 April, 2002) where the case was reported.

35 For a discussion of issues central to the concept of diversity, see Fredman 2005 p.13.

'social, localised' conception of it?[36] Is it not against the precepts of equality to treat those who are socially unequal equally, until they are made equal?[37] Should not the principle of equality accept the factual inevitability of difference and accommodate the actuality of societal relationships,[38] especially for instance, within the contextual subject of the family?

It is often acknowledged today, that cultural context and even a plurality of parallel legalities operating simultaneously must be taken into account if legal frameworks are to function satisfactorily. However, in an effort to meet the demands of equality, the realities of social relationships may have to be ignored and brushed aside, in the hope that things would conform to this ideal (Walby 2004 p.4). This is most striking in the area of the western approach to family law, which seems to disregard the actual and the very real inequalities of family relationships. Family law is dominated by consequentialist/utilitarian themes. Here the fundamental questions that could be considered are: Is it legitimate for the legislature and the judiciary to try to change tradition and social reality? How far can concessions be given to culture and tradition and yet at the same time the principle of equality be upheld? Are measures, such as 'affirmative action' for 'protecting the vulnerable' commensurate with the principle of equality?

The principle of equality challenges culture and tradition and rightly so, but, especially in relation to weaker parties, a protective approach to be adopted by the courts must be allowed to mitigate the standardising impact of this principle, as long as the courts are dealing with those who are in fact not equal. It is an axiom of our times that men and women are categorically equal partners. However, being the weaker party in marriages - and this is the case in most societies whether admitted or not - women should be protected by law, both by the legal legislative framework, and by the work of the courts.

One does not have to locate the issues in the framework of the binary opposition of multiculturalism versus feminism, universalism versus cultural relativism or secular versus religious practices, to challenge the notion of equality, when family realities point in a different direction. This should not be regarded as an attempt to associate women with the protection of the cultural and traditional or religious

---

36 See a summary discussion on equality and inclusiveness versus equality and difference in Toddington 2008 p.49.

37 For a critique of 'equal treatment' as opposed to 'same treatment' see Squires 1999; and for the lack of protection for women inherent in treating everyone in the same way, see Phillips 2001 p.249 and Phillips 1992.

38 For a discussion of the neglect of the private sphere as a fundamental source of gender inequalities, see Pateman 1989 and Nussbaum 1999.

values. Neither is the secular normative framework, though it threatens cultural values, regarded here as an undesirable development. On the contrary, tradition and culture inimical to social and economic injustice to women should be eliminated categorically (Okin et al. 1999). However, it is also worth remembering that family laws can never hope to be totally neutral, secular or pluralist. Rights discourse can strengthen the politics of gender justice; but in the process women must be protected. Otherwise the rhetoric of equality turns against women's interests. Can the courts search for 'egalitarian justice'? Can judges override solutions and principles encoded in private law codifications or other laws by using the weapon of interpretation, when the official provisions do not live up to what they regard as 'socially just'?

Casting our eyes to the work of the Commission on European Family Law (CEFL), can we say something on harmonisation in this context?[39] Let us first take note of the fact that family law is predominantly about values. In secular societies moral values that reflect religious positions, do not disappear. Maybe in our day religion is on the decline in the predominantly secular Western Europe, but this is happening at best at different speeds in different societies. It is also worth remembering that religion has been traditionally a major source of conflict between European countries historically. Protestant, Catholic and Eastern Orthodox Christianity divided Europe into North and South, and East and West.[40] In many of the countries in Europe today, in spite of secularism at the level of the legal systems, there are divided religious structures following the patterns of multiculturalism, also exacerbated by large-scale migrations from outside the EU. Each country has a multifaceted culture and internally, law and culture do not mirror one another.

An interesting scale of values came to light in a survey we carried out juxtaposing some selected systems to the General Principles on divorce and maintenance drawn up by the CEFL. The scale ranged from a Lutheran population with an ex-socialist secular legal system (Estonia); a Roman Catholic population with an ex-socialist legal system (Lithuania); a number of secular legal systems with Evangelical Lutheran populations (the Nordic countries); a predominantly Roman Catholic population with a secular legal system (France); a predominantly Protestant Anglican population with a secular legal system (England and Wales); a mixed Presbyterian Protestant - Roman Catholic population with a secular legal system (Scotland); a Roman Catholic population without a secular legal system (Malta); to a Muslim population with a secular legal system (Turkey). The impact of the

---

39 The following observations are a summary of the final assessment part of our work juxtaposing some legal systems to the General Principles drawn up by the CEFL in the area of divorce and maintenance. See Örücü 2007 pp.233-254.

40 See further on what factors divide Europeans, Guibernau 2001 pp.14-19.

values these beliefs embody can be traced in their present family laws — secular or not — and regardless of their membership of the civil law or common law families. The differences reflect historical developments, cultural and religious differences and ideological preferences.

All the above tells us is that 'the common core' is very limited, and any General Principles to harmonise family law in Europe relying on common core research will be of little use. Therefore, the only effective type of harmonisation today can be top-down intervention reflecting a vision for the future with provisions based on the 'better law' approach. This may provide a desirable modern legal framework, but could be regarded as unacceptable in today's multiculturalist societies, since in our day, there is no longer one socio-culture in any one country. For instance, assumptions relying on working women, equality, women capable of supporting the family and self-sufficiency, relate to the values and realities of some societies and not to all. We might consider these values as highly desirable, but does not cultural diversity necessitate that legal diversity should be maintained? In pressing for transformation of family life, bottom-up strategies are crucial, though there might be an eventual 'norms diffusion' and 'identity change' and European integration may have a transformative effect on the laws of the Member States and various cultures therein. After all, multiculturalism itself is an evolving concept.

Family life and family law may have an instrumental dimension but their emotional dimension is more prominent. The famous EU slogan, 'unity in diversity' means that there must be a mutual understanding and acceptance of this diversity. In the type of project we were dealing with, it would be difficult to generate a popular response in favour of a harmonised Europe-wide family law, harmonised through Principles, which seemingly reflect the value system of a particular worldview, drafted by a committee of legal experts. Therefore, it was commendable that a number of issues were left to the competence of national legislators and the courts. Yet, Europeans do need standardised approaches and solutions for at least cross-border relationships. Thus, we end up in a dilemma.

Concluding Remarks

The issue of multiculturalism in a western unitary nation state connotes catering for diverse cultures within its borders -at times with rules inimical or even repugnant to the official state law- demanding recognition, while at the same time aiming towards maintaining a 'national identity'. For the EU however, the issue of multiculturalism connotes catering for an increasing number of diverse nation states -themselves struggling to come to terms with diverse internal cultures- in a multicultural framework external to the nation states, while at the same time aiming towards building 'a European identity', 'European citizenship', and in the long run, 'a common European culture'.[41]

Nevertheless, the following questions await resolution: When official law meets cultures different to the dominant value system it represents, what should it do? Is it true that only trans-cultural and morally neutral rules can work successfully in a multicultural society? Can a legal system of the modern type be independent of social and cultural systems? Can defending multiculturalism be regarded solely as reactionary conservatism? Are multicultural policies a threat to liberty and equality? Can liberal democracies accommodate minority groups without sacrificing peace and stability (See generally, Murphy 2011)?

The main demarcation lines are clearly drawn within domestic laws by Constitutions, and within Europe and within the EU by the demands of human rights and 'ever closer integration'. Domestic courts will become even more important as tuners of the law in the coming years, in their efforts to cope and to create the necessary 'fit' between law and culture.

A pragmatic and cosmopolitan approach would say that in a globalising world, there is an advantage as well as an inevitability in convergence, that the fundamental values represented by universal standards of human rights should override all other claims to 'exceptionalism', that cultural diversity which can be regarded as 'the spice of life', should stay cultural and not reflect into the legal world, that there should be overarching legal systems all striving towards transnational, regional, inter-communal levels bringing a uniformity of modernity to the legal world which can accommodate multiculturalism in society. At no stage should multiculturalism impede the progress of the law towards these aims, otherwise it becomes 'the bane' of legal systems. The pursuit is towards ideals of rationality, harmony and reform using a selection of the legal rules and materials best suited to the task. Internal group norms repugnant to some overarching sense of natural justice and morality will not be enforced. A society can only remain healthy, if diversity does not threaten unity of purpose. There can be only room for 'qualified legal pluralism', embodying recognition, tolerance and respect.

In her book 'Ordering Pluralism', Delmas-Marty asks whether we can move beyond the relative and the universal to build order without imposing it, to accept pluralism without giving up on a common law in the 21st century? Opting neither for utopian fusion nor for illusory autonomy, *Ordering Pluralism* is her answer: creating a common legal area by progressive adjustments that preserve dignity.

---

41 See in general, Llobera 2001 p.193. It has been suggested however, that instead of basing the model around the traditional model of a State or a Nation, we should be more inventive and create a new and different model for Europe. See Beck & Giddens 2006 and Joerges 2004.

Since an immutable world order is impossible, 'the imaginative forces of law' must be called upon to invent a flexible process of harmonisation that leaves room for protecting common values' (Delmas-Marty 2009). Will this be the remedy to our woes?

Indeed, moral pluralism, value pluralism, ethnic pluralism and cultural pluralism are part of social reality and have to be not only tolerated, but preserved. The translation of these into legal pluralism however, carries with it fundamental problems and may not be in the best interests of progress towards the targets of achieving a universal, comprehensive, internally reconcilable and cohesive moral or political unit (See Robertson 1992; Robertson 1995 p.38; Featherstone 1995). As we have also seen in the issue of equality, the fit will always be uncomfortable.

Bibliography

Beck, U & Giddens, A. (2006) 'L'Europe telle qu'elle est: un point de vue cosmopolitique', in *Raison Politique* 5, pp.7-15.

Chiba, M. (ed.) (1986) *Asian indigenous law in interaction with received law*, KPI, London.

Chiba, M. (1989) *Legal Pluralism: Towards a general theory through Japanese legal culture*, Tokai University Press.

Delmas-Marty, M. (2009) *Ordering Pluralism: A Conceptual Framework for Understanding the Transnational Legal World*.

Dick, C. (2011) 'A Tale of Two Cultures: Intimate Femicide, Cultural Defences, and the Law of Provocation', in *Canadian Journal of Women and the Law,* 23(2), pp.519-547.

Donlan, S.P. (2011) 'The Mediterranean Hybridity Project: Crossing The Boundaries of Law and Culture', in *Journal of Civil Law Studies,* 4.

Featherstone, M (1995) *Undoing Culture: Globalization, Postmodernism and Identity*.

Fredman, S. (2005) 'Double Trouble: Multiple Discrimination and EU Law', in *European Anti-discrimination Law Review*.

Gessner, V. (1994) 'Global Legal Integration and Legal Cultures', in *Ratio Juris,* 7.

Gibbon, J.L. & Calderia, G.A. (1996) 'The Legal Cultures of Europe', in *Law and Society Review,* 30.

Gladwin, T. (1964) 'Cultures and Logical Process', in W. Goodenough (ed.), *Explorations in Cultural Anthropology: Essays in Honour of George Peter Murcock*.

Griffiths, J. (1986) 'What is legal pluralism?', in *Journal of Legal Pluralism and Unofficial Law,* 24, pp.1-56.

Guibernau, M. (2001) 'Introduction: Unity and Diversity in Europe', in M. Guibernau (ed) *Governing European Diversity*.

Harlow, C. 'Voices of Difference in a Plural Community', in *American Journal of Comparative Law,* 50, pp.339-367.

Hannerz, U. (1990) 'Cosmopolitans and Locals in World Culture', in M. Featherstone (ed.), *Global Culture: Nationalism, Globalization and Modernity*.

Howard, R. (1993) 'Cultural Absolutism and the Nostalgia for the Community', in *Human Rights Quarterly,* 15, pp.315-338.

Jantera-Jareborg, M. (2009) 'Family Law in a Multicultural Sweden – the challenges of migration and religion' in M. Dahlberg (ed), *Uppsala – Minnesota Colloquium: Law, Culture and Values*.

Joerges, C. (2004) 'Challenges of Europeanization in the Realm of Private Law: A Plea for a New Legal Discipline', in *E.U.I. Working Paper Law,* 12.

Jones, R. & Gnanapala, W. (2000) (eds.), *Ethnic Minorities in English Law*.

Llobera, J.R. (2001) 'What Unites Europeans', in M. Guibernau (ed) *Governing European Diversity*.

Menski, W. (2002) 'Ethnic minority studies in English law', in R. Jones & W.

Gnanapala (eds.), *Ethnic Minorities in English Law*.

Murphy, M. (2011) *Multiculturalism: A Critical Introduction*, Routledge Contemporary Political Philosophy.

Nelken, D. (2004) 'Using the Concept of Legal Culture', in *Australian Journal of Legal Philosophy*, pp.1-28.

Nussbaum, M.C (1999) *Sex and Social Justice*.

Okin, S.M. et al. (1999) (eds.), *Is Multiculturalism Bad for Women?*

Örücü, E. (2010) 'Diverse Cultures and Official Laws: Multiculturalism and Euroscepticism?', in *Utrecht Law Review*, Special Issue, pp.75-88.

Örücü, E (2008) 'Judicial navigation as official law meets culture in Turkey', in *International Journal of Law in Context*, 4(1).

Örücü, E. (2007) 'The Principles of European Family Law Put to the Test: Diversity in Harmony or Harmony in Diversity?' in E. Örücü & J. Mair (eds.), *Juxtaposing Legal Systems and the Principles of European Family Law on Divorce and Maintenance*, pp.233-254.

Örücü, E. (2002) 'Waat wet en cultuur elkaar ontmoeten: cultureel pluralisme, juridisch pluralisme en pragmatisme', in *Culturele diversiteit, Justitiele verkenningen*, 5(2), pp.96-107.

Pateman, C. (1989) 'The Patriarchal Welfare State', in C. Pateman (ed), *The Disorder of Women: Democracy, Feminism and Political Theory*.

Phillips, A. (2001) 'Feminism and Liberalism Revisited: Has Martha Nussbaum Got It Right?' in *Constellations*.

Phillips, A. (1992) 'Universal Pretensions in Political Thought', in M. Barrett et al. (eds.), *Destabilizing Theory: Contemporary Feminist Debates*.

Robertson, R. (1992) *Globalization: Social Theory and Global Culture*.

Robertson, R. (1995) 'Glocalization: time-space and homogeneity-heterogeneity' in M. Featherstone et al. (eds), *Global Modernities*.

Santos, B.S. (2002) *Toward a New Common Sense: Law, Science and Politics in the Paradigmatic Transition* 2nd edn.

Sefton-Green, R. (2010) 'Multiculturalism, Europhilia and harmonization: harmony or disharmony?', in *Utrecht Law Review*, Special Issue, pp.50-67.

Squires, J. (1999) *Gender in Political Theory*.

Toddington, S. (2008) 'Universalism, Multiculturalism and the Rule of law', in *Student Law Review*, 54.

Walby, S. (2004) 'The European Union and Gender Equality: Emergent Varieties of Gender Regime', in *Social Policy*, 11(1).

Wilhelmsson, T. et al. (2007) (eds), *Private Law and the Many Cultures of Europe*.

Dialogue and Multicultural Dynamics: Challenges to Hearing Cultures in Conversation

Donal Andrew Carbaugh[42]

Introduction

This essay explores dialogue as a form of communication which is widely praised, yet one with roots in various cultural traditions. The themes are both conceptual as we ask what dialogue indeed is, and empirical as we examine its preferred form and meanings in different cultural contexts. Both the ideas about dialogue and studies about actual dialogic exchanges are treated throughout the paper. The major objectives are to discuss dialogue as an ideal yet uniquely localized form for communication which tends to amplify the presumption of common purposes while muting the differences in its cultural preferences.

This essay is organized into five parts: the first gives some background about studies which treat human social engagement in cross-cultural perspective, both those about communication more generally, and dialogue specifically; the second explores the different forms and meanings of dialogue as these are at play in two major theorists of dialogue, Martin Buber and Carl Rogers; the third reviews some of the major findings about dialogue when viewed in cross-linguistic and cross-cultural perspective; the fourth analyzes cultural differences in a particular televised dialogic exchange between Finnish and American participants; and the fifth discusses basic tensions in dialogic conduct regardless of its content, whether political, religious, racial or whatever.

---

42 Donal Carbaugh is Professor of Communication and Director of the Graduate Program in Communication at the University of Massachusetts Amherst. He is currently a Samuel F. Conti Faculty Research Fellow, which is the highest award for research, at the University. He has also been a finalist for the university's outstanding teaching award. In 2007-2008, he was Fulbright's Distinguished Professor and Bicentennial Chair of North American Studies at the University of Helsinki, Finland. From 2005-2010, he was a member of the Research Advisory Group for the Security Needs Assessment Project of the United Nations Institute for Disarmament Research in Geneva. In 1992, he was elected Visiting Senior Member at Linacre College, Oxford University, England, which is a lifetime position. His general interests focus upon cultural philosophies of dialogic communication, the environment, and the ways culturally distinctive practices get woven into international and intercultural interactions.

Background: Communication in Cross-cultural Perspective

In a very important way, communication is what people in different places have made of it. There are places in northern Europe, central Finland in particular, where verbal exchanges are occasionally punctuated by periods of silence, a kind of socially shared quietude which is shared together, with these silences being affirmations of the importance of the social relationships among those who are co-present. There are places in the Caribbean, Antigua in particular, where people speak together in an animated way all at the same time, simultaneously, a kind of contrapuntal conversation, which is appreciated and enjoyed (Scollo 2012; Shields-Brodber 2001). There are places in the Pacific Islands, Fiji in particular (Brenneis and Pradath 1975), where communication can take the shape of a song, and the songs are turned into contests among competing religious groups, with the goal of the contest being to make the other group so mad that they will cry!

Yes, communication is indeed what people in different places have made of it. There are of course differences not only in silences, simultaneous talk, and song, but also in the language people will speak. In Europe, while the European Union can come together through utterances of French, or English, the EU is also extremely diverse linguistically as over twenty-languages are declared as official within it. And there are more than that which are active within the union. As an example, in Finland there are two designated national languages, Finnish and Swedish. But there are other languages spoken frequently within the nation as for example English is used in many international contexts, as is at times German, or French, or even Estonian. When one travels north in Finland, to the international territory of Lapland, the indigenous Sami language is audible as are other languages, and other dialects of any one of these languages. A well-known statement about regional uses of English in Finland is that the further east one goes, into Karelian Finland for example, the more voluble become Finnish speakers. Going west from Karelia, into the central Hame region, and into Ostrobothnia, one finds a quieter use of Finnish, talk assuming less time of sociable interaction. So the variety is evident not only between and among languages, but within them as well.

The situation of diversity in communication and cultural variety in a language becomes more deeply pronounced when one begins examining the varieties which are available within any one particular language. English is perhaps the most pronounced example. As English has been used around the world, it has been uniquely tailored and designed by people to meet their local circumstances. A few months ago, I was part of a wonderful intercultural and international meeting in Shanghai, China. While the conference proceedings were held in English, the topics addressed at times brought varieties of English to the table. One researcher was studying generally the challenges in teaching English in China, and discussed in detail how English was being taught by him at his Chinese university. Considering the challenges very carefully, he concluded that the Chinese classroom became extremely complicated with questions about what indeed is "standard" English? British English, then American English, and then Australian English were considered carefully by him, and brought into his discussion. He noted differences among these, and how each would affect the specific program he taught in grammar, spelling, vocabulary, and pronunciation to mention only a few. Finally, unable to meet multiple such standards simultaneously and perhaps in a fit of exasperation, he concluded that he should quit trying to select just one of these varieties, nor should he try to teach all of these other varieties together. He wondered: Why not make his classroom the best it could be, focused on the teaching of Chinese English! While there are limits to such a solution, there is also facility in it. Such a dynamic requires something of a standard(s) that is adapted to its local circumstances. With it comes questions of use, of local form, meanings, situated preferences. Such considerations are important, with this being a rather typical example.

Studies of communication which have examined communication and its cultural varieties have long noted such differences. Within the United States, scholars have studied African American vernacular, Black English, or Ebonics as a culturally and racially based variety of English. Similar studies have been done of Native American uses of English, and of course of many Native American languages as well. Each has its own preferred vocabulary, forms of use, and range of meanings.

How do we study such variety so that communication and its cultural variability can be held in view? What we have found is this: Communication is a radically cultural phenomenon; it varies of course by language, by culture, and by nation, yet it also varies within languages, within societies, and within nations. If we do not take this into account, we risk looking over, or talking over that diversity, holding one in view at the expense of the others. Emphasizing only "the one" risks dishonoring the others whose ways we should seek or indeed need to understand.

The importance of the point is amplified once we see that our ways and means of communicating are deeply and inextricably tied to our meanings about ourselves, the ways we believe we should act, our relations with others, our feelings about things, and at base the way we see the nature of things. To understand our communication, we must understand what people have made of it. In so doing, we strive to understand specifically our human culture(s), those means and meanings of practice which each people believe, and which they value as so significant and important to them.

This is especially the case when it comes to one valorized form of communication which is being championed around the world today, accompanied as it is by a strong feeling of hope, with pleas for it being ever so widespread, often through a version of Global English. We speak of course about Dialogue.

Dialogue According to Martin Buber and Carl Rogers With a Nod to Mikhail Bahktin

In 1957, two giants in the philosophy and practice of dialogue met on a stage at the University of Michigan in the United States (Anderson and Cissna 1997). One was Martin Buber, a Jewish philosopher of dialogue and a highly influential religious thinker of his day. The other, Carl Rogers, was an American psychologist, one of the most well known clinical psychologists in American history. Each was a champion of dialogue, and each left a legacy in the study and practice of dialogue which reverberates throughout many such discussions to this day. For about an hour and a half on April 18th, the two discussed dialogue together.

I want to focus here on only a few passages from their transcribed exchange as a way of introducing some thoughts about dialogue in cross-cultural perspective. Even as each man was deeply engaged in advancing a kind of dialogic practice, the background and experiences each brought with him uniquely colored just what could count, for him, as dialogue.

Let us begin with the American psychologist, Carl Rogers, who characterised dialogue in section 27 of the transcribed exchange, prominently for him, as "an effective moment in a therapeutic relationship" (Anderson and Cissna 1997 p.29). In such a "dialogic moment," individuals would meet as subjective, whole persons, who hide nothing, who are accepting of each other, and in the process would reach a kind of clarity which was missing before, with a result of that clarity being the possibility or increased likelihood of personal change. These qualities characterised dialogic communication for Rogers and its immediacy in a moment of therapeutic interaction.

In his discussion with Martin Buber, Rogers emphasised that even in a therapeutic relationship, it is important to treat each other as equals, with quintessential moments of therapy being best as an equal meeting of two individuals. This sort of relationship, in this type of interaction, Rogers argued, allows change to occur, especially as the therapist listens and gives the client the permission to change, and to grow. The promise of dialogue, in short, is to place individuals - if momentarily - into equal relations with others so they can conquer problems both personal and societal.

Martin Buber brought another view about dialogue to this exchange. According to him, dialogue is a "certain mode of existence" (p.32). As he responded to Rogers, he emphasised that a therapist and a client are "not equals," both are caught within a "real situation" that, to some important extent, "cannot be changed." In this sense, dialogue is "hampered by tragedy," that is, by some real, prior condition which is an exigency for the therapeutic session, and that real situation, outside of the therapeutic moment, establishes limits and boundaries that cannot be changed. Buber says, "I give into dialogue; yet in it I come to a wall, a boundary, a limit" (p.54). He insists in such situations, a therapist and a client are not equals, with certain things being outside the scope of possible change.

Dialogic communication for Buber thus involves speaking as two different persons, with each being involved in a social and historical situation. It is crucially important, therefore, from Buber's view, that each is heard and understood not only as an individual, but as a person who is caught in a larger social and historical environment. Persons, as such, come to dialogue, as do therapists and clients, in ways that are unequal and within limited conditions that cannot be changed. As persons in dialogue, each acts within social circumstances, yet also we are inevitably caught in conditions which may permit some movement, but limit movement in others. As a Jewish intellectual in the wake of the Second World War, Buber was undoubtedly speaking ever so mindful of recent horrific circumstances.

The Russian author of dialogue, Mikhail Bahktin, wrote similarly of "dialogic overtones" (Bahktin 1986 p.92), that is, how the words we speak bring with them echoes of our larger social scene, or deeper meanings from a larger whole of which our dialogic moments are inevitably a part. The views of the American psychologist, Carl Rogers, the Jewish philosopher, Martin Buber, and the Russian philologist, Mikhail Bahktin, all bring with them echoes of their social and cultural worlds. As each discusses and employs a dialogic view, each also brings with them cultural premises of their own, divergent presumptions not only about what dialogue is, but indeed what it can be.

Dialogue in Cross-cultural and Cross-linguistic Perspective

Dialogue, today, is what we might call a powerful key term. It is pervasive in its use, prominent as well as potent in its applications as people call for inter-religious dialogue, political dialogue, a dialogue on race, or on education or on just about anything else. The hope in this form of communication is a productive response to ethnic conflicts, political divisions, religious intolerance, or cultural differences. Indeed, there is much currency to the term, much prominence in its use, and much potency presumed through its form. But what does this term identify as a form of action? What preferences for conduct, for relations, for action itself are so presumed?

What we have discovered in studying dialogue in cross-linguistic perspective -including studies in Chinese, English, Hungarian, Japanese, Korean, Russian as well as some in Blackfoot and Finnish- is, like with Rogers and Buber, that this form of communication brings with it culturally variable preferences. And these preferences extend not simply to the kind of communication people desire and expect when engaged in "dialogue," but beyond that to deeper messages about social relationships and to the conduct of the person. In other words, as people plea for dialogue, they also, knowingly or not, are making a plea for a system of social relations and rightful action among people, with all of this couched, to some degree, in the terms of a local language and culture (Carbaugh, Boromoisza-Habashi, & Ge 2006; Carbaugh, Nuciforo, Saito, & Shin 2011).

The general point can be formulated in this way: pleas for dialogue and dialogic action are in other words pleas for a particular configuration of social relations and institutions, including a standard for proper conduct and action. The particularities at play, however, in any one language, or in any one variety of a language are considerable, and these local particularities often hide from those making such a plea. To illustrate the point, I summarize below the range of specifics we have found in various cultural discourses which make a plea for dialogue. Each cultural and/ or linguistic system shapes and forms these features in their own particular ways, and thus the range of particularities is crucial to understand when dialogue is being advocated, especially in multicultural scenes.[43]

First, there are several ***meanings being expressed about communication practices*** when "dialogue" or a term translated as something like "dialogue" is being used. These are the most literal and explicit meanings at play:

1. The terms refer to face-to-face, verbal co-productions, between two or more parties.

2. The practices being referenced range from cooperative interactions, to competitive debates.

3. An ethos of mutuality of exchange (or interdependence) pervades these practices.

4. The predominant tone or feeling is socially collaborative, and varies from serious and formal to informal.

5. The predominant channel is face-to-face conversation, but also includes writing, scripted and spontaneous practices, as well as various electronic

---

43 The following summary draws from an earlier article (Carbaugh, Nuciforo, Saito, and Shin, 2011, p.101-104). The passages from that article are slightly revised for purposes of this paper.

media (newsprint, internet, radio, television).

6. Structuring norms include speaking in a sincere, informative, and ably expressive way about one's views; and listening in a way that is open to the views, and to the emotions of others.

7. Goals of the practice vary widely from producing harmony, to winning a verbal contest, to informing participants about issues, problem-solving, clarifying the nature of the issues, presenting a range of views, developing shared understanding, mutual trust, resolving a conflict in a mutually satisfying way, transforming social circumstances, establishing a common goal, affirming and/or repairing social relationships, to establishing future actions.

8. The practices of "dialogue" are conceived to be of varying importance, but most are deemed highly efficacious, yet the locus or site of the efficacy varies: in some cases, the weightiness is in the relations among the participants (as more important than the information exchanged), in others, the weightiness is in the topic being addressed (as presumably weighty e.g., societal issues, political, economic matters); in still others, the weightiness concerns value in the form of the social activity getting done (and is not so much focused on the topic of discussion); or further, the weight is in the balance between clarity of the information expressed, the agreement being forged, and the emotion involved in its expression.

In addition to these meanings about communication, there are *more implicit meanings being expressed about sociality, social relations, or social institutions*. These are active in these cultural discourses in more of a metaphorical or figurative way. That is, as people talk about the importance of "dialogue," they are also saying something about the arrangement of social identities, relations, and possibly institutions. These meanings can be formulated as follows:

1. The dialogic form of practice gives voice to various social identities: Political or social opponents; high status participants e.g., scholars, officials; guests and hosts; disputants and intermediaries; employers and employees.

2. The form presumes social relations of equality, or as moving in some senses toward equality.

3. The form can activate various social institutions: Political-governmental, religious, educational, friendship, therapeutic, health, entertainment media (radio, television, theatre, opera).

4. The dialogic form is designed to balance relations among people including, within social scenes, their social and emotional self.

Finally, there is a range of ***premises these terms activate about proper conduct and personhood***. As with the meanings above about sociality, these are largely taken-for-granted, and are as a result expressed more implicitly and metaphorically. The first three formulations, here, operate as an interactional exigency, or occasioning antecedent for dialogue as a social form. These can be formulated as follows:

1. Persons can be insincere, conniving, or inappropriately inexpressive.
2. Persons can act on the basis of their own selfish interests, on the basis of an imbalance of power, or in other imbalanced ways.
3. The above are ultimately limited, immoral, or bad.
4. Persons need forms of social interaction which are sincere, informative, expressive of their views, AND, receptive to the views of others.
5. Persons need forms of social interaction which are educational (disseminate information widely) and socially productive (advance mutual interests in socially productive ways).
6. Persons need forms of social interaction which balance informational needs and social care.
7. These needs are attached to various philosophical, literary, and cultural traditions (axioms of particularity and of actuality).

The meanings above suggest a range of possible features that are active when people call for "dialogue." Such a plea is inevitably made, and interpreted through the specific communication code of one's language and culture. In other words, when heard, the plea for "dialogue" can play in distinctive ways through specific languages, or specific varieties of one's own language, carrying into one form of communication here (e.g., problem-solving in Korea, agreement in Turkey), and another there (e.g., clarifying information in Russia; or social care in Japan). Further, the plea can signal change within a society in what is deemed proper public dialogue as movement from the Finnish "vuoropuhelu" (taking turns talking about an important topic) to "keskustelu" (where the interactive quality of the exchange is amplified over the clarity of the topic being discussed) (see Carbaugh, Boromisza-Habashi, and Ge 2006 p.38-39). The variety of features being summarized above can help sensitize us to the particular meanings active in and about dialogue. Across various languages and cultural discourses, a wide range of possible meanings can be active. Clearly there is much more work to be done in order to understand what is getting said through one coding of dialogue, and how it relates to others.

Cultural Identities in a Televised Context: A Failed Dialogue

Perhaps the most popular and famous American television news program of all time is "60 Minutes." It has run since September 24, 1968 and based upon ratings it would be the most successful television program ever. The format of the hour-long program is typically in three segments, each telling a story about a recent issue, event, or person. One such segment was titled, Tango Finlandia, and was designed to tell a story about Finns and Finland for an American audience. The participants in the parts of this segment I discuss below are the American reporter from "60 Minutes," Morley Safer, an American reporter who was living in Helsinki, Finland at the time of the broadcast, Terri Schultz, a prominent Finnish songstress in Finland's public culture, Arja Koriseva, and a popular Finnish media personality, Jan Knutas. As Safer engaged the others through questions, a story was collaboratively created concerning Finns and Finland. This same broadcast appeared in English in the United States and in Britain (as in the numbered lines below); it also appeared in Finnish in Finland (as in the lines marked "a" below). Without further introduction, let's listen to one exchange which occurred near the beginning of the broadcast segment.[44]

> *SAFER*: *((Voiceover))*
> Terri Schultz is an American reporter *h
> a) *Amerikkalainen toimittaja Teri Schulz*
>   who's lived in Helsinki for three years
> b) *on asunut Helsingissä kolme vuotta.*
>   Even though she now speaks the language (.)
> c) *Vaikka hän puhuukin suomea,*
>   the **ice** has yet to be broken.
> d) *keskustelua ei ole helppo aloittaa.*
>   SAFER: ((Cut to interview))
>   they resist even shaking hands?
> e) *He eivät suostu kättelemäänkään.*
>   *SCHULTZ*: oh my yeah definitely *h I wonder yeah
> f) *Eivät todellakaan.*

---

44 The transcription conventions used below are the following: hhh marks an outbreath; (.) marks a brief pause which of longer is indicated by a number in the parentheses such as a half-second pause being (.5); bold letters mark a vocal emphasis; an ~ indicates sounds are produced quickly and tightly together; lines are broken to indicate a natural pause in the vocal performance.

Shaking hands I think is~is~is pretty intense for them

g) *Kättelyllä on heille paljon painoarvoa.*

But try to hug a Finn *(h)*

h) *Mutta yritäpä halata suomalaista.*

if you've ever tried to hug a Finn, they're very **ugherr** (.)

very (.5) shaky.

i) *Siitä he järkyttyvät.*

SAFER: ((Voiceover))

even Arya Koriseva

j) *Jopa Arja Koriseva,*

a Finnish songstress and hardly a **wall** flower (.)

k) *suomalainen laulaja ja kaikkea muuta kuin ujo,*

is **comfortable** in Finland's icy reserve

l) *nauttii suomalaisten jäisestä varauksellisuudesta.*

KORISEVA ((*Cut to interview*))

we have like a **wall** here

m) *Meillä on tässä seinä.*

We try to **hh* look at you and (.5)

watch~wh(h)o~y(h)ou~a(h)re~

w(h)hat~y(h)ou~(h)are (laughing)

n) *Me tarkkailemme sinua*

before we dare to come to you and **h*

o) *Ennen kuin uskaltaudumme*

speak with you (.)

p) *puhumaan.*

and I guess the American people (.5)

are more like (.5)

q) *Amerikkalaiset sanovat:*

hi(.) who are you. where are you from.

r) *"Hei, kukas sinä olet?"*

nice meeting you. I love you

s) *"Hauska tavata. minä rakastan sinua."*

(hhhhhhh) ((loud laughter))

((Footage of Safer and Knutas))

SAFER: it strikes me uh traveling around this country that (.)

t) O*len matkustellut täällä*

people are **terribly** shy (.)

particularly **the men**

u) *ja etenkin miehet vaikuttavat ujoilta.*

KNUTAS: ((Voiceover))

among ourselves

we think that is the natural way to be.

v) *Ajattelemme, että on luontevaa*

not to sort of (.)stick out

w) *olla erottumatta joukosta.*

It's easy to see that from coming from another country *hh

x) *Muualta tulevat*

you think of it as shyness

y) *pitävät sitä ujoutena*

and it probably is **yes**

z) *Sitä se varmaankin on*

A detailed analysis of this segment appears in a monograph I am near completing. For purposes of this paper, let me make a few observations. To begin, notice that this section of the broadcast appears in what Mikhail Bahktin might call a speech genre of reporting culture.

An American voice: The American speakers use words like the following to describe Finns, Finland, or Finnish comportment: the American reporter in Helsinki talks about the "[Finnish] ice" (line 5), "they resist even shaking hands" (7), which is "pretty intense for them" (9), with a "hug" being even more so (10-12). The American reporter, Safer, discusses Finns as "terribly shy, particularly the men" (32-33). Through these utterances, Finns are verbally portrayed by Americans as rather cold, uncomfortable socially, and shy.

A Finnish voice: However, if we listen to the Finnish participants in this segment, we hear the matters differently. The Finnish songstress Arja Koriseva explains a Finnish stance for proper conduct when approaching others, when wanting to interact with them: waving her hand between herself and Safer she says, "we have like a wall here" (18), we look and watch before we dare approach another to speak to them (19-23). Jan Knutas, the Finnish media personality explains that Finns have "a natural way " of being (35) which is not to "stick out" (36). Through these utterances we have expressed and hear a proper Finnish stance for conduct: It is proper to exercise reserve with others, to watch others carefully before approaching them, so one does not impose oneself upon the other, nor stick out oneself.

A Finnish reply to the American voice: Also in this segment, we find Finnish speakers responding to American (mis) characterisations of Finns. Ms. Koriseva playfully contrasts her Finnish voice with an American one which is relatively direct as it says things like "hi, where are you from, nice meeting you, I love you" followed by much laughter (24-27). Similarly, Knutas is careful when he explains that Americans may characterize Finnish ways as "shyness," "you think of it as shyness" (38) and "it probably is" (39). Through these utterances, the Finnish speakers show a verbal dexterity by acknowledging how the Americans are portraying them, yet they also contrast that American portrayal with their reserved own, which is never quite grasped or expressed by the Americans in the segment above, or elsewhere in the broadcast.

Utilising some of the features of dialogue discussed in the prior section provides some tools – with cross-linguistic and cross-cultural currency - for understanding the above. For example, if dialogue is to involve an ethos of mutuality in the exchange, while listening to others so to capture their view of the matter, the above is a failure. Nowhere in it do the Americans express a Finnish view of the matter to which the Finns unequivocally consent. [While Knutas gestures in this direction with his last line, later in the broadcast he realizes the Americans do not get his point, in fact Safer is caught by Knutas laughing inappropriately to which Knutas responds, "that's not funny."] Similarly, if dialogue involves social identities on a somewhat equal footing, or in an expressive understanding one of the other, the above is a failure. Regarding the proper dialogic conduct of persons, if this involves being receptive to others' views, properly educational and productive about the matters at hand, being balanced in informational needs and in the care of others, the above is further a failure. While the segment might be entertaining to American viewers, it does so at a high risk of caricaturing Finns and Finnish ways with American viewers (unlike Finns) not knowing the report is perhaps a caricature. And so, as a news report about Finns and Finland, we have, on several dimensions, a failure in dialogue.

Dialectical Tensions in Dialogue

When employed by people of various cultural backgrounds, communication is pitched and combined in deeply different ways. As the exchange above makes clear, one objective can be to entertain while the other is to tell the truth. Communication is, as a result, subjected to classic dialectical and cultural tensions. Another such tension can be the push in one direction to maintain the face of those involved, and to do so the truth may need muted, even elided. Studies of Chinese communication report the degree to which such a stance is deeply cultural within this tradition (Blum 2007). As in the example of the SARS epidemic, the truth of the matter was treated as secondary relative to that of saving face. Some forms of public communication operate similarly in Russia and the Arab world (Carbaugh 2005; Griefat and Katriel 1989). Other systems of communication, or ways of speaking, prioritize truth telling, no matter what its consequences (Katriel 1987). Katriel's study of Israeli "dugri" speech, speaking directly about the facts of the matter, is only one case in point. A similar symbolic theme of "being open and honest" is active in prominent North American scenes (Carbaugh 1988, 2005). And so it is with dialogue, whether about culture, religion, race, health, education, or whatever, what one can and should say as such is tutored, as was Rogers' or Buber's, by one's traditional ways. And while there may be tension and stress between entertaining, telling the truth, or face-work, how one resolves the tension as a practical matter typically resides within one's customary ways. We must be mindful of such tendencies, especially our own, and not blindly use them as a standard for the conduct and judgment of others, as others are accustomed to acting differently. Because of this, the differences in cultures and traditions in dialogue, we must be deeply educated in the variable, possible features which are active, as those summarized above. Thinking and acting with them, should help us embrace rather than ignore the diversity in our dialogues, moving onward with the range of our human cultural worlds in view.

Bibliography

Anderson, R. and Cissna, K. (1997) *The Martin Buber – Carl Rogers Dialogue: A new transcript with Commentary,* Albany, New York: State University of New York Press.

Bakhtin, M. (1986) 'The problem of speech genres' In M. M. Bakhtin, M. Holquist, V. McGee, & C. Emerson (Eds.), *Speech genres and other late essays,* pp.60-102, Austin, TX: University of Texas Press.

Blum, S. (2007) *Lies that bind: Chinese truth, and other truths,* New York: Rowan and Littlefield Publishers.

Brenneis, D. and Padarath, R. (1975) '"About those scoundrels I'll let everyone know": Challenge singing in a Fiji Indian community', in *Journal of American Folklore,* 88, pp.283-291.

Carbaugh, D. (1988) *Talking American: Cultural discourses on Donahue,* Norwood, NJ: Ablex Publishing Company.

Carbaugh, D. (2005) *Cultures in conversation,* London and New York: Lawrence Erlbaum Publishers.

Carbaugh, D., Boromisza-Habashi, D., and Ge, X. (2006) Dialogue in cross-cultural perspective. In N. Aalto & E. Reuter (eds.), Aspects of Intercultural Dialogue, pp.27-46, Koln, Germany: SAXA Verlag.

Carbaugh, D., Nuciforn, E., Saita, M., & Shin, D. (2011) 'Dialogue in cross-cultural perspective: Japanese, Korean, and Russian discourses', in *Journal of International and Intercultural Communication,* 4 (2), pp.87-108.

Katriel, T. (1986) *Talking straight: Israeli "dugri" speech in Sabra culture,* Cambridge University Press.

Scollo, M. (2012) Antiguan contrapuntal conversation in the Bronx, New York, Paper presented at the international conference, The ethnography of communication: Ways forward, Creighton University, Omaha, Nebraska, June 10-14.

Shields-Brodber, D. (2001) Contrapuntal conversation and the performance floor, In R. Le Page & P. Christie (eds), *Due respect: Essays on English and English related creolesin the Caribbean in honor of Professor Robert Le Page,* pp.208-218, University of West Indies Press.

Part 2

MULTICULTURALISM IN CONTINENTAL EUROPE

Was European Multiculturalism Destined to Fail?

Anya Topolski[45]

> ***Romeo****: For here lies Juliet, and her beauty makes*
> *This vault a feasting presence full of light.*
> *Death, lie thou there, by a dead man interr'd.*
> *How oft when men are at the point of death*
> *Have they been merry! which their keepers call*
> *A lightning before death: O, how may I*
> *Call this a lightning? O my love! my wife!*
> *Death, that hath suck'd the honey of thy breath,*
> *... O, here Will I set up my everlasting rest;*
> *And shake the yoke of inauspicious stars*
> *From this world-wearied flesh. Eyes, look your last!*
> *Arms, take your last embrace! and, lips, O you*
> *The doors of breath, seal with a righteous kiss*
> *A dateless bargain to engrossing death!*
> *Come, bitter conduct, come, unsavoury guide!*
> *Thou desperate pilot, now at once run on*
> *The dashing rocks thy sea-sick weary bark!*
> *Here's to my love! O true apothecary!*
> *Thy drugs are quick. Thus with a kiss I die.*
> ***[Romeo Dies.]***

---

45 Dr Anya Topolski is a FWO postdoctoral fellow at the Centre for Ethics, Social and Political Philosophy of the Higher Institute of Philosophy at the KU Leuven, Belgium. She studied biochemistry and philosophy at McGill University in Canada and in 2008 defended her PhD thesis entitled: A Political Ethics of Intersubjectivity: Between Hannah Arendt, Emmanuel Levinas and the Judaic (KU Leuven). Her thesis was awarded the 2009 Auschwitz Stichting prize and is being prepared for publication. Her areas of interest are ethics, politics, feminism, and Jewish thought. Her current research involves the deconstruction of the discourse of Judeo-Christianity in relation to European identity formation and its symbolic role in propagating Islamophobia.

As a foreigner, one often plays the role of spectator in the drama that is Europe's story. As all of Europe's 'others', even those that have lived here for dozens of generations, it is clear that this is the token role that one is permitted to perform. While my particular appellation of x-pat (a euphemism that grants me the basic respect often denied immigrants who have another skin colour or a lower balance in their bank accounts) allows me to be engaged spectator, a la Immanuel Kant, this is not the case for most of Europe's 'others'.[46] These others are forced to play the role of Juliet. And as the leaders of Europe's three most important nations have recently declared, multiculturalism -like Juliet- is dead. Yet, as Shakespeare reminds us in this tragedy of star-crossed lovers, Romeo swallows the poison only because he thought Juliet to be dead. Is it possible that Europeans are committing the same grave error? Multiculturalism, like Juliet, may not really be dead (at least not until the end of the play). So why has the public accepted the rhetoric of multiculturalism's death so easily? One might even ask whether it was ever really alive in Europe.

Has multiculturalism really failed or rather, as I will argue, was multiculturalism **destined to fail** in Europe. It is my contention that Europe's so-called multiculturalism is actually an economically driven series of tolerance demanding top-down policies, which prevented multiculturalism from developing in any bottom-up or horizontal manner. Tolerance, which is what Europe has striven for, is not enough. While a firm believer in the ideals of multiculturalism, it cannot be forcefully introduced without the people's support and without the possibility of redefining collective identities, such as national or trans-national identities. Without openness to alterity, such a top-down approach is equivalent to constructing a ticking time bomb, to be set-off by a (financial) crisis, as it did in the 1930's. Sadly, European history looks like it might repeat itself. If we want to prevent this, we must first prevent Juliet's death. Can we transform this tragedy into an ode for Europe? Can Europe transform its tale of tolerance and exclusion to one of respect and relationality?

While I do not have the arrogance to presume to know the answer, I would like to suggest a first step in this paper. While the Canadian model is far from perfect, it is far better than what I see and experience every day in the heart of Europe. What my trans-Atlantic home has taught me is that for multiculturalism to flourish, it must arise from the bottom-up and mature horizontally. Multiculturalism requires a radical openness to the other who forces one to ask oneself very difficult questions, questions that may require one to challenge and change one's identity. This type of questioning, change and growth cannot take place on soil that remains poisoned by the past. If Europeans really wish to embrace and create a culture of respect for

---

46 Take for example the 23 sans-papiers who are now on a hunger protest in Brussels who are being told they do not even have this right (see http://www.dewereldmorgen.be/artikels/2012/04/02/wat-baten-kaars-en-bril).

diversity, I believe that they, together with their 'others' must begin to collectively examine the roots of xenophobia in Europe in order to re-construct Europe's story. Europe rushed (and was forced by 'the allies', in the post-war years, to reconstruct itself – both literally and symbolically. There was no real time and space for the pain and shame of the Shoah to be unreservedly and openly addressed and expressed. This is not only true of Europeans; it is equally true of the survivors, their children and grandchildren – my self-included. While I do not wish to open the Pandora's box that is today symbolised by Israel, it seems to me that this is case and point of the failure of all those who experienced the trauma of the Shoah to give themselves time and space to understand its full effect on their psyches and actions. As an engaged spectator witnessing the rise of Islamophobia in Europe (and in Israel), it is now more apparent than ever that these emotions remain rooted in the culture and need to be addressed before there is any hope of saving multiculturalism, and for that matter, Europe.

Turning to the task at hand, I would like to develop this rather complex narrative in four distinct steps. Firstly, I will briefly consider the story of European multiculturalism; focussing on the case I am most familiar with, that of Belgium. Secondly, I will clarify the differences between multiculturalism and tolerance and argue that Europe's model is the latter and not the former. Thirdly, I will return to my roots and consider the Canadian model of multiculturalism in order to demonstrate the importance of bottom-up approaches, flexible identity narratives and maintaining the separation of economics and politics. Finally, I hope to reflect on the lessons we might draw from Canada and consider a possible first step to be taken by those inhabiting Europe, legally or otherwise, to ensure that the past does not repeat itself.

The Story of European Multiculturalism

While the vast majority of European nations have sought unity in the post-war period, policies relating to immigration, integration and multiculturalism in each nation-state have been far from united. This of course makes perfect sense when one considers that each country has different needs, borders, economic realities, degrees of homogeneity, histories etc. In a recent paper,[47] Keith Banting, one of the scholars responsible for the Multicultural Policy Index (MPI), along with Will Kymlicka, argued that the MPI contradicts the discourse of current politics, which has declared multiculturalism in Europe to be dead. While policy is undoubtedly important, the discourse cannot be underestimated. Discourse not only determines future policy and funding, it also has -on a daily basis- a negative effect on the

---

47 I am indebted to his current work, which he was kind enough to share with me in its unpublished form.

subjective well-being of immigrants by supporting a symbolic space that is radically intolerant to difference. Furthermore, these authors agree that Europe has taken a recognizable 'multiculturalist turn' in the last few decades of the 20th century (Banting, Johnston Kymlicka and Soroka 2006; Vertovec and Wessendorf 2010). Setting aside my disagreement temporarily, let us consider their account before focussing on the Belgian case.

Although recognisably provisional, they define multiculturalism within liberal-democracies as state policies that go further than upholding the rights of its citizens. It is this going-beyond in the form of 'recognition, support or accommodation for ethnocultural minorities to maintain and express their distinct identities'.[48] Based on the results of the MPI, they claim that the majority of European countries adopted multiculturalist policies in the last three decades and that there has been no significant change since 2000 (with the exception of Netherlands), with many countries reporting an increase in multiculturalism (among which they include Belgium). Intriguingly, they admit that certain countries, such as Germany, have never really embraced multiculturalism. At the national level there is clear hostility to institutionalised pluralism, and at the local level multicultural initiatives have only emerged in cities where there are large immigrant populations (Kraus and Schönwälder 2007). Exemplary is the fact that:

> Mother-tongue education was not introduced as a minority right but in order to enable guest worker children to reintegrate in their countries of origin. The fact that it continues to exist after this policy has been abandoned demonstrates the persistence of once-established structures as well as the continuing demand for such classes, but it is probably also due to the support of 'multiculturalist' officials and teachers. (Schönwälder 2010 p.160)

---

48 "Multiculturalism Policy Index, http://www.queensu.ca/mcp/, 31/3/2012" The Multiculturalism Policy Index (MCI) limits itself to 8 criteria noting that: "As with all cross-national indices, there is a trade-off between standardisation and sensitivity to local nuances." We take the following eight policies as the most common or emblematic forms of immigrant MCPs:

1) constitutional, legislative or parliamentary affirmation of multiculturalism, at the central and/or regional and municipal levels;
2) the adoption of multiculturalism in school curriculum;
3) the inclusion of ethnic representation/sensitivity in the mandate of public media or media licensing;
4) exemptions from dress-codes, either by statute or by court cases;
5) allowing of dual citizenship;
6) the funding of ethnic group organisations to support cultural activities;
7) the funding of bilingual education or mother-tongue instruction;
8) affirmative action for disadvantaged immigrant groups.

While the MPI takes the German case to be exceptional, I see it as representative of Europe's so-called multicultural turn. Immigrants, even those 'invited' as in the case of the guest workers, were **tolerated** in the post-war years as they were economically necessary and it was inappropriate, given the recent horrors of the Shoah, to express any sentiments of in-hospitality. Yet as the memory of the Shoah faded and with increasing economic downturns, the veil of forced tolerance slowly began to fade. While the more progressive governments scrambled to address this situation by introducing multicultural policies in the 80s and 90s these remained limited, top-down and a band-aid solution that often prevented public debate on issues, past and present, that were long overdue. This band-aid, not surprisingly, could not withstand the political events of the early 21st century whether the May 2001 riots in the UK, 9/11, the headscarf debate, the 2004 Madrid bombings and murder of van Gogh, 7/7, the 2005 cartoon controversy and Paris riots etc. These events, in combination with increased immigration, partially as a result of the worldwide economic crisis, have led to what is today referred to as 'the multiculturalism backlash'. Yet this backlash presupposes that Europe had in fact taken a multicultural turn, and that German is exceptional. Let us now take a closer look at the Belgian case to consider how exceptional it really is.

While the events prior to WWII cannot be underestimated, we must start somewhere. In 1945, Belgium, like most European nations, was at a loss to understand what had happened under the cover of war – not only across the continent as well as within its own borders (between the different linguistic, religious and political groups). While prior to the war Belgium had approx. 3.9% foreigners (mostly from neighbouring countries, eastern Europe and Italian coal workers), this number changed radically between 1946-49. As coal was the major energy source in the post-war period and Belgium did not have enough men to work in the mines, workers were sought first among the German prisoners of war, and secondly by inviting 77,000 southern Italians and 20,000 Poles to come work. Even with the economic recession of 1948 and a series of deathly mining accidents in the late 40s, Belgium continued to welcome its 'poorer' European neighbours (Caestecker 2001).[49] Most likely due to their limited geographical locations, the taboo imposed on any form of racism, and the shared values, this first wave of immigrants -most of whom were also Catholic-

---

49 The other non-economic and much smaller immigration group in this period was the arrival of former colonial subjects from Congo (much like the Indonesia who came to the Netherlands in this period or Northern Africans to France etc).

occurred without great tensions.[50] While they did not speak the language of the land, and were much poorer, they were willing -without protest- to do the jobs that Belgians refused to do and thus contribute to the country's economy. It was also an unspoken assumption that they would return to their homelands when no longer necessary.

The second wave of 'guest worker' (a term that is in desperate need of deconstruction) seems to have been less harmonious. It became clear, in the late 50s that the Belgian economy was in need of another kind of worker, an unskilled one to do hard labour, construction work in the cities, in the ports, and in the care-sector. Thus starting in the early 60s, bilateral agreements were made between first with Spain and Greece, and then (when these European nations could not provide the needed numbers of economic 'slaves) with Morocco and Turkey. The Ministry of Labour engaged in intense recruiting by publishing the brochure 'Living and Working in Belgium' in 1964:

> **Workers, welcome in Belgium!** Are you considering coming to work in Belgium? ... We Belgians are delighted that you are willing to contribute your labour power and your intelligence to our nation... Moving to a new country inevitably brings some adjustment problems with it. These initial difficulties will be more easily overcome if you have a normal life, i.e. a family life. Belgium is a country where labour is well paid, where life is very comfortable especially for families... In any case, we would like to reassure you that you are welcome among us in Belgium (*my trans.*)

Not surprisingly many foreigners, whose opportunities in their own countries were far from attractive, responded rapidly and positively to this warm invitation to become a Belgian 'guest-worker'. Most Belgians, in this time of economic growth, were more than happy to temporarily welcome these foreigners. All this came to an abrupt end in 1969 with another economic, this time oil related, crisis. This led, in 1974 -much like in other European countries- to a complete immigration halt (which is still officially in effect today). All those in Belgium before the freeze were regularised and given work permits but as of 1974 only work-permits were accorded to educated immigrants (i.e., x-pats, from Asia, North Americans etc.)

---

50 One of the most striking differences between the two waves of immigrants is how they, or their children, are referred to today in political circles. Elio di Rupo, the current prime minister, the son of Italian immigrants is considered Belgian of an Italian origin. Saïd el Khadraoui, a MEP from Belgium, whose mother is Belgian and father is Moroccan is referred to as a Moroccan born in Belgium. The discourse, of which this is just and example seems to reveal the refusal to accept the second wave of immigrants, and their Belgian born offspring, as Belgians much like in France as was recently demonstrated when Sarkozy, as well as the media, refused to refer to the Toulouse murderer as a French citizen.

and, in accordance with EU law, those from the EU. As of 1974, only the families of the 'guest-workers' were permitted to apply to be reunited as were a limited number of refugees and asylum seekers (again in accordance with UN law). What is significant is that Belgians, both the people and the politicians, believed that this freeze would solve the 'so-called migration problem'. They had not considered firstly, the number of family reunification requests; secondly, the fact that the 'guest-workers' had interpreted the invitation as permanent rather than temporary and thirdly, the impact of their experiences on those who had 'stayed behind' but who, like all human beings, wished to better their lives.

To a great extent, the current demographics are the result of these policies and this historical narrative. While approx. 3% of Belgium's current population, many of these 'guest workers' are now elderly, uneducated (they were never permitted to study as they had to work incredibly long and often illegal hours), un-integrated (as no effort was made for them to integrate as it was presumed they would leave at some point), and some are quite dependant on the health care system (because of physical ailments resulting from their poor working condition). These same workers are now publically scolded for not integrating and learning the language of their 'host' state. By contrast, their Belgian born children are young, educated, and have made great efforts to integrate (which is not easy with the growing hostily). Yet unlike their parents they do not feel that they are guests in Belgium and thus must behave according to the etiquette dictated by their host. They feel, having imbibed the liberal discourse of rights that have the right to feel at home in Belgium (the right to have-rights as Arendt calls it). Subjectively, as almost every recent poll has made clear, they do not feel welcome in Europe (EUMC 2006). There is seemingly a great deal of frustration among the children of the second wave of 'guest workers' (many feel that Europe is redefining itself to explicitly exclude them such as with the proposal to refer to a 'Judeo-Christian' tradition in the recent failed constitution). They rightly point out that the first wave 'guest workers', and their children, who were mostly Christian, have not been attacked by politicians and the media calling for the end of multiculturalism and have never been asked to leave Belgium. They sense the unspoken and inhuman expectation that it would be better for Belgium if they would simply 'go home' now that the economy does not need them. For them, even as unwelcoming as it is, Belgium is their only home. Thus, while there may be multicultural policies in Belgium and Europe, there is almost no multicultural spirit. In a word, the experience of these primarily Muslim offspring of the second-wave of 'guest workers' is that they are being ***tolerated*** as collateral damage caused by the needs of the economy. But as any Jew in Europe after the Shoah will state, ***tolerance*** is not enough, human beings need and deserve more. Tolerance does not prevent violence (and genocide) in times of crisis. Clearly the lessons of the Shoah about dehumanisation which one would have hoped and presumed had been learned by Belgians, and Europeans, have not. It seems that once again economic growth trumps all ethics.

Multiculturalism is not Rooted in Tolerance!

Moving away from history, far from my area of expertise, to the realm of philosophy where I feel more 'at home' – it is time to disentangle the meaning of multiculturalism from that of tolerance.[51] My claim is that Europe since the late 1970s, with notable exceptions, has couched a culture of tolerance in multicultural rhetoric and policies. Melanie Phillips seems to agree when she states "Multiculturalism became the driving force of British life, ***ruthlessly policed*** by an ***army of bureaucrats enforcing*** a ***doctrine*** of ***state-mandated virtue*** to promote racial, ethnic and cultural balkanisation" (2006 ***emphasis added***). This approach has further stifled the debate about Europe's historical violent reactions to difference, which may be adding fuel to the fire of today's backlash. This top-down approach, to be found primarily in policies and political rhetoric, is a necessary condition of multiculturalism but is not a sufficient one. What is essential for multiculturalism is that an openness to alterity -both within and without- arises from the bottom-up and flourishes in a horizontal manner. The latter cannot be introduced by force as it calls for a taxing commitment to reflexivity, individually and collectively (better yet relationally). Without this commitment and without the possibility of redefining collective identities, such as national or trans-national identities, multiculturalism is but masked tolerance.

This type of radical openness is rooted in respect for the other and not tolerance. Concretely, I do not want my gender, faith-commitments or political views tolerated by those whose gender, and faith or opinions are part of the majority culture. I want to be respected for being a woman, a Jew and a left-winger. Multiculturalism cannot possibly flourish if differences are not seen as enriching. This is also why multiculturalism struggles in times of crisis when people are locked into the politics of fear that often re-defines and reduces the potential richness of alterity to a threat. The necessary condition of multiculturalism, which is to a great extent lacking in Europe, is the openness to the other, an openness that forces one to ask oneself very difficult questions and to allow oneself to be vulnerable to critique. This re-thinking of identity is the key to the possibility of multiculturalism. So what does re-thinking identities mean?

Let us begin by looking at a recent example of political rhetoric in the UK that

---

51 With the exception of some thinkers, among other sociologist Frank Furedi, who have recently made valiant efforts to redefine the notion of tolerance, returning it to its radical roots in classical Lockean liberalism and thereby rescue it from its current abuse as exemplified by the language of 'zero-tolerance'.

refuses such openness *prima facie*. In the by now infamous June 16th 2007 Economist Bagehot article, David Cameron, then the Conservative Party leader, attacked the creed of multiculturalism (again the theological language) as it 'deliberately weakened our collective identity'. In other words, Cameron creates and reaffirms the most binary, polemic and exclusionary of identity narratives, that of us vs. them, often used in war rhetoric without even considering and leaving open the possibility of a relational identity. The Conservative Party it seems realised how successful this us vs. them frame is, speaking as it does to our animal-like instincts, and continues to use today.[52] This language and exclusionary logic clearly has inspired both Merkl and Sarkozy to make similar claims (one of the rare occasions in European history that these three centres of power are in such agreement). This us vs. them rhetoric seems to dominate current political discourse in Europe, as documented by Prins and Slijper (2002; 2010), and it is my contention that this frame prevents the possibility of relationality (Topolski 2008; 2011; 2012), that is a re-thinking and possibly re-construction of one's own identity, whether as an individual or as a nation. Without such a possibility there is no hope for popular multiculturalism to arise and complement potential policies. Without such openness, prevented by us vs. them thinking all that is left is tolerance, with its inherent instability and invisible -in good times- mask of hatred.

The Canadian Multicultural Identity

Given the difference between multiculturalism and tolerance, and the heavy demand the former places on individuals and society as a whole, one must ask, does a multicultural society exist? While the obvious answer is that no society is perfectly harmonious, the Canadian case is interesting in that it embraces multiculturalism, both bottom-up and top-down, and has not experienced the European backlash to any flagrant extent (Banting 2006; Kymlicka 2007). Before I begin, let me admit I am clearly biased. Growing up in Canada I was brainwashed, like so may others, by the ethos of the multicultural mosaic. I learned it, I lived it and to be honest, since moving to Europe I love it. While I had many doubts in Canada, raised by our treatment of the First Nations, the Sri Lankan boat people and the current immigration preference for 'skilled' workers, in contrast to what I have recently observed – I am beginning to wonder whether I should give up hope of making

---

52 In 2008, in The Daily Mail, Cameron warned, "Multiculturalism had dangerously undermined Britain's sense of identity and brought about 'cultural apartheid'". Simply put, multiculturalism is not part of Britain's identity or story; it is foreign to British culture. Furthermore, it has led to a form of apartheid – a word loaded with meaning in the public's mind – cultural apartheid, the term culture being the acceptable term for ethnic, religious, or racial difference.

Europe my home.[53] So what is, with admittedly rosy coloured glasses that make the Canadian model that is striking? I would like to briefly focus on three related points. First, the combination of top-down and bottom-up approaches; second, the flexible identity narrative; and third the distinction between economic and politically motivated multiculturalism.

The Canadian story of multiculturalism is one with a hidden history (which is all too often the case in foundational myths, see Honig 2003). What is often forgotten is the original form of this policy; one of bilingualism and biculturalism clearly privileged the traditional French and English majorities in Canada. The non-traditional, or newer minorities reacted publically claiming that this policy was exclusive and did not fit *their* definition of Canada. The fact that they felt empowered and included enough to do so is a testament to Canadian multiculturalism, and what is more important is that they succeeded in changing the nature of the policy which was to become Trudeau's 1971 policy of multiculturalism. This is perhaps the greatest evidence of the bottom-up approach in Canada.[54] Thus not only was this top-down

---

53 If I am asking others to be self-critical and open to the criticism of others (as the ethics implicit in this paper requires), it seems only fair do the same. There are three distinct points I wish to express, each of which is strongly subjective and thus difficult to convey. First, I like so many non-Europeans am attracted to the idea of Europe, with its history and culture, an attraction that even with an awareness of all of its flaws cannot be denied. Second, having left Canada a decade ago, I have a naïve vision of Canada; from a distance – mainly by means of the media – it seems that since I have left, it is moving away from its ideology of alterity towards a more economic model of immigration. The third 'confession' is the most complex as it occurs at an almost sub-conscious level. I have begun to realize that since moving to Europe my Canadian 'brainwashing' is starting to fade. Sadly, this is not a good thing. Taking a bus in Toronto, the most multicultural city in the world, I never once would have doubted my safety or worried about being robed. Since moving to Belgium, these questions often cross my mind most often when there are dark-skinned men on the bus with me. I hate this subtly racist daimon in my head, and silence it as quickly as possible, that seems to have been produced by living in a culture where such thinking is common, where it is repeated daily in the media, etc.

54 What is also worth noting is that these policies differ from those concerning Canada's national minorities, the Quebecois and First Nations. The policy defined the goals of multiculturalism as:

- to "assist members of all cultural groups to overcome cultural barriers to full participation in Canadian society";
- to "promote creative encounters and interchange amongst all Canadian cultural groups in the interest of national unity"; and
- to "assist immigrants to acquire at least one of the Canada's official languages in order to become full participants in Canadian society".

While the phrasing recognises that there are barriers, and thus implicitly a distinction between us and them, it is a porous barrier and one which is meant to be eliminated by means of encounter and exchange between all groups. These are taken from Prime Minister's statement to the Canadian parliament declaring the policy (Trudeau 1971 p.8546).

policy adapted because of critique from the bottom, it was also first drafted because of the demand from the citizens expressed both on the streets and at the poll box in the end of the 1960s. This period was one of social and political protests in which Canadians demanded a revolution in civil rights (Kymlicka 2007). This change was further solidified, in terms of policy, in 1988 in the preamble to the Canadian Multiculturalism Act, a text whose impact extends far beyond the courthouse and has a real impact on political discourse and public opinion (Eliades 2007). What this case makes clear is that the Canadian model is one in which there is a dynamic exchange between top and bottom, that is between policy and public opinion, and as such a healthy balance of both top-down and bottom-up approaches to multiculturalism.[55]

This brings me to my second claim related to flexible identity narratives. This flexibility is critical to the openness to alterity I referred to above. Since the 1970s, the Canadian national narrative has been re-constructed as one that celebrates diversity, an identity to which every newcomer can contribute – hence the metaphor of the mosaic. This national identity avoids the type of us vs. them frame that can often be politically problematic. According to Irene Bloemraad, "Canadian multiculturalism legitimates immigrants' multiple identities, provides resources to community organisations that promote citizenship and participation, and orient leaders of ethnic communities towards a language of inclusion" (2006 p. 84). Other evidence in favour of this inclusive identity narrative is the high rate of naturalisation in Canada – approx. 85%, as compared to 40% in the US and even lower in most European countries (Tran, Kustec and Chui 2005). Furthermore, while many European countries require that those wishing to be naturalised break ties with their land of origin or religion, this is seen as detrimental in Canada. Canadian immigrants are instead asked to add a dash to their identity thus Polish-Canadians or Muslim-Canadians etc. Identity in Canada is seen as additive rather than aporetic, it is relational rather than exclusive. It is this re-constructed identity, and its accompanying myths and symbols, which creates the openness necessary for bottom-up multiculturalism. Perhaps the clearest evidence for this case is the positive correlation between national identity and immigration, with both direct and indirect positive impacts of national identity in favour of immigrants in Canada (Johnston et al. 2010).[56]

Closely related to the identity issue is the fact that multiculturalism in Canada is

---

55 This also implicitly suggests that Europe's current democratic deficit may be closely related to the multiculturalism backlash.

56 Unfortunately, that is for Europe, there is evidence that this narrative flexibility and openness to additive identities is something deemed detrimental in societies founded on largely ethnic terms 'in contrast to societies built by waves of immigration (Citrin and Sides 2008).

driven by politics rather than economics. While there is no doubt that economics plays a role in Canada, as is clear from the new and problematic category of 'skilled workers', this remains secondary in terms of the national narrative. One of the strongest proofs for this is the fact that "Canada has the highest proportion of foreign-born legislators in the world" (Adams 2007 p.69). Multiculturalism in Canada is much more than a policy; it is an identity for all Canadians, new and old. It is – as it were – the glue that binds citizens together in a common project. It is thus first and foremost political and is as such less threatened by periods of crisis, economic or other.

Is There Hope for Europe?

One of the distinct advantages of being raised by a family of survivors is that I am committed, even against all odds, to believe there is always hope (perhaps it helps that Jews have a positive philosophical anthropology unencumbered by the original sin). Nonetheless, the situation in Europe -as observed by an engaged spectator- is dire. It is from this vantage point that I wish to propose a small, but necessary, *first step* towards creating space for the bottom-up approach, which I believe is greatly lacking in Europe. As I have demonstrated, this type of multiculturalism requires a radical openness to the other, a willingness to be criticized and a commitment to re-constructing one's narrative. While there is no doubt this is an immense undertaking, and a lot to ask in times of crisis, let us not forget that crisis means both danger and opportunity. The first, small step, I wish to propose, by ways of conclusion, is one that asks Europeans, both insiders and outsiders, to begin to deconstruct its narrative -a first necessary step to an re-construction- and to do so without trying to silence or erase what is either shameful or painful.

While Europe has a very extensive history, and in this sense a rich culture and heritage to want to hold on to, it would be misleading to deny that Europe has not always had to re-write its story (Pocock 1994; Hay 1966; Judt 1996; Perkins 2004). More importantly, this process does not mean denying its past and traditions, rather it means re-framing them by considering other perspectives and voices. Europe, contrary to its myth, has always had changing borders, newcomers, and thus new narratives. In this vein, there is certainly hope for Europe. Yet hope is not sufficient unless there is a sincere desire to engage in a collective process of historical reflexivity. Just as one constructs the self by means of a narrative, all those that call themselves Europeans must engage in a collective reconstruction of their narrative – if they wish to avoid repeating their past mistakes (Demos 2011). While the Shoah is but one such sore spot, it is -given the rise of Islamophobia today- an obvious place to start.

Bibliography

Adams, M. (2007) *Unlikely Utopia: The Surprising Triumph of Canadian Pluralism*, Toronto: Viking.

Balibar, É. (2003) *We, the People of Europe?: Reflections on Transnational Citizenship*, Trans. James Swenson, Princeton: Princeton University Press.

Banting, K. (2010) 'Is There a Progressive`s Dilemma in Canada? Immigration, Multiculturalism and the Welfare State', in *Canadian Journal of Political Science*, 4(43), pp.797-820.

Banting, K. and Kymlicka, W. (2006) *Multiculturalism and the Welfare State: Recognition and Redistribution in Contemporary Democracies*, Oxford: Oxford University Press.

Banting, K., Richard, J. & Kymlicka, W., Stuart, S. (2006) 'Do Multiculturalism Policies Erode the Welfare State: an Empirical Analysis' in Keith Banting and Will Kymlicka, eds, *Multiculturalism and the Welfare State: Recognition and Redistribution in Contemporary Democracies*, Oxford: Oxford University Press.

Bloemraad, I. (2006) *Becoming a Citizen: Incorporating Immigrants and Refugees in the United States and Canada*, Berkeley: University of California Press.

Caestecker, F. (2001) *Alien Policy in Belgium, 1840-1940: The Creation of Guest Workers, Refugees and Illegal Aliens*, Berghahn Books.

Citrin, J. & Cara, W., Brian, D. (2001) 'The Meaning of American National Identity' in Richard D. Ashmore, Lee Jussin, and David Wilder, eds. *Social Identity, Intergroup Conflict, and Conflict Reduction.* New York: Oxford University Press, pp.71-100.

Demos Think Tank: http://www.demos.co.uk/publications

Eliadis, P. (2007) 'Diversity and Equality: the Vital Connection' in Keith Banting, Tom Courchene and Leslie Seidle, eds., *Belonging: Diversity, Recognition and Shared Citizenship in Canada,* Montreal: Institute for Research in Public Policy.

Eumc European Union Agency for Fundamental Rights Agency (2006) *Muslims in the European Union: Discrimination and Islamophobia.*

Hay, D. (1966) *Europe: The Emergence of an Idea*, London: Harper Torchbooks.

Honig, B. (2003) *Democracy and the Foreigner*, Princeton: Princeton University Press.

Johnston, R. Keith, B. & Kymlicka, W., Stuart, S. (2010) 'National Identity and Support for the Welfare State', in *Canadian Journal of Political Science,* 2(4) pp.349-377.

Judt, T. (1996) *A Grand Illusion?: An Essay on Europe*, New York: NYU Press.

Kraus, P. and Schönwälder, K. (2006) 'Multiculturalism in Germany: Rhetoric, scattered experiment and future chances' in Keith Banting and Will Kymlicka, eds,, *Multiculturalism and the Welfare State: Recognition and Redistribution in Contemporary Democracies*, Oxford: Oxford University Press.

Kymlicka, W. (2007) 'Ethnocultural Diversity in a Liberal State: Making Sense of the Canadian Model(s)' in Keith Banting, Thomas Courchene and Leslie Seidle, eds., *Belonging? Diversity, Recognition and Shared Citizenship in Canada,* Montreal: Institute for Research on Public Policy.

Mpi (2012) *Multiculturalism Policy Index,* http://www.queensu.ca/mcp/.

Pagden, A. (2002) *The Idea of Europe: From Antiquity to the European Union,* Cambridge: Cambridge University Press.

Perkins, Mary A. (2004) *Christendom And European Identity: The Legacy Of A Grand Narrative Since 1789.* Walter De Gruyter Inc.

Pocock, J. (1994) 'Deconstructing Europe', in *History of European Ideas,* 18(3) pp.329–345.

Prins, B. and Slijper, B. (2002) 'Multicultural Society Under Attack: Introduction', in *Journal of International Migration and Integration,* 3(4), pp.313–28.

Schönwälder, K. (2010) 'Germany: integration policy and pluralism in a self-conscious country of immigration' in Steven Vertovec and Susanne Wessendorf, eds., *The Multiculturalism Backlash: European discourses, policies and practices,* London: Routledge.

Soroka, S. & Richard, J., Keith, B. (2007) 'The Ties that Bind: Social Diversity and Cohesion in Canada', in Keith Banting, Thomas Courchene and Leslie Seidle, eds., *Belonging? Diversity, Recognition and Shared Citizenship in Canada.* Montreal: Institute for Research on Public Policy.

Topolski, A. (2012) http://www.opendemocracy.net/anya-topolski/does-it-get-more-transparent-than-this.

Topolski, A. (2011) 'An Ethics of Relationality: Destabilising the Genocidal Frame of Us vs. Them', in *Preventing Genocide: Root Causes and Coping Strategies* (forthcoming).

Topolski, A. (2008) 'Creating Citizens in the Classroom: Hannah Arendt's Political Critique' in *Ethical Perspectives.* Leuven: Peeters Publishers, 15(2), pp.259-282.

Tran, K. & Stan, K., Tina, C. (2005) 'Becoming Canadian: Intent, Process and Outcome' in *Canadian Social Trends,* Ottawa: Statistics Canada, Catalogue, 76 no. 11-008.

Trudeau, P. (1971) Statement to the House of Commons on Multiculturalism' in House of Commons, *Official Report of Debates,* 28th Parliament, Third Session, 8 October: 8545-46.

Wessendorf, S. (2010) *The Multiculturalism Backlash: European Discourses, Policies and Practices.* Taylor & Francis.

Wodak, R. et al. (2008) *The Discursive Construction of National Identity.* Edinburgh: Edinburgh University Press.

Public Figures of Islam in Europe: Perspectives on Multicultural Public Individuals

Cagla E. Aykac[57]

In contemporary Europe, the issues related to multiculturalism focus mostly on the claims of migrants, and more specifically of Muslims living in Europe, rather than indigenous groups or nations without states (Kymlicka 2007 pp.49-59). Why this focus on Islam? First, since the 1970's there has been the development of a 'demand' of Islam that came with the settling of migrants from Muslim countries in Europe (Dassetto, Maréchal and Nielsen 2001). This demand took multiple forms and contributed to the development of a wide range of 'supply' of Islam (Haenni 2005) such as associations, mosques, books, journals and Internet sites. Further, in the 1990's, Islam became 'public' in Europe (Gole and Ludwig 2006). Islam went from being perceived as external and anachronic to Europe to becoming internal to it. This 'interpenetration' involves shared space and time, and mutual transformations that create tensions that can take different shapes, from creativity to violence (Gole 2005). It is the 'interpenetration' of Islam and Europe, the proximity and the changes taking place both in Europe and in Islam that raise new issues and fears.

What is today known as the 'crisis of multiculturalism' is debated from a theoretical perspective in academic circles, and it is also discussed in public spheres by contemporary political leaders, as well as by public figures, writers, journalists, and thinkers, and it is transmitted through the mass media (Lentin and Titley 2011). The notion of the crisis of multiculturalism refers on the one hand to state policies about how to accommodate difference and on the other it permeates public debates and contributes to shaping opinions on how to 'live together'. The areas where these debates take place and opinions are formed are separate from the state and economics and are central to thinking existing democracies (Fraser 1992 pp.109-142). Nancy Frazer defines these areas as a 'theater in modern societies in which

---

57 Cagla E. Aykac is Assistant Professor in the Department of Political Science and Public Administration of Fatih University. She holds a PhD in Sociology from the Ecole des Hautes Etudes en Sciences Sociales (EHESS) in Paris. She received her Bachelors' degree from Brown University and her Masters' degree from Boğaziçi University, and has worked as an independent researcher for institutions such as the Open Society Institute (OSI), the Centre for European Policy Studies (CEPS), the Ecole des Hautes Etudes en Sciences Sociales (EHESS) and the European Research Council (ERC).

political participation is enacted through speech' (Fraser 1992 p.110). In this paper, rather than focusing on formal party politics and state policies, I look at public debates on multiculturalism, at the shape of debates, at who participates and under what conditions, as these issues are central to thinking democracy.

The Rushdie Affair is a landmark in what concerns theoretical and public debates on multiculturalism in Europe. These landmark moments multiplied in the following years, 9/11, 7/7, the murder of Theo van Gogh or the Danish Cartoons affairs are all similar types of moments. The Rushdie Affair continued to unfold since 1989 and it is today considered key in understanding the current debates on multiculturalism. According to Kymlicka, the Rushdie Affair, more than any single event, led people to question the nature of multiculturalism (Kymlicka 1995 p.19). The content of the book, the intentions of the writer, the fatwa for his killing, the burning of the book in public are important issues on which there is much literature. Here, however, I would like to draw attention to the fact that the affair developed around a multicultural individual, Salman Rushdie, and his cultural production, the novel, *the Satanic Verses*. Rather than focusing on the content of the affair, the intentions of the author or the positions of various social and political actors, I propose to look at the ways in which this affaire lead to the development of new spaces where the opinions about the accommodation of difference are debated in Europe. I underline that the affaire developed around the work of a multicultural European individual and I argue that this opened up an era in which there was an increase in the number of individuals that became public in Europe by making active references to Islam and that their incursions in the public sphere altered the ways in which debates about multiculturalism take place in Europe.

The Rushdie Affair developed in a transnational fashion in the 1990's and left marks in local, national, and global spheres. It created clear-cut positions: at first, one felt compelled to take position, for or against Rushdie, for or against the *fatwa* of Ayatollah Khomeini, for or against the burning of the book, for or against racism, for or against multiculturalism. However, it also opened an era of doubt and incertitude: standing against the fatwa while understanding the feeling of offense of parts of the population and being shocked by both the racist discourses that circulated and the burning of the book in public all together meant that many people did not know how to position themselves on the multiplicity of issues raised by the Rushdie Affair. These dynamics led to the opening of new spaces where alternative articulations took place. The Rushdie Affair highlighted that a theoretical limit had been reached and that this border also involved clashes in daily practices. Further, the affaire was transmitted in the international and local media; it unfolded in a highly visual and performative manner. It reinforced civilisational discourses and exacerbated racial dynamics, creating new camps and new social borders. It opened a space where public condemnations of multiculturalism could be expressed while also opening up new venues and opportunities for minorities to express their claims in public. The Rushdie affair opened space in Europe both for individuals who would speak up in defense of multiculturalism and for those who would speak against it and condemn Islam as a set of values opposed to the European ones. It was instrumental in the development of the debates on multiculturalism and highlighted the central role of writers and thinkers in the formation of opinions. It created a demand of people who would speak about Islam in public and this bears weight on the ways in which multiculturalism is debated in Europe.

Salman Rushdie had many heirs of Muslim origin who would speak about their beliefs and their political views on contemporary Europe. Tariq Ramadan, for example, argues that the Rushdie Affair (along with the Iranian Revolution and the first headscarf affair in Creil in France) was key in his 'coming out' in public as a Muslim believer. Although he kept his faith 'private' up until in then, in the beginning of the 1990's he felt that he should stand by his beliefs in public. He argues that this led to changes in the ways in which he was perceived in Europe; he went from being seen as a model citizen, to being seen as a potential threat. Tariq Ramadan penetrates public debates in Europe in pretty much the same ways as Salman Rushdie, through scandals and controversies. Ayaan Hirsi Ali is another one of these public figures that took advantage of the demand of people who would speak about Islam in public in the 1990s. Multicultural individuals that speak a mixed language of belonging came to maturation and developed the skills necessary for public roles in the 1990's in Europe where public structures and social networks fit to receive them had been established.

People like Salman Rushdie, Tariq Ramadan and Ayaan Hirsi Ali embody in a dramatic, caricatural, and hyper mediatised way some of the central issues that multiculturalism poses in Europe, they contribute to the shaping of opinions, and they shed light on relations of power that are at play. Tariq Ramadan and Ayaan Hirsi Ali both hold strong positions on why, how, and how much to accommodate or not accommodate the demands of the divers Muslim communities living in Europe. While Ramadan argues that multiculturalism is the only path possible in Europe and that it is urgent to create a sense of European Muslim citizenship by focusing on notions of equality and justice, Hirsi Ali argues that multiculturalism poses a great threat to European values and liberties and that Muslims need to adopt European values and be assimilated by force.

Following the paths of public individuals like Salman Rushdie, Tariq Ramadan and Ayaan Hirsi Ali shows that debates on multiculturalism crystallise in the form of scandals. Speaking about Islam in public in Europe implies accepting to get involved in controversies. The notion of scandal involves the public denunciation of an event and divisions into opposing camps; it is a conflict-laden moment of social transformation in which there are shifts in the positions of the accused and the accusatory (De Blick 2005 p.17). Further, for scandals to develop, there must be on the one hand matter to create controversies and on the other there also needs to be actors that have the means to express their discontent in public (Thompson 2000). As such, the scandals that develop around these public figures are constructed around certain themes and they are dealt with through different structures: The issue of how to relate to Islamic sources of knowledge is central to the debates, and the figure of the Prophet Mohammed is central. Gender issues permeate all the debates on multiculturalism. Anti-semitism and racism in general figure entangled in the web of controversies while mobility and security are also some of the major themes treated. Further, it is impossible to think about multiculturalism in contemporary Europe without taking into the role of modern media and technology. The media and technology offer mobility and the possibility to reach always-larger audiences. It also creates alternative public spaces and allows for new forms of subjectivity to emerge (Mandeville 2001). According to Gluckman, scandals test the limits and the border of belonging to a group and question its internal hierarchies (Gluckman 1963 pp.307-316).

The issues concerning multiculturalism are debated in a context in which there are asymmetries of power and in which identities stand on the forefront. The debates do not take place among 'equals'; and they tend to look more like trials taking place in a court room in which the 'accused' need to answer to any question asked; identity figures on the forefront of the debates and so does private life and practices. This leads to public debates where political propositions are measured by looking at values, intentions, affiliations, and character more than political ideas and practices. The debates rarely take the shape of a rational discourse that would have as its objective consensus on solutions to common issues education, health, justice or equality. Rather they become scandalous, offensive and highly emotional multilateral monologues where each party defends his own 'worldview'.

The debates about multiculturalism also develop through rumors and suspicions. The novel *The Satanic Verses*, became a central piece in delineating the debates on multiculturalism but it was not read by many of the people involved in the controversy, as it was forbidden in many places, it took years to translate, and parts and pieces of the text were used selectively. Analogously, Tariq Ramadan affirms that most of his opponents have not read his opinions and interpret them out of context; he also argues that the same goes for those who portray his grandfather as an extremist without reading his writings. This means that while texts and sources are central in debates on multiculturalism, they are rarely approached with a critical or analytical mind. At the same time, there is a demand for information and knowledge, and there are spaces for information to circulate. Today in Europe it is difficult to think the issue of multiculturalism without taking into account the central position of books and the production and transmission of knowledge.

Private life experiences are as important as political propositions for gaining access to public debates on multiculturalism. There is a demand for 'biographical data' and this shapes public debates in Europe. Whether these narrations are autobiographical or biographical, and whether they are true or not, talking about private life seems to be necessary for gaining access to the public. To gain access to the public, one is asked to talk about family relations, friendships, life choices, and day-to-day experiences, making personal lives become public and identities known, in all their complexity. The fact that Tariq Ramadan is the grandson of Hassan al-Banna, one of the central figures of 20th century Islamism, is a legacy that gives him both legitimacy among Muslim publics and creates suspicion in Europe. He is asked to answer questions about the religious views and political program of Hasan al-Banna in public, but he is also summoned to talk about his feelings for him and his emotional attachment to his grandfather. Alternately, the fact the Ayaan Hirsi Ali gives ample details about her childhood as an African Muslim girl who was subject to genital mutilation and forced to marry a cousin she had never seen, gives her a legitimacy to speak in public about the plight of Muslim women, and the dangers posed by Islam.

There is thus an increase in the demand in Europe for individuals to speak in public about their personal experiences of Islam and about their religiosity. This demand is divers. On the one hand it concerns individuals who will speak 'against' Islam. Hirsi Ali speaks at great length about how she was born into Islam and raised in fear and how she progressively lost her faith and left Islam. She talks of the death threats that she received for having left the faith and of the weight of knowing that her colleague, Theo van Gogh, was murdered for producing the film *Submission Part I* with her. It is based on these experiences that she argues that the 'illiberal' practices of Muslims should not be accommodated in any way in Europe. Hirsi Ali argues that migrants need to change, and that Europe should force the assimilation of Muslims in terms of mentality, education, critical thought, and hygiene. On the other hand, there are also strong demands for individuals who can give insight on how to live in Europe as a believer. Tariq Ramadan for example draws attention to how to accommodate being a good European citizen and a pious Muslim. As mentioned above, coming out in public about being a believer involved being excluded from certain spaces. There is a demand from believers to defend and justify their positions with reference to Islamic sources of knowledge, as well as political events but it is their intentions and character that remains the focus of discussions. Today, in Europe, Muslims, ex-Muslims and non-Muslims all contribute to the shapes of discourses on multiculturalism in Europe. Talking in public about religious beliefs is a contemporary trend, almost a necessity to gain access to the public, and there is always a price to pay.

These individuals are also ready and willing to use their images and their bodies to gain access to the public. Public multicultural subjects use their bodies as they embody the reality of European multiculturalism. There is an aura of ambiguity around them, they are difficult to situate geographically but also in terms of their style. The 'looks' of multicultural subjects are central for their access to the public. The 'satanic' looks of Salman Rushdie are highlighted while Ayaan Hirsi Ali's 'extraordinary beauty' is expected to look 'very fine on the cover of magazines' (Buruma 2007); and Tariq Ramadan 'fascinates the media' with his ease in speech in divers languages and seductive allure while attempts to determine whether he is 'an angel or a devil' (Kepel 2008 p.248) remain central. Through these public figures, there are new forms of masculinity and feminity that appear in Europe. For Hirsi Ali, migrants come from another time, they have serious diseases, and they are ignorant, illiterate, and limited in their capacities to think and to act. She portrays Muslim men as being violent, brutal, infantile, irresponsible, and illiterate. In her account, Muslim women are portrayed as being victims and reproducers of oppressive Islamic norms. Hirsi Ali launches herself as a disfranchised victim, a woman who was once oppressed and then managed to liberate herself through the opportunities available in Europe. She tries to engrave in all minds the violence that take place according to her systematically in Muslim culture. Her public discourse is challenged by Muslim feminist women who argue that it is possible to be a woman, a believer and an active citizen at the same time. Tariq Ramadan challenges the very stereotype of the Muslim man described by Hirsi Ali. He stands as a pious intellectual, sober, elegant man with a sense of humor and strong debating skills. New forms of masculinity and feminity that challenge the stereotypes and the norms of feminity and masculinity appear in Europe, men and women's bodies are highly sexualized and their intellectual credentials and capacities for action stand on the forefront.

The growing numbers of public figures of Islam in Europe do not share a common group identity, ethnicity, gender, a form of religiosity, or nationality. They illustrate the diversity in origins and modes of beliefs of the wide category of 'Muslims in Europe.' They are highly 'integrated' in Europe, they position themselves as autonomous independent European subjects; they refuse institutional ties, or they use institutional ties in passing. Their associations with political parties or transnational movements are often partial and transitory. Ayaan Hirsi Ali for example first became a researcher in the Wiardi Beckman Foundation, a research institute in the Netherlands linked to the social-democrat party, the PvdA. But she quickly found her herself in conflict with the multicultural policies of the party that she judged to be 'blind' to the dangers posed by Islam in Europe. Her political positions lead her to dissociate from the party and get involved with the rightist Volkspartij voor Vrijheid en Democratie (VVD), that holds a strong anti migrant stance. According to her, minorities should be forced to emancipate, group identities should be rejected and the individual should be placed back at the center of the social structure. Tariq Ramadan's association with the Muslim Brotherhood and his claims of autonomy are looked at with suspicion. His refusal to get involved in the Conseil Français du Culte Musulman (CFCM) which he criticised for not being representative of Muslims in Europe and for being a tool of the French government to control Muslims is also quite illustrative. Being a multicultural subject involves being dynamic and fluid between groups; relations to places, peoples, and groups can be transitory. They make sense only as long as they serve a purpose; they can be activated and disactivated depending on need. Being excluded can sometimes increase public capital, and dissociations from institutions or networks can be beneficial and necessary. Beyond 'integration' it is sometimes rejection that gives public legitimacy. The activation and disactivation of associations creates an 'aura of ambiguity' that fascinates but also creates suspicion which leads to efforts to 'unmask' multicultural subjects.

The issue of language is of course central in the debates on multiculturalism in Europe. It is central in trying to measure the degree of 'integration' of migrants through the creation of mandatory language courses and citizenship courses. However, today, beyond learning local languages, idioms and references, multicultural subject ought to be able to navigate between languages and intellectual references. These skills are necessary for interacting with European intellectuals, political figures, and popular figures in spaces such as universities, newspapers, magazines, mosques, cultural associations, think tanks, and the Internet. Multicultural subjects share their experience with Europeans that often do not have the same degree of mobility and flexibility as they do. While knowing French or Dutch is still presented as being a measure of the capacity to 'integrate', actually, knowing Arabic, Turkish, and other languages alongside European languages are much needed skills for European multicultural subjects. The limitations of those who can speak only one language in Europe are increasingly being outlined. However linguistic flexibility might lead to new forms of criticism and can been perceived as a threat. Tariq Ramadan is for example accused of *taqiyya,* which in France translates as 'double speech' and this accusation is based on the idea that he holds different speeches in English or French than in Arabic. Mobility is central, whether it is geographic, linguistic, or intellectual as new platforms for debates and spaces for the transmission and construction of knowledge appear.

Being 'translocal' is central for multicultural subjects; they have to be 'rooted' while at the same time to have a grasp of transnational affairs and debates (Mandeville 2001)[58]. The local and transnational dimensions of the public scandals that develop around these individuals feed on each other. The Rushdie Affair for example revived debates on race and class in England, as well as discussion on education and the construction of mosques. It also led to a revival of debates on colonial relations, multicultural politics and legal issues: on this occasion, it was the law on blasphemy that came under scrutiny. The debate between Tariq Ramadan and Nicolas Sarkozy in 2003 revived discussions about the institutionalisation of Islam in France through the creation of the CFCM, and the issue of anti-Semitism with references to the history of the Vichy regime in France. In the Netherlands, the debate around the diffusion of the film *Submission Part I* and the murder of Theo van Gogh revived the debate on multiculturalism as they were set by Pym Fortuyn, and led to a revival of debates on of the tradition of 'abusive criticism' and homosexuality. The increase in the numbers of public figures of Islam in Europe challenges the ways in which history is told in Europe.

Multiculturalism today does not concern only individuals who go from a place of origin to a host country. Migration can no longer be seen as a linear path with a point of departure and a land of arrival; there are returns, multiple entries, new opportunities and many obstacles to movement. The presence of multicultural public subject forces proximity with countries outside of Europe; it becomes impossible for Europe to think itself in isolation of the countries like the Egypt, Pakistan, India or Somalia. These public figures give references to the places they come from and the places they have been through; they contribute to the circulations of experiences and histories that are still marginalized in Europe. Their tales contribute to reviving the notion of the *Umma* and to 'decentralising Europe' (Sayyid 1997 and 2003). The national unit is challenged from inside, and through increasing and diversifying transnational forms of belonging. The European anguish about border control might be linked to the reality that these borders are porous to ideas as they are to individuals and the efforts to close those borders are having important consequences in what concerns democracy in Europe.

Questions of security are posed in a whole series of different ways for all people who intervene in public on issues related to Islam. The public figures of Islam in Europe all live under a certain form of surveillance, in hiding, or under high pressure. The threats to their mobility and threats to their lives might come from governments, organisations, institutions, or other individuals. Salman Rushdie

---

58 Mandaville uses the term 'translocal' with references to the work of Arjun Appadurai, "Disjuncture and Difference in the Global Cultural Economy" in Mike Featherstone (ed.) (1990), Global Culture: Nationalism, Globalization and Modernity, London: Sage.

talks at great length about the intimate reality of living in hiding, the sense of shame, frustration, and fear. The death threat issued against him was delivered by the Ayatollah Khomeini, and involved official and non-official organs. Hirsi Ali, who has also received explicit death threats, argues that it is necessary for more people to take risks in order to 'reform' Islam. In 1995, Tariq Ramadan was refused entry into the French territory because he was suspected of supporting terrorist groups, and in 2004, he was refused a visa for the US where he was invited to teach at the University of Notre-Dame, in the framework of the Patriot Act. He argues that the French government has been trying to impeach his movements for more than ten years, following him and threatening those associations that would invite him to speak. In the European context all public individuals are subject to the general politics of fear and control that are being deployed. Uncertainty, danger and risk seem to be the load of many multicultural subjects.

In this paper, rather than focusing on formal party politics and state policies on multiculturalism, I tried to focus on the shape of public debates on the issue. I argued that in the 1990's, the dynamics created by the Rushdie Affair opened up spaces for public figures to intervene on issues related to living together in Europe. A demand for individuals from minority groups who would speak in favor of multiculturalism emerged in parallel of a demand for people who would speak against it. These individuals might not share common ethnicities or forms of belief but they share similar ways of entering public debates, mostly through scandals and controversies. They are autonomous, flexible, versed in more than one language, highly attractive and ambiguous. They are ready to talk about their private lives to gain access to the public. They must have a strong grasp on local and national affairs while being able to refer to transnational dynamics and being proficient in using modern media and technology. Their modes of belonging challenge nationalist narratives and force revisions of European history and reality. Mobility and security are the load of public multicultural subjects; they enter public platforms knowing that there are political as well as personal risks involved.

Bibliography

Appadurai, A. (1990) 'Disjuncture and Difference in the Global Cultural Economy' in Mike Featherstone (ed), *Global Culture: Nationalism, Globalization and Modernity*, London: Sage.

Appignanesi, L. and Maitland, S. (eds) (1989) *The Rushdie File*, London: Fourth Estate.

Allievi, S. & Nielsen, J. (eds) (2003) *Muslim Networks and Transnational Communitiesin and across Europ*, Leiden: Brill.

Asad, T. (1990) 'Ethnography, Literature, and Politics: Some Readings and Uses of Salman Rushdie's The Satanic Verses', in *Cultural Anthropology*, 5(3), pp.239-269.

Buruma, I. (2007) *Murder in Amsterdam: The Death of Theo van Gogh and the Limits of Tolerance*, London: Atlantic Books.

Calhoun, C. (ed) (1992) *Habermas and the Public Sphere*, Cambridge: MIT Press.

Dassetto, F. & Maréchal, B. & Nielsen, J. (eds) (2001) *Convergences musulmanes: aspects contemporains de l'islam dans l'Europe élargie*, Louvain-la-Neuve: Academia Bruylant, L'Harmattan.

De Blic D. & Lemieux C. (2005) 'Le scandale comme épreuve. Éléments de sociologie pragmatique', in *Politix,* 3(71), pp.9-38.

Deltombe, T. (2005) *L'islam imaginaire: la construction médiatique de l'islamophobie en France 1975-2005*, Paris: La Découverte.

Fassin, É. (2006) 'La démocratie sexuelle et le conflit des civilizations', in *Multitudes*, 3(26), pp.123-131.

Fassin, É. (2008) 'Ayaan Hirsi Ali, 'Voltaire des temps modernes?' La chronique d'Eric Fassin, *Regards*, http://www.regards.fr/article/?id= 3056.

Fourest, C. (2004) *Frère Tariq: Discours, stratégie et méthode de Tariq Ramadan*, Paris: Grasset.

Fraser, N. (1997) *Justice Interruptus: Critical Reflections on the 'Postsocialist' Condition*, New York, London: Routledge.

Fraser, N. (1992) 'Rethinking the Public Sphere: A Contribution to the Critique of Actually Existing Democracy', in Craig Calhoun (ed) *Habermas and the Public Sphere*, Cambridge: MIT Press, pp.109-142.

Geisser, V. (2005) 'A propos du double langage de Tariq Ramadan » dans le dossier « Tariq Ramadan: islamiste ou citoyen ?', in *Politis*.

Göle, N. & Ammann Ludwig (eds) (2006) *Islam in Public: Turkey, Iran, and Europe*, Istanbul: Bilgi University Press.

Göle, N. (2005) *Interpénétration : L'Islam et l'Europe*, Paris : Galaade Editions.

Göle, N. (2000) 'Snapshots of Islamic Modernities', in *Daedalus,* 129(1), Research Library Core, pp.91-117.

Gluckman, M. (1963) 'Gossip and Scandal', in *Current Anthropology*, IV (3), p.307-316.

Gresh, A. & Ramdan, T. (2000) *L'islam en questions*, Paris: Babel.

Haenni, P. (2005) *L'Islam de marché: l'autre révolution conservatrice*, Paris: Editions duSeuil et La République de Idées.

Hirsi Ali, A. (2006) *Ma vie rebelled*, Paris: Nil Éditions.

Hirsi Ali, A. (2005) *Insoumise*, Paris: Editions Laffont / Pocket.

Kepel, G. (2008) *Terreur et Martyre: Relever le Défi de Civilisation*, Paris: Flammarion.

Kymlica, W. (ed) (1995) *The Rights of Minority Culture*, Oxford: Oxford University Press.

Kymlicka, W. (1995) *Multicultural Citizenship: A Liberal Theory of Minority Rights*, Oxford: Oxford University Press.

Landau, P. (2005) *Le Sabre et le Coran: Tariq Ramadan et les Frères musulmans à la conquête de l'Europe*, Paris: Edition du Rocher.

Mandaville, P. (2001) *Transnational Muslim Politics: Reimagining the umma*, London: Routledge.

Mandaville, P. (2003) 'Towards a critical Islam: European Muslims and the changing boundaries of transnational religious discourse' in Allievi, S. & Nilesen, J. (eds) *Muslim networks and transnational communities in and across Europe*, Leiden: Brill.

Modood, T. & Werbner, P. (eds) (1997) *The Politics of Multiculturalism in the New Europe*, London: Zed Books.

Moors, A. (2005) 'Submission', in *ISIM Review*, 15, pp.8-10.

Nielsen, J. (2003) 'Transnational Islam and the integration of Islam in Europe', in Allievi, J. & Nieslen, J. (eds.) *Muslim networks and transnational communities in and across Europe*. Leiden: Brill.

Parekh, B. (2000) *Rethinking Multiculturalism: Cultural Diversity and Political Theory*, London: Macmillan.

Pipes, D. (1990) *The Rushdie Affair*, London: BrickLane.

Ramadan, T. (2003) *Les Musulmans d'Occident et l'Avenir de l'Islam*, Paris: Sindbad/ Actes Sud.

Ramadan, T. (1999) *To Be a European Muslim*, The Islamic Foundation Press.

Roberston, R. (1992) *Globalization: Social Theory and Global Change*, London: Sage.

Rushdie, S. (2003) *Step across this Line*, London: Vintage Books.

Rushdie, S. (1991) *Imaginary Homelands*, London: Penguin Books.

Rushdie, S. (1988) *The Satanic Verses*, London: Vintage Books.

Sayyid, B. (1997, 2003) *A Fundamental Fear: Eurocentrism and the Emergence of Islamism*. London, New York: Zed Books Ltd.

Spivak, G. C. (1993) *Reading the Satanic Verses Outside the Teaching Machine*, New York: Routledge.

Politics, Labour Markets, and the Feasibility of a Multicultural Spain

Francisco Beltran[59]

Introduction: A Simplistic Debate

One feature of the contemporary debate on immigrants' integration is a certain simplification when discussing the number of available options the recipient societies have at their disposal. In the last decades of the twentieth century it seemed countries could choose from a vast array of models ranging from extreme versions of multiculturalist laissez-faire to equally radical varieties of assimilationist requirements on their foreign-origin residents. However, after the 9/11, London and Madrid attacks, the murder of a Dutch film director known for his anti-Muslim public stance, riots in the UK and France involving immigrant communities, and certain cases of violence -also involving immigrant families-, all made public by the European and North American media, the integration alternatives set appears to have grown smaller. Now it seems we may only either keep arguing for the virtues of the multiculturalist model or support some sort of assimilationist social goals. It is either one extreme or the other.

In Europe at least, the assimilationist positions -not always known by this name- seem to be in the lead. Angela Merkel declared recently that the attempt to build a multicultural society in Germany had been a complete failure (BBC 2010); Nicolas sarkozy is now supporting the idea of 'monoculturalism' as a better route for immigrants' integration in France (Fassin 2011); David Cameron said multiculturalism had failed in the UK as well, warning Muslim groups against not embracing liberal values (Wright and Taylor 2011); the former Italian prime minister Silvio Berlusconi declared a few days after the 9/11 attacks that Western civilisation was 'superior to Islamic culture' (Henneberger 2001). In most of these pronouncements the usage of terms such as 'multiculturalism' or 'integration' is at least very vague, and often embodies a mixture of ideological principles with political calculations.

---

59 Francisco Beltran is a Lecturer in Political Science at the Universitat Oberta de Catalunya (Barcelona) and Research Fellow at the Institute for European Studies, University of British Columbia (Vancouver). Degrees in Political Science (UNED, Madrid) and Economics (UV, Valencia), MA in Government and Theory of Democracy, and PhD in Political Science (both from the UAM, Madrid). Main fields of research: comparative politics of immigration and integration.

The political debate on integration and multiculturalism in Spain is also taking place along the lines summarised above. In the last electoral campaign in Catalunya, the current Spanish prime minister, Mariano Rajoy, declared that immigration was among the three top issues 'of great concern' for Spaniards, advocating the introduction of an 'integration contract' similar to the French one. Actually, immigration was the fourth issue mentioned by respondents in the CIS (the national center for the study of public opinion) barometer, well behind unemployment, the economy and politicians. In a previous campaign in 2008 he affirmed that Spain had too many immigrants (Cué 2010).

This paper wants to briefly address some of the dimensions usually not mentioned in the simplified and biased political debate on multiculturalism. In this regard, it will identify in the Spanish context some policies and aspects worth taking into account if the goal is to minimize social conflict and increase opportunities for all in a diverse, multicultural society.

The Conceptual Framework

Of the many concepts vaguely or misleadingly employed in the political and academic debate on multiculturalism, there are four in particular that are essential in my approach: multiculturalism, assimilation, integration, and the idea of a 'two-way street'. I will also address the concept of social mobility at a later point.

There are those who think of multiculturalism as a situation in which all members of a given society enjoy equal cultural rights. Furthermore, they say, the state legally acknowledges all cultural manifestations on an equal basis. Others equate multiculturalism with communitarianism (González 2007 p.125). However, many communitarian authors give an implicit support to cultural relativism, whereas most multicultural theorists, and certainly all the liberal ones, usually endorse an idea of multiculturalism compatible with the rule of law and liberal freedoms. Also, we could think, broadly, of multiculturalism as a matter of recognition of traditionally marginalised groups. 'Multicultural society' would be a different kind of concept, a value-neutral one that merely describes the diversity in a given society (Johansson Heinö 2011 p.11). Assimilationists, on the other hand, consider governments must uphold a strict idea of equality before the law and cannot grant special rights to ethnic or cultural communities or recognize them as distinct groups (González 2007 p.125).

Integration is a difficult term to define in a few words. The *Migrant Integration Policy Index*, for instance, links migrants' integration with a situation in which they 'have equal opportunities to lead just as dignified, independent and active lives as the rest of the population' (MIPEX 2011). Surely, enjoying equal opportunities to fulfil your goals in life is an important and necessary condition to achieve integration but often, while we look at the big picture of integration policies at the macro level, we also tend to neglect significant factors that may result in success or failure at the individual level. For instance, do policymakers consider immigrants individually or as members of a cultural group when implementing their integration policies? The answer to this question is not easily captured by the MIPEX indicators, nor relates directly to multiculturalist or assimilationist integration models. Defining a succesful integration process is more related to the particular social, political and economic characteristics of a given society than we may sometimes think. In another work, I explain how the idea of integration is understood very differently in Scandinavia and in North America (Beltrán 2010).

Lastly, just a quick note on the expression 'two-way street'. Broadly speaking, 'two-way street' refers to the idea of integration being a matter of both recipient society and new, foreign-born residents making an effort to mutually accommodate to each other's norms and customs. If the goal is to avoid the creation of the so-called 'parallel societies' this is also a necessary condition, though the extent and specific forms the accommodation will take place in the society should be determined through a democratic, participatory process. For instance, what counts exactly as the norms and customs which characterize Spanish culture? It is also worth noticing that 'two-way street' is a commonly-used expression when politicians speak of integration, though they sometimes mean something closer to assimilation when they use it.

Integration as a Multidimensional Process

Integration is neither a synonym of multiculturalism nor an euphemism for assimilation. A succesful integration process requires, at a minimum, compliance with the receiving society's laws, and often much more than that, but it should be also viewed as a multidimensional experience and addressed simultaneously from political, social and economic angles. I will review jointly these three dimensions in the Spanish case, plus a fourth one dealing with collective vs. individual identities at the end of the paper.

The 2011 edition of the *Migrant Integration Policy Index* reviews seven kinds of policies dealing with migrants' integration at a national level. Spain fares relatively well in the index and finds itself among the top third of the countries surveyed.

Spain is below the average score in relation to access to nationality, requiring ten years of residence to be elegible, and granting citizenship at birth after two generations. Regarding permanent residence, non-EU individuals are required to have been residing in Spain for at least five years and prove to have a basic income.

On the other hand, it is easier now for former students to settle in the country and look for a job (Huddleston and Niessen 2011 pp.20 ff).

Spain is on a par with immigration countries on family reunion policies, as it has expanded elegibility for spouses at partners (though there is a limited elegibility for parents and grandparents). Procedures are relatively short, and conditions (ability to suport the family and housing) are the same that are required to Spanish nationals for family life (Huddleston and Niessen 2011 p.14).

The Spanish Constitution guarantees equal political liberties to all individuals residing in Spain. The 2009 Immigration Law extends these liberties to all immigrants, including the undocumented ones. However, non-EU national do not have the right to vote on local elections, as EU citizens do (Huddleston and Niessen 2011 p.18). Immigrants are not represented in the national or regional parlaments and executives, and play a negligible role in the organisation of traditional political parties. This is common in Europe (with important differences among countries), and could be related to a variety of factors, among them, identity questions, the more centralized party model in Europe and, particularly in the Spanish case, the fact that it has only been an immigration country for the last 15 years (Mollenkopf and Hochschild 2009 p.20). Also, consultative bodies play a lesser role than in certain other European countries in influencing immigration and integration policies in Spain.

Regarding anti-discrimination policy, and though both the national government and regional executives have their own anti-discrimination plans and campaigns, Spain is in a weak position due to the poor institutional design of its *Consejo para la Igualdad de Trato y la No Discriminación* (Council for Promotion of Equality and Non-Discrimination) (Consejo para la Igualdad de Trato 2012). Contrary to the powerful anti-discrimination bodies in other European countries, the Spanish Council is not independent from the government and its mandate consists in giving advice to the victims and carrying out investigative tasks (Huddleston and Niessen 2011 p.24). However, and though discrimination and acceptance may point to very different social attitudes, immigrants do not face overt rejection in Spain, nor Spaniards consider immigration as big an issue as some politicians assert. According to the CIS barometer, 14 per cent of Spaniards think immigration is a problem for the country, and only 3,7 per cent think of it as a personal problem (CIS, both figures for October 2010). According to the European Commission Eurobarometer, the percentange of Spaniards who think immigration is a problem for the country or a personal problem is 8 and 4 per cent, respectively (Eurobarometer, figures for Fall 2010).

In the education realm, a decentralised policy in Spain for which regional governments are responsible, schooling both at primary and secondary levels is granted to all immigrant children, including the undocumented ones. On the other hand, Spain fares badly in the sub-field of intercultural education. The introduction in 2009 of a mandatory 'Education for citizenship and human rights' subject -which the newly elected conservative governments has vowed to eliminate-, improved somehow this situation. It would also be an improvement if schools also taught immigrants' languages and cultures to immigrant children, as Northern European countries do, for instance (Huddleston and Niessen 2011 p.16).

The education level attained by the parents is crucial in the school performance of immigrant children. Besides parental educational attainment, the language spoken at home seems to be also a decisive factor explaining differences between immigrant and native children at school. While school systems in traditional countries of immigration -such as Canada or Australia- seem to do well at removing educational gaps besides those related to family background, those in regions such as Southern Europe, which has been a net recipient of immigrants only for the last 15 years and is still adapting its social institutions to the new situation, have fared worst. On the other hand, immigrants arriving to the traditional countries of immigration have usually attained higher levels of education than those settling in, say, Portugal or Italy. In 2008, first generation immigrants in the UK had completed, on average, 13,9 years of full time education, while the figures for Spain, Italy, Portugal and Greece, were 12,2 years, 11,1 years, 9,2 and 9,6, respectively (Dustmann et al. 2011 p.28). Since parental educational attainment and language spoken at home are some of the essential elements explaining immigrants' social mobility in the host country, we can conclude education systems in countries such as Spain should make an effort to compensate for parent's educational background, particularly in the field of language proficiency, and to provide 'better information to immigrants about educational paths and possibilities for their children' (Dustmann et al. 2011 pp.23-24).

Lastly, the MIPEX report looks at the labour market mobility policies. Spain scores high in basic equal access to the labour market and in labour rights, since all residents should -in principle- enjoy equal conditions (Huddleston and Niessen 2011 p.12). However, the Spanish economic recession and the skyrocketing unemployment figures have had a high impact on immigrant workers. We shall see more in detail how the Spanish labour market has contributed to immigrants' integration or hindered it.

Important as these policies are for a succesful integration process, we also need to look more closely at the characteristics of the Spanish labour market, and at the role of the social mobility processes of migrants as compared to natives.

Often, the importance of labour markets in the integration realm is overlooked. To be sure, immigrants need to find a job if they aspire to lead an independent life, but sometimes it seems that social and political measures are the only ones needed for the achievement of a successful integration process. This is particularly true in Europe, and less so in North America or Australia, which could be related to the different traditional role of governments and distinctive political cultures in these regions, European countries being more interventionist in the social and economic life of their societies and, say, the US or Canada less so. However, labour market performance might be a better variable to assess integration than the percentage of the national budget allocated to integration policies each year. In turn, individual economic performance depends on many of the variables mentioned before.

Since, in principle, immigrants have the same access to the Spanish labour market than natives, which other barriers prevent them from integrating on an equal basis in the labour force? De la Rica and Amuedo distinguish three types of barriers -social, linguistic and economic- which may hinder immigrants' opportunities in the labour market (De la Rica 2011; Amuedo and De la Rica 2007 p.281-282). Due to lack of data in the first two cases, they study the third type of barrier, finding that immigrants (both men and women) 'appear significantly less likely to be employed than similarly skilled natives', though this gap depends on gender and origin, being 15 per cent for men and 4 per cent for women, 8 per cent in the case of African immigrants, and negative in the case of Latin American women (which means they are more likely to be employed than native women). The gap changes with time as well. The longer they stay in Spain, the smaller the employment rate gap between Latin Americans and natives, while the gap is less dependent on the length of the stay in the case of African immigrants. This difference could be linked to linguistic reasons (Latinos already speak the language while Africans do not) and discrimination. Latinos and Asians integrate quickly in terms of employment and also in terms of 'occupational upgrading' (though at a slower pace), while Africans do not. This means that policies specifically oriented to facilitate the integration of immigrants of African origin into the labour force would be much needed, in particular in the field of training and education in the abilities demanded by the Spanish employers.

In another work, De la Rica and Ortega study the economic and cultural gaps between certain groups of immigrants and natives. They reach the conclusion that in relation to the variables studied (educational attainment, marriage age, inter-ethnic marriage, gender gaps in education and employment, fertility, language proficiency and social participation), Latinos are the ones with the lowest cultural distance to the Spanish norms, while Moroccans and immigrants from other Muslim countries show large differences in some of these dimensions. However, the length of the stay in Spain and the education level may alter these gaps dramatically. Also, these differences appear to be lower for younger generations of immigrants (De la Rica and Ortega 2009 p.19). Lastly, D'Amuri and Peri find that, with similar levels of educational attaintment, immigrants tend to be employed in different occupations: an increase in the share of foreign-born workers makes natives move to occupations with a relatively higher content of interactive tasks -technical, professional, clerical, sales-, while immigrants occupy those with a higher content of manual tasks, such as crafts, machine operations, assembly, domestic help and care (D'Amuri and Peri 2010 pp.31-32).

One quick note on the nature of Spanish labour market in relation to immigrants' integration and social mobility. The dual character of Spanish labour market is well known. One part of employees enjoys a high labour protection and is very difficult to dismiss. Another part is hired on temporary, unstable contracts with very low protection. Immigrants are disproportionally represented among the latter. For instance, While 55,6 per cent of native workers enjoy a permanent contract, only 38,6 of Asian-origin workers, 38 per cent of Latinos, and 27,5 per cent of African-origin workers do (De la Rica 2011; INE 2012). This labour duality has combined with a prolonged and deep economic recession to produce one of the highest unemployment rates in recent Spanish history, 22,85 per cent of the working age population in the fourth quarter of 2011 (INE 2012). Due to the particular economic structure and competitive advantages of Spain, most of the jobs created in the previous economic boom were in sectors like tourism and residential construction, low-skilled occupations that attracted many immigrant workers. These are precisely the kind of jobs that have disappeared during the crisis, leaving a sizable proportion of immigrants (and natives) unemployed. Since the Spanish economy cannot usually compete in the international markets in globalised, high-value industries (apart from some successful multinational companies which are not among the labour-intensive ones), most of the jobs it offers to immigrants during boom times are low-skilled, low-paid ones. On the other hand, one of the characteristics of Spanish society is a low social mobility, since, while the absolute mobility is not that low, individuals usually find themselves moving upwards in specific social brackets, never jumping to a higher social group (Marqués and Herrera-Usagre 2010 pp.71-72). Taking all this into account, it is easy to conclude that immigrants tend to remain for long periods of time at the bottom of the socio-economic ladder.

Complexity and Identity

To properly assess how (and if) all these elements combine into preventing immigrants from fully enjoying the opportunities to flourish in Spain, we would need better data. This data can only come from better designed statistical instruments that reflect the current social and ethnic variety of the country. Equally important is the fact that, aside from the three or four largest cities, we can only speak of first generation immigrants, Spain being a country of very recent net immigration. Therefore, we will only be able to properly study many of the dimensions of the social integration of immigrants we have mentioned in this paper when second and third generations have started their professional lives.

Returning to the initial goal of this paper, we may nevertheless conclude that to achieve the succesful social integration of new Spaniards and residents and reduce the amount of social conflict we tend to associate with an increasingly diverse society, we cannot frame the debate in simplistic, biased terms such as 'multiculturalism or assimilation', in the first place. Secondly, we need to address the barriers to integration in regard to the aforementioned social, political and economic dimensions, being careful not to think that a successful path to integration consists exclusively on political measures or extending the scope of our assistance instruments (i.e. social benefits) to the newly arrived. The inclusiveness of our welfare states being very important, allowing, promoting, and encouraging immigants' access to the labour markets in equal terms with the native workers is crucial.

Last but not least, identity is an essential factor, and here I refer to both the immigrant's personal identity and the collective identity of the host society. Individuals who behave substantially differently from their fellow citizens in moral and social terms tend, at the very least, to enjoy less social opportunities. This is particularly true in the case of immigrants with a strong sense of ethnic identity. Alberto Bisin and others, for instance, study the social penalty in terms of reduced labour market opportunities of immigrants with strong ethnic identities in several European countries (2011 p.13). However, no society should require from its new members to renounce any cultural features they consider part of their identity, provided their manifestation does not infringe the law. As mentioned before, deciding which social and moral norms should be part of a country's legislation is a matter of democratic deliberation in which both immigrants and natives' voices should be heard. However, governments should avoid trying to *protect citizens from themselves*, be they natives of immigrants, and intervene only when a specific norm or custom is undoubtedly harmful to an individual, not when we believe it is alien to our own *ancestral* traditions or to the customs we are familiar with. Equally important, open identity societies, by definition those in which formal and informal requisites to be considered a full member are not very strict, make the integration of immigrants easier than those with a more closed identity, with their rigorous cultural and/or ethnic criteria for inclusion. This is particularly true for second generation immigrants, for whom expectations regarding equal treatment, respect and a sense of belonging are usually higher than for their parents (González 2007 p.28). European societies are, generally speaking, not very open in relation to their national identity, which many citizens derive from ethnic and cultural treats. In this regard, some assimilationist manifestations and speeches on the importance of tradition in our collective identity, which leading members of the now governing conservative party in Spain made when addressing immigration issues during the last electoral campaign, are not pointing towards an open, inclusive approach.

Therefore, if the proclamed goal is achieving a thriving diverse society and the route to that goal is based on a 'two-way street' integration process, it is a contradiction to speak of multicultural societies, multicultural not in the sense employed in this paper but as a synonym of 'parallel societies', living side by side with different moral and social norms. However, requiring complete assimilation and leaving the cultural elements of identity at the door is also a contradiction. Open identity societies, flexible and freely, self-chosen individual identities,[60] may not solve all the problems associated to our contemporay diverse societies, but are certainly a much better road to success.

---

60 For a communitarian defense of culture as an essential element of an individual's identity, see Sandel, M. J. (1998), Liberalism and the limits of justice, Cambridge: Cambridge University Press; for a theoretical argumentation that carries that defense to the extreme, see Huntington, S. P. (1996), The clash of civilisations and the remaking of the world order, New York: Simon and Schuster; for a discussion based on individuals as valuing their cultural and ethnic origins but not deriving their value as human beings from being a member of a given ethnocultural group, see Sen, A. (2006), Identity and violence, London: Allen Lane.

Bibliography

Amuedo, C., and De la Rica, S. (2007) 'Labour market assimilation of recent immigrants in Spain', in *British Journal of Industrial Relations*, 45(2), pp.257-284.

BBC (2010) 'Merkel says German multicultural society has failed', *BBC* [online], 17 October, available at: http://www.bbc.co.uk/news/world-europe-11559451 (accessed 15 January 2012).

Beltrán, F. (2010) *The government of Valencia's immigrant integration policies: a comparative report*, Vancouver: Institute for European Studies, UBC.

Bisin, A., et al. (2011) *Ethnic identity and labor-market outcomes of immigrants in Europe*, Centre for Research and Analysis of Migration, Working Paper No. 03/11.

CIS barometer (2010) available at http://www.cis.es, (accessed 10 February 2012).

Consejo para la Igualdad de Trato y la No Discriminación (2012), available at: http://www.igualdadynodiscriminacion.org.

Cué, C. (2010) 'El PP ensaya en la campaña catalana su discurso más duro en inmigración', *El País* [online], 11 November, available at: http://elpais.com/elpais/2010/11/11/actualidad/1289467027_850215.html (accessed 15 January 2012).

D'Amuri, F., and Peri, G. (2010) *Immigration and occupations in Europe*, Centre for Research and Analysis of Migration, Working Paper No. 26/10.

De la Rica, S. (2011) 'Social and Labour Market Integration of Ethnic Minorities in Spain', in Martin Kahanec and Klaus F. Zimmermann, eds., *Ethnic diversity in European labor markets. Challenges and solutions*, Chentelham: Edward Elgar Publishing Ltd.

De la Rica, S., and Ortega, F. (2009) *Economic and Cultural Gaps among Foreign-born Minorities in Spain*, IZA Working Paper No. 4115.

Dustmann, C., et al. (2011) *Educational Achievement of Second Generation Immigrants: An International Comparison*, Centre for Research and Analysis of Migration, Working Paper No. 16/11.

Eurobarometer (2010) available at: http://ec.europa.eu/public_opinion/index_en.htm, (accessed 10 February 2012).

Fassin, E. (2011) 'Nicolas sarkozy en marche vers le "monoculturalisme"', *Le Monde*, 22 February.

González, R. (2007) 'Más allá del multiculturalismo y la asimilación', in *Política Exterior*, Vol. XXI, No. 116, March/April.

Henneberger, M. (2001) 'Berlusconi stands by remarks on Islam', *The New York Times* [online], 29 September, available at: http://www.nytimes.com/2001/09/29/international/europe/29ROME.html?scp=1&sq=Berlusconi%20stands%20by%20remarks%20on%20Islam&st=cse (accessed 15 January 2012).

Huddleston, T., and Niessen, J. (2011) *Migrant Integration Policy Index III. España*, Brussels: Migration Policy Group.

INE (National Statistics Institute) (2011) available at: http://www.ine.es (accessed 10 February 2012).

Johansson Heinö, A. (2011) *Integration or assimilation*, Stockholm: Timbro.

Marqués, I., and Herrera-Usagre, M. (2010) 'Are we More Mobile? New Evidence of Intergenerational Class Mobility in Spain During the Second Half of the 20th Century', in *Revista Española de Investigaciones Sociológicas*, 141, pp.43-73.

MIPEX (2011) available at: http://www.mipex.eu, (accessed 10 February 2012).

Mollenkopf, J., and Hochschild, J. (2009) 'Immigrant political incorporation: comparing success in the United States and Western Europe', in *Ethnic and Racial Studies*, 33(1), pp.19-38.

Wright, O., & Taylor, J. (2011) 'Cameron: my war on multiculturalism', *The Independent* [online], 5 February, available at: http://www.independent.co.uk/news/uk/politics/cameron-my-war-on-multiculturalism-2205074.html (accessed 15 January 2012).

Alevis' Struggle for Recognition in Turkey: An Analytical and Normative Assessment

Devrim Kabasakal Badamchi[61]

Introduction

The recognition of Alevism has been one of the most pressing problems in Turkish politics for the last couple of years. Alevis consitute a faith based group which differentiates itself from the mainstream Sunni sect of Islam. Whether Alevism is a separate sect of Islam is still debated among Alevis and Sunni theologicians, yet Alevis claim that they have a distinct and different belief system which dates back to the time of Ali, son-in-law of Prophet Muhammed. They maintain that Ali was the legitimate heir to the Prophet Muhammed instead of EbuBekir. Moreover, Alevis, like Shia Muslims, recognise the twelve Imams.

Starting from the early 90s, Alevis became more visible as a group which raises claims for recognition. They demand that *Cemevis* be recognised as places of worship by the state authorities. Moreover, they have demands regarding the content and the way of delivery of the compulsory religious education in primary and high schools. They also demand that the Madımak Hotel – a hotel in which 35 Alevis were killed during the 90s- be renovated as a Museum to remember the people who were killed and the catastrophic event. In this paper, I aim to analyse the Alevi's demands of recognition from a theoretical and normative perspective. The question I aim to answer is: How can Alevis justify their cultural and religious claims as claims that deserve public recognition? My goal is to build the theoretical framework on Nancy Fraser's account of recognition as equal status. Therefore I argue that Nancy Fraser's prominent approach on recognition is a good starting point to understand and assess the issue of Alevi recognition in contemporary Turkey.

The paper is founded on three parts. In the first part, I argue why and how Nancy Fraser's account of recognition is superior to other approaches- Taylor and Honneth- in understanding claims for recognition. In the second part, I deal with the description of the Alevi's recognition problem and analysis of the demands of Alevis in Turkey. In the third part, I am concerned with the application of the Fraserian account of recognition to the case of Alevi's recognition in Turkey. This

---

61 Devrim Kabasakal Badamchi is an assistant professor at the Department of Political Science and Public Administration, Izmir University, Turkey. She teaches history of political thought and contemporary political theory. She published on toleration and its international aspect, the idea of toleration in the works of John Rawls and Jurgen Habermas.

would mean dealing with the ways in which Alevis could justify their claims and possible normative and practical proposals for the Alevis' recognition in Turkey.

Recognition and Nancy Fraser's Account of Status Model

For the last couple of years, the meaning of politics has been challenged from various dimensions. First of all, the traditional understanding of citizenship has been criticised due to its weak capacity for political participation. It is suggested that citizenship should be understood with a greater emphasis on civic virtues and political participation (Kymlicka 2002 p.327). The second challenge towards the traditional conception of citizenship refers to its capacity to take into account cultural pluralism and diversity. This second criticism has been discussed under various labels: 'politics of difference', 'identity politics', 'multiculturalism', and 'the politics of recognition' (Kymlicka 2002 p.327).

However, as I mentioned, the challenges were regarding the very nature of our understanding of politics. Broadly speaking the challenges addressed the fact that modern societies are indeed marked by cultural pluralism and diversity and that politics of today must consider this fact as relevant in its analysis. This debate found a fruitful vein within critical theory: it led to a debate on the nature of political struggle of the excluded /oppressed. Today, it is commonly accepted that the significance of cultural difference and diversity is a significant motive for political struggle and theory should consider this when making analysis of descriptive and normative sort.

Nancy Fraser, along with Axel Honneth and Charles Taylor, is among the theorists who developed a theory of recognition to understand and evaluate the current struggles for recognition under contemporary conditions of modernity. In this section of the paper, I analyse the aspects of Fraser's account of recognition by contrasting them with the theories of Taylor and Honneth. This analysis will constitute the justification why I have chosen Fraser over the other theorists to examine the Alevi situation in Turkey.

I claim that I agree with Fraser on the argument that, by giving equal importance to the analysis of status both in the realm of redistribution and recognition, her theory is superior to the theories of Taylor and Honneth who tend to examine the struggles for recognition by remaining within the realm of identity; under-emphasizing the role of status hierarchy in the realm of redistribution and recognition. In this vein, I argue that Fraser's theory of recognition provides a deeper and broader terrain on which we can understand and evaluate the contemporary struggles for recognition.

In his famous essay ***Politics of Recognition***, Charles Taylor explains what a politics of recognition in the public sphere could mean. He develops his argument by referring to a universal idea of equal respect and dignity. In the public sphere, for him, we need to refer to the idea that each person is worth equal respect and dignity due to the human potential that all humans share (Taylor 1994 p.41). In the case of politics of difference, for him, this would mean that all human beings have the equal potential to form and define one's own identity as an individual (Taylor 1994 p.42). This means we should show equal respect to all actually developed cultural practices and cultures as well. Taylor analyses the politics of recognition truly as a matter of identity and culture. Although he begins with a universal appeal to the notion of respect, he ends up evaluating the issue of recognition as an issue of cultural self-realisation and due respect that has to be shown regarding such a realisation rather than an issue of status subordination.

In his well-known exchange with Nancy Fraser *Redistribution or Recognition*, Honneth claims that one needs to refer to a conception of good life to criticise any kind of injustice that Fraser mentions (Honneth 2003 p.114). We will see Fraser's reply to this later in the paper yet; I would like to add that one needs to distinguish two aspects in a theory here. It might be true that each excluded group refers to a conception of good life when going through a struggle to gain equal rights of recognition. This is truly a matter of how groups justify their claims for recognition. However, a theorist when developing a theory about recognition, I think, he/she has to avoid relying on any notion of a good life in an age where we have diverse collections of good lives competing. Relying on a notion of good life might prevent us from evaluating the highly pluralistic nature of today's politics realistically.

Secondly, Honneth, like Taylor, remains within the realm of identity politics when evaluating the matter of recognition. For him, the purpose of social equality is to enable personal identity-formation of all members of society (Honneth 2003 p.177). Enabling the self-realisation of all persons in a society is the basic aim of equal treatment of all subjects in a given society. Persons are recognised within specific spheres of life on the basis of certain principles: the principles of love, equal legal treatment, and social esteem. "In order to be able to actually make use of their autonomy, individual subjects are in a certain way entitled to be recognised in their neediness, their legal equality or their social contributions, according to the kind of relation at issues" (Honneth 2003 p.181). I think this sophisticated analysis of Honneth about recognition is mainly concerned with the realm of identity and its politics. As Honneth puts it quite openly, the individual self- realisation and its conditions are the basic motivation in his theory. Both three principles of recognition address the issue of the satisfactory fulfillment of one's own identity rather than status hierarchy and domination.

In **Redistribution or Recognition**, Fraser rightly points out that both Honneth and Taylor consider the issue of recognition as a matter of self-realisation: 'Being recognised by another subject is a necessary condition for attaining full, undistorted subjectivity' (Fraser 2003 p.28). She claims that unlike Honneth and Taylor, she considers the issue of recognition as an issue of social status. This means she considers recognition as a matter of justice. As long as there are institutionalised patterns of cultural value that define certain groups as inferior and wholly other, we talk about misrecognition and status subordination. I think this way of seeing the problem is quite helpful in evaluating the situation of Alevis in Turkey but I will come to that point specifically in the last section of the paper.

The status model of recognition considers misrecognition as an institutionalised relation of subordination, which prevents one from participating as a peer in social life (Fraser 2003 pp.29-30). For Fraser, this model has advantages over Honneth's and Taylor's self-realisation models. For her the advantages can be listed as follows:

1. Justifying claims of recognition as a morally binding under modern conditions of value pluralism. There is no common conception of good life.

2. Locating the wrong in social relations rather than in individual or interpersonal psychology.

3. Avoids the view that everyone has an equal right to social esteem. What it does entail is that everyone has an equal right to pursue social esteem under fair terms of equal opportunity.

4. Integrating of claims of recognition with claims for the redistribution of resources and wealth. (p.2)

The first point perfectly applies to Honneth and Taylor as a criticism of their theories of recognition since both theories rely on a conception of good that the goal of society is to provide the sources of self-realisation for everyone. Fraser's account, in this sense, does not build upon such a conception of the good life, rather her theory considers justifying claims for recognition as morally binding under the condition of pluralism in which various conceptions of good life compete. For sure, this makes her theory more plausible when we consider the conditions of the highly pluralistic age in which we live today.

It might be argued that the second criticism does not treat the theories of Taylor and Honneth fairly since both Honneth and Taylor also deliberate the significance of social relations in building up of self-esteem and self-realisation. However it seems true that they rely heavily on interpersonal psychology.

In regard of the third point, it is obvious that Fraser starts from a rights based theory rather than a theory that is founded on any notion of a good life. That is why for her, the equal right to pursue social esteem under fair terms of equal opportunity is significant. As a liberal, she emphasises the right of choice of an individual – whether to pursue a specific way of life or not- given the conditions of equal opportunity. And as for the fourth point, I think one of the most significant aspects of her theory of recognition is that she incorporates claims of redistribution with claims of recognition. The way she sees the issue of recognition is through the idea of redistribution.

To sum up, Fraser's account of recognition as redistribution has advantages over the theories of Honneth and Taylor in general. In particular, I claim that this Frasersian account can be applicable to understand and evaluate the issue of recognition of the Alevis in Turkey. This point will be clear in the last section of this paper where I apply Fraser's account of status model to the Alevis' struggle for recognition in Turkey.

Alevis and Their Demands

What is Alevism?

It seems difficult to come up with an easy and common description of Alevism. For some groups, Alevism is a sect of Islam that contains mainly heterodox components of the faith. For others, Alevism is a totally distinct belief system that is quite different from Islam.

> Although practiced differently in various parts of Turkey, Alevi belief is marked by a mystical understanding of religion that emphasises a deeper spiritual message of the Qur'an; an internalized sense of God that can be attained through the Alevi path; the overwhelming love for Ali, Muhammad's cousin and son-in- law who is revered as the keeper of the mystical knowledge; the commemoration of the martyrdom of Hasan and Hussein, Ali's sons; and the practice of a communal ritual named *cem* in which men and women participate. (Ozyurek 2009 p.236)

The relationship between Alevis and the central authorities has been tense throughout history. Although Ottomans treated these heterodox groups more or less in a peaceful manner until the early 19th century, with the slaughter of Bektashi Jannisaries in 1826, Bektashi orders were made illegal and the Kizilbash were massacred. During the time of Turkish Republic, Alevi Bektashi groups were relaxed since the mass persecutions of the state authorities stopped. However, hundreds of Alevis were killed by Sunni Muslim and Turkish nationalist fanatics in Sivas (1978 and 1993), Kahramanmaraş (1978), Çorum (1980), and Gazi in Istanbul (1997)

(Ozyurek 2009 p. 237).

Today, Alevis constitute 10 to 30 percent of the 70 Million Turkish population. Beginning from the 1980s; we can talk about an Alevi revivalism, which constitutes the efforts to redefine Alevi identity as well as raising claims to Turkish authorities for recognition. We may identify the general reasons behind this revival of Alevism. According to Erman and Goker, the first reason is related to the fall of Communism and its effect on Leftists who were close to Alevism (Erman and Goker 2000 p.99). Alevism became an alternative social movement and Alevism as a cultural social identity came to the center of the agenda rather than socio-economic concerns. The second reason has to do with the rise of Sunni political Islam in Turkey beginning from the mid -1980s. Alevism, together with Sunni Kemalism were considered as a counterforce to the rising political Islam.

Furthermore, the presence of military confrontation between PKK (the Kurdistan Workers Party) and Turkish military forces fostered the revival of religious identity of the Kurdish population who was forced to migrate to the metropolitan cities (Erman and Goker 2000 p.99). The Kurds in the big cities began to emphasise their Aleviness as a religious identity in the public discourses. Lastly, Erman and Goker state that we should also consider developments regarding the late modernisation in Turkey such as newly developing media services and the funding of powerful Alevi associations by the Alevi members of a newly growing urban elite. (p.100). In addition, Turkey's convergence with the EU democratic norms and standards has a positive effect on the status of Alevis in Turkey (Grigoriadis 2006 p.454). Issues such as the nonrecognition of *Cemevis* and the absence of any reference to Alevis in religious textbooks were addressed by EU Commission reports.

Within this environment of revivalism of Alevi identity, Alevis began to raise certain claims as part of their struggle for recognition. I analysed the news on the websites of the two major Alevi associations *Cem Vakfı* and *Pir Sultan Abdal Kultur Dernegi* to outline the main demands of Alevis from different strands. In line with this, I examined the reactions that the two mentioned associations gave to the state's take up on the Alevi issue that is stated on the final report of the Alevi workshops that were held during the last couple of years.

The Demands of Alevis for Recognition

All the demands of the Alevis are founded on the claim to be treated as equal citizens and equal recognition on a social, cultural and political basis. We might group their demands into four categories: the demands about the places of worship, the demands regarding the abolition of compulsory religious education, the demands regarding the Madımak Hotel and lastly the demands regarding the status and practices of the Directorate of Religious Affairs.

One of the most pressing claims of the Alevis is that the *Cemevi* (the house of gathering) must be officially recognised as a place of worship like mosques, synagogues etc. On the websites of both *Pir Sultan Abdal Kültür Derneği* and *Cem Vakfı*, we found a strong support of the Alevis' claims that *Cemevis* should be regarded officially as places of worship. In this sense, for instance, Hüseyin Güzelgün (n.d.), the President of the *Pir Sultan Abdal Kültür Derneği*, declares that the *Cemevi* is an indispensable right of the Alevis to be recognised as equal citizens in Turkey. On the websites of both associations, they refer to the court decision that states that Çankaya Cemevi Yaptırma Derneği (Çankaya Associations for Building *Cemevis*) cannot be closed down because *cemevis* have been the places of worship for centuries for Alevis and, the regulation that labels *cemevis* as places of worship should not be considered against the Constitution. The history of the court decision dates back to a couple of years ago. The Ministry of Interior sent a warning to the Governer of Ankara saying that the regulation that declares *cemevis* as places of worship should be abolished from the regulation of the Çankaya Cemevi Yaptırma Derneği. The warning mentions that declaring cemevis as places of worship is against the decree of the Directorate of Religious Affairs. Upon this warning, the directorate of associations of the Governorship of Ankara sent a notification to the Çankaya *Cemevi Yaptırma Derneği* for the abolition of this particular regulation. After a certain time, the Directorate took the case to the prosecutor with the excuse that the association did act to make any changes. The Court decided that there is nothing against the law in the regulation of the Çankaya Cemevi Yaptırma Derneği (n.d.). Although there is a court decision on the side of the Alevis, the official legal status of the *cemevis* as worshipping places is not recognised. Alevis consider this demand as a legitimate cultural, religious demand for recognition as equal citizens.

The second demand of the Alevis is regarding the abolition of compulsory religious education in primary and high school education. In Turkey, the religious instruction was first introduced in schools in the 1940s. 'It was first of all applied to the first two classes of middle school (*ortaokul*) and later extended to other classes. At first, children belonging to families who wished their children to attend religious instruction lessons had to bring a letter from their parents. This was later switched around so that the letter had to be sent by those who wished their children to be exempt from attendance at religious instruction classes' (Bozkurt 1998 p.111). With the 1982 Constitution, religious education was made compulsory for all primary and middle schools. Upon this practice, 'textbooks prescribed clearly display a fusion of Turkish nationality with the Sunni religious approach' (Bilici 1998 p.69).

According to Cemal Şahin (n.d.), the general Secretary of the *Pir Sultan Abdal Kültür Derneği*, through compulsory religious education, the Alevi children are taught under a specific sect of Islam and are assimilated. For him, compulsory religious education is also against the principles of secularism since in a secular state; the state cannot make the propaganda of any religious sect or religion. These statements are in line with the Alevis' claims that only a specific sect of Islam which is Sunni is being taught in religious classes and this is against the right of equal recognition of Alevi citizens. For them, abolishing the compulsory religious education will contribute to the recognition of Alevis as equal citizens.

Another demand of the Alevis is regarding the status of the Directorate of Religious Affairs. As a basic characteristic of secularism in Turkey, religion has been controlled by the state while, at the same time, a particular version of Islam, which is Sunni and Hanefi, is promoted within the boundaries and rules that the state defined. The directorate of Religious Affairs worked for that purpose. 'Today, the Directorate of Religious Affairs, which promotes and serves Sunni Islam, has a larger budget than many ministries, approximately one billion dollars. In 2005, the directorate employed 60.000 imams in Turkey and abroad and funded 4221 Qur'anic schools. Yet, Alevis …receive none of these services' (Özyürek 2009 p.10).

There are two main Alevi positions on the status of the Directorate of Religious Affairs: the first position claims that the constitution of the Directorate of Religious Affairs should be rearranged in order to leave room for the representation of the Alevis. This position is mainly supported by *Cem Vakfı*. According to this association, each faith should be able to establish its own association within the composition of the Directorate of Religious Affairs. They claim that religion should be a public service for Alevi citizens and that a certain amount from the general budget should be dedicated to that purpose (Dogan n.d.).

The second position claims that the Directorate of Religious Affairs should be abolished since it is against the principles of secularism. This thesis is supported by *Pir Sultan Abdal Kültür Dernekleri* and a couple of other associations such as *Hacı Bektaş Veli Dernekleri*, *Semah Kültür Çevreleri*, Şahkulu Sultan Dergahı, *Karacaahmet Sultan Dergahı* and Kurdish Alevi journals such as *Hedef* and *Zülfikar* (Keskin 2010 pp.2-3). For these associations, as a matter of principle, a secular state should not support any particular faith group by economic and other means. In regard to both positions on the status of the Directorate of Religious Affairs, we might say that the demand is about equal recognition on a cultural and religious basis. Both arguments favor equal treatment from state concerning the Alevi and all other faith based groups are concerned.

Lastly, I aim to concentrate on a rather specific demand. 'In July 1993, a conference on the occasion of the Alevi *Pir Sultan Abdal* festival was attacked by a mob of Islamist fanatics. The hotel which served as a venue for the event was set on fire and thirty seven participants died.' (Grigoriadis 2006 p.454) Since then, this event remained as a symbol of Alevi struggle in the minds of Alevi people. All Alevi groups desire that this hotel should be re-constructed as a museum to remember this horrible event and all other events that resulted with the death of Alevi people. This is a demand from the state authorities to remember and make remember this catastrophic event as part of a common memory in the country.

In regard of all these demands of Alevis, the state organised a series of workshops between June 2009 and January 2010. As said, these workshops were organised to establish a terrain of dialogue and try to come up with solutions with which the whole nation could be satisfied (Çelik 2011). These workshops brought together various actors such as academicians, theologians, civil society organisations, representatives of the media, politicians, Alevi – Bektashi religious leaders, Sunni intellectuals, representative of Turkish Alevi citizens who live abroad, civil society organisations from Sivas and the relatives of the people who died in Sivas.

In the final report of the workshops, it is stated that many improvements had occurred regarding the demands of the Alevis due to the dialogic terrain that was established. It is stated that the Madımak Hotel was passed to the hands of the public and made an eminent domain (Çelik 2011). Secondly, it is mentioned that a revised content of the religious textbooks which is compatible with the criteria of pluralism and objectivity would be prepared by an Alevi Commission. Moreover, it is mentioned that a consensus emerged among the participants of the workshop with regard to the status of the *cemevis* about the necessity to establish a legal status for them.

The results of the workshops were highly debated by the major Alevi associations in Turkey. For instance, the president of the Alevi Bektashi Federation Fevzi Gümüş and former president of *Pir Sultan Abdal Kültür Derneği* Kazım Genç declared that the Government's attempts regarding the recognition of Alevis failed (2011). Gümüş says that the situation of the Madımak Hotel did not meet up the demands of the Alevis since the Government was not willing to convert the building into a museum.

Moreover the Alevi community is not satisfied with the solution of the workshop on the compulsory religious education. Especially for *Pir Sultan Abdal Kültür Derneği*, the problem could not be resolved until compulsory religious education is totally abolished. (*Evrensel*, 1 April 2011) The general secretary of Education and Science of the *Pir Sultan Abdal Kültür Derneği* considers the Government's attempt to revise the content of the compulsory religious education as a misrecognition of the demands of the Alevis. He says the Alevis demand that the compulsory religious education be abolished (2011). For the President of the *Cem Vakfı*, although it is a significant attempt, the new information that is said to be added regarding Alevism in the textbooks is not enough (Doğan 2011).

Alevis also criticised the fact that the report did not come up with a reasonable solution for the status of the *cemevis*. For them, mentioning the need to assign a legal status and recognising a place as a place of worship are two different things. In the report, it was implied that there is only one place of worship for the Muslims which is the Mosque, and this is unacceptable for the Alevis ('Alevi Raporu Açıklandı', 2011).

As we consider the final report of the Alevi Workshop and Alevis' reactions to it, we might say that the workshop was not able to meet the basic demands of the Alevi Community. Especially on the issue of the abolition of the directorate of Religious Affairs, no steps were taken at all. Regarding the other matters such as the recognition of the *cemevis* as places of worship and the abolition of compulsory religious education, we can say that no remarkable steps were taken. Given this situation, Alevis demands are still in need of satisfaction and it seems a long and rigorous struggle is waiting them.

As said, the aim of this paper is to analyse and assess the demands of Alevis from a particular theoretical perspective, which is the theory of recognition of Nancy Fraser. I claim that Fraserian account of status model is quite helpful in understanding and evaluating the issue of recognition of the Alevis in Turkey. In the next section the paper, I apply Fraser's account of recognition to the case of Alevis' struggle of recognition.

Justification of the Claims for Recognition and the Case of Alevism

The normative core of Nancy Fraser's conception of recognition is parity of participation. For participatory parity (equal participation) to be possible, two conditions should be available: "the distribution of material resources must be such as to ensure participants' independence and voice" and "the second condition requires that institutionalised patterns of cultural value express equal respect for all participants and ensure equal opportunity for achieving social esteem" (Fraser 2003 p.36). The first condition is called the objective condition of participatory parity and the second condition is called the intersubjective condition. Keeping this normative foundation in mind, Fraser says

> ...which people need which kind(s) of recognition in which contexts depends on the nature of the obstacles they face with regard to participatory parity. That, however, cannot be determined by an abstract philosophical

practical intent of overcoming injustice (p.47).

In line with this, both referring to Fraser's theory as a social critical theory, which is normatively oriented and benefiting from the empirical analysis of the Alevi case for recognition, I aim to draw practical and normative solutions to the problem. Below I try to demonstrate in which manner the Alevis can justify their claims that deserve public recognition from a normative point of view.

The concept of participatory parity is quite significant for us to evaluate the situation of the Alevi case. The solution to the Alevi problem should be solved with an intention to ensure equal participation of the Alevis in the public realm and various social domains. To ensure this, equality in receiving religious services like Sunni people seems to be significant, or at least not being discriminated on the basis of the choices of religion is important for equal participation. Certainly, in this respect, the Directorate of Religious Affairs seems to be a big obstacle in front of achieving participatory parity since it does not allocate resources equally to Sunni and Alevi citizens. In this sense, the present situation of the Directorate of Religious Affairs violates the first objective condition of participatory parity in the Fraserian terminology.

The misrecognition of *cemevis* as places of worship violates both objective and intersubjective conditions of participatory parity. First of all, it prevents the allocation of resources on an equal basis for the Alevis. Alevis cannot benefit from the services that are provided for the Mosques, churches and synagogues such as free water and property tax breaks. It violates the second intersubjective condition of participatory parity because the misrecognition of *cemevis* as places of worship could lead to a loss in social esteem among the Alevi members of the society.

Compulsory religious education violates the second intersubjective condition of participatory parity since only the Sunni sect is promoted in the compulsory religious courses, which leads to an assimilation of the Alevi students into a specific sect of Islam. In other words, we might say that compulsory religious education creates an institutionalised pattern of cultural value that does not express equal respect for all participants of a community and does not allow Alevi students the equal opportunity for achieving social self-esteem.

Lastly, we might add that the establishment of the Madimak Hotel as a museum is really significant to show equal respect for all the Alevi citizens and ensure equal opportunity for them to achieve social esteem. The catastrophe that happened in the Madimak Hotel in Sivas became a social event that is in need of collective remembrance which is quite significant for the social identity of the Alevi citizens. That is why the suspension of the hotel's conversion into a museum would violate the second intersubjective condition of participatory parity.

I tried to demonstrate that, from a Fraserian point of view, the Alevi claimants must show, that 'the institutionalisation of majority cultural norms denies them participatory parity' (Fraser 2003 p.41). However, this is not enough for a legitimate justification of the demands. Moreover, the Alevi claimants need to show that they do not deny participatory parity of the Alevi citizens whose rights they fight for as well as all other citizens. In this sense, Alevi claimants need to have a democratic discourse and mentality which gives equal respect to all cultures and identities. According to the status model of Fraser, this is the condition of any claim that deserves public recognition.

Conclusion

In this paper, I analysed the Alevis' struggle for recognition in terms of outlining their demands from the Turkish authorities. I referred to the status model of Fraser as a normative theoretical framework for determining the way in which the Alevis can justify their claims that deserves public recognition.

I concluded that Alevis could justify their demands by referring to the fact that regarding all their demands, the objective and intersubjective condition of parity of participation is violated. They need to demonstrate that for equal recognition, first the distribution of material resources in a society should allow each participant's independence and voice and secondly, institutionalised forms of cultural value should treat all the participants with equal respect and equal opportunity for achieving social esteem.

Bibliography

Bilici, F. (1998) 'The Function of Alevi- Bektashi Theology in Modern Turkey', in *Alevi Identity- Cultural, Religious and Social Perspectives*, ed. Tord Olsson, Elizabeth Özdalga and Catrine Roudvere, Swedish Institute in Istanbul Transaction, Vol.8.

Bozkurt, F. (1998) 'State –Community Relations in the Restructuring of Alevism' in *Alevi Identity- Cultural, Religious and Social Perspectives*, ed. Tord Olsson, Elizabeth Özdalga and Cathrine Roudvere, Swedish Research Institute in Istanbul Transaction, Vol. 8.

Bülbül, K. (2011) 'Rapor Beklentileri Karşılamadı', Etkin Haber Ajansı, [online], 31 Mart 2011, available at: http://www.alevihaberajansi.com/index.php?option=com_content&task=view&id=11528&Itemid=51(accessed 18 January 2012).

Çelik, F. (2011) 'Alevi Çalıştayları nihai raporu açıklandı', [online], 5 April 2011, available at: http://www.farukcelik.com.tr/index.php?page=faaliyetleridetay&id=44032 (accessed 18 January 2012)

Doğan, I. n.d., 'Prof. Dr. İzzettin Doğan'ın AİHM ile ilgili Basın Toplantısı', [online], available at: http://www.cemvakfi.org.tr/tum-haberler/prof-dr-izzettin-dogan%E2%80%99in-aihm-ile-ilgili-basin-toplantisi/ (accessed 17 January 2012).

Doğan, I. (2011) 'Doğan'dan Alevi Çalıştay Raporu'na Eleştiri', Cumhuriyet, [online], 5 April 2011, available at: http://www.cumhuriyet.com.tr/?hn=231180 (accessed 13 April 2012).

Erman, T. and Göker, E. (2000) 'Alevi Politics in Contemporary Turkey', in *Middle Eastern Studies*, 36(4), pp. 99-118.

Fraser, N. and Honneth, A. (2003) *Redistribution or Recognition- A Political-Philosophical Exchange*, London, New York, Verso.

Grigoriadis, Ionnas N. (2006) 'Political Participation of Turkey's Kurds and Alevis: A Challenge for Turkey's Democratic Consolidation', in *Southeast European and Black Sea Studies*, 6(4), pp.445-461.

Gümüş, F. and Genç, K. (2011) 'Çalıştay Raporu Kabul Görmüyor', Etkin Haber Ajansi, [online], 31 March 2011, available at: http://www.alevihaberajansi.com/index.php?option=com_content&task=view&id=11529&Itemid=5 (accessed 18 January 2012).

Güzelgün, H. (2010) 'Cemevi Vazgeçilmez Bir Haktır', [online], 24 October 2011, available at: http://www.pirsultan.net/haber_detay.asp?ID=4391 (accessed 17 January 2012).

Keskin, Yahya M. (2010) Alevi Bektaşilerin Diyanet İşleri Başkanlığı'nda Temsil Önerisine İlişkin Alevilerin Tutumları Üzerine Bir Alan Araştırması (Elazığ Örneği), in *EKEV Akademik Dergi*, 14, p.42.

Kymlicka, W. (2002) *Contemporary Political Philosophy- An Introduction*, Oxford, New York, Oxford University Press.

Özyürek, E. (2009) 'The Light of the Alevi Fire was Lit in Germany and then Spread to Turkey- A transnational Debate on the Boundaries of Islam', in *Turkish Studies*, 10(2), pp.233-253.

Şahin, C. (2011) 'Zorunlu Din Dersleri Evrensel Hukuka Aykiridir', [online], 20 September 2011. Available at: http://www.pirsultan.net/haber_detay. asp?ID=4350 (accessed 17 January 2012).

Taylor, C. (1994) 'The Politics of Recognition' in Amy Gutmann ed. *Multiculturalism-Examining the Politics of Recognition*, Princeton University Press.

http://www.pirsultan.net/haber_detay.asp?ID=4369 (accessed 17 January 2012)

Evrensel (2011), "Alevi Açılımı Muhabbetten İbaret", [online], available at: http://www.alevihaberajansi.com/index.php?option=com_ content&task=view&id=1153 (accessed 18 January 2012).

2011, 'Alevi Raporu Açıklandı', Etkin Haber Ajansi, [online] 31 March 2011, available at: http://www.alevihaberajansi.com/index.php?option=com_content &task=view&id=11526&Itemid=51 (accessed 18 January 2012).

Diverse Feminisms in Turkey: Secular, Ethnic and Religious Women's Movements[62]

Omer Caha[63]

Introduction

Feminism has continuously developed in Turkey since mid-1980s through street activities, publications, movies, alternative associations and consciousness-rising activities. About a decade after its emergence, it reached a crossroad of gender, ethnicity, religion and secularism which led to a divergence within women's movements in Turkey. Three divergent movements seen in that respect are 'secular Turkish feminism', 'Kurdish feminism' and what is called 'Islamic feminism'. Each of these groups has formulated women's identity in different ways and emphasised different issues and problems associated with women in Turkey. This study aims at drawing attention to the main differences between three women's movements in Turkey. The central issues of this paper revolve around the following questions: What are the sociological and ideological reasons that make them different? Why have they taken part in different camps? And, what kind of issues does each women's movement defend?

The Development of Feminism in Turkey

It is generally accepted that an indigenous feminist movement developed during the last decades of the Ottoman Empire (Çakır 1995). It played an important role even during the early years of the republican regime established in 1923, in obtaining rights for women (Çaha 2010). But the basic care of the Republican political elite to create a homogeneous nation from the Ottoman legacy made it impossible for this movement to survive longer. Women who took place in this movement were enforced by the government to end their activities and abolish their association Union of the Turkish Women in 1935. After then Turkish women gave support mostly to the modernisation attempts of the state at least until 1970s within the framework of official ideology. During 1970s, grown up in ideological environment of the time, an active women movement developed under the banner

---

62 The first draft of this paper was presented in a conference on "Class in Feminism", Dubrovnik-Croatia, 5-7 May, 2007.

63 Omer Caha (Professor of Political Science) is currently teaching at Yildiz Technical University, Department of Political Science and International Relations, İstanbul, Turkey. He has several books and articles on the issues such as democratisation, political behaviors, Islam and politics, civil society, ethnicity, women movement, Turkish politics etc. both in English and in Turkish.

of leftist movements, struggling for a socialist regime. But the military intervention of 1980 excluded political ideologies from public sphere including that of left, Islam and ethnic nationalism and thus served the creation of a neutral public sphere.

The new public sphere, being an opportunity ground for new identities and special right-based attempts, gave chance to the women who were once active in the leftist movement to develop a new identity and a new movement (Tekeli 1989 p.37). Based on the development of the educational and communicational possibilities, women who were active once in the left movements became able to claim rights special to women. Issues such as the right for abortion, divorce on demand, punishment of beating women at home, equality in the familial life, nurses for working women, elimination of the legal norms against women, sexual rape in the marriage life, and assault in the public sphere all were emphasised by these women in 1980s.[64] One can say that the women who sought for prestige under the banner of ideological groups of 1970s started to shift their attention to struggle for self-realisation and self-identity in the public domain. They were these women who started feminism in the mid-1980s.

Starting from 1985 onwards feminists started to hold some street activities. They, for the first time in Turkey, celebrated the International Women's Day on March 8, 1985.[65] In the same year the feminist movement crystallised into three distinct streams -egalitarian, socialist and radical feminists- each attempting to publish different journals and develop different discourses. Although they varied in different branches, they devoted their energy together to various actions in the streets of different cities from 1986 onward. Feminist actions have brought together almost all groups of women around issues mentioned above. Feminist movement has been popularised, across the country, through various street activities. Being a new movement in Turkey feminism influenced social groups from other ideological spectrums to discuss women's problems from their own lenses. Women's problems as a sociological issue, indeed, became one of the most popular topics in the agenda of academia as well as that of media in 1980s.

The development of feminism can be divided into two periods. In the first period,

---

64 The abortion was legally forbidden until 1983. Women were given this right in 1983 under the influence of pressures put by women groups on government. The right for divorce in demand was given through the revision of Civil Code in 2000. This revision was done under the pressures of women groups as well.

65 In Turkey, women's day was officially celebrated on 5th of December every year. This was the anniversary of the right of vote given to women by ruling elite in 1935. But after feminist groups start to celebrate women's day on 8th of March every year Turkish government has also started to celebrate this day as women's day. Today 8th of March is officially being celebrated every year.

which continued throughout 1980s, it basically gave emphasis over street activities. Therefore, a protesting feminism was seen during that time. However, after 1990s feminists have tended to be institutionalized. Feminist groups trying to publicise their voice in the streets during 1980s through campaigns and protests seem to push their stamp over more permanent activities through establishing institutions and centers during 1990s. Women's library in Istanbul, department of women's studies in different universities, women's shelters, associations and foundations in different cities are of this kind. Their activities have still continued in this direction.

In short, after 1990s feminist groups came to publicise their voice in institution-based activities and in international platforms more than in the streets (Kara 2006). As a part of this they have regulated the 'Festival for Women Movies' every year since 1998 and they regularly take place in the meetings organised by the United Nations (Kardam and Ecevit 2002 p.98). The most important contribution of institution-based feminism in Turkey is seen in their achievement to impact government to make a fundamental revision in the legal norms. The fundamental revision done in Civil and Penal Codes in 2000s is noteworthy to mention as one of the prominent outcomes of feminist politics in Turkey.[66]

In the post-1990 period the voices of different feminist women have been heard through different journals stressing on different issues. Even though Kurdish women constituted an arm of Turkish feminist movement in 1980s they decided to depart from Turkish feminists on the basis that they have not represented women of Kurdish ethnicity in 1990s. The tension between secular Turkish feminist groups and Islamic women's movement goes back further. Although they were influenced from feminist groups, Islamic women have always preferred to stay distant from Turkish feminist groups and *vice versa*. The reason why a distinction is apparently seen between Turkish feminist groups and Islamic women's movement is perhaps hidden in tension seen between Islam and secularism in Turkey (Badran 2005). While feminists launched protests against deep-rooted reasons behind women's oppression, Islamic feminists gave struggle for receiving rights to attend school with their headscarves in 1980s. In order to understand the difference between three feminist currents one should illuminate the basic discourses of each in more detail.

The Basic Discourses of the Turkish Feminism

Although Turkish feminist groups are varied as egalitarian, radical and socialist it is noteworthy to remark that they have some common characteristics that are

---

66 For a detailed study on the new norms coming through the revision of the Civil and Penal Codes on behalf of women see http://www.die.gov.tr/tkba/mevzuat.htm

associated to the specificity of their experiences in the Turkish context.[67] The most distinct characteristic of Turkish feminism is visible in its vigorous attempt to represent itself as an element of public sphere. The privacy it urges has created a place of assault and battery, marital rape and women's exploited domestic labor. In that respect, Turkish feminists have tried to abolish the boundaries between public and private worlds. They briefly argue that what is known as the "private" is the locus of power for every man and the locus of patriarchy, which is a crude form of biological determinism.

As an extension of the politics of partaking in the public life, Turkish feminists imposed a great credit over the equality of women with men in the public realm. Participating in public life means mainly two things for them: preserving their liberty and achieving an equal status with men. They attempt mainly to develop a democratic theory based on civil equality that undermines the differences between the sexes so that full citizenship for women can be secured. The realisation of its aim means the transformation of sexual division of labor and norms of femininity and masculinity. Although this seems a unique characteristic of Turkish liberal feminists, radical and socialist feminists also articulate this view as the basis of "rights" for women.

A further particular feature of Turkish feminism is being strongly against political lesbianism. Turkish feminists project emancipation not through institutions separating women from men, but through strengthening the links between men and women on the basis of sexual relations. It should be underlined that some radical feminists in the West took lesbian sexuality as a way to challenge the ideological, political and economic bases of male supremacy. For them, lesbianism was the symbol of patriarchal rejection. However, Turkish feminists formulate the rejection of a patriarchal culture through sexual liberty. Sexual liberty for the Turkish feminists means mainly to have control over their own bodies and to obtain the freedom of having sex with men. Indeed, emancipation for almost all feminist groups means sexual liberty in that sense in the case of the Turkish context.

Still another distinctive characteristic of Turkish feminism is that it is in favor of secularism. In being against Islamic domination in the Turkish context, particularly in the post-1980 period, feminist women denounced that they should remain against Islamic-religious groups and preserve a secular government in Turkey. They feel themselves indebted to the virtue of a republican-secular society whose basic

---

67 One should remember that the mainstream current in Turkish feminism is egalitarian feminism. Radicals seem to be marginal and in the form of small groups. Socialist feminists are influential mostly in academia.

principles were laid down by Kemalists on behalf of women.[68] Some of Turkish feminists, briefly, see Islam as a strong challenge to women and, therefore, they prefer a secular society in which women would easily achieve their aims. It should be noted that despite this general attitude of Turkish feminists against domination of Islam in Turkish society, some of them gave support to female students to attend universities with their headscarf during the end of 1990s.

It seems that the peculiar characteristics of Turkish feminism are originated in the historical-cultural background of the Ottoman women. As it is well known, Ottoman society was divided into two sub-universes: the universe of men and the universe of women. This resulted in the division between those who hold authority and those who do not (Mernissi 1985 p.138). This division after the sixteenth century of the Ottoman Empire resulted in the emergence of the harem institution, which secluded women from social life and led them to live among themselves, coming in contact only with the male members of their family. Moreover, the existence of the polygamy as an institution in the Ottoman society stands as another historical experience in the subconscious of Turkish women. These particular experiences of the Turkish women are seen to be the most plausible reasons behind the fact why Turkish feminist groups are against political lesbianism and are formulating sexual liberty as the means of their emancipation.[69] In short, participation into the public life on the basis of equality with man and being together with man in the public life seem to be the most essential care of Turkish feminist groups.

Kurdish Feminism: A Reactionary Women's Movement in Turkey

Kurdish feminist groups were a part of women's movement seen in Turkey through 1980s and they participated in almost all activities organised by Turkish feminist groups. But starting from 1990s onward they went to free themselves from Turkish feminist groups on the basis that Turkish feminist groups did not represent them, nor they allow them to represent their identity as Kurdish women. The issues they stress on seem to be quite different from those defended by Turkish feminist groups. They give quite different meanings to such issues as identity, body, violence, language, motherhood, birth, homeland, tradition, schooling, etc.

In order to scrutinise the basic characteristics of Kurdish feminism one should first look at the Kurdish ethnic movement developed after 1980s. Kurdish issue

---

68 This is perhaps the reason why some feminists have tended to declare the reforms done by the state for women in the early years of the Republic as "state feminism".

69 It is necessary to remark that although the harem institution was limited almost with the ruling class it has larger influence over the sub-conscious of Turkish women.

as a problem seems to be closely related to the nation-building process in Turkey. Kemalists, as the founder of Turkish republican regime, denied any differentiation in Turkey and defined their target to establish a uniform nation blind to any difference when they established republic. One of the most victimised groups of this project has, in the long run, been Kurds who are assumed to be about nearly one fifth of the total population. All citizens lived in Turkey have been defined Turk officially and no group has been given the right of education and publication in their own language. All ethnic groups were denied the right to give name to their children or their locations in their own language until the start of reforms toward Turkey's integration in EU. This, indeed, has increasingly given rise to a tension between state and pro-Kurdish movements for a long time during the Republican regime.

Starting from 1984 onwards an ethnic movement has developed under the banner of Kurdish Labor Party (PKK), through violated activities. This group, having gun-power, started a war against state and led the kill of more than 30 thousand people from both sides in Turkey. Some Kurdish groups also established a political party named Democratic Labor Party (*Demokratik Emek Partisi*/DEP) in the beginning years of 1990 to struggle for ethnic rights in legal platform. Being banned by the Constitutional Court, this party has been followed by others over the line of the same ideology. The present party established over this tradition is Democratic Society Party (*Demokratik Toplum Partisi*/DTP). Both movements have promoted the development of a Kurdish women's movement as their arm. They gave support to the Kurdish women to hold various actions in the streets. One of the women groups supported by DTP was Saturday Mothers, who launched sitting actions in 1995 persistent for three years in Taksim, Istanbul. Through these kinds of actions these women demanded from government to find out their lost husbands or sons (Açık 2002 p.302). While some Kurdish women have identified themselves with Kurdish ethnic movements, some others claimed that these movements have not represented them as women. This is the ground given rise to the development of Kurdish feminist movement.

In 1990 some of Kurdish women established the Independent Kurdish Women Group (*Bağımsız Kürt Kadın Grubu*) and they claim that their voice has been smothered by and among Turkish feminists. When coming to 1996 Kurdish women started to publish some journals in order to express themselves in the public life. Journals like *Roza* (rose), *Jujin* (a word referring to the mixture of hedgehog and woman, symbolizing the defense of women), *Ji Bo Rizgariya Jiyan* (For the Freedom of Women) and *Jin u Jiyan* (Woman and Womanhood) were published with this aim. Kurdish woman groups mostly stress, in these journals, on such issues as traditions and customs oppressing Kurdish women, racism of dominant groups, war in the South East of Turkey, violence against women, honor crimes, and migration from the East and South of Turkey to the metropolitan cities. It can be said that the journals mentioned above constitute the avenue for Kurdish feminist groups to develop a different identity and a different movement from Turkish feminists.

Those women who published these journals separate themselves from Turkish feminism, from the Kurdish nationalist movement and from men (Arat 2000). In order to develop their own identity as the women of an oppressed ethnicity these women indicate reaction to both Kurdish movement and the women's movement in Turkey. They try to free themselves from the man of Kurdish movement as women. On the other hand, they dissociate themselves from women within Turkish feminist groups as ethnic women. Therefore, one can easily say that they try to construct their identity over their attitude to reject hegemony of the men of their own nation (Kurdish man) and the hegemony of the women of their own gender (Turkish women). What these journals refuse is clearly seen in the slogan used by *Roza* in its cover. The journal presents itself in its cover as "Kurdish Women's Journal against Genderism and Racism". Genderism here refers to the Kurdish men, while racism refers to the Turkish women.

Kurdish feminists criticise Turkish women movement on the basis that they do not consider ethnic difference between women. They blame Turkish feminist groups of having ignoring the women of other ethnicity. For them feminism with no ethnic identity is naturally understood as Turkish feminism. The women of other groups are neglected. Thus the common discourse of women serves the women of dominant nation and hereby covers their difference (Yelda 1996 p.31). The general approaches used by Turkish feminist movement, they argue, bring general lenses that cannot be able to see what Kurdish women have lived (Roza 1999 p.3). The struggle of the women from oppressor nation against problems women faced in general neglects the racist dimension of the system against Kurdish women. And this for them "made the women of oppressing nation blind to see the racist and destructive characteristics of the system. They even don't see, hear and speak how we as their Kurdish counterparts live rape and sexual harassment under boots of the solders in the region" (Jujin 1997 p.27). In order to reach a true emancipation of women, they argue, women movement should be abstracted from all forms of dominant powers and discourses.

Kurdish feminists also criticise Kurdish ethnic movement. The reason why they criticise Kurdish ethnic movement is that similar to Turkish feminism the men of this movement are not in the aware of their difference as women. They perceive women as asexual and neutral actors and demand from women to be in the second position in their movement. The leadership and top positions in Kurdish ethnic movement, they argue, are shared by men. What expected from women in this movement is to follow up their decisions. This is the reason why one of the writers wrote in *Roza* denounces that "men are the slaves of the Turkish state, but we sisters are the slaves of slaves and we are expected to fight for so-called asexual utopia" (Doğan 1996 p.6).

Kurdish feminist women perceive identity and body in a different way from Turkish feminists. When they define their identity they give reference to the special experience they have lived as women of different and oppressed ethnicity. This seems to be the reason why they passionately escape from an essentialist understanding of women. They define themselves not women but "ethnic women". This means that they have a double identity and two identities matches in their body. This makes them perceive body in a different way as well. Similar to Turkish feminist groups they struggle to take the control of their body. But different from Turkish feminists they perceive that the control of body does not serve only sexual freedom for women, however, it also serves the continuation and survival of Kurdish nation. For Turkish feminist groups the control of body refers to the autonomy of women against culture and tradition. However, it refers not only to autonomy of women but also to the transmission of Kurdish culture, language and national values to the next generations. Therefore, they strongly react to the birth control mechanism on the basis that birth control is operated by Turkish state to control Kurdish population.

Kurdish feminist groups can also be distinguished from their Turkish counterparts on the issue of motherhood. The motherhood for them is not a traditional institution that should be left out for them; however, it is an essential institution functions for the endurance and even survival of a nation. Some women's journals, sympathetic towards Kurdish ethnic movement as in the case of *Yaşamda Özgür Kadın* (Free Women in Life), mystify motherhood. This journal defines Kurdish mothers as the goddess of Kurdish nation (Açık 2002 p.285). Because they are mothers who animate a nation and make it survive. Motherhood, criticised by some of Turkish feminists as a traditional role, comes to be defended by Kurdish feminists as an institution serving the production as well as reproduction for Kurdish people and thus constituting a bridge between current population and the coming generations. They criticise Turkish feminists for being ignorant of this. It is denounced by *Roza* that "Turkish feminism's focus of interest becomes 'traditional roles' rather than 'genocide in the womb'. This is the white face of looking from outside, above and missionary. It is white feminism not to see the double oppression (sexism and racism), how they strengthen each other and not to display a racist face, and leaving the priority to sexism" (Roza 1998 p.5).

Kurdish feminists argue that motherhood does not mean anything important for Turkish feminists, because they are not assimilated like the Kurds. The most essential resisting tool against assimilation policy of the state is motherhood which transmits language, culture, national conscious and national values of Kurdish people to the next generations. In order to protect the image of motherhood alive in the conscious of Kurdish people some women groups, as mentioned above, launched street activities with the names Saturday Mothers (*Cumartesi Anneleri*) or Peace Mothers (*Barış Anneleri*) and journals mentioned above frequently give news from their actions.

Language and education policies are other areas that distinguish Kurdish feminist groups from their Turkish counterparts. Some Turkish feminist groups gave support to the state in East and South East in its attempts to school Kurdish women. A project started by the state in 1990s, named Multi Purpose Social Center (Çok Amaçlı Toplum Merkezi), attempted to literate Kurdish women through some courses and to teach them Turkish language, birth control mechanisms and some hand-made arts. Turkish feminist groups support this project on the basis that this project will enable Kurdish women to participate in the public life and thus will support them to go out of family, which is an oppressive ground for women. Kurdish feminist groups, however, strongly reacted to that project on the claim that it will assimilate Kurdish people. They see women as a bridge mediating between existing Kurds and coming generations. Therefore, the state policy aiming at educating Kurdish women, on Turkish language, is perceived by them as a trap against Kurds. They went to criticise Turkish feminists as being the women of oppressive nation and playing a negative role for Kurds in that play (Karayazgan 1998 p.8). Education on the basis of Turkish language means, for them, assimilation of the Kurds. They argue that the Turkish state has been able to assimilate Kurdish men through education and military service and thus integrate them into the public life. However, they are women who have succeeded to stand out of this assimilation policy. The project, therefore, will assimilate women as well.

In short, Turkish feminist groups are criticised by Kurdish feminists on the claim that they have an essentialist understanding of women. As part of this understanding they perceive that all women have the same problems and they project to emancipate women within the framework of general policies. Thus acculturation of women by means of modern schools and their articulation in the public sphere over the basis of equality with men becomes their basic target. However, moving from the claim that they are essentially different from men and from the women of dominant nation Kurdish feminists try to dissociate women from public sphere and keep them as the agent of traditional values. Women are formulated as the agents who protect their own language, costumes, culture and traditions. The rejection of traditional roles has not served emancipation of Kurdish women. On the contrary, traditional roles are perceived to be medium that protect Kurdish women, and thus their identity against assimilation policy of the state.

Islamic Women's Movement: From Street Actions to Islamic Feminism

The development of Islamic women's movement seems to be a reaction as well as a by-product of the policies followed by Turkish governments in the post-1980 period. The dissemination of educational networks through liberal policies created an opportunity ground for religious groups to get power in economic and political senses and to articulate in the activities associated to the public sphere. The activities they undertook might be ranged from education to media and from industry to trade. Media and educational network disseminated in Turkey made a ground for religious women to gain an appearance in the public domain as well. Female students, educated in modern schools, started to be immensely seen in universities during 1980s. When they attempted to attend universities with their headscarves they were strongly reacted and tried to be pushed back by Kemalist elites on the basis that the headscarf was a symbol of revolt used by these students against secular regime in Turkey.

The massive actions of female students supported by men, either student or not, started in 1984 when they were banned to attend classes with their headscarves in Ankara Divinity Faculty. When the ban was broadened to other universities the street protests were disseminated across the country. Although governments from central right tried to liberate headscarf in universities they could not be able to succeed it completely. This was because of the double power seen in Turkey, i.e., the separation between the realm of state and that of politics. Being a part of state military elite has always been reactive to the headscarf on the basis that it has symbolized the reaction to the secular system of Turkey. Nevertheless to say, some universities allowed female students to attend class with their headscarves until 1997. But the military maneuver in politics during the 28th February process of 1997, which is defined as post-modern coup by Turkish media, brought a strict ban on headscarf in all Turkish universities, as well as in public offices. This took a severe reaction of religious women and they started to organise massive protests in streets against this decision. The ban in Istanbul University, which is the greatest university in Turkey with its ninety thousands students, made Beyazıt Square, found in front of university, the center place for such actions. The protests organised by female students were supported by different social groups including some of secular feminist groups as well. One of the most prominent and original actions was 'freedom chain' launched through holding hand in hand in all cities in the country at the same time. It is estimated that several million people joined this protests across the country.

Religious women have, indeed, been politicised through such activities in Turkey. While the traditional religious norms advise them stay in domestic domain with traditional roles, these women converted such teaching and attempted to articulate in the public life. As described by a religious columnist these kinds of activities made religious women represent the "generation of 98", which is used by her to be allusion to the "generation of 68" (Eraslan 2002 p.261). The ban on headscarf and struggle against it has promoted religious women to reach a political consciousness as well as a self identity. One can say that the movement developed by these groups served the fabrication of self-realisation and individual-based identity. The transition seen among religious women is defined by the same columnist as being a transition from "sisterhood to individuality", and from "community to civic movement" (Eraslan 2002 p.245).

Headscarf has, indeed, become a controversial issue making a cleavage between Kemalist and Islamic groups after 1980. Kemalist elites, particularly women elite in academia, define it as a symbol of revolt against secular system and therefore wage a war against it in public sphere. On the contrary, religious women claim that headscarf is a religious decree commended in the Qur'an and they are covered not for political reasons but for the sake of religion (Nişancı 2006). Some women academicians like Nilüfer Göle (1998) and Elizabeth Özdalga (1998) argue that headscarf has become a medium that enable religious women to participate into the public life. The headscarf used by female students seems to be a modern version of traditional veiling and modern life in the public sphere. Headscarf, in that sense, has become the synthesis of tradition with modern. It legitimises the integration of women into the public life in the eyes of traditional sections on the one hand, and gives women the feeling of security in the public life on the other.

As mentioned above the liberal policies followed up in the post-1980 created a ground of opportunity for almost all social groups to depict themselves in the public sphere. One of the beneficiaries of this was religious women's groups. Religious women have gradually depicted themselves in the public sphere through political, economical, intellectual and educational activities. The Welfare Party (*Refah Partisi*), which was banned by the Constitutional Court in 1997 on the claim that it became the center of revolt against secular system, motivated the political mobilisation of a large number of religious women. It is estimated that about 400 thousands women were affiliated only in Istanbul organisation of the Party (Eraslan 2002 p.268). It is generally accepted by the students of Turkish politics that Welfare Party was the most successful party in motivating women for such a mobilisation.

Media is another platform that makes the visibility of religious women possible in the public sphere. A number of journals have been published by the religious groups. Such journals as *Kadın ve Aile* (Woman and Family), *Bizim Aile* (Our Family), *Prenses* (Princes), *Kadın Kimliği* (Women's Identity) and *Mektup* (Letter) have been published by these groups since mid-1980s (Mardin 1998). Some of these journals are supported by male writers. The first three journals have tried to develop a woman identity matching traditional roles with modern ones. They idealised an educated, but at the same time a religious woman who has traditional roles. Although they have not denied the working of women in the public domain frankly they argue that the natural role of women is motherhood. In order to fulfill this role best the most appropriate alternative for women is to stay at home and to take care of their children.

The last two journals, on the contrary, have been published only by women and they seem more sensitive to the women issue. *Mektup* is published by a group of women with slogan over its cover "from women to women or men, everybody". The basic care of women who publish this journal is to disseminate the message of Islam by means of women. They formulate a militant identity for women who care not for the sake of their own benefit only but that of Islam as well. Unlike these journals the *Kadın Kimliği*, took women's identity as the central care of its struggle. The journal mainly emphasises over such issues as problems lived by modern women, women's identity and problems with essentialist understanding of women as well as over pornography, advertisement, education, poverty and human rights from women's point of view. This journal frequently opens it page to the secular feminists as well as to those intellectuals who struggle for human rights in order to find out a common platform with them. The journal has an egalitarian standpoint which envisages the equality of women with men in every respect.

Religious women have also expressed themselves through a number of associations that they established. Starting from the beginning of 1990s onwards they have established some associations to support the struggle against ban on headscarf as well as to give support to the women's identity. Three prominent of these are the The Association for Human Rights Against Discrimination *(Ayrımcılığa Karşı Kadın Hakları Derneği/AK-DER)*, the Capital City Women's Platform *(Başkent Kadın Platformu)*, and the Rainbow Women's Association *(Gökkuşağı Kadın Derneği)*. These associations give struggle against the oppression of the state over the headscarved women on the one hand, and they strive against the traditional roles given to Muslim women on the other. Those adhered these associations are, indeed, politically active and intellectually sophisticated women. They pronounce their identity as "Muslim women" who believe into the equality of women with men. They pay a special care to the articulation of women into the public sphere as a medium for self-realisation of women.

Some of the women taking place under the roof of such associations have paid attention to the problems lived by Muslim women under the pressure of traditional understanding of Islam. These women are known as the representative of what is called "Islamic feminism" (Moghadam 2002). A group of women published the journal *Ayçe* (a female name in Turkish) during the end of 1980 became avenue of such women. Later, during 1990s and 2000s most of the women who established The Capital City Women's Platform have been known as Islamic feminists. The co-founder of this association Hidayet Tuksal, an academician in Ankara Divinity Faculty, has passionately criticised the traditional understanding of Islam and the domination of men over women (Akagündüz 2006). Women known as the representative of Islamic feminism in Turkey basically portrayed the idea that the traditional roles of women have not been originated from Islam but rather from a male culture. They criticized religious men's attempts that accorded the roles of housewife and motherhood only to women. However, they argue, Islam does not bring such a division of labor based on gender definitions. Therefore, they insisted that their struggle for participation into the public life should be tolerated by the religious men as well as by Kemalist elites. Being equal to men in public domain as well as in domestic life is their basic target.

The discourses of Islamic feminists can be summarised into three points. They are firstly the advocate of taking place in the public life through education and profession. In order to be able to do this they demand from the system to open a room for them and to accept them as they are. Secondly, they have reacted to the traditional roles given to women in the name of Islam. For them neither Islamic theory nor its application during the lifetime of the Prophet has accorded women in the secondary position to men. They believe, however, that Islam gives women equal status with men in respect to capacity and human dignity. The last point they emphasise is the essentialist understanding of women coming through the lenses of modernisation. They argue that as Muslim and women of third world countries they have different identity as well as different categories of human rights (Aktaş 2006). From the essentialist point of view headscarf seems to be a traditional symbol-keeping women in the prison of traditions. However, they argue, headscarf might liberate women, because of the fact that it is women's personal choice. Any choice taken by women should be tolerated as their right. This is the point of their divergent with secular feminist groups. They criticise Turkish secular feminist groups for being alien to their choices as Muslim women.

Whither the Wall Among Women's Movements in Turkey?

As it is argued above there is a controversy and disagreement among three women's movements in Turkey. Each of these movements has its own agenda and priorities. One should remember that the modernisation project followed by Turkish state seems to be an important factor behind this. One of the ultimate goals of the Turkish modernisation was to create a nation with only one color that is a nation having the same language, religion and even political choice. A tension has been seen, as an extension of this politics, between secular and religious sections and hereby between the women of these groups. Defining their place in the secular camp, Turkish feminists frequently take stance against religious women. In particular, when political regime is assumed to be under threat of religious groups the women of secular camps become too sensitive and even aggressive against religious groups. In such cases they come to struggle with their counterparts. The 28th February process was the peak of such a cleavage and the ground of a struggle against two groups of women. Most of feminist groups gave support to secular groups in struggling against headscarved women even though it cost them to return home back.[70] The tension seen between Kurdish and Turkish feminist groups is relatively less. This is, importantly, due to their mutual leftist and secular background. This indicates that the ideological background of women is influential, in the case of Turkey, over their position and attitude even though they struggle almost against the same problems.

Despite the existence of a clearly apparent wall among three feminist groups, in Turkey, there are some mechanisms that bring them together (Negron 2006). One of such mechanisms is the democratisation of the country. In particular the process of Turkey's integration into the European Union created a ground for women of different groups to meet in the same platforms. The reforms done within framework of Copenhagen Principles have enlarged the democratic ground in Turkey and this, indeed, played a critical role in the erosion of the wall among women's groups. Democratic ground has made them understand each other and thus led a transition among women's groups from conflict to competition (Çaha and Karaman 2006). One can say that the European Project has served the development of an arena of communication among different women's movements in Turkey.

The local problems that women groups struggle against seem to be another mechanism that make women of different sections meet in the same platform. Such problems can be seen at least in three different and interrelated areas. First, they all together bring some important issues from the back streets into the open and raise them for public discussion. Issues such as abortion, wife battering, honor crimes, marital rape and molestation are examples of this kind that all women's groups struggle against. Second, women of different groups redefine the deep-rooted codes of social institutions as in the case of gender analysis, the subordination of women, the traditional role of women and try to replace them with new meanings. Finally, women of different groups have put pressure on political parties and the government to take a stand in emphasising women's issues and in creating new institutions in

---

70 During the 28th February process thousands of women were dismissed from public offices since they were headscarved. These women, thus, were forced by the state to turn back home.

that respect. The revision done in the legal norms on behalf of women are the outcomes of their common attempts.

Feminist women of different classes have pressed their stamp over the traditional definition of the unified public sphere in Turkey. In the official ideology the importance is always given to the need for "homogeneity" of citizens under the fear that social differentiation would tend to undermine commitment to the general interest. This picture in the politics of the Turkish state seems to be reversed by different women's movements in the aftermath of 1980 period. They have done this by articulating in discourses drawing attention to "difference" developed mainly against the universal claim of the Enlightenment used by Kemalist elites. They reacted to the basic institutions that the state elite appropriated as worth getting for their purposes. Turkish women's groups have tried to develop a heterogeneous public sphere which seems to be the only way to ensure that political life will not exclude persons or groups that have been excluded from the public sphere in the past. In such a public domain the recognition and the appreciation of differences in the context of configuration with power become the ultimate goal. The contribution of diverse feminist groups in developing a multi-public domain is, indeed, their most focal and joint support to the development of civil society in Turkey as well.

Bibliography

Açık, N. (2002) 'Ulusal Mücadele, Kadın Mitosu ve Kadınların Harekete Geçirilmesi: Türkiye'de Çağdaş Kürt Dergilerinin Bir Analizi', in *90'larda Türkiye'de Feminizm*, ed. Aksu Bora and Asena Güldal, İstanbul: İletişim.

Akagündüz, Ülkü Ö. (2006) 'İslami Feminizm: Adı Var Kendi Yok', in *Aksiyon*, 587 (March 6).

Aktaş, C. (2006) 'White Western Women Elitism of Feminism', Symposium on *New Perspectives for Human Rights*, organised by Mazlum-Der and Human Rights Review, İstanbul, Turkey, (May 27-29).

Arat, Y. (2000) 'From Emancipation to Liberation: The Changing Role of Women in Turkey's Public Realm', in *Journal of International Affairs*, 54(1), pp.107-127.

Badran, M. (2005) 'Between Secular and Islamic Feminism/s: Reflections on the Middle East and Beyond', in *Journal of Middle East Women's Studies*, 1(1) (Winter), pp.6-28.

Çaha, Ö. (2010) *Sivil Kadın: Türkiye'de Sivil Toplum ve Kadın*, Ankara: Savaş Yayınları.

Çaha, Ö. and Karaman, L. (2006) 'Civil Society under a Strong State Tradition Towards the Integration into the European Union: The Case of Turkey', in *Process of EU Enlargement in the 21st Century: New Challenges*, eds. Peter Terem and Ömer Çaha: Banska Bystrica: University of Matej Bel.

Çakır, S. (1995) Osmanlı *Kadın Hareketi*, Istanbul: Metis.

Doğan, S. (1996) 'Evet, Erkekler Türk Devletinin Köleleri Ama Biz Bacılar Kölelerin Kölesiyiz...', in *Roza*, 1(2) (May-June).

Eraslan, S. (2002) Uğultular... Silüetler', in *90'larda Türkiye'de Feminizm, 90'larda Türkiye'de Feminizm*, ed. Aksu Bora and Asena Güldal, İstanbul: İletişim.

Göle N. (1998) *Modern Mahremiyet*, Istanbul: Metis Yayınları.

Tanrıkulu, S. (1997) *'Dilimi Bilsen Beni Anlayabilir misin?'*, in *Jujin: 2 Aylık Kürt Kadın Dergisi, 3–4, p.27.*

Kara, N. (2006) '80 ve 90'larda Türkiye'de Feminist Hareketler', in *Kadın Çalışmaları Dergisi*, 1(3) (September-December), pp.16-39.

Karayazgan, Ayşe G. (1998) 'Biz Kadınlar Diyememek Bir Türlü?' in *Pazartesi*, 38 (May).

Kardam, F. and Ecevit, Y. (2002) '1990'ların Sonunda Bir Kadın İletişim Kuruluşu: Uçan Süpürge', in *90'larda Türkiye'de Feminizm*, ed. Aksu Bora and Asena Güldal, İstanbul: İletişim.

Kutluata, Z. (2003) 'The Politics of Difference Within the Feminist Movement in Turkey as Manifested in the Case of Kurdish Woman/Feminist Journals', İstanbul: Bogazici University, Unpublished Master Thesis.

Mardin, Aslı D. (1998) *Hanımlar Aleminden Roza'ya: Kadın Süreli Yayınları Bibliyografyası (1928-1996)*, İstanbul: Kadın Eserleri Kütüphanesi ve Bilgi Merkezi.

Mernissi, F. (1985) *Beyond the Veil: MaleFemale Dynamics in Muslim Society*, London: Al Saqi Books.

Moghadam, Valentine M. (2002) 'Islamic Feminism and its Discontents: Toward a Resolution of the Debate', in *Signs: Journal of Women in Culture and Society*, 27, pp.1135–1171.

Negron, M. (2006) 'Converging Agendas? Dialogue Between Muslim and Secular Activists in Turkey's Women's Movement', Symposium on *New Perspectives for Human Rights*, organized by Mazlum-Der and Human Rights Review, İstanbul, Turkey, (May 27-29).

Nişancı, E. (2006) 'Modern Türkiye'de Kadın Kimlik Tasarımı', in *Kadın Çalışmaları Dergisi*, 1(1), (January-April), pp.106-116.

Özdalga, E. (1998) *Modern Türkiye'de Örtünme Sorunu Resmi Laiklik ve Popüler İslam*, İstanbul: Sarmal Yayınevi.

Roza, 'Kürt Feminizmi', 3, 15 (Ferbuary-March).

Tekeli, Ş. (1989) '80'lerde Türkiye'de Kadınların Kurtuluşu Hareketinin Gelişmesi', in *Birikim*, 3 (June 1989).

Yelda, 'Kadın Örgütlenmesi'nden Önce Kadın Dayanışması', in *Roza*, 1, 2 (May-June).

Part 3
MULTICULTURALISM IN THE UK - I

Does Ethnic Diversity Lead to Community 'Inter-Ethnic Tensions'? Reconciling the 'Contact' and 'Threat' Hypotheses: Ethnic Diversity and the Moderating Effects of 'Inter-Ethnic Contact' and Community Disadvantage Amongst White British Individuals in England and Wales

James Laurence[71]

Introduction

Over the past 10 years the UK has experienced a significant demographic shift in the ethnic composition of its populace: current mid-year 2009 estimates put the percentage White British population in England at 83%, from 87% in 2001[72]. This demographic shift has brought a substantial shift in both the *public* and *political* discourses surrounding issues of race and ethnicity, coalescing around the idea that this increasing ethnic diversity poses a 'threat' to 'social cohesion' in the UK (Cheong et al. 2007). In 2011, the newly-elected Conservative Prime Minister, David Cameron, declared that "[u]nder the doctrine of state multiculturalism, we have encouraged different cultures to live separate lives, apart from each other

---

71 Dr James Laurence is a post-doctoral research fellow at University of Manchester. He recently completed his PhD exploring whether community ethnic diversity has a negative effect on indicators of local 'social cohesion' at Oxford University. During this period he wrote a report for the UK Department of Communities and Local Government on the predictors of 'social cohesion', worked as a consultant for the Birmingham Strategic Partnership on the relationship between diversity and social cohesion, and collaborated on the 'Managing Cultural Diversity' project at Oxford. He is currently working on a project analysing the social effects of recessions for a joint Manchester-Harvard University collaboration.

72 Office for National Statistics (ONS) 'Current Population Estimates' by Ethnic group: mid-2001 and mid-2009.

and the mainstream" with the effect of "weakening our collective identity". This sentiment has also been proclaimed in France and Germany, where Angela Merkel stated that "the multicultural concept" in which individuals "live happily side by side, and [are] happy to be living with each other…has failed, and failed utterly". We have thus witnessed a shift in "the tone of the debates and policy initiatives on immigration and asylum…away from multiculturalism to [an] assimilationist and monoculturalist" framework (Cheong et al. 2007 p.26), entering a phase in which the mood is now "not one of valuing diversity but of avoiding conflict" (Modood 2010).

The much longer academic literature on the relationship between community ethnic diversity and 'inter-ethnic relations', however, is far more mixed than the *political* discourse suggests. The range and mix of results has led a number of scholars to conclude that "the vast empirical literature has notprovided a definite answer as to which effect [i.e. 'contact' or 'threat'] prevails" (Dustmann and Preston 2001 p.354; Rothbart and John 1993). Thus, it is far from clear as to whether increasing ethnic diversity stimulates positive or negative 'inter-ethnic attitudes'.

The main aim of this paper is thus to explore whether increasing community diversity leads to greater or weaker 'inter-ethnic relations' amongst the majority, White British, population in England and Wales. We posit that one reason *why* the current literature is so mixed is that it tends to make an assumption about diversity's effect (i.e. whether 'contact' or 'threat' is occurring) based solely on the direction of the relationship between community ethnic diversity and *mean* levels of 'inter-ethnic relations' i.e. a positive direct relationship indicates that the 'contact' hypothesis is in operation and a negative relationship indicates 'threat'. Few studies actually directly test the mechanisms purported to account for the effect of contextual diversity on individual 'prejudice'.

We suggest that, theoretically, it is feasible that *both* the 'contact' *and* 'threat' hypotheses are in operation and the direction and strength of the relationships between community diversity and *mean* levels of inter-ethnic attitudes might be a product of: (1) the strength of the negative effect of diversity; (2) if 'contact' is occurring (and the proportion of individuals experiencing 'contact'); (3) the relative size of the positive effect of 'contact' on attitudes; and (4) that diversity's effect may be *conditioned* (i.e. moderated)by whether 'contact' occurs or not. We aim to directly interrogate these theories, through the application of multi-level regression models, by exploring the *mediating* and *moderating* role of individual-level 'contact' in the relationship between their level of community diversity and their inter-ethnic attitudes. In doing so we hope to contribute to the academic debate on whether increasing community diversity aids or undermines 'inter-ethnic relations' and the wider debate on whether increasing diversity undermines community 'social cohesion' in the UK.

Theoretical Framework

The 'Threat'/'Contact' Hypothesis Dichotomy

The debate between the effects of living in a diverse environment and levels of 'inter-group feeling' tends to be polarised around the 'threat' (or 'conflict') hypothesis and the 'contact' hypothesis. The 'conflict' (or 'threat' hypothesis) broadly posits that "a superordinate group (e.g., whites) becomes more racially hostile as the size of a proximate subordinate group increases, which putatively threatens the former's economic and social privilege" (Oliver and Wong 2003 p.568; Blalock 1967; Bonacich 1972; Stephan et al. 1998; Esses et al.1998). This general theory can be differentiated into 'symbolic' (or 'cultural' threat) hypotheses (Stephan et al. 1998; Zarate 2004), and the 'realistic/perceived group threat' hypothesis (Blumer 1958; Blalock 1967; Sherif et al. 1961; Bobo 1988; Esses et al. 1998). Although nuances exist between the exact mechanisms at work (e.g. 'resource-based', 'cultural') the conclusions of these theories are the same: that living in a diverse environment will stimulate prejudice.

On the other side of the debate is the 'contact' hypothesis, whereby interaction, and the formation of ties between *different* ethnic groups, leads to a reduction in prejudice and the formation of positive inter-group attitudes (Pettigrew and Tropp 1998; 2000; Hewstone 2003; 2009; Gaertner et al. 1996. Allport's (1954) original formulation involved four strict conditions under which 'contact' should take place to reduce prejudice. A recent meta-analytical review by Pettigrew and Tropp (2006 p.766) found that while 'contact' under these pre-conditions "achieved a markedly higher mean effect size", 'contact' under *any* situation tended to have a significant positive effect on inter-group attitudes. The 'contact' theory follows that living in a more diverse community increases the likelihood of 'contact' between ethnic groups; therefore high ethnic diversity should be, contrary to the 'threat' hypothesis, associated with *less* prejudice, as it provides greater opportunities for the formation of 'inter-ethnic ties'.

Most studies make assumptions about which theory applies (and therefore *which* mechanisms are in operation e.g. 'contact' or attitudes of 'threat') based on the *direction* of the relationship between increasing 'community' diversity and *mean* levels of 'attitudes' in a 'community' (Putnam 2007; Lancee and Dronkers 2009; 2010; Oliver and Mendelberg 2000; Stein et al. 2000; Oliver and Wong 2003; Dustmann and Preston 2001). Thus, if individuals, on average, report greater 'tolerance' in diverse areas it is *assumed* that inter-ethnic 'contact' is in operation. If individuals report, on average, lower 'tolerance' in diverse areas is *assumed* that attitudes of 'threat' are being fomented.

The current evidence for how contextual diversity affects 'prejudicial' attitudes is relatively mixed. Studies have found that living amongst greater concentrations of ethnic out-groups is associated with *more* 'prejudicial attitudes' (i.e. evidence for the 'threat' hypothesis: Schaefer 1975; Giles and Buckner 1993; Dustmann and Preston 2001; Taylor 1998) *less* 'prejudicial attitudes' (i.e. evidence for the 'contact' hypothesis: Oliver and Wong 2003; Welsch et al. 2001; Laurence and Heath 2008); and still more studies have found *conditional* results (Oliver and Wong 2003; Biggs and Knauss 2011; Bledsoe 1995; Bowyer 2009; Dixon 2006; Stein et al. 2000). The mix of results has led a number of scholars to conclude that"the vast empirical literature has notprovided a definite answer as to which effect prevails" (Dustmann and Preston 2001 p.354; Rothbart and John 1993).

Reconsidering the 'Contact'-'Threat' Dichotomy: a 'Unified Theory'

The 'contact' and 'threat' hypotheses, at first appraisal, appear paradoxical: why would increasing exposure to ethnic out-groups foment prejudice (through perceptions of 'threat') if, with increasing exposure to out-groups, comes an increased likelihood of 'contact' (and thus 'prejudice reduction') (Oliver and Wong 2003; Stolle et al. 2007). Yet, as demonstrated above, there is a substantial body of research finding evidence for both theories (at both the individual and community level) (Brown and Hewstone 2005; Pettigrew andTropp 2006; 2008; González et al. 2008).

We posit that one possible explanation for this apparent paradox (and for the mixed evidence-base) is that: *whether* an individual living in a more diverse community reports more, less, or no difference in 'inter-ethnic attitudes' (compared to an individual in a more homogeneous community) may depend on *whether* they actually experience inter-ethnic 'contact' or not. Most studies simply infer whether 'contact' is occurring based on the comparative *mean* levels of 'tolerance' amongst all individuals in diverse communities. However, it is quite feasible to imagine that some individuals do and some do not experience 'inter-ethnic contact' in diverse communities. Potentially, those individuals that *do* experience 'contact' may report comparatively greater 'tolerance' whilst those who do *not* experience 'contact' may report greater 'prejudice'; in other words, in diverse communities, both the 'contact' and 'threat' hypotheses may be in operation. Such a relationship would be difficult to partial out when simply analysing *mean* levels of 'tolerance' across levels of community ethnic diversity.

Scenario One: the Mediating Effects of 'Contact'

In embracing the idea that *both* the 'threat' and 'contact' hypotheses may be operating, we can formulate a new set of possible scenarios to understand how diversity relates to mean levels of 'tolerance' in a community. The first scenario is that living amongst higher concentrations of ethnic out-groups in a community stimulates 'threat' and thus increases levels of prejudice amongst residents i.e. diversity has a direct negative effect on 'tolerance'. However, at the same time, living amongst higher concentrations of ethnic out-groups may also increase the likelihood of inter-ethnic 'contact' (which in turn reduces levels of prejudice). Under this scenario, inter-ethnic 'contact' would *mediate* the negative effect of % out-group on levels of 'tolerance'.

A number of European studies have found significant, negativedirect relationships between concentrations of ethnic out-groups and forms of 'prejudice' (suggesting the 'threat' hypothesis is in operation). However, at the same time, they demonstrate that 'contact' increases in environments with higher proportions of out-groups, and that such 'contact', in turn, reduces 'prejudice' (suggesting the 'contact' hypothesis is *also* in operation) (Schlueter and Wagner 2008; Schlueter and Scheepers 2010). Such work has suggested 'contact' therefore *mediates* the negative effect of '% out-group in an area' on 'tolerance' i.e. that while higher proportions of ethnic out-groups stimulate 'threat' (and thus 'prejudice'), such effects are suppressed by the fact that it also stimulates 'contact' (and thus 'tolerance').

Scenario Two: the Moderating Effects of 'Contact'

The key point in this first scenario ('contact' as *mediator*) is that *diversity has a potentially negative effect on all individuals*. However, this effect can be suppressed by greater 'inter-ethnic contact' in diverse areas. The second scenario differs from this in suggesting that *diversity may not affect all individuals equally*; the effect of living in a diverse area itself may actually *depend on whether an individual possesses 'inter-ethnic' ties or not*.

Under this scenario, amongst individuals who do not possess 'inter-ethnic' ties, increasing diversity may foment 'threat' and thus increase 'prejudice'. Individuals who do not possess 'inter-ethnic' ties would therefore experience a direct negative effect of contextual diversity on 'tolerance'. However, individuals who do possess 'inter-ethnic' ties would not report greater 'prejudice' at higher concentrations of ethnic out-groups i.e. increasing community diversity would have a weaker (or *no effect*) on levels of 'prejudice' amongst those with 'inter-ethnic ties'. In this second scenario 'contact' would therefore act as a *moderator* of ethnic diversity.

Very few studies have explored the *moderating* effects of 'contact' on community diversity. In the US, Stolle et al. (2008) found evidence that 'contact' positively moderated diversity's negative effect on 'neighbour trust'. In the UK, Laurence (2009) found 'contact' positively moderated diversity's relationship with community 'inter-ethnic relations', although crucially they did not disaggregate by ethnicity[73]. We intend to adapt this theory and explore the moderating effect of inter-ethnic 'contact' on diversity's relationship with 'inter-ethnic attitudes' amongst White British individuals (for whom, as the 'majority' ethnic group, 'threat' should play a greater role). This has not yet been explored in the literature. Exploring the mediating and moderating effects of 'contact' is a significant addition to the field as, unlike the majority of studies, *we do not need to infer whether 'contact' is occurring (or not) simply based on whether diversity has a positive or negative direct effect on mean levels of 'tolerance' in a community.*

Structure of Analysis

The primary aim of this paper therefore is to test our 'Unified Theory' of community diversity's relationship with 'inter-ethnic relations', observing: (1) whether *both* the 'threat' and 'contact' hypotheses are in operation; and, depending on (1), whether (2) 'contact' acts as a *mediator* or *moderator* of diversity's effect. At the heart of this framework is the role played by 'inter-ethnic contact'[74]. The first step is to establish the direct effect of community diversity on *mean* levels of 'inter-ethnic relations' in a community (as conducted in much of the literature). We then want to test for the two tenets of the 'contact' hypothesis: (1) that living amongst a higher proportion of ethnic out-groups (a lower proportion of co-ethnics) is associated with a greater likelihood of possessing 'inter-ethnic' ties; and (2) that possessing 'bridging' ties is associated with more positive 'inter-ethnic attitudes'. Together, this constitutes a test of the 'contact' hypothesis (as understood in the diversity literature). The third step is then to explore the 'unified theory' of diversity's effect. If 'contact' acts as a *mediator* of diversity's effect we would expect to see either: (1) a positive effect of diversity grow weaker or become negative (i.e. the greater likelihood, and positive effect, of 'contact' in *more* diverse communities accounts for why diversity has a positive relationship with 'inter-ethnic relations'); or (2) a negative effect of diversity to grow stronger (i.e. the mediating effect of 'contact' in diverse areas is suppressing the true negative effect of diversity on 'inter-ethnic relations'). If 'contact' acts as a *moderator* of diversity's effect, then upon including an interaction term between individual-level 'contact' and community-level diversity, we should

---

73 Laurence (2009) found, amongst all individuals, that those who possess 'inter-ethnic ties' report higher 'tolerance' in diverse communities compared to those who do not. However, non-White individuals living in 'diverse' communities are more likely to be residing with co-ethnics (thus experiencing, in theory, less 'threat') and are more likely to possess 'bridging' ties (compared to Whites, due to shear probability). Therefore, it is unclear as to whether the moderating effect was spurious.

74 We do not have psychological measures of 'threat' in our dataset. Therefore, significant negative relationships between 'diversity' and 'relations' will have to be assumed (based on theory) to be originating from 'threat'.

see that diversity has a stronger negative effect amongst individuals who do not possess 'inter-ethnic contacts'. We restrict our analysis to White British individuals only as the 'contact', and especially 'threat', hypotheses are purported to have greater resonance with the 'majority' ethnic community.

Measures and Methodology
Data Sets and Key Individual Measures

To empirically test our questions we utilise the 2005 Citizenship Survey (CS) covering England and Wales. This data set contains our individual (level-1) measures of 'inter-ethnic relations', alongside all individual-level controls. All the community (level-2) data is obtained from the 2001 UK Census.

The 2005 CS provides two questions with which to analyse 'inter-ethnic attitudes': 'to what extent do you agree or disagree that this local area, (within 15/20 minutes walking distance), is a place where people from different backgrounds get on well together?' and 'Would you agree or disagree that this local area (15/20 minutes walking distance) is a place where residents respect ethnic differences between people?'. Both questions are answered on a scale of 'strongly agree', 'agree', 'disagree' and 'strongly disagree'. One way to both confirm the consistency of these two measures and also minimise biases from measurement error, is to explore, using factor analysis, whether they form a robust index of 'inter-ethnic attitudes' (**Table 1**). This index provides a more sensitive measuring instrument than analysing the two variables separately.

Table 1 –Factor Analysis of 'Inter-ethnic Relations' Measures

Variable	Factor I	Uniqueness
Respect Ethnic Differences	0.866	0.25
Different Backgrounds get along well	0.866	0.25
Eigen Value	1.49	

These measures of 'inter-ethnic attitudes' differ to some extent from other measures of 'inter-ethnic attitudes' used in the literature (e.g. attitudes towards inter-ethnic marriage, feeling thermometer scores towards ethnic groups, etc.). However, in a separate piece of analysis it was found that these questions were strongly influenced by personal 'inter-ethnic attitudes'[75]. These questions may also help to mitigate

75 The only dataset that contains these questions as well as questions on personal feelings towards ethnic out-groups is the 'Managing Cultural Diversity Questionnaire' (as yet unreleased). Permission to compare these measures was kindly given by Professor Miles Hewstone.

'social desirability biases' through asking for an individual's appraisal of ethnic groups in their community (as opposed to their own personal 'prejudice')[76].

The CS contains one question which will allow us to capture inter-ethnic 'contact': "what proportion of your friends is from the same ethnic group as you: 'all the same', 'more than half', 'about half', or 'less than half'?" This 'proportional measure' of inter-ethnic *to* intra-ethnic 'contact' sets an artificial zero-sum relationship between the two which is problematic. Therefore, to minimise these problems we will transform it into a binary measure of 'inter-ethnic contact' (compared to no 'contact' ties)[77].

Community Level Measures

As we our looking at these relationships amongst White British alone, our key measure of the ethnic composition of the community will be % non-White British. We also control for a range of possible confounding community-level variables, including: rate of residential turnover (calculated by adding together the inflow and the outflow of persons in an area) per 1,000 people; whether the neighbourhood is found in a town, or urban, (compared to a rural) area; density of population per hectare; % aged 65 years old and above; and level of crime (the IMD Crime Domain).

We also include two indices of disadvantage (derived from a factor analysis of indicators of community-disadvantage present in the literature (Patterson 1991; Sampson and Wilson 1995; Messer et al. 2006; Putnam 2007; Sturgis, et al. 2011)). These include: % economically active but unemployed, % female lone-parent households, % 'long-term unemployed/never worked', % social housing, % with no qualifications, and % in elementary/process occupations. As demonstrated in **Table 2**, the indicators load on to two distinct measures of disadvantage: 'disadvantage 1' (factor 1) and 'disadvantage 2' (factor 2)[78].

---

76 A further issue with these questions is that they were not asked to individuals who reported that 'the area they lived in was all the same race'. Therefore, an individual's response to these questions will be based on actual experience of living in an (at least marginally) diverse community.

77 This involves aggregating the options 'more than half', 'about half', and 'less than half of my friends are from the same ethnic group' into a single category of 'possess at least one friend from a different ethnic group'.

78 We experimented with both oblique and orthogonal rotation. Both reported almost identical factors; however, we report the results from the orthogonal rotation.

Table 2 - Factor Analysis of 'Community Disadvantage' Variables

Factor	Eigen Value		Proportion	Cumulative
Factor1	2.81		0.69	0.69
Factor2	1.44		0.35	1.04
Variable	Factor 1	Factor 2		Uniqueness
% Unemployed (Economically Active)	0.86	-		0.18
% Social Housing	0.73	-		0.28
% L/T Unemployed and Never Worked	0.87	-		0.22
% Female Lone-Parent	0.72	-		0.28
% No Qualifications	-	0.73		0.24
% Elementary/Process Occupations	-	0.76		0.40

Note: Factor loadings below .4 are suppressed in the table; Orthogonal Varimax Rotation (Kaiser On)

Individual-Level Controls

At the individual-level we control for age, sex, and household income. We control for education (comparing the effect of possessing no qualifications (baseline) with possessing: foreign qualifications, GCSEs (d-e), GCSEs (a-c), A-levels, Higher Education, or a Degree). To control for Social Class we collect individuals into three 'Socio-Economic Group' categories (comparing the effect of being 'non-manual' (baseline) with being 'manual' or 'other'). We also control for whether an individual is married and how many children they have. Additionally, we control for whether the individual was born in the UK, and the length of time they have lived in their community. Finally we control for tenure (comparing the effect of owning one's property (baseline) with possessing a council tenancy, a housing association tenancy, or private renting).

Geographic-Level of Analysis: Community and Outcomes

In our analysis of the 2005 CS, an individual's community is measured at the Middle Super Output Area (MSOA) level[79]. MSOAs are statistical areas defined by the Office for National Statistics (ONS) with a minimum population of 5,000 residents and an average population of 7,200. This area-level corresponds closely to the area an individual is instructed to think of when answering questions on 'inter-ethnic relations' in their community ('within 15/20 minutes walking distance')[80]. However, the 2005 CS also possesses a question on 'what proportion of people in your 'local area' (within 15/20 minutes walking distance) are the same ethnic group as you?' With this we will test the robustness of our models.

Methodology

Our analysis can be simply stated as an attempt to explore whether differences in the level of *community*-level 'diversity' are associated with differences in *individual*-level reports of 'social cohesion' in the community. It will therefore contain both individual-level (level-1) and community-level (level-2) units. This nested structure of our data violates a fundamental assumption of multiple-regression analysis that the residuals are *independent* and introduces the potential of biased standard errors (Putnam 2007; Gelman and Hill 2007). To cope with this we will apply hierarchical (multi-level) modelling techniques (Carle 2009; Snijders and Bosker 1999).

Level 1 Model:

$$Y_{ij} = \beta_{0j} + \beta_{1j} X_{ij} + r_{ij}$$

Level 2 Model:

$$\beta_{0j} = \gamma_{00} + \gamma_{01} Z_j + u_{0j} \} \text{ Random Intercept}$$

$$\beta_{1j} = \gamma_{10} + \gamma_{11} Z_j + u_{1j} \} \text{ Random Slope}$$

Results

Establishing the Core Relationships: Direct Effects and the 'Contact' Hypothesis

Table 3 displays the results from a series of multi-level regression analyses amongst White British individuals in England and Wales. All individual-level controls are included in the models although are not displayed in the tables. The first step of our analysis is to establish the relationship between increasing % community non-

---

79 Due to issues of confidentiality related to the use of small-area identifiers the MSOA is smallest level at which IPSOS MORI would release the data.

80 Although there is no data on the average size (in km) of MSOAs, by observing a large number of MSOAs mapped on to towns and cities we can see most appear, on average, around 0.8 km2 or slightly under.

White and *mean* 'inter-ethnic attitudes'. In **Model 1** we see that, after controlling for all individual- and community-level variables, increasing % non-White in the community has a weak negative but non-significant relationship with individuals' 'inter-ethnic attitudes'. If our analysis was to stop here we would suggest that we find no evidence for the 'contact' hypothesis and only very weak evidence for the 'threat' hypothesis. Instead, it is higher community disadvantage (especially 'Disadvantage 2') that appears to undermine 'inter-ethnic relations'.

Table 3 – Multi-level Regression Analysis; White British Individuals

Dependent Variable:	Model 1 Relations Index	Model 2 'Bridging' Ties	Model 3 Relations Index	Model 4 Relations Index
Density (MSOA)	0.01	0.026	0.012	0.008
Turnover (MSOA)	0.002	-0.071	0.004	0.009
% Aged 65+ (MSOA)	-0.02	-0.003	-0.022	-0.023
cf. Village (MSOA)				
Town (MSOA)	0.008	0.027	0.006	0.008
Urban (MSOA)	-0.043	0.045	-0.041	-0.039
Disadvantage 1 (MSOA)	-0.021	0.152	-0.023	-0.03
Disadvantage 2 (MSOA)	-0.197****	-0.122	-0.195****	-0.192****
IMD Crime (MSOA)	-0.044	0.087	-0.046	-0.044
% non-White GB (MSOA)	-0.036	0.451****	-0.041	-0.11***
'Contact' (Individual-level)			0.044***	0.087****
'Contact' * % non-White GB				0.101***
% change in MSOA div.			+23%	
N (Individ.)	3540	3540	3540	3540
N (MSOAs)	1000	1000	1000	1000

Notes: ****$P<0.001$; ***$P<0.01$; **$P<0.05$; *$P<0.1$; all models include 'individual-level' controls (although not reported in the results); *standardized* coefficients

Our next aim is to establish whether the 'contact' hypothesis is in operation. **Model 2** predicts the likelihood of possessing an 'inter-ethnic contact' (using logistic regression as the measure is dichotomous). We see that White GB individuals living in communities with higher proportions of non-White GB individuals are significantly more likely to possess 'inter-ethnic ties'[81]. This confirms the first tenet of 'contact' hypothesis as applied in the literature: that individuals living in more diverse communities are more likely to form 'inter-ethnic ties'.

We are assuming from this that the reason higher % non-White GB is significantly associated with 'contact' is that ties are being formed in the neighbourhood. However, the positive relationship between % non-White GB and 'contact' may be a product of 'selection effects' e.g. White British individuals who already possess 'inter-ethnic ties' (and are thus likely more 'tolerant') may be morelikely to *select into* 'diverse' communities. These counter-arguments are difficult to unpick using cross-sectional data; however, we will discuss possible implications of selection effects further on.

Our next aim is to establish the second tenet of the 'contact' hypothesis. **Model 3** replicates **Model 1** but also includes our measure of 'inter-ethnic contact'. First of all we see individuals with 'inter-ethnic ties' are significantly more likely to possess positive 'inter-ethnic attitudes'. This empirically confirms the second tenet of the 'contact' hypothesis. Based on **Models 2** and **3** we see that White GB individuals living amongst greater proportions of non-White GB are *more* likely to possess 'inter-ethnic ties', and these individuals are *more* likely to report positive 'inter-ethnic attitudes'. Thus, even though increasing % non-White GB has a negative (but non-significant) direct effect on 'inter-ethnic attitudes'; the 'contact' hypothesis does appear to be in operation.

Testing the 'Unified Theory': 'Contact' as Mediator or Moderator

We turn now to exploring the 'Unified Theory' of diversity's relationship with 'inter-ethnic relations'. The first test is whether 'contact' acts as a *mediator*. Potentially, increasing proportions of non-White GB in the community does not have a significant negative effect on 'inter-ethnic attitudes' because whilst diversity may stimulate 'threat', at higher levels of diversity individuals are also more likely to possess 'inter-ethnic ties' (and thus report greater 'tolerance'), suppressing the true negative effect of diversity (rendering it non-significant). When we add 'inter-ethnic contact' into our model (**Model 3**) we find it substantially *mediates* the effect of % non-White GB in the community (*increasing* its negative effect by 23%). This suggests the true effect of diversity is being suppressed by the greater occurrence of 'contact' in diverse communities. However, diversity's effect *remains* relatively weak and non-significant. Therefore, even accounting for the counteracting positive effects of 'contact', 'tolerance' is still *not* significantly lower in diverse communities.

---

81 This relationship is holds if we look at the likelihood of 'all Whites' possessing 'inter-ethnic ties' as the proportion of 'non-Whites' increases

The second scenario in the 'Unified Theory' is that the effect of rising proportions of non-White GB may be different for individuals *with* and *without* 'inter-ethnic ties' (i.e. 'contact' *moderates* its effect). In **Model 4** we test for this by including an interaction term between % community non-White GB and whether an individual possess 'inter-ethnic ties' or not. We observe that the direct % non-White GB term now becomes more strongly negative and is now significant (*p value*: 0.01) while the interaction term is positive and significant (to a 0.01 level)[82]. This finding suggests that living amongst higher proportions of non-White GB has a significantly stronger *negative* effect on 'inter-ethnic attitudes' amongst White GB individuals *without* 'inter-ethnic ties'. To understand how this relationship manifests itself across different proportions of non-White GB, we will create a series of *predicted* scores (**Figure 1**). To aid our substantive understanding of these relationships we will look at the *predicted* scores of 'disrespect for ethnic differences'. These *predicted* scores are based on a full model (identical to **Model 4**, **Table 3**) where 'respect' is the dependent variable[83].

Figure 1 – Predicted % 'disagree/disagree strongly' that residents 'respect ethnic differences' at grouped-% non-White GB, by possession of 'inter-ethnic ties'; amongst White British

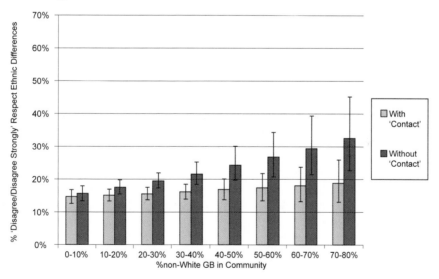

Notes: All other individual and community variables set to mean

---

82 We also substitute our MSOA diversity measure for the 'self-rated measure of diversity' ('what proportion of people are of the same ethnic group as you…all the same, more than half, about half, less than half'). We create an interaction term between 'inter-ethnic ties' and 'subjective diversity' and find the interaction term strong, positive and significant (0.195***).

83 diversity*'inter-ethnic tie': 0.244***

Figure 1 demonstrates the *relative* effect of diversity based on whether a White British individual possesses an 'inter-ethnic tie' or not. The main take-away is that increasing proportions of non-White GB in a community are only associated with growing negative 'attitudes' if an individual does not possess 'inter-ethnic ties'. In other words, increasing % ethnic out-group has *no significant* effect on levels of 'tolerance' amongst White British individuals *with* 'inter-ethnic ties'. Before we move on to discussing the implications of these findings we will look at the final aim of this paper: re-examining the role of community disadvantage.

Re-introducing Community Disadvantage

Our current analysis demonstrates that communities with higher rates of 'Disadvantage 2' report lower *mean* levels of 'tolerance' (although communities with higher rates of 'Disadvantage 1' do not). This provides evidence that prejudice can also arise as a psychological response to economic and physical duress, stimulating what Oliver and Mendelberg (2000) term 'interracial material competition' (Bettelheim and Janowitz1964; Fromm 1941; Sales 1973). As suggested in the literature, we might expect that "[a]s racial integration is a greater [or perceived to be a greater] material threat to residents of low status neighborhoods, racial animosity in [more diverse] settings may be higher" (Oliver and Mendelberg 2000 p.375) i.e. increasing concentrations of non-White GB would have a stronger negative effect in low SES areas. We therefore aim to test this in the UK.

Above we demonstrated that whilst, on average, 'inter-ethnic attitudes' are not significantly higher or lower in more diverse communities, % non-White GB in a community *does* appear to have a negative effect on levels of 'tolerance' amongst individuals who do not possess 'inter-ethnic ties' i.e. vulnerability is focused amongst those without 'contact'. Based on this, we posit that increasing proportions of ethnic out-group in a community may actually have a stronger negative effect if found in more disadvantage communities, but that this effect will be concentrated *amongst individuals who do not possess 'inter-ethnic ties'*. We will therefore also test this idea. **Table 4** shows the results of a new series of multi-level regression models exploring these questions.

Table 4 – Multi-level regression predicting 'tolerance' index and testing for diversity/disadvantage/'bridging' ties interactions; White British; standardised coefficients

	Model I	Model 2	Model 3	Model 4
Dependent Variable:	*Relations Index*	*Relations Index*	*Relations Index*	*Relations Index*
Density (MSOA)	0.014	0.008	0.009	0.007
Turnover (MSOA)	0.003	0.009	0.006	0.007
% Aged 65+ (MSOA)	-0.012	-0.023	-0.0169	-0.016
cf. Village (MSOA)				
Town (MSOA)	0.009	0.008	0.004	0.004
Urban (MSOA)	-0.021	-0.039	-0.027	-0.027
Disadvantage I (MSOA)	-0.010	-0.03	0.008	-0.045
Disadvantage 2 (MSOA)	-0.143****	-0.192****	-0.137****	-0.137****
IMD Crime (MSOA)	-0.032	-0.044	-0.032	-0.03
% non-White GB (MSOA)	-0.043	-0.11***	-0.119****	-0.122***
'Contact' (Individual-level)		0.087****	0.108****	0.095****
'Contact' * % non-White GB		0.1***	0.122***	0.117***
% non-White GB * Disadvantage I	0.002		0.001	-0.084**
'Contact' * Disadvantage I			-0.062**	-0.002
% non-White GB * Disadvantage I * 'Contact'				0.119***
N (Individ.)	3540	3540	3540	3540
N (MSOAs)	1000	1000	1000	1000

Notes: ****p<0.001; ***P<0.01; **P<0.05; *P<0.10; all models include 'individual-level' controls (although not reported in the results); *standardized* coefficients

Model 1 (Table 4) tests whether living amongst higher proportions of non-White GB in a community has a stronger negative effect on 'inter-ethnic attitudes' if found in communities with higher rates of 'Disadvantage 1'. However, the interaction term ('% non-White GB * Disadvantage 1') is not significant[84]. We next want to test whether this interaction is present but only amongst individuals who do not experience 'contact'. **Model 2** re-establishes the main relationship so far (identical to **Model 4, Table 3**) (including the '% non-White GB * 'inter-ethnic ties'' interaction). In **Model 3** we add in interaction terms between 'Disadvantage 1 * 'inter-ethnic ties'', and '% non-White GB * Disadvantage 1' (necessary for the eventual '% non-White GB * Disadvantage 1 * 'inter-ethnic ties'' interaction). In **Model 4** we add in our interaction term testing whether the effect of % non-White GB is *moderated* by: (1) the level of 'Disadvantage 1'[85] and (2) whether an individual possesses 'inter-ethnic ties' or not (that is our "inter-ethnic ties' * % non-White GB * Disadvantage 1' interaction term). We now see that this interaction is significant, strong and negative[86].

To best illustrate what these findings imply, we generate a series of *predicted* probabilities of 'disrespect for ethnic differences' across different concentrations of % non-White GB. However, we subdivide these predicted probabilities by: (1) whether an individual possesses 'bridging' ties; *and* (2) the level of community 'Disadvantage 1' (**Figure 2**).

---

84 Neither did we find a significant interaction between % non-White GB and 'Disadvantage 2'.

85 We also experimented with testing the interactive relationships with 'Disadvantage 2'. These are significant until we control for the interactive relationships of 'Disadvantage 1' at which point they disappear.

86 We also performed a likelihood-ratio test between **Model 3** and **Model 1** (Prob> chi2 = 0.000). Suggesting adding the three-way interaction term into the model provides a significantly better model fit than simply controlling for the 'bridging ties * diversity' interaction.

Figure 2 – Predicted % 'disagree/disagree strongly' that residents 'respect ethnic differences' across grouped-% non-White GB, by possession of 'inter-ethnic ties' and level of Community 'Disadvantage 1'; White British

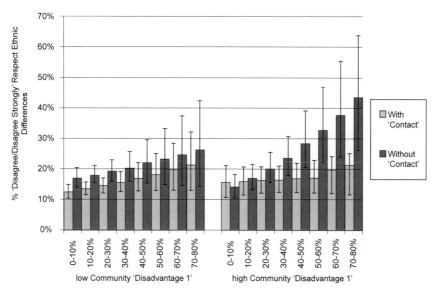

Notes: All other individual and community variables set to mean; 'low' disadvantage is approximately -1 SD below the mean; 'high' disadvantage is approximately +1 SD above the mean;

Previously, we demonstrated that increasing proportions of non-White GB in a community *do* undermine 'inter-ethnic attitudes' but *only* amongst White GB individuals *without* 'inter-ethnic ties'. The results from **Figure 2** show us that this was premature. We now see is that in communities with 'low' levels of 'Disadvantage 1', regardless of whether an individual has 'inter-ethnic ties' or not, increasing % non-White GB in a community is not associated with significantly greater reports of 'ethnic tensions'. In other words, in less disadvantaged communities, % non-White GB has no effect on 'inter-ethnic attitudes' (regardless of 'contact')[87]. Instead, we see living amongst increasing proportions of ethnic out-group only has a stronger negative effect in communities with 'high' levels of disadvantage i.e. it is only in more disadvantaged communities that the negative effect of % non-White GB is sufficiently 'charged' to undermine 'inter-ethnic relations'. However, within more disadvantaged communities, this negative effect is only present amongst individuals *without* 'inter-ethnic contact'; White GB individuals who do possess 'inter-ethnic ties' are essentially immune from the negative effects of increasing diversity.

---

87 We ran extensive robustness tests to explore whether the small increase in 'disrespect' (around 7%) at low (or medium) levels of 'Disadvantage 1'was significant but found it was not.

In sum, these results suggest there is no direct effect of % non-White GB in 'low' disadvantage communities i.e. the 'threat' hypothesis does not appear to operate in more affluent areas. However, it does appear as if 'threat' is in operation in more disadvantaged areas i.e. there is a direct negative effect of % non-White GB in disadvantaged communities. Yet, in such areas, possessing 'inter-ethnic ties' essentially renders individuals immune to this effect i.e. increasing % non-White GB has no negative effect on individuals in disadvantaged communities who *do* possess 'inter-ethnic ties'.

Discussion and Conclusion

The primary aim of this paper was to explore whether White British individuals, living in more diverse (i.e. lower % co-ethnic) communities report, on average, more positive or negative 'inter-ethnic attitudes'. Our analysis demonstrated that, on average, White British individuals living in communities with greater proportions of non-White British report slightly (but not significantly) more negative 'inter-ethnic attitudes'. Based on the 'contact'/'threat' theoretical framework, and assuming the same structure as much of the current literature in this area, we would have concluded that there is some evidence that increasing diversity stimulates 'threat', no evidence of the 'contact' hypothesis, but overall that neither theory is substantiated. In sum, we would simply assume there is little evidence that increasing diversity significantly effects 'inter-ethnic tensions' in the UK.

We posited, however, that simply studying differences in mean 'attitudes' across levels of diversity to assume either 'contact' or 'threat' may mask the fact that both processes could be in operation i.e. a 'Unified Theory' of diversity. Far from neither process being in operation, we actually find evidence that *both* the 'contact' and 'threat' hypotheses operate with increasing community diversity.

Our results demonstrate that White GB individuals living in communities with greater proportions of ethnic out-group are more likely to possess 'inter-ethnic ties', and individuals with such ties are more likely to report positive 'inter-ethnic attitudes' i.e. evidence for the 'contact' hypothesis. However, this 'inter-ethnic contact' doesn't just *mediate* (and thus suppress) diversity's true effect but actually *moderates* it. We find that amongst individuals who do *not* possess 'inter-ethnic ties', increasing proportions of non-White British has a significant negative effect on 'inter-ethnic attitudes' i.e. evidence for the 'threat' hypothesis. However, increasing proportions of % non-White British in a community has no effect amongst individuals *with* 'inter-ethnic ties'. Essentially, such 'ties' acts as a buffer, rendering individuals 'immune' to the potential negative effects of increasing diversity. Thus, the apparent zero-effectof diversity on *mean* reports of 'tolerance' we found at the outset masks the fact: it is not that diversity has no negative effect (as we might have mistakenly assumed based solely on the *means*), but that the sum of both the processes of 'threat' and 'contact' is that, on average, there is no significant difference between more diverse and more homogeneous communities.

Crucially, however, we actually find that higher levels of diversity only appear to have a negative effect in communities at higher levels of community disadvantage. Equally, it is therefore only in more disadvantaged communities that 'contact' *moderates* this effect. In other words, the potential 'threat' that increasing diversity may stimulate is much greater in more disadvantaged communities. This seems intuitively correct as we would expect that (the perception of) competition will be greater in areas where socio-economic resources are fewer (Oliver and Mendelberg 2000). However, the fact previous studies did not pick up such an interaction may be because it is concentrated amongst those *without* 'inter-ethnic ties'. We can summarise our proposed 'pathways of effect' diagrammatically for White British individuals (**Figure 3**: green symbolises a *moderating* effect).

Figure 3 - 'Key Pathways of Effect'

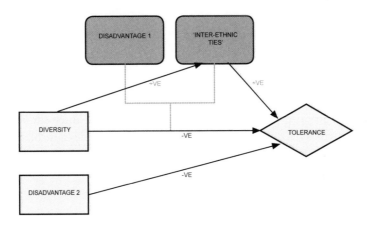

To summarise, we suggest that the apparent paradox between the 'contact' and 'threat' hypothesis can be reconciled by the understanding that *both* processes are likely in operation with increasing diversity. Based on this analysis, we suggest that the relationship between community diversity and *mean* levels of 'prejudice' (after full controls) is a function of: (1) the baseline level of 'inter-ethnic attitudes' in more homogeneous communities; (2) the strength of the direct negative effect of diversity on 'attitudes' (i.e. the effect of 'threat'); (3) the proportion of individuals with 'inter-ethnic' ties in diverse areas; and (4) the size of the *moderating* effect of 'contact' on diversity's effect. We would also add to this list, based on this current analysis at least: (5) the distribution of diverse communities across levels of disadvantage; and

(6) the strength of the moderating effect of community disadvantage on diversity. The sum of the relative levels of these pathways is what together produces the apparent zero-effect of diversity in the UK.

Changes in any one (or combination) of these pathways could lead to a different *mean* relationship between diversity and 'inter-ethnic attitudes'. However, crucially, this would not preclude the fact that both 'contact' and 'threat' are in operation. Potentially, such differences may account for some of the conflicting evidence for the 'threat' and 'contact' hypotheses in the current literature. It may be that in many of these studies (including those that found positive, negative, or no relationships), we would find that both 'threat' and 'contact' are in effect. Differences across *mean* levels of 'prejudice' may simply be down to different levels of pathways.

This paper also has wider implications for the current debate on diversity and 'social cohesion' in the UK. Firstly, we find that, on average, 'inter-ethnic tensions' are not significantly higher in more diverse communities. Secondly, however, it would be potentially dangerous to simply take this relationship to imply that increasing diversity cannot lead to growing tensions in communities as our evidence suggests it can. However, it is not simply greater proportions of ethnic out-group itself which appears to stimulate 'tensions', but diversity *coupled with* disadvantage. Crucially, there is nothing inherently problematic about different ethnic groups co-residing that appears to simulate 'tensions'. Furthermore, this research shows that the same force potentially dividing communities (i.e. increasing diversity) in more disadvantaged areas also simultaneously provides opportunities to *prevent* 'intolerance' from growing[88] (i.e. increasing rates of 'inter-ethnic contact'). Increasing diversity is unique in that it functions as a possible cause of, and solution to, negative 'inter-ethnic attitudes'.

---

88 As discussed, this assumes a causal relationship i.e. as diversity in an area increases individuals have an increasing likelihood of forming 'inter-ethnic' ties.

Bibliography

Allport, G. W. (1954) *The Nature of Prejudice*. Reading, MA: Addison-Wesley.

Bettelheim, B. and Janowitz, M. [1950] (1964) *Social Change and Prejudice*, New York: Macmillan Co.

Biggs M. and Knauss, S. (2011) 'Explaining Membership of the BNP: A Multilevel Analysis of Contact and Threat', in *European Sociological Review* (forthcoming)

Blalock Jr., H. M. (1967) *Toward a Theory of Minority-Group Relations*, New York: Capicorn Books.

Bledsoe, T., Welch, S., Sigelman, L. and Combs, M. (1995) 'Residential Context and Racial Solidarity among African Americans', in *American Journal of Political Science*, 39, pp.434-458.

Blumer, H. (1958) 'Race prejudice as a sense of group position', in *Pacific Sociological Review*, 1, pp.3-7.

Bobo, L. (1988) 'Group conflict, prejudice, and the paradox of contemporary racial attitudes', in P. A. Katz and D. A. Taylor (eds.), *Eliminating racism: Profiles in controversy*. New York: Plenum Press.

Bonacich, E. (1972) 'A Theory of Ethnic Antagonism: The Split Labour Market', in *American Sociological Review*, 37, pp.547-59.

Bowyer, B. (2009) 'The Contextual Determinants of Whites' Racial Attitudes in England', in *British Journal of Political Science*, 39, pp.559-86.

Brown, R. and Hewstone, M. (2005) 'An integrative theory of intergroup contact', in *Advances in Experimental Social Psychology*, 37, pp.255–343.

Carle A. C. (2009) 'Fitting multilevel models in complex survey data with design weights: recommendations', in *BMC Medical Research methodology*, 9, pp.49.

Cheong, P. H., Edwards, R., Goulbourne, H. and Solomos, J. (2007) 'Immigration, social cohesion and social capital: A critical review', in *Critical Social Policy*, 27, pp.24-49.

Dixon, J. C. (2006) 'The Ties That Bind and Those That Don't: Toward Reconciling Group Threat and Contact Theories of Prejudice', in *Social Forces*, 84, pp.2179–2204.

Dustmann, C. and Preston, I. (2001) 'Attitudes to ethnic minorities, ethnic context and location decisions', in *The Economic Journal*, 111, pp.353-373.

Esses, V. M., Jackson, L. M. and Armstrong, T. L. (1998) 'Intergroup competition and attitudes toward immigrants and immigration: An instrumental model of group conflict', in *Journal of Social Issues*, 54, pp.699-724.

Fromm, Eric (1941) *Escape from Freedom*, New York: Holt, Rinehart, & Winston.

Gaertner, S. L., Rust, M. C., Dovidio, J. F., Bachman, B. A. and Anastasio, P. A., (1996) 'The contact hypothesis: The Role of a common ingroup identity on reducing intergroup bias among majority and minority group members', in J. L. Nye and A. M. Brower (eds.), *What's social about social cognition?* Newbury Park: CA Sage.

Giles, M. W. and Buckner, M. (1993) 'David Duke and Black Threat: An Old Hypothesis Revisited', in *Journal of Politics*, 55, pp.702-713.

Gonzalez, K., Verkuyten, M., Weesie, J. and Poppe, E. (2008) 'Prejudice towards Muslims in the Netherlands: Testing integrated threat theory', in *British Journal of Social Psychology*, 47, pp.667–685.

Hewstone, M. (2003) 'Intergroup contact: Panacea for prejudice?', in *Psychologist*, 16, pp.352-355.

Hewstone, M. (2009) 'Living apart, living together? The role of intergroup contact in social integration', in *Proceedings of the British Academy*, 162, pp.243-300.

Lancee, B. and Dronkers, J. (2009) 'Ethnic diversity in neighbourhoods and individual trust of immigrants and natives: A replication of Putnam (2007) in a West-European Country', in M. Hooghe (ed.), *Social capital and social cohesion. Interdisciplinary theoretical perspectives*. Brussels: Royal Academy of Sciences.

Lancee, B. and Dronkers, J. (2010) 'Ethnic, religious and economic diversity in the neighbourhood: explaining quality of contact with neighbours, trust in the neighbourhood and inter-ethnic trust for immigrant and native residents', in *Journal of Ethnic and Migration Studies*, (forthcoming).

Laurence, J. and Heath, A. (2008) *Predictors of community cohesion: Multilevel modeling of the 2005 citizenship survey*, London: Department of Communities and Local Government.

Laurence, J. (2009) 'The effect of ethnic diversity and community disadvantage on social cohesion: a multi-level analysis of social capital and interethnic relations in UK communities', in *European Sociological Review*, 27, pp.70-89.

Messer, L., Kaufman, J., Laraia, B., O'Campo, P., Burke, J., Eyster, J., Holzman, C., Culhane, J. and Elo, I. (2006) 'The development of a standardized neighborhood deprivation index', in *Journal of Urban Health*, 83, pp.1041-62.

Modood, T. (2010) We need a multiculturalism of hope. *The Guardian*, 24th September.

Oliver, E. J. and Wong, J. S. (2003) 'Racial Context and Inter-Group Prejudice in a Multi-Ethnic Setting', in *American Journal of Political Science*, 47, pp.567-582.

Oliver, J. E. and Mendelberg, T. (2000) 'Reconsidering the environmental determinants of white racial attitudes', in *American Journal of Political Science*, 44, pp.574-589.

Patterson, E. B. (1991) 'Poverty, income inequality, and community crime rates', in *Criminology*, 29, pp.755-776.

Pettigrew, T. F. and Tropp, L. R. (2008) 'How does intergroup contact reduce prejudice? Meta-analytic tests of three mediators', in *European Journal of Social Psychology*, 38, pp.922–934.

Pettigrew, T. (1998) 'Intergroup Contact Theory', in *Annual Review of Psychology*, 49, pp.65-85.

Pettigrew, T.F. and Tropp, L.R. (2006) 'A meta-analytic test of intergroup contact theory', in *Journal of Personality and Social Psychology*, 90, pp.751–783.

Pettigrew, T.F. and Tropp, L.R. (2000) 'Does intergroup contact reduce prejudice: Recent meta-analytic findings' in S. Oskamp (ed.), *Reducing prejudice and discrimination*. Mahwah, NJ: Lawrence Erlbaum.

Putnam, R. D. (2007) '*E Pluribus Unum*: Diversity and Community in the Twenty-first Century The 2006 Johan Skytte Prize Lecture', in *Scandinavian Political Studies*, 30, pp.137-174.

Rothbart, M. and John, O.P. (1993) 'Immigration and race; recent trends', in B. Edmondston and J. S. Passel (eds.), in *Immigration and ethnicity: The integration of America's newest immigrants*. Washington D.C.: Urban Institute Press.

Sales, S. (1973)'Threat as a Factor in Authoritarianism: An Analysis of Archival Data', in *Journal of Personality and Social Psychology*, 28, pp.44-57.

Sampson, R. J. and Wilson, W. J. (1995) 'Toward a theory of race, crime, and urban inequality', in J. Hagan and R. D. Peterson (eds.), *Crime and Inequality*. Stanford, CA: Stanford University Press.

Schaefer, R. T. (1975), 'Regional differences in prejudice', in *Regional Studies*, 9, pp.1-14.

Schlueter, E. and Scheepers, P. (2010) 'The Relationship between Outgroup Size and Anti-Outgroup Attitudes: A Theoretical Synthesis & Empirical Test of Group Threat and Intergroup Contact Theory', in *Social Science Research*, 39, pp.285-295.

Schlueter, E. and Wagner, U. (2008) 'Regional Differences Matter: Examining the Dual Influence of the Regional Size of the Immigrant Population on Derogation of Immigrants in Europe', in *International Journal of Comparative Sociology*, 49, pp.153-173.

Sherif, M., Harvey, 0. J., White, J., Hood, W. and Sherif, C. W. (1961) *Intergroup conflict and cooperation: The robbers cave experiment*. Norman, OK: University Book Exchange.

Snijders, T. and Bosker, R. (1999) *Multilevel Analysis,* London: Sage

Stein, R., Post, S. and Rinden, A. L. (2000) 'Reconciling context and contact effects on racial attitudes', in *Political Research Quarterly*, 53, pp.285-303.

Stephan, W. G., Ybarra, O., Martinez, C. M., Schwarzwald, J. and Tur-Kaspa, M. (1998) 'Prejudice towards immigrants to Spain and Israel: An integrated threat theory analysis', in *Journal of Cross-Cultural Psychology*, 29, pp.559-576.

Stolle, D. Stuart, S. and Johnston, R. (2008) 'When Does Diversity Erode Trust? Neighborhood Diversity, Interpersonal Trust and the Mediating Effect of Social Interactions', in *Political Studies*, 56, pp.57-75.

Sturgis, P., Brunton-Smith, I., Read, S. and Allum, N. (2011)'Does Ethnic Diversity Erode Trust? Putnam's 'Hunkering Down' Thesis Reconsidered', in *British Journal of Political Science*, 41, pp.57-82.

Taylor, M. C. (1998) 'Local racial/ethnic proportions and white attitudes: numbers count', in *American Sociological Review*, 63, pp.56-78.

Welch, S., Sigelman, L., Bledsoe, T. and Combs, M. (2001) *Race and Place: Race Relations in an American City*, Cambridge: Cambridge University Press.

Zarate, M. A., Garcia, B., Garza, A. A. and Hitlan, R. T. (2004) 'Cultural threat and perceived realistic group conflict as dual predictors of prejudice', in *Journal of Experimental Social Psychology*, 40, pp.99-105.

Rants Against Multiculturalism Caught on Camera in Britain: Racism Without Races?

Fred Dervin[89]

Introduction

This is how Indian Nobel Prize winner Amartya Sen (2006 p.152) describes his arrival in Britain in 1953: 'I recollect (with some fondness, I must admit) how worried my first landlady at Cambridge was about the possibility that my skin color might come off in the bath (I had to assure her that my hue was agreeably sturdy and durable), and also the care with which she explained to me that writing was a special invention of Western civilisation ("the Bible did it")'. In the early 2000s such recollection, exemplifying a strongly ideological *us vs. them* discourse, would probably puzzle and upset most people – especially the reference to skin colour. Multiculturalism, as a political, educational and scientific approach to *diversities*, has generalized since the 1950s, in Britain and elsewhere, and brought about changes to the way the 'Other' is perceived and treated.

In the 1990s the French philosopher Etienne Balibar (1995) foretold an alternative form of differentialist and negative discourses in relation to multiculturalism - **racism without races**. This paper reflects on this prediction by examining a series of rants against multiculturalism in Britain in 2011/2012. Caught on camera, these rants were mediatized and circulated via the Internet (YouTube). Appearing day after day in autumn 2011 in the media, especially around one of the culprits, Emma West, these rants seem to have marked a new level of public aggression towards the 'Other'.

In this article, I am interested in two sets of questions:

1. What do these rants tell us about how multiculturalism is perceived today? What misconceptions about multiculturalism can be identified in these rants?

2. How did people react to the rants, i.e. onlookers in the videos but also

---

89 Fred Dervin is Professor of Multicultural Education at the University of Helsinki (Finland) and Director of the Education for Diversities (E4D) research group. He specialises in language and intercultural education, the sociology of multiculturalism and linguistics for intercultural communication and education. Dervin has published extensively on identity, the 'intercultural' and mobility/migration. His latest books: Politics of Interculturality (co-edited with Anne Lavanchy and AnahyGajardo, Newcastle: CSP, 2011) and Impostures Interculturelles (Paris: L'Harmattan, 2012). http://blogs.helsinki.fi/dervin/

the journalists reporting the rants, the newspaper readers, and politicians? How is multiculturalism defended and/or criticised?

Following Eric Fassin's suggestion as to how social scientists can tackle racism, I am trying to describe and explain rather than claim to find a clear-cut answer to what causes racism or rather than merely denounce the rants (2006 p.27).

Reassessing Multiculturalism and the Old and Tired Concept of Culture

Does the existence of a diversity of cultures, which might pass each other like ships in the night, count as a successful case of multiculturalism? Sen (2006 156)

In recent years, the idea of *clash of civilisations,* which was presented by political scientist Samuel P. Huntington (1996), has received a considerable amount of criticisms worldwide, especially in research milieus. For A. Appadurai (2006 pp.115-116), its main default is that it gives an image of multiculturalism where "The world appears as a large series of slowly moving cultural glaciers, with sharp contrasts at their boundaries and little variety within". He adds that by doing so, thinkers like Huntington remove "history" and "culture" to the analytical box and leave geography as the only "walking stick" to rely on (2006 p.164). Appadurai's critique seems to be shared by many thinkers and researchers who are interested in multiculturalism. Yet there seems to remain many "misunderstandings" and "misconceptions" about the notion.

The first aspect is related to "variety within". Anthropologist N. P. Pieterse reminds us that well before the accelerated multiculturalism of the last decades, European countries, amongst others, combined 'people that have been conventionally amalgamated under a political heading (such as Celts, Franks, and others in "France")' (2004 p.33). He concludes therefore that "national identities are *mélange* identities". For Laplantine and Nouss (1977 p.21) national "purity" has no anthropological value and is contradictory to the *mélange* history of Europe – and beyond!

In relation to how multiculturalism is conceptualised, one of the remaining problematic concepts -which composes the word- is culture. According to many scholars in different fields, the concept is "introverted" (Pieterse 2004 p.82), potentially dangerous and it easily leads to "infinite blunders" (Debray 2007 p.27). Following the bomb attacks in London in 2005, political and gender theorist Anne Phillips proposed to consider multiculturalism "without culture" (2007). She claims that 'we should be far more wary about promoting the notion of people as products of their culture' (2007 p.67) as it makes the concept too stable and fixed. In a later publication, *Culture and Gender* (2010), Phillips argues that this 'flawed' use and understanding of culture 'misrepresents what is frequently a contested activity' (ibid. 5). Another important point that she makes is that culture can serve as a way of "walling" certain people and groups and thus discriminating against them and not allowing them to take part in societal interactions. Finally culture is often called upon before non- and/or misunderstandings (Phillips 2007 p.65).

It also appears that the notion of hybridity (or *mélange*) hasn't been taken seriously in research on multiculturalism. Pieterse (2001 p.221) asserts that the only occasion during which the notion is used is to highlight "superficial confetti culture and glosses over deep cleavages that exist on the ground". Hybridity from inside and from outside is often ignored in multiculturalism most probably because of "the fetishism of boundaries that has marked much of history", Pieterse argues (ibid.). For R. Brubaker (2004 p.9) this all leads to a 'multichrome mosaic of monochrome ethnic, racial, or cultural blocks'.

The hybridity argument is also shared by Amartya Sen (amongst others) in his book *Identity and Violence* (2006), who criticizes "high theory" for contributing to the 'boxing' of individuals. The economist and philosopher reminds us that individuals are influenced by many different elements in their "reasoning" and that 'we need not lose our ability to consider other ways of reasoning just because we identify with, and have been influenced by membership in a particular group' (ibid. p. 34-35). What Sen worries about is the reduction of "many-sided human beings into one dimension" (ibid. p.12), which has been a tendency in many strands of research on multiculturalism (cf. Dervin 2011). If we go back to Anne Phillips, this sole dimension is often equated to people's "culture": "national culture" for "Westerners", something else for the rest (Amselle 2010).

Racism Without Races?

In their recent book entitled *The Crises of Multiculturalism: Racism in a Neoliberal Age*, Lentin&Titley (2011) assert that we are now witnessing post-racial multiculturalism. By doing so, they agree entirely with what Balibar in the 1990s had envisioned (cf. introduction). For Lentin and Titley (ibid.), the notion of culture, used in a solid and fixed manner (cf. culturism/culturalism, Dervin 2012), is increasingly used in attacks on multiculturalism and thus could be substituting the concept of race – which has been central in anti-racist language – in some parts of the world. They also maintain that the concept of race could be 'hidden' behind these discourses of culture (ibid.), and the "boundary maintenance" that goes with them (Barth 1969). As such many studies – starting in anthropology – have showed how culture is used to create, strengthen and maintain boundaries and borders 'through the enactment of contrasts with others' (Eriksen 1995 p.435).

Going back to Phillips' book *Culture and Gender* (2010), the scholar demonstrates clearly how cultural difference is used as a way of establishing hierarchies between people: 'There are said to be 'better' and 'worse', 'more advanced' and 'more backward' cultures' (2010 p.20). In her earlier book (2007 p.82), the case of cultural defense in legal matters according to which a person's cultural background can provide an important explanation as to why they committed a crime is used to show how so-called 'cultural traditions' can justify crimes against women. This is 'practiced' in the USA, Canada and the UK. The French anthropologist Amselle (2010 p.79) also notes that in many countries decision-makers often determine which culture or language suits 'minorities' and wonders if this does not represent a way of controlling them and making sure that they do not find an 'important place' in society.

So there seems to be a strong agreement amongst many researchers that culture is a 'contemporary avatar' of race and racism (Fassin 2006 p.37). Yet this is not the only element of post-racial multiculturalism. As such other forms of essentialisation can serve the same purpose: language (Kumaravadivelu 2008), localism (Pieterse 2004), attitudes to education (Abdallah-Pretceille 1986) and dichotomies such as East-West. A strong reaction to methodological nationalism (i.e. the nation as the sole explanation to individual's behaviours, thoughts, values, etc.) is felt in the social sciences, instead, a division of the world in two clear-cut regions (the West and the East) seems to be taking over in some research contexts. However as Sen (2006 p.129) puts it: 'given the cultural and intellectual interconnections in world history, the question of what is "western" and what is not would be hard to decide'.

Data and Methodology

In this paper, I am interested in testing the ideas developed in the previous sections in relation to rants against multiculturalism in British public transporting 2011/2012. I am analysing four videos but also newspapers articles and comments left by viewers on YouTube. All of the videos were secretly or openly filmed by onlookers (other passengers). The rants analysed here (4) were reported for the first time in the British newspaper *The Daily Mail* on these dates:

> 29th Nov. 2011 - a woman sitting on a tram between Croydon and Wimbledon.
>
> 30th Nov. 2011 - a woman sitting on a train between London and Manchester.
>
> 1st Dec. 2011 - a woman sitting on a London underground tube carriage.
>
> 6th February 2012 - a woman sitting on a London underground tube carriage.

All the articles on *the Daily Mail* website contain the videos of the rants. These videos show exclusively female renters. A quick search in YouTube retrieved several other rants against multiculturalism featuring men but also 'minorities' (e.g. an "Asian" vs. a "Black" lady). It is impossible to give the actual dates of the rants except for the 6.2. Rant which is believed to have been filmed on January 23 2012 according to the Daily Mail. The video of the first rant on the underground was uploaded on YouTube by a friend of the victim in June 2011 (*Daily Mail* 1.12.2011). The duration of the videos varies between 2 to nearly 10 minutes. We need to bear in mind that parts of the rants are missing as e.g. 'my friend only realised this was worth filming after about 10 minutes of her rant' (a victim's friend).

In order to analyse the data, I use a linguistic form of discourse analysis which derives directly from linguistic approaches: utterance theory (inspired by philosophy of language) and dialogism (inspired by Bakhtin's work). Utterance theory is interested in how language relates to context and its users but also how discourse is constructed through intersubjectivity (Marnette 2005 p.19). By analysing the use of various pronouns, adjectives, adverbs but also verbs, one can examine how one individual constructs ideas with and through others. Dialogism works hand in hand with utterance theory as it allows researchers to identify the various explicit or implicit voices that compose discourse (Hermans 2004). These voices are represented by so-called "in/direct speech" (a quote, words borrowed from other people, etc.). It is through the analysis of utterances and dialogism that one can look below the surface level of discourse and make contradictions, identifications and instabilities emerge. According to Lakoff (1990 p.1), 'language is politics, politics assigns power, power governs how people talk and how they are understood'. The data I propose to analyse represents archetypes of unbalanced situations: all the female ranters are white and they are addressing people who are presented as 'minorities'.

Racist Rants and/or Rants Against Multiculturalism?

Media Treatment of the Rants: Constructing Reactions Against Multiculturalism

Let us start with the articles reporting the rants. My first interest is in the titles of the articles:

'You're not British because you're black': Woman charged with racially aggravated harassment after vile rant aboard tram (29.11)

'You're in my country now, talk my language': Second woman filmed 'hurling vile racist abuse' (30.11)

'BNP, that's me, now f*** off': Vile race rant No.3 caught on camera as ANOTHER woman hurls abuse on a train (1.12)

Woman filmed hurling racist abuse at Tube passengers in yet ANOTHER video of a vile rant on London transport (6.2.)

We notice that the four articles use the words "racist" and "racially" to describe the contents of the videos. Also the fact that the ranter is a woman in each case is mentioned (note the capitalisation of *another* in articles 3 & 4). In three of the articles the direct voices of the ranters are heard: "you're not British because you're black", "you're in my country, now talk my language" and "BNP (British National Party), that's me, now f*** off". The first quote refers to skin colour, the second one to language while the third one refers to afar-right British party, known for its anti-immigration ideas.

What did the women do and who are the victims? It is interesting to see that, in the way the rants are reported, the same actions took place across the rants: "hurling racist abuse", "making xenophobic insults" and "jabbing fingers at the victims". Note that **racist abuse** and **xenophobic insults** seem to be used interchangeably by the journalists. In terms of who is verbally attacked, it is also interesting to notice that all the victims are men. Besides some of them appear to be "foreigners" (Russians, "Middle eastern men" and Asian passengers). In the Emma West video the target is a group of passengers but no mention of nationality is made. The problem with these classifications is that we are not sure if the victims are all foreigners or British. At least in two of the videos some of the attacked people insist that they are themselves "British".

While reading the articles, it often appears unclear who posted the rants on YouTube (use of the passive voice: "has been posted online"), except for two of the videos (29.11 and 1.12). For the 1.12 video the newspaper lets "a friend of the victim" nicknamed Optimess Prime talk: "I am posting this video to show how this woman *racially* abused my friend on the London Underground during a busy period (…) the reason as to why she became agitated is because my friend was having a quiet conversation with his friend in Russian and she was sitting in front of them". The event is also labeled 'racial' by the friend and he gives the reason why she started ranting: the use of a foreign language.

Now let's turn to the direct voices that are reported by the newspaper in the four articles. Few direct voices are heard from the other passengers ('Keep your mouth shut') and the victims ('Welcome to London!'). One journalist includes the voice of one YouTube viewer who says: 'As a white British male, I feel disgusted to even be associated with this woman by my race and nationality'. In the four articles around 20 direct quotes from the ranters are inserted or repeated. The following table classifies these quotes in terms of what difference(s) they claim between the ranter and the 'Other' and in terms of argument(s) against multiculturalism:

Difference	Quote
Language	- "Learn the lingo and then think about coming back you ******* ┌*****" - "You're in my country now, talk my language. Don't f****** talk your ****, talk my language. You ****, ****"
Nationality/origins	- "None of you are ****ing English. Get back to your own country. Sort your own countries, don't come and do mine" - "where do you come from? F****** like, f****** all over the world"
Skin colour	- (At one point she claims passengers in the carriage are) "****ing burnt people" - "You're not British because you're black"

Argument against	Quote
Illegality	- "I'd like to know if any of you are f****** illegal, I'm sure 30 per cent of you are. It's taking the f****** p***" - "I hope they f****** catch up with you and shove you off" - "This is what we've got to put up with… that's what we don't like about you people. I'll show you what kind of government lets people like you in" - "I shall punch you in the f****** face. Ninety per cent of you are f****** illegal. I wouldn't mind if you loved our country"
Economy	- "We have got enough of you ******* muppets in our country, stealing out jobs, ******* taking the English jobs" - "Yeah, welcome to London, get all the benefits, get everything free. Yeah loser, that's the only reason you are here" - "As long as you're f****** working, and not claiming benefits"

Three 'canonical' differences are mentioned by the ranters: language, nationality and skin colour. Apart from the two references to skin colour, no mention of specific countries, languages or religions was identified in the reported voices. The targets thus appear to include people from "all over the world". Interestingly, although the concept of culture has been much discussed in scholarship on multiculturalism, the word doesn't appear a single time. The arguments against multiculturalism are rather classical (*stealing our jobs, claiming benefits*).

The article published on 29.11 reproduces a transcript of Emma West's rants. After having compared what the journalist calls "the horrific transcript" with the video, it is interesting to see that the ranters' interlocutors are absent from the transcription. Let me take two excerpts that do not appear in the article. In the first one, while the ranter is arguing with a woman ("You ain't ****ing British. **** off. You're black You ain't British, you're black"), another woman intervenes and says:

> Will you calm down because you're ****ing waking up my baby up! So do you wanna shut your mouth? Look shhhh. And now you're waking my baby up and I am English what have you got to say to me? ****all! Now shut your mouth!

Interestingly, the white woman intervenes for herself ("I am English what have you got to say to me?") but not to defend the passengers who are being abused.

In the next excerpt, which was deleted from the transcription, the ranter interacts aggressively with another passenger. She has just asked the people around her to "Go back to where you come from, go back to ****ing Nicaragua or where ever you come from". The other passenger says:

> If we don't come here you guys don't want to work
> You guys don't want to work. We have to do the work for you. Go and work!

The use of the pronoun "we" here serves the same purpose as in the ranter's use of *we/our*: to place a boundary between in-groups and out-groups. Interestingly, the same woman repeats several times that she is British when the ranter questions who she is ("you're not British! You're black!"), thus including herself in the "we" that she claims doesn't want to work.

Transcriptions of the Rants and Comments Left by Viewers: Unstable and Multifaceted Racism

This section concentrates on the rants as they appear in the videos posted on Youtube. Most of the videos start with an aggressive tone: two about language ("You're in my country now talk my language talk my language ****"; "Learn the linguo and think about coming back you ****ing retard don't ****ing wind me up"); one about origins ("What has this country come to? A load of black people and a load of ****ing Polish. A load of ****ing in"). The fourth one begins with a justification as to why the woman is ranting: "She pushed me she ****ing pushed me". Based on the video it is impossible to say who pushed who and how the argument started.

In terms of interaction, the videos differ amply. Two of them contain violent arguments between the ranter and the man who is filming her and the ranter and a large group of passengers. In the remaining videos the ranters hurl insults at a small group of passengers (Russians and Middle eastern men) but none of them really respond to them. The argument between the ranter and the man who is filming on the underground is based on origins. The ranter is surrounded by two "Asian" men (according to the *Daily Mail*) and we assume that the person who is filming is acquainted with them. The ranter says that she is British but that she lives in the "United Nations". Following this revelation, they have the following discussion about origins:

> Man: You know you have no right to ask me if I am British none of your business
> Ranter: But you're asking me but I am not allowed to ask you
> Man: It's not your country anyway
> Ranter: Yeah we've been overtaken by people like you.

As we shall see later on, the ranter's last argument was identified in most rants. In the video about the Middle Eastern men being harassed because they speak Arabic, a few passengers try to intervene. They are met with the following: "I don't even want to hear you **** off lady you don't even know what you are talking about **** off".

As asserted earlier on, what is surprising about the rants is the similarities in terms of settings but also arguments used against multiculturalism. The question of origins is found in all the rants: "Where do you come from?"; "You ain't English. No, you ain't English either. You ain't English. None of you's ****ing English"; "Go back to where you come from, go back to ****ing Nicaragua or where ever you come from". Another argument is that of the number of immigrants in Britain is overwhelming for her: "Yeah we've been overtaken by people like you"; "this is my British country until they/we let you lot come over" (note the interesting use of "my" in this quote). Finally, the aspect of language was found in all the rants: "You're in my country now talk my language talk my language". Again the use of the first person possessive pronoun says a lot about the *us vs. them* game taking place in the rants (Eriksen 1995).

To finish with, I would like to examine a few comments that were left on YouTube with the videos. Of course we need to be careful with such comments, as they are anonymous and often quite playful. Yet I believe that they can provide us with interesting features of discourses on multiculturalism. Based on a discourse analysis of the comments, I retain five types of comments: racist, anti-racist, (neo-) colonizing, comments about language and meta-analysis of the rants. Let us start with the racist comments. Many of the racist comments defend the ranters (e.g. "luv this lady cause she is standing up and speaking her mind"). These comments range from a mere "White power" to a long racist comment about the Blacks, Muslims and Jews. Interestingly the author of the latter claims that his comment is not racist: "Return them back to their native country, and everyone is happy! Well this is not a racist comment, it's only not acceptable, letting other people coming to your country, for what? So they can destroy it, stealing your stuff? Etc.".

The second element found in the comments counterbalance these comments – even though they are less frequent. Two of these comments stand out. The first one is a reply to the viewer who claims that his racist comment is not racist: "well it kind of is a racist comment, when you say "black people" you make out that all black people aren't English in which case some have family trees that date back to 200 years ago you're also making out that all black people steal and destroy other people's property for argument's sake, what if a black man has a family and has a paying career of 35 thousand pounds per year, what do they do, just get up and leave? Black are just like all other people". The latter part of the comment illustrates well a constructionist approach to multiculturalism (cf. section 1). The other comment, which opposes the ranter's arguments, seems to have been posted by a foreigner who works in the UK (s/he writes: "IM MOVING BACK TO ****ING POLAND"). The argument s/he uses is very close to that of the passenger on the tram whose words were not reproduced in the Daily Mail: "If she wanna do something about the benefits then she should tell all the British **** to get their assess to work and educate themselves so that they get the qualification they like". By doing so s/he also essentialises British people. Besides racist and anti-racist comments, many viewers include references to British (neo) colonisation in what they have to say. References to history are many: "The Brits were not upset when they took over half the world and made people work for them, now were they?"; "The reason we are here lady is because you guys were in my country for 200 years. I am just helping return the favour!" Other comments link history and today's situation: "Didn't U.K. robbed countless wealth from them in colonial age? The world's largest bloodsucker left south Asia extremely under-developed, and then they can play hypocritical high class and moral in front of the world". This viewer ends her/his comment with 'Yeah, perfect Olympic Ads...'

As we have seen throughout the article, language is an omnipresent argument against multiculturalism. This is also reflected in the comments with people, on the one hand, supporting the idea that one should learn the local language ("I don't like her way of talking but I think also that if I decided to move to another country *I have to respect this new country* and at least try to learn there *language...*") and, on the other, people "throwing back" at British people the fact that they don't speak any other language than English ("we go to Spain and Italy on holidays we don't speak Italian or Spanish when we are there do we?"). Another discussion in relation to language revolves around the right to speak a foreign language in private circumstance: "People have the right to speak whatever language they want in private conversations, which is what it was when they were on the train". Yet this viewer argues that "It's a different matter if they're at work, there they should speak the native language with co-workers, customers, etc."

I have labeled the final type of comments "meta-analysis of the rants". In a way what some of the viewers do is that they analyse the rants by identifying the contradictions, the ideology behind the arguments used by the ranters, and the situations. The first meta-analysis concerns contradictions in the ranter's line of argument: "funny how they are taking all the English jobs yet they are only here for the benefits can't have it both ways stupid ****". The next one touches upon typical aspects of anti-multiculturalism: "love how she throws in the benefit argument at the end". Finally one viewer wonders about the sociolinguistic similarities between the ranters: "why do these woman all sound the same?! They all come from the same council estate or something?"

Conclusion

This article was an attempt to describe and explain violent rants against multiculturalism in Britain that had been discussed heavily in the media. My starting point was the claim that many societies are now experiencing post-racial multiculturalism and that this has an influence on discourses on racism (Balibar 1995; Lentin&Titley 2011). In reviewing and reassessing multiculturalism it became clear that the concept of *culture* was central in this new phenomenon – rather than **race.**

The data that I have analysed seem to corroborate the idea of post-racial racism. I could identify only one reference to "race" in the videos but many references to language skills, nationality and the legal status of immigrants. This reference derives from a confusion between nationality ("You ain't British!") and skin colour ("you're black!"). Of course, we need to bear in mind that many "racist with race" thoughts might also be hiding behind the omnipresent question "where are you from?" in the rants. The newspaper articles and the comments left on YouTube tended to brand the rants as **racist** – even though race was rarely mentioned in the criticisms of the ranters. As we saw, another 'hidden' confusion was contained in the remark made several times by of one of the attacked persons in one of the videos about immigrants having come to Britain to do the work that "English people" do not want to do – even though she kept repeating that she was British herself.

It thus appears that the concept of racism has taken on a different meaning in our times of accelerated multiculturalism. Yet the 2011/2012 rants do not confirm the idea that culture is central in discourses on multiculturalism. Neither was the argument of non-/mis-understanding across "cultures" present. Boundaries and borders between the ranters and their victims rely on such aspects as nationality, origins and language. In a way all these elements represent archetypical components of the Modern Era as Michel Maffesoli (2010) or Zygmunt Bauman (2004) have described them in opposition to Postmodernity or Liquid Modernity. These rants appear to be remnants of these eras; a seemingly apparent inability to cope with multiple identities, hybridity and confusion as to who is "within" and "outside". They also symbolise strong power relations between the so-called "native" and the "minorities". Interestingly too is the fact that religion was not mentioned as single time, even though it has been used heavily as a counter-argument against multiculturalism, especially in relation to the Muslim faith.

To conclude I would like to comment on the difficulties faced by researchers when they work on such events. As such it was very challenging to describe and analyse the 'actors' in the videos. The discourses or images contained do not allow identifying them and I feared that I might fall into the same trap as the ranters as a white scholar if I put a label on who they are. For example, some passengers spoke in a strong accent in English but this can't allow us to classify them as foreigners (they might have a British passport, they might have been born in Britain). The same goes for the 'Asian looking' passengers. It was in fact easier to examine how the newspapers qualified them and to deconstruct their discourses. This is an important message about the ethics contained in researching racism and multiculturalism (Fassin 2006).

Bibliography

Abdallah-Pretceille, M. (1986) *Versunepédagogieinterculturelle*, Paris: PUF.

Amselle, J., L. (2010) *Rétrovolutions*, Paris: Stock.

Appadurai, A. (2006) *Fear of Small Numbers: An Essay on the Geography of Anger*, Duke University Press.

Balibar, E. (1991) 'Is there a neo-racism?' in E. Balibar andI. Wallerstein (eds.), *Race, Nation, Class*, London: Verso, pp.17–28.

Barth, F. (1969) 'Introduction', in F. Barth (ed.), *Ethnic Groups and Boundaries: The Social Organization of Culture Difference*, London: George Allen &Unwin, pp.9–38.

Bauman, Z. (2004) *Identity*, Cambridge: Polity.

Brubaker, R. (2004) *Ethnicity Without Groups*, Harvard: Harvard University Press.

Debray, R. (2007) *Un mythecontemporain: le dialogue des civilisations*, Paris: CNRS.

Dervin, F. (2011) 'A plea for change in research on intercultural discourses: A 'liquid' approach to the study of the acculturation of Chinese students' in *Journal of Multicultural Discourses*, 6(1), pp.37–52.

Dervin, F. (2012) *Impostures interculturelles*, Paris: L'Harmattan.

Eriksen, T. H. (1995) 'We and Us: two modes of group identification', in *Journal of Peace Research*, 32 (4), pp.427–436.

Fassin, D. (2006) 'Nommer, interpreter. Le senscommun de la question raciale' in D. Fassin and E.Fassin (eds.), *De la question sociale à la question raciale*, Paris, La Découverte, pp.27–43.

Hermans, H. J. M. (2004) 'Introduction: the dialogical self in a global and digital age', in *Identity*, 4(4), pp.297–320.

Huntington, S. P. (1996) *The Clash of Civilizations and the Remaking of World Order*, New York: Simon & Schuster.

Kumaravadivelu, K. (2008) *Cultural Globalization and Language Education*, Yale University Press.

Lakoff, R. (1990) *Talking Power*, NY: Basic Books.

Laplantine, F. andNouss, A. (1977) *Le métissage*, Paris: Flammarion.

Lentin, A. andTitley, G. (2011) *The Crises of Multiculturalism: Racism in a Neoliberal Age*, NY: Zed Books.

Maffesoli, M. (2010) *Le temps revient, forms élémentaires de la postmodernité*, Paris: DDB.

Marnette, S. (2005) *Speech and Thought Presentation in French: Concept and Strategies*, Amsterdam: Benjamins.

Phillips, A. (2007) *Multiculturalism without Culture*, Oxford: OUP.

Phillips, A. (2010) *Culture and Gender*, Cambridge: Polity.

Pieterse, N. P. (2001) 'Hybridity, So What? The Anti-Hybridity Backlash and the Riddles of Recognition', in *Theory, Culture and Society*, 18(2–3), pp.219–245.

Pieterse, N. P. (2004) *Globalization and culture: Global mélange*, Lanham, MD: Rowman and Littlefield.

Sen, A. (2006) *Violence and Identity*, New Delhi: Penguins.

Faith in the Suburb: Discourses of Identity and Extremism in the Royal Borough of Kingston upon Thames, UK

Rupa Huq[90]

Introduction

Popular wisdom has long held that religion is in decline in the western world with the advance post-enlightenment rationalisation (Bruce 2003) yet the story of Britain's move to a modern multicultural society is underscored by its multi-faith character with religious practices having played a key role in diasporic identity formation. Britain's capacity to accommodate cultures is a cornerstone of the diversification it has undergone since the twentieth century and as it has gone from having one dominant Christian denomination in faith terms to its current patchwork of all faiths and none. It is an inescapable fact that religion has been an important aspect of most major migrant groups that has helped to both define and solidify them. There is a need to consider faith groups in wider (sub) urban, national as well as trans-national networks of social organisation. Perhaps the religion that this applies most clearly to is Islam with its concept of global umma connecting Muslims across the world in sometimes political demands. Even before the domestic instances of terrorism in 2005 that became known as 7/7 it was widely perceived that Britain's Muslims were subject to "unprecedented scrutiny and examination" (Choudhury 2002 p.71) following the September 11th US terrorist attacks. In this sense British Muslims face unprecedented civic and spiritual challenges. This chapter focuses on the affluent south west borough of Kingston upon Thames using qualitative research findings resulting from some 60 interviews conducted by a team of three upon a purposive sample there from 2008-10 funded by the UK government Preventing Violent Extremism programme looking at Muslim lives in the borough. Transcript material covers Muslim identities and fundamentalism before making conclusions about manifestations of Islam is in an outer-London borough.

Kingston Case Study

Kingston, or to give it its full legal-administrative title the Royal Borough of Kingston upon Thames (RBK), is often seen as an archetypally suburban borough

---

90 Rupa Huq is Senior Lecturer in Sociology at Kingston University. She is author of (2006) Beyond Subculture: pop, youth and identity in a postcolonial world, Routledge, Oxon. Her next book will be On the Edge: reconsidering suburbia (2012), Lawrence and Wishart, London.

as seen in classic television sitcom "The Good Life", famously set in its Surbiton district. It is then reliant on the city of London for jobs etc but is also distinct from it with a primarily residential character. The mere mention of Kingston evokes suburban associations in both geographic literal spatial and attitudinal/cultural senses. Yet the 2011 Census results are likely to show that demographically Kingston now numbers significant minority populations of Tamil, South Korean and Muslim backgrounds unsettling the key presumption of suburbia in classical academic sources as ethnically homogenous unlike the more diverse mix that is to be found in the inner city. Kingston with its reputation for being a peaceable suburban London borough is not usually automatically associated with being a hotbed of Islamic or indeed any type of extremism, as borne out by the Place Survey for London Councils (Ipsos Mori 2009) investigating quality of life and local public services across all the 33 London Boroughs. 83% in Kingston replied that in their local area people of different backgrounds got along well together, 85.3% general satisfaction recorded with area. But Kingston came lowest of all boroughs of people wishing to be more involved in local-decision-making. This suggests a stable population and self-contained locality.

Most existing published research into Islamism and youth disengagement have been conducted in more obviously "ethnic" areas eg the "pathfinder" borough of Hounslow (Cantle 2007). Nonetheless many high profile foiled terror plots in recent years have taken place at Kingston Crown court, due in part to its comparatively new building and proximity to the A3 arterial road for fast access to central London. Whist frequently the US terrorist attacks of 9-11 are seen as pivotal in shaping Islamic diaspora identity in the west (Werbner 2002) our research took place almost a decade later making the incident beyond younger respondents recollection. Attitudes to the Government's Preventing Violent Extremism policy initiative and the roots of radicalism were covered in most detail by a Kingston-raised former extremist as outlined below.

Suburban Settlement, Muslims and the Mosque

Classic theories of the suburb in both the UK and US construct it as a safe haven away from undesirable influences which include ethnic minorities and multiple deprivations. Yet present-day Kingston is now as a first destination site eg amongst South Koreans working for large international companies who have settled in the borough with no prior UK migration history. This Bangladeshi postgraduate student interviewee who moved from east London with his family in the 1980s described how the restaurant trade had been a motivating factor. There was a perception voiced that Bangladeshis in Kingston and its environs were those who had "made it" rather than the more down at heel counterparts in the multiple-deprivation blight districts such as Tower Hamlets.

There weren't very many [Bangladeshi] families when I was very young – maybe 4 or 5. While I was growing up there were more and more Bengali families came because Surrey is a goldmine for Bangladeshi restaurants and they all do really well because it's a wealthy county and they all like Indian food so a lot of families started emerging I'd say from mid 90s onwards there was this kind of rush, they'd say, it's too far from east London... well we work in Surrey, we have a business in Surrey, we might as well move there so people actually moved out from East London and set up businesses in Byfleet, Weybridge, Tadworth, Epsom, places like that... Bengalis in Epsom are actually growing to a higher more accelerated level than Bengalis in Kingston but the number of Muslims in Kingston has significantly increased since when I was young.

Another interviewee, a Bangladeshi aged 21 who was an undergraduate at Imperial College praised Kingston for being ethnically mixed but recognised that there was a degree of conscious or subconscious segregation at play in choice of residential district. When asked if the stereotype of Kingston as white leafy suburban borough was still valid he answered:

Erm well now I think it is but the values, the white leafy values are still around as you seem to have all the white people live in a certain area, and all the Asians and Africans they all to seem to live in an area like you have all the Koreans live in New Malden, all the Sri Lankans live in Coombe and everywhere, all the Africans seem to be living in Cambridge estate. I don't know if it's a financial thing or cultural thing then you have all the English people tend to be living Kingston Hill or nearer town, the Charter Quay development and everything so obviously there are the different sectors but people you know they cope with it, there's no you know difference or resistance or anything.

Kingston Mosque or masjid is a mainstream Sunni Mosque. Even though it is not necessarily representative of all Kingston Muslims many of our interviewees in official positions referred us to the mosque. The committee member we spoke to was at pains to stress its inclusive nature:

I stood down as chair of the mosque, the vice chair is a black man and do you know the number of Punjabis who've said 'why have you got a black chairman?' and yet he's far more scholarly than I am. He knows the Qur'an far better than I do, prays 5 times a day and all that, except a Somali doesn't have a big beard, his hair doesn't grow. It never grows; it's just a growth. On Eid we have a black brown and white Imam, did you know that?

Some interviewees perceived it to be a 'Pakistani' mosque while others felt more comfortable to pray at home or attend events at Regents Park, the central London mosque. Kingston Mosque has a good relationship with the local authority and police and is seen by officialdom as encouraging diversity and thus as an important tool in the engagement process but it is only the tip of the iceberg in terms of the borough's Islamic population. Also present in Kingston are Ahmadiyya Muslims who follow different prayer rituals and suffer long term experience of not being accepted as an Islamic faith by more mainstream Muslims to the point that they are persecuted in other countries. The Ahmadiyya Mosque is in the neighbouring south London borough of Merton. Cultural differences raise the difficulties of the concept of a single demarcated Muslim community in Kingston or indeed anywhere. This mosque committee member saw the rural/urban divide as the most important:

> The majority who came here from the 60s, 70s came here from rural areas of Pakistan and Bangladesh. If they came from a big city say Bombay it would have been different... if they come from rural lands, how do they cope with completely different structures?

Yet we now have a second and third generation - the children and grandchildren of these original pioneering first generation settlers that outnumbers them. The majority of Muslims in the UK are now British-born with English as their first language. This necessitates the asking of new questions such as managing the multicultural settlement of the post-colonial settlement rather than immigration per se which is a more pressing concern for settled populations. When during the 2010 General Election campaign Gordon Brown was on the receiving end of a voter in Rochdale questioning what he was doing on immigration (the Mrs Duffy incident) it was migrants from the post-2004 EU accession countries that was referred to not people of the new Commonwealth, immigration itself is becoming a less – to use the old cliché – 'black and white issue' with categories such as the UK Polish migrants who are often collapsed in 'other EU' for statistical purposes as they are legitimately entitled under freedom of movement to work with the same entitlements and benefits as the UK population. Other newer groups include the Somalis who are of Muslim backgrounds.

Politicisation of Islam

Recent years have witnessed much debate around the headscarf eg government minister Jack Straw calling it a barrier to communication. Most female participants we questioned on the topic reported increased experience of discrimination when wearing a headscarf.

> You get comments and name-calling, especially when you've got your hijab on it and I live in Surbiton where its predominantly English people, I think I am the only one with the headscarf sticking out there. (Focus Group December 2009)

Another time was on the bus. I was just doing my A-levels. I wore the Jilbab for two and a half years and this lady looked at me and said, in a very patronising way "Are you not hot, wearing that?" And I said "No I'm not, but even if I was it's something for me to be bothered about and for you to just ignore, you just mind your own business." And to be honest the Jilbab, it's like this light material. And just you get this assumption that I'm being forced to suffocate myself in the way I dress. And I said "no I'm not sweating. There's nothing wrong with me." And she said "oh god, I don't know how you put up with it. Luckily it was my stop, so I got off. (Focus Group, November 2009)

Beard-wearing males (Muslim sand non-Muslim) reported similar instances of hostility.

Instances of bodies such as the Jewish Board of Deputies, Hindu Forum of Britain and the Muslim Council of Britain being consulted by governments underline how faith can intersect with social and political incorporation. On a more personal-individual note, we did hear remarks from participants that their experience of discrimination or racism had increased since 9/11 (eg reports of "dirty looks" in the immediate aftermath of the events referred to by one hijab wearing woman), younger interviewees had no real memory of these events that occurred a decade ago. Many participants also reported a qualitative change in the type of racism they were experiencing. Thus, whereas beforehand, their experience of racism tended to be focused on their ethnicity, it was now quite clearly focused on religion and its perceived association with terrorism.

E: I think before 9-11 we were all Asian yeah, now it's just them or us.

U: Like that Sikh guy who's joined the BNP; they're united by the common hatred of Muslims. I think they're trying to now promote him to say "look we've got our token sikh guy who's part of the party.

There is an argument that Islam more than other religions is a 'way of life' or complete code of personal conduct and that more than ever to be a Muslim in current times has become a political statement. This identification with a wider international issues has been called "imaginaries from the margin" by Pnina Werbner (2002 p.101) who in her work on diasporic Pakistanis in Manchester draws a parallel between their identifications with homeland struggles and diasporic Jewish support for the Israeli extreme right and Irish-American republicanism. Another significant aspect we found in our conversation with young people that not only that particular age groups (especially older teenagers and younger adults) were particularly exposed to prejudice against Muslims, but that this experience seemed to politicise young people and affect the way in which they could explore their faith. With regard to the former, many young Muslims reported how the constant confrontation with such issues has made them much more political:

> I think Muslims are now compelled to have an awareness of politics as well, because of the questions we always have to answer. Such as "why did 9/11 happen, why did July the 7th happen?" And I feel that if Muslims don't research these questions, and have answers to these questions prepared, it's almost like people are going to continue with the stereotyping, what they've got in their mind. You kind of have to become political. I was never political, but people expect me to have an opinion on what happened.

In addition to this such experiences also hampered young people in the exploration of their faith, afraid of coming across or being classed as extremists young people and in particular young men tended to self-censor the events they went to or the people they got involved with:

> I'm not involved in any of the [Islamic] groups at Kingston. I sometime go to talks and lectures, and I go to like the Islamic week but I'm not really part of the society. I think mum would be very worried about extremism, she's always saying don't get too involved with any group, do what you need to do, you know go and pray or, OK, go to some talks if you want to. But even if I go to a talk I have to tell them [parents] what it is. Everyone knows that universities are hotspots for youngsters to get into radical stuff so you're careful.

> My mum was more worried about my brother getting involved than me when he started at university. So he didn't really go to talks or even pray. But he isn't really religious, so it didn't matter. But it was still funny that my mother was so worried that she'd rather have him out of that scene altogether. Even if it was a talk, she'd ask him like a 100 questions, like what is it about, who is [the speaker], do you really know who he is, where is he from, what's his background? So before he answered all these hundreds of questions he'd just rather just not go. He is more religious now. But my mum was fine with that, because it happened after uni, and in a more private way, so that was fine. (Female respondent, undergraduate at Kingston University).

Although flashpoint events such as the September 11th terrorist incidents in the US and the 7-7 London bombings in London have propelled Islamic extremism into the public eye the interviewee Amin, who the next section focuses on, traced the historical period of extremism's emergence to geopolitical events earlier in time.

> I've got sisters I used to hang round with them a lot and with their friends, we'd go to places like [secular music-based] Asian events but it shifted. It shifted with the Rushdie affair. It shifted with the Gulf war. It shifted with Bosnia. These are all 90s. Bosnian Muslims, they're white but they're Muslims getting annihilated, do you see what I mean? Bang bang bang bang

bang. The 90s was the period where radicalisation in Britain prevailed. Now it's been curtailed because there's Prevent, think tanks, there's this, there's that but the 90s was mental that's when I got sucked in, I got sucked into the wave. So did a lot of these guys.

Interview With an Extremist: Case Study of "Amin" on His Rise and Fall Within Hizb ut-Tahrir

Hizb ut-Tahrir (HT) is among the best-known Islamist groups in the UK. There is almost now an industry of former members who have since published and broadcast their revelations on the other side eg Hussain (2007). The group's strategy in the 1990s when Amin joined was entryism onto higher and further education courses then after having infiltrating to identify, persuade and then groom potential members as he described:

> I first came across them at Kingston college... they have a pseudo intellectual style and it's very stimulating when you're 16, 17 years old because they come to you and say all ideas of what you had when you were growing up are a fabrication. Islam is actually a political ideology. If you look at the history of Islam this is actually what happened. If you look at the life of the prophet he was a statesman or a politician, he united the tribes... Islam had an empire stretching over a thousand years. Islam gave rise to Algebra, Islam gave rise to astronomy, Islam gave rise to libraries, universities, conquests so all of these things struck me as really romantic notions of my own identity that I didn't know, that I was never really exposed to.

Amin told us he became a full member on beginning his degree course at SOAS rising to be recruiter for University of London. He was at pains to deny that it was a paintballing group of testosterone-filled thugs. The educational interface confirms that statement of the female interviewee above of universities as potential sites of radicalisation. Amin rejected the proposal that the group be proscribed by the government:

> I don't think anything should be banned. I'm against censorship. With HT first of all they're not enough of a threat so if you ban them you're only giving them more legitimacy because they don't share any love for the government so if the government turns around and bans them it'd be like a huge victory for them. They'll get more popular... I don't want them to be banned, they should definitely be debated, they should be given a platform to be exposed. They do go on Newsnight every now and again HT.

The opposition to the Iraq war and subsequent success of campaigns such as that of George Galloway running on the anti-war Respect ticket in the heavily-Muslim parliamentary seats of Bethnal Green and Bow in 2005 and Bradford West in 2012 is evidence of the domestic echoes at home of events abroad. Thus although the 'Preventing Violent Extremism' (PVE) agenda applies to events within UK borders such activity often occurs as a consequence of far off happenings to the point that there can be said to be a constitution of a global political brand of Islam. Amin attributed the impetus for joining such groups to a pan-Muslim underclass rather than the social standing of individual members who had been implicated in terrorist plots.

> RH: But why is it suburban people who've been to private school?
> A: Yeah but there is no class distinction between suburban Muslims and urban Muslims or rural Muslims... I don't think it's that. It's less to do with where one is situated in Britain but more to do with Britain... unintentional mismanagement. Historical process results in their alienation, disenfranchisement. If we take the most extreme example of the Tavistock Square suicide bomb. These guys before they died left a message saying we're doing this for our brothers around the world, we're doing this to fight oppression. This is a profound political message. Their entire endeavour was political and the constituency if you like that they ascribe themselves to was not in England, necessarily. It's this sort of global umma, global community of Muslims so they identify themselves as Muslims before anything else and more than that they saw Muslims as suffering the consequences of foreign policies of the sort of post-colonial world. They saw these corrupt rulers that the ex-colonies put in place after they left. It's actually quite a sophisticated political critique of the global world as it stands today. They felt that pain to such an extent that they were willing to give up their lives for it and that's where the religion comes and kicks in... ideas of afterlife and reward.

Amin was critical of think tanks that had been set up to tackle extremism since PVE's institution such as the Quilliam Foundation:

> I think it's more of a springboard to launch their political careers than actually [anything else]... on.... Islamism, fighting Islamism, Islamists, the trouble with Islamists... the problem is ideas from Saudi. No! All of this has a place in the history but that is not the problem... People are becoming radicalised because of the way they feel inadequate in this fucking country... their exposure to the world, their interaction with British society isn't enough for them for them to feel part of this society and so they look for alternatives. They have no affinity for this country, this country made no efforts to give them affinity. These people are angry something's happened.

Acknowledgement of the grievances that result at home from events occurring abroad has taken place at the highest level of the civil service. A leaked letter from Michael Jay, the Foreign Office permanent under-secretary, to the cabinet secretary, Sir Andrew Turnbull from 2004 well before the UK's own 7/7 incidents warns that

British foreign policy could be a driver for discontent in the Muslim community, "especially in the context of the Middle East peace process and Iraq" (Bright 2005). The letter speaks of "potential underlying causes of extremism that can affect the Muslim community, such as discrimination, disadvantage and exclusion. But another recurring theme is the issue of British foreign policy, especially in the context of the Middle East peace process and Iraq." The content mentions both Hizb ut-Tahrir and Al Majaharoon as benefiting from this in membership terms, concluding that 'British foreign policy and the perception of its negative effect on Muslims globally plays a significant role in creating a feeling of anger and impotence among especially the younger generation of British Muslims.' The Open Society Institute's report of 2005 for example is sub-headed 'discrimination and disadvantage'. These comments concur with what Amin told us about his reasons for joining Hizb ut-Tahrir. It is probably most accurate to characterise this as grievance-led with an added divine dimension i.e. accountability before your creator. Amin stressed that he had been principally attracted to Hizb ut-Tahrir for chiefly intellectual reasons before rising up within the ranks. He had also had negative dealings with Kingston mosque as a child and claimed that he had been beaten by the man that ran their madrassa-school which stopped him attending the masjid altogether.

Whilst at first sight then 'Islamic extremism' all appears to be one political bloc here the differences of strategy, tactics and theological opinion are explained. The exit strategy of Amin Hossain was described as a process rather than a critical incident:

> The thing that impressed me about HT was they gave me an idea of my own identity that was based on something that I was completely ignorant of. When I found out more details of that history it appeared to me how erroneous their narratives were and I started questioning those narratives to them and nobody really gave me a satisfactory answer but I was bound to the organisation because I thought it was a religious duty. I wanted to nourish this desire for spirituality and I thought I was doing it with them so even though I was intellectually unimpressed with them after a couple of years I felt it was my religious duty to be with them for lack of an alternative.

Amin's story substantiates the argument of Hari (2005) who said of the 7/7 bombers ' There are no simple materialist solutions: these men were not poor, they were not persecuted, they were not personally humiliated. No; if we want to find explanations for why people living in safe suburban streets would act this way, we have to realise the extraordinary, intoxicating power of political ideas.'

Future Fault-Lines: Continuity and Change in Suburbia

This 7/7 series of domestic mainland acts of terrorism during the course of a single morning in London in 2005 shocked the world. As the identities of the bombers

who caused death and injury on the London transport network were uncovered
The *Bucks Herald* Newspaper commented 'when news filtered through that
suicide bomber Germaine Lindsay - the deadliest of the four London bombers
- was an Aylesbury resident, the town was stunned...' (Jackson 2007). Here both
Islam becomes the new enemy within and it is within suburbia. One image that
continually replayed on news bulletins showed an iconic red London bus ripped
apart by a bomb. This appeared to with all the reassuring images of Britishness and
its associations with safety and security. Stereotypical notions of what we take to be
'the suburbs' in the UK have long been seen as linked to quintessential Englishness
eg as seen in John Major's declaration: "Fifty years on from now, Britain will still
be the country of long shadows on cricket grounds, warm beer, invincible green
suburbs, dog lovers and pools fillers".[91] Yet recent years have seen our received
notions of both the concept of "suburbia" and "Englishness" become somewhat
unsettled. *The Sun* newspaper on 6.7.08 depicted a map of knife crime incidents
in London which showed such activity clustering around the periphery. This shows
the suburbs coming into line with the cities they are by-product of: an inevitability
matched by the gentrification (i.e. suburbanisation) of the inner city.

Much was flawed about this project. Whilst attitudes to the (Labour initiated)
government Preventing Violent Extremism Strategy (known commonly as
'Prevent') were meant to be a key research question, the majority of respondents
were unaware of the programme that external organisations from all sides have
been quick to condemn. The right-wing pressure group the Taxpayers Alliance
(2009) have claimed "Giving councils millions of pounds to dole out to hundreds
of community groups clearly creates a massive risk that money will be wasted
or finance groups hostile to Britain's liberal, democratic values." Meanwhile the
left-leaning think tank the Institute of Race Relations have asserted that Prevent
constructs the Muslim population as a 'suspect community', fosters social divisions
and is counter-productive in reducing the risk of political violence (Kundnani
2008, 2009). Indeed singling out Muslims has helped confirm their isolation. If
the research were replicated it would be interesting to include[92] east European (i.e.
white) Muslims and[93] converts into the sample as they were regrettably absent.

These findings demonstrate that Muslims in Kingston are not a singular entity
but a community of communities. They also show the importance of education in
faith formation and the intersection of religion with politics. Suburbia's detractors
perceive it to be ultimately boring and nondescript. Multitudes of adjectives have

---

91 From http://www.number10.gov.uk/output/Page125.asp

92 '*Radical Islam* as bad as the *BNP says Cameron*' at http://www.dailymail.co.uk/news/
    article-432186/Radical-Islam-bad-BNP-says-Cameron.html

93 Is Radical Islam a mirror image of the BNP? at http://www.newstatesman.com/polls/721

accordingly been used alongside the word "suburb" and its derivatives eg "dull", "sleepy", "dead". When Bertrand Russell came up with the short story title "Satan of the Suburbs" (1953) it was meant to highlight the incongruity of devilish goings on in the outer reaches which are more frequently perceived of as being innocuous, inoffensive and generally mild. Manifestations of extremism in suburbs in recent years include Islamic fundamentalism and far right politics in eg the east London borough of Barking and Dagenham. The extent to which fear in suburbia now clusters around extremism as well as the more enduring suburban phobia of crime (Taylor 1995) can be seen in the fact that Poynting et al (2004) called their Australian based study *Bin Laden in the Suburbs: Criminalising the Arab Other*. Yet the demands of the far right in British politics have also been described as similarly grievance-led eg by David Cameron when in opposition. In conclusion there needs to be a sensitive exploration of the barriers and discriminatory practices described above that can feed the discontent that can be a driver extremist group recruitment and public policy needs to minimise these for all. As well as British society encouraging diversity and difference commonalties need to be stressed in a plural society of self-confident citizens of multiple ethnicities and religious backgrounds who have no need to resort to extremism as an imagined solution to their problems. The suburbs may be at the margins spatially but as over 80% of Britons live in them they need to shift centre-stage of policy-makers concerns.

Bibliography

Bright, M. (2005) 'Leak shows Blair told of Iraq war terror link', *Observer*, 28 August 2005, available at: http://www.guardian.co.uk/politics/2005/aug/28/uk.iraq

Bruce, S. (2002) *God is Dead: Secularization in the West*. Oxford: Blackwell.

Cantle, E. (2007) 'A Window on Extremism: Young People in Hounslow - A study of identity, social pressures, extremism and social inclusion', commissioned by London Borough of Hounslow

Choudhury T. A. (2002) *Monitoring Minority Protection in the EU: The Situation of Muslims in the UK*. Budapest: Open Society Institute.

Clapson, M. (1998) *Invincible Green Suburbs, Brave New Towns: Social Change and Urban Dispersal in Postwar England*, Manchester: Manchester University Press

Hari, J. (2005) "The best way to undermine the jihadists is to trigger a rebellion of Muslim women", *The Independent, 15 July 2005,* available at: http://richarddawkins.net/articles/2957-the-best-way-to-undermine-the-jihadists-is-to-trigger-a-rebellion-of-muslim-women-and-establish-energy-independence

Hussain, E. (2007) *The Islamist: Why I Joined Radical Islam in Britain, What I Saw Inside and Why I Left*. London: Penguin.

Institute of Race Relations (2010) 'Evidence to the UK parliamentary select committee inquiry on preventing violent extremism', in *Race and Class*, 51(3), pp.73-80.

Ipsos, M. (2009) 'Life in London: Report on the 2008/09 Place Survey findings for London', [online], available at: http://www.londoncouncils.gov.uk/London%20Councils/LondonPlaceSurveyReportLifeinLondonFINAL.pdf

Jackson, A. (2007) 'The Bucks Herald 1963 - Present day', [online], 15 March 2007, available at: http://www.bucksherald.co.uk/newspaperhistory/The-Bucks-Herald-1963-.2051918.jp

Kundnani, A. (2008) 'Islamism and the roots of liberal rage', in *Race and Class*, 50(2), pp.30-68.

Kundnani, A. (2009) *Spooked: How not to Prevent Violent Extremism*, London: *Institute of Race Relations*, available at: www.irr.org.uk/spooked

Open Society Institute (2005) *Muslims in the UK* Policies for Engaged Citizens. Budapest: Open Society Institute.

Poynting, S., Noble, G., Tabar, P. and Collins, J. (2004) *Bin Laden in the Suburbs: Criminalising the Arab Other* Sydney, Australia: Institute of Criminology.

Russell, B (1953) *Satan in the Suburbs and Other Stories*. London: Bodley Head

Taxpayers Alliance (2009) Council Spending Uncovered II - No. 5: Preventing Violent Extremism Grants, available at: www.taxpayersalliance.com/Prevent.pdf

Taylor, I. (1995) 'Private Homes and Public Others: An Analysis of Talk about Crime in Suburban South Manchester in the Mid-1990s', in *British Journal of*

Criminology, 35(2), pp.263-285.

Werbner, P. (2002) *Imagined Diasporas among Manchester Muslims,* Santa Fe: James Currey & School of American Research.

BAME Political Representation in the UK

Nader Fekri[94]

Definitions

Throughout this paper we use the current term BAME, (Black, Asian, and Minority Ethnic) to refer to those people who do not define themselves as being White using the 2001 Census definitions. So although there are many communities who consider themselves, and are classed as "ethnic minorities" including Irish, Polish, German, American, South African, Australian, Italian, and French, (each with more than 100,000 people and in the case of the Irish more than two-thirds-of-a-million) they are excluded from this study. Similarly the Jewish population, although arguably a distinct ethnic grouping, nevertheless are discounted because the overwhelming majority classify themselves as White.

So we shall be focussing on those people who are: Asian or Asian British including, Indian, Pakistani, and Bangladeshi; Black or Black British including Caribbean and African; Mixed, including White and Black Caribbean, White and Black African, White and Asian; Chinese; Arab; and Any other ethnic group.

A Historical Overview of the UK's BAME Population

Black people have been living in the British Isles since at least Roman times. There are records of African legionaries being based near Hadrian's Wall in northern England under the Emperor Septimius Severus around the year 210 CE. Africans continue to appear in British history. In 862 CE the Annals of Ireland record the landing of black slaves, ('fear gorm' in Irish, or 'blue men') by Vikings returning from raids on Spain and "Mauritania" (North Africa).

In the 1500s records of an African community appear in the records of the Scottish

---

94 Nader Fekri was born in Iran and moved to Britain as an eight-year-old, to live on the south coast, before moving to Manchester to attend university where he read History and Politics. He has worked variously as a researcher, teacher, and university lecturer, teaching at universities across Britain and Europe, most recently at the University of Bradford. His research interests lie in Post-War British Politics and Society. He has been a member of Calderdale Council since 2004 and served as Deputy Mayor, before being elected as Mayor in 2011.He is a school governor in Hebden Bridge and a magistrate in Halifax. He is a pacifist and humanist and a supporter of Amnesty International, Médecins Sans Frontières, and the National Secular Society. In his spare time, he enjoys solving The Guardian cryptic crossword, reading Modern European Detective Fiction, and following the trials and tribulations of Tranmere Rovers FC.

court at Holyrood, some of whom probably came from Portugal, where trading in African slaves had been going on throughout the previous century. In 1596, Queen Elizabeth wrote to the mayors of various cities ordering them to expel "blackamoors" people from the land. However, it was the growth of the British Empire that caused numbers to swell in the 17th and 18th centuries.

South Asians have been living in Britain for more than four centuries, stretching back to the founding of the East India Company, (EIC) in 1600. Indian sailors, at first recruited in small numbers to fill the shortage arising through death or desertion in India of white sailors, crewed the Company's East Indiaman ships. Many of these mariners jumped ship in British ports to escape ill-treatment and their second-rate service conditions, under Asiatic Articles, which paid as little as one-fifth of the wages for European seafarers. As the British Empire expanded, African and Afro-Caribbean slaves were ferried across the seas to work on plantations in the Caribbean or the Americas.

Others, in much smaller numbers, were ferried into the ports of London, Liverpool, and Bristol, on the same ships that brought imperial products to enrich the national economy. Indian housekeepers, servants, and nannies were brought over by British families returning from India; European men, many having made their fortune in India, often returned home with Indian wives and children. Visitors, envoys, and supplicants seeking redress against the East India Company, visited Britain.

Teachers came to Britain to teach Oriental languages, as did a number of Indian emissaries and other visitors. Increasing numbers of largely professional Indians came to Britain. Some as a result of the political, social, and economic changes brought about under colonial rule. Others came out of a sense of inquisitiveness to see the land of their rulers, or in the case of the princes, on official visits or for pleasure.

Students, some on scholarships, came to obtain vital professional qualifications to enable them to gain entry into the structures of colonial hierarchy back home. Some, having qualified, stayed on to practice their professions in Britain. Entrepreneurs came to seek economic opportunities. Political activists brought the struggle for colonial freedom to London, the centre of imperial power.

By the mid-19th century, there were at least 40,000 Indians living in the UK, of whom 25,000 were lascar sailors. By the turn of the 20th century, this had increased to around 70,000, of whom more than 50,000 were lascar sailors. The Great War drew more than one million Indian troops to serve overseas, of whom 130,000 served in France and Belgium, and of those almost 9,000 died. Similarly, despite the level of support for the war effort from the British West Indies, the War

Office was initially hostile and reluctant to accept black West Indians. However, by the end of the war more than 15,000 West Indians had been recruited and sent to serve as members of the British West Indies Regiment, (BWIR). The inter-war period saw a growth of both working-class and professional migration to Britain. By then Asian organisations and institutions, places of worship, 'ethnic' shops, and restaurants had also been established.

During the Second World War, many men from the West Indies had fought for the "mother country" but returned to civilian life with few opportunities. Their sense of patriotism, coupled with the need to find work, steered them towards the UK. Despite an apparent official reluctance to allow immigration from the fast-disappearing empire, the government could not recruit enough people from Europe and turned to these men. On 22 June 1948, the MV Empire Windrush docked at Tilbury in London, with 492 Jamaican workers on board. Many had returned to re-join the RAF; others had been encouraged by adverts for work. The workers quickly found jobs, as there was a shortage of workers, indeed the local London paper's report was headlined "Welcome Home". The day marked what would become a massive change to British society, the start of mass immigration to the UK and the arrival of significant numbers of different cultures. In the decade to follow, 125,000 West Indians had arrived. By the end of the Second World War, several thousand Asians had been living in Britain for generations, and an 'Asian Community' of some 55,000 was in existence. When India gained her independence in 1947, Asians began arriving in the UK in large numbers, more than 60,000 arrived before 1955, many of whom drove buses, or worked in iron foundries, or textile factories.

Later arrivals opened corner shops or ran post offices.

The flow of Indian immigrants peaked between 1965 and 1972; boosted in particular by Idi Amin's sudden decision to expel all 80,000 Indians from Uganda more than 30,000 Ugandan Asians migrated to the UK. By the beginning of the 21st century, there were BAME professionals, industrial workers and labourers, students, and activists, traders, merchants, and entrepreneurs, artists and writers. The BAME community is not a homogeneous community. There are different religious, ethnic, and linguistic communities from south Asia and the diaspora in Africa and the Caribbean. Others were born here, some having families across the racial divide.

The History of Parliament

Parliament in the UK can trace its roots to at least 1066, when William of Normandy introduced a feudal system, by which he sought the advice of a council of tenants-in-chief and ecclesiastics before making laws. In 1215, the tenants-in-chief secured Magna Carta from King John, which established that the monarch might not raise taxes without the consent of his royal council, which gradually developed into a parliament. In 1265, Simon de Montfort introduced the idea that power-holders are responsible to an electorate, although only landowners were allowed to vote.

Over the centuries, the English Parliament progressively limited the power of the monarchy, culminating in the English Civil War in the mid-17th century. For centuries, Parliament consisted of a small landowning elite whose priorities were their own power and prosperity. From the 18th century onwards, the social changes brought about by industrial growth and the decline of agriculture meant that the demographic landscape of Britain had changed.

With these changes came demands from the working and middle classes for equality and fairness in representation. Even as late as the beginning of the 20th century only a small minority of men were entitled to vote in parliamentary elections. Parliament was dominated by rich landowners and reflected their interests. Their priorities were to defend their property rights against taxation and state interference. Social disorder was not tolerated. Women did not have any right to vote at all. The growth of industry in the 18th century brought great change to the country, its people and their aspirations. Towns and cities increased in population as factories grew in number and people were drawn to work in urban areas as agriculture declined.

This led to further inequalities in representation in Parliament. Urban areas such as Birmingham and Manchester had no Members of Parliament while small villages which had once been important in the Middle Ages sometimes sent two representatives to Parliament. A sense of injustice and a growing political consciousness contributed to a small but growing demand for parliamentary reform. As the 19th century progressed there was an increasing recognition that some parliamentary reform was necessary. The Representation of the People Act 1832, known as the first Reform Act or Great Reform Act, among many things, broadened the franchise's property qualification in the counties, and created a uniform franchise in the boroughs. Limited change had been achieved but for many it did not go far enough. The 1832 Reform Act proved that change was possible, but among the working classes there were demands for more. The growth and influence of the Chartist Movement from 1838 onwards was an indication that more parliamentary reform was desired.

However, the call for universal manhood suffrage or 'one man, one vote' was still resisted by Parliament and the second Reform Act, passed in 1867, was still based around property qualifications. There was no question of campaigning for the right to vote for women too. They were still excluded. The 1867 Reform Act granted the vote to all householders in the boroughs and reduced the property threshold in the counties. Men in urban areas who met the property qualification were enfranchised and the Act roughly doubled the electorate in England and Wales from one million to two million men.

Parliament's resistance to 'one man, one vote' was partly overturned in 1884 with the third Reform Act, which established a uniform franchise throughout the country. However, one section of society was still completely excluded from the voting process, women. To be truly representative, Parliament still had changes to make. However, it was not until 1918 that women achieved suffrage, (aged 30 and above), and it was to be another decade, in 1928, that they gained the prize of voting on equal terms as men. It is against this background of Empire, immigration, settlement, enfranchisement, entitlement, and equality that we now look at the representation of BAMEs in the House of Commons.

BAME Candidates and MP's

BAME involvement in parliamentary politics dates back to the end of the 19th century. The first Indian MP to win a seat in parliament was Dadabhai Naoroji, who had moved to England and joined the Liberal Party becoming elected MP for Finsbury Central in London in 1892 by three votes, and then losing the seat at the following general election three years later. Although he promised that his first duty would be to his constituents, he made no secret of the fact that he would also be representing 250 million of his fellow subjects in India. In 1895, Mancherjee Bhownagree became Conservative MP for Bethnal Green. He was re-elected in 1900, but unlike his fellow Parsi, Naoroji, Bhownagree was a supporter of British rule in India and opposed the campaign for Home Rule. Bhownagree retired from politics after being defeated in the 1906 General Election. It was to be nearly two decades for the House of Commons not to be all white. The third BAME elected to parliament was Shapurji Saklatvala. In 1922, Saklatvala was elected Labour MP for Battersea North. He narrowly lost his seat in 1923 but was re-elected as a Communist in 1924 and served as an MP until 1929. At that election the Labour Party refused to support Communist Party candidates, and their candidate Stephen Sanders easily defeated Saklatvala. Between them these three men represented the whole political spectrum.

It was to be two decades for any BAME candidate to even stand for Parliament. The first BAME candidate put up for election by a major party after the Second World War was a colourful [sic] character called Sirdar Colonel Karam Singh Bahr Ahluwalia who stood for the Liberals in Willesden West in 1950. He managed a relatively reasonable, respectable 2,853 votes or 5.1%, but he nevertheless lost his deposit. Dr David Pitt (later Lord Pitt) contested Hampstead in the 1959

General Election he was the first person of African descent to be a parliamentary candidate, standing as the Labour candidate for the north London constituency of Hampstead. In this election, issues of race were injected into the campaign, and he was defeated by the Conservative candidate, Henry Brooke. During the course of the campaign, Pitt received racist death threats, as did his family; however, despite the racist abuse, he refused to withdraw from the race. He again represented the Labour Party in 1970, contesting Wandsworth Clapham, which had been seen as a notionally safe seat for Labour. In what many believe many believe was a racially sensitive campaign, the Conservatives won the seat.

In 1970, there were also three ethnic minority candidates who stood for the Liberal Party including in the northern cities of Bradford and Sheffield. In February 1974 the Labour Party put forward a Pakistani, Councillor Bashir Maan from Glasgow, to contest East Fife and the Liberal Party proposed Dhani Prem in Coventry South-East. However, neither of these candidates had any chance of winning. In the October 1974 general election there was only one ethnic minority candidate, Cecil Williams who stood for the Liberal Party in Birmingham Sparkbrook.

In the 1979 general election there were five ethnic minority candidates put forward by the three main political parties: one Labour candidate, two Liberals, and two Conservatives. This was the first time since 1945 that the Conservative Party had nominated ethnic minority candidates. In the event, none of the candidates was elected because they contested seats where they had no chance of winning. There was a step change in the early 1980s in terms of ethnic minority candidates. In the 1983 general election there were eighteen ethnic minority candidates who stood for the four major parties four Conservatives, six Labour, four Liberal, and four for the Social Democratic Party (the SDP had been formed in 1981 as a moderate break-away from the Labour Party). However, as in 1979, no ethnic minority candidate contested a winnable or 'safe' seat, with the exception of Paul Boateng for Labour who fought Hemel Hempstead, a notionally winnable seat on the basis of the re-drawn boundaries.

Breakthrough

In 1987, Britain saw the election of the first Asian MP since 1929 and the first African-Caribbean MPs ever. The number of BAME candidates fielded by the main parties did not rise dramatically, twenty-eight selected compared to eighteen in 1983, fourteen Labour, six Conservative, six SDP, and two Liberal (the latter two collectively known at this election as the Alliance). What made these elections qualitatively different from almost any other before was the selection of six of Labour's candidates for winnable or "safe" seats, of whom four were successful.

Keith Vaz, a Cambridge-educated solicitor of Goan parentage, won Leicester East, and is the longest standing Asian Member of Parliament. Diane Abbott was a former councillor and the first-ever African-Caribbean woman MP, who won Hackney North and Stoke Newington. Bernie Grant, a Labour councillor and leader of the London Borough of Haringey won Tottenham. The fourth victor was Paul Boateng, who had already stood in Hemel Hempstead in 1983, and was successful in Brent South, having been a member of Greater London Council for Walthamstow. Labour would probably have taken a fifth seat with a BAME candidate had not Sharon Atkin (Nottingham East) been sacked for insulting the Labour Leader, Neil Kinnock, at a rally shortly before the campaign opened. Her replacement narrowly failed to win the seat.

There was much pressure and expectation on this quartet of BAME MPs, who were also closely watched not only by their own party, but also the other major parties, and of course the electorate both white and BAME. Their mistakes and failures would be magnified beyond reasonableness and any slip would be used to delay the entry of more BAMEs to the House of Commons. David Pitt's defeat in the 1970 election when he lost a "safe" Labour seat is a good example of how political parties became spooked in giving a safe seat to a BAME candidate for fear of losing it.

The 1992 general election saw a small increase in the number of successful candidates from BAME communities compared with the 1987 election. The number fighting as incumbents or in seats held by their parties was eight whereas it was only three in 1987. This increase in the number with good prospects was accompanied by a slight drop in the total number standing for the major parties from twenty-nine to twenty three.

These included five Labour incumbents (the four victors of 1987: Abbott, Boateng, Grant, and Vaz plus the victor of the Langbaurgh by-election) plus Piara Khabra, who had been adopted for the safe Labour seat of Ealing Southall. The Conservatives selected Nirj Deva in the safe seat of Brentford and Isleworth, and John Taylor for the marginal seat of Cheltenham. The Liberal Democrats (as the Liberals had become following their merger with the Social Democrats) again selected BAME candidates in hopeless seats.

The result was the success of Abbott, Boateng, Grant, and Khabra for Labour and Nirj Deva for the Conservatives making him the first Conservative BAME MP for nearly ninety years. The surprise was the failure of Kumar to hold on to Langbaurgh against a heavy push by the Conservatives. Rather less surprising was the sight of the local Cheltenham Conservative Association refusing to wholeheartedly back Taylor, a well-respected London barrister, with an at times openly racist whispering (nay shouting) campaign against their own candidate, and so allowing the Liberal

Democrats to take the seat on the night.

The 1992-97 parliament saw a substantial increase of constituency-centred arguments over the adoption of BAME and especially Asian candidates in particular. Especially bitter disputes occurred in seats where long serving white MPs were due to retire and/or pressure among Asian activists had served to bring forward retirement decisions. This kind of setting had initially been witnessed in the late 1980s in Ealing Southall, where Sydney Bidwell's departure had created a valuable opportunity for Asian candidates in 1992. Now the focus was on seats such as Birmingham Sparkbrook (where Roy Hattersley was about to step down), Bradford West (where Max Madden had been successively re-elected), and Glasgow Govan (where boundary changes meant that the sitting white MP had to contest the nomination). Many of these selection contests threw up allegations of dirty tricks, usually centring on claims (usually unfounded) of bogus Asian membership drives. It was obvious that Labour was beginning to see a pattern of contested nominations involving racial bitterness.

This in itself was not particularly new; in the 1920s and 1930s similar battles had been waged over the motives of Irish recruits to British political parties, and in the 1940s and 1950s over Jewish involvement in the Labour Party. The Asian-centred rows of the 1990s apparently appeared to continue this trait. The 1997 election witnessed a significant expansion in the numbers of black and Asian parliamentary candidates (a record 44 were selected among the three major parties, up from 24 in 1992). The real focus, however, was on those in promising seats, with a likely scenario of three, perhaps four, additional minority members joining the ranks of those elected in 1992 and 1987.

The period of the Labour rule, 1997-2010, saw all three parties re-assess their attitudes and policies towards both the BAME vote and BAME representation. In the case of the Labour party, a consolidation of groups such as the Black Sections, and the descendants of the Labour Party Race and Action Group (LPRAG). The Conservatives, have had their Anglo-Asian Conservative Society, and the Anglo-West Indian Conservative Society, whilst the Liberal Democrats have the Ethnic Minority Liberal Democrats. All of these groups have tried to shape and influence their respective parties' policies and priorities dealing with BAME communities. Increasingly, as the "ethnic minority" vote became ever-more important to win a larger number of seats then the various hierarchies within the three main political parties themselves threw themselves into the necessary task of courting that vote. Gaining more BAME parliamentary candidates and (hopefully) more BAME MPs was to be one method here that vote would be delivered.

However, there was often extreme reluctance amongst the membership of all three parties to anything that smacked of favouritism or "reverse discrimination", and so frequently many progressive or "positive action" policies were stymied. Consequently, there was a barely perceptible rise in the number of BAME MPs from nine to fifteen, and although many were arguing for the lesson of All-Women Shortlists (used by Labour in 1997 in half of their winnable seats) this seemed to fall on deaf ears.

Conclusion

Until David Cameron's bold use of the "A List", political parties generally tend to select them in the BAME concentration areas. This is misguided at best. Firstly, the BAME communities are not a homogeneous group; increasingly in the 21st century, and especially after the impact of the Iraq War, they tend to vote on a party basis and those party allegiances are becoming looser. Secondly, this approach is seen by many activists both white and BAME as being both tokenistic and patronising. Thirdly as recent research has shown, the "ethnic penalty" is disappearing and having BAME candidates in primarily white areas as initially shown by Dr Ashok Kumar in the 1991 Langbaurgh by-election, shows that political parties are serious about their BAME candidates and that they are not merely putting them forward to harvest BAME votes.

The current composition of the Commons does not reflect society. In 2008, Parliament acknowledged this problem by stating "the disparity between the representation of women, ethnic minorities, and disabled people in the House of Commons and their representation in the UK population at large", and formally established a Speaker's Conference to "consider and make recommendations for rectifying" these anomalies. The argument for widening representation is three-fold to ensure justice, effectiveness, and enhanced legitimacy. A more diverse House of Commons would make better decisions and solve problems more effectively, because it would be able to draw upon a wider range of experiences and insights.

There is a problem, not only because of unfairness or lack of balance but because we miss out on the input from the rich nature of the cultures that make up this country. The problems and challenges that the government faces today are not being solved by the best resource available, the totality of the perspectives of the diverse British public. MPs must represent all their constituents regardless of their background, personal circumstances, or political allegiance. Every good MP recognises this duty and will do the best they can to meet their constituents' needs. Yet, although individual MPs work hard to represent the breadth and depth of their constituents' concerns and experiences, the absence of a wide cross-section of society in the House of Commons means that the legislature as a whole, perhaps through MPs' ignorance, inattention, or a collective failure of the imagination, overlooks the needs and concerns of specific groups. In these circumstances its decisions and actions may be considered less legitimate than they would otherwise be.

There is a widespread perception that MPs, and Parliament itself, are divorced from reality. There is little sense that Members understand, or share, the life experiences of their constituents. Restoring public faith in Parliament is of crucial importance to the future of democracy. Ensuring a diverse representation within Parliament is one way to rebuild trust and restore a dialogue between Parliament and those whom it represents. It is clear that there is a long way to go to rebuild the House of Commons and to make it the efficient, effective, and credible legislature it ought to be.

Appendices

Appendix 1: List of BAME MPs in The House of Commons

NAME	PARTY	FIRST ELECTED	CONSTITUENCY
Dadabhai Naoroji	Liberal	1892	Finsbury Central
Mancherjee Bhownagree	Conservative	1895	Bethnal Green North East
Shapurji Saklatvala	Communist	1922	Battersea North
Jonathan Sayeed	Conservative	1983	Mid Bedfordshire
Diane Abbott	Labour	1987-	Hackney North and Stoke Newington
Paul Boateng	Labour	1987	Brent South
Bernie Grant	Labour	1987	Tottenham
Keith Vaz	Labour	1987-	Leicester East
Ashok Kumar	Labour	1991	Middlesbrough South and East Cleveland
Nirj Deva	Conservative	1992	Brentford and Isleworth
Piara Khabra	Labour	1992	Ealing Southall
Oona King	Labour	1997	Bethnal Green & Bow
Mohammad Sarwar	Labour	1997	Glasgow Central
Marsha Singh	Labour	1997	Bradford West
Mark Hendrick	Labour	2000-	Preston
David Lammy	Labour	2000-	Tottenham
Parmjit Dhanda	Labour	2001	Gloucester
Khalid Mahmood	Labour	2001-	Birmingham Perry Barr
Parmjit Singh Gill	Lib Dem	2004	Leicester South
Adam Afriyie	Conservative	2005-	Windsor
Dawn Butler	Labour	2005	Brent South
Sadiq Khan	Labour	2005-	Tooting
Shahid Malik	Labour	2005	Dewsbury
Shailesh Vara	Conservative	2005-	North West Cambridgeshire
Virendra Sharma	Labour	2007-	Ealing Southall
Rushanara Ali	Labour	2010-	Bethnal Green and Bow
Rehman Chishti	Conservative	2010-	Gillingham and Rainham

Helen Grant	Conservative	2010-	Maidstone and The Weald
Sam Gyimah	Conservative	2010-	East Surrey
Sajid Javid	Conservative	2010-	Bromsgrove
Kwasi Kwarteng	Conservative	2010-	Spelthorne
Shabana Mahmood	Labour	2010-	Birmingham Ladywood
Lisa Nandy	Labour	2010-	Wigan
Chi Onwurah	Labour	2010-	Newcastle upon Tyne Central
Priti Patel	Conservative	2010-	Witham
Yasmin Qureshi	Labour	2010-	Bolton South East
Anas Sarwar	Labour	2010-	Glasgow Central
Alok Sharma	Conservative	2010-	Reading West
Chuka Umunna	Labour	2010-	Streatham
Paul Uppal	Conservative	2010-	Wolverhampton South West
Valerie Vaz	Labour	2010-	Walsall South
Nadhim Zahawi	Conservative	2010-	Stratford-on-Avon
Seema Malhotra	Labour	2011-	Feltham and Heston
Imran Hussain?	Labour	2012-	Bradford West

Appendix 2: BAME Candidates at UK General Elections 1892-1945

General Election, July 1892

D. Naoroji	Liberal	Finsbury Central	50.0%	1st

General Election, July 1895

M. Bhownagree	Conservative	Bethnal Green NE	51.6%	1st
D. Naoroji	Liberal	Finsbury Central	43.7%	2nd

General Election, September/October 1900

M. Bhownagree	Conservative	Bethnal Green North East	53.4%	1st

General Election, January/February 1906

M. Bhownagree	Conservative	Bethnal Green North East	34.0%	2nd

General Election, November 1922

S. Saklatvala	Communist	Battersea North	50.5%	1st

General Election, December 1923

S. Saklatvala	Communist	Battersea North	49.6%	2nd

General Election, October 1924

S. Saklatvala	Communist	Battersea North	50.9%	1st

General Election, May 1929

S. Saklatvala	Communist	Battersea North	18.6%	3rd

General Election, October 1931

S. Saklatvala	Communist	Battersea North	8.9%	3rd

Appendix 3: BAME Candidates at UK General Elections 1945-1983

General election, February 1950

K. Ahluwalia	Liberal	Willesden West	5.1%	3rd

General Election, October 1959

D. Pitt	Labour	Hampstead	28.3%	2nd

General Election, June 1970

D. Pitt	Labour	Wandsworth Clapham	40.4%	2nd
G. Musa	Liberal	Bradford East	2.5%	3rd
P. Singh	Liberal	Sheffield Hallam	7.3%	3rd

General Election, February 1974

B. Maan	Labour	Fife East	15.0%	3rd
D. Prem	Liberal	Coventry South East	11.7%	3rd

General Election, October 1974

C. Williams	Liberal	Birmingham Sparkbrook	9.8%	3rd

General Election, May 1979

F. Saleem	Conservative	Glasgow Central	16.4%	3rd
N. Saroop	Conservative	Greenwich	33.3%	2nd
R. Singh	Liberal	Coventry North East	4.9%	3rd

General Election, June 1983

H. Gardener	Conservative	Newham North East	27.8%	2nd
P. Le Hunte	Conservative	Birmingham Ladywood	27.1%	2nd
P. Nischal	Conservative	Birmingham Small Heath	21.0%	2nd
S. Popat	Conservative	Durham North	24.0%	3rd
J. Sayeed	Conservative	Bristol East	40.5%	1st
R. Austin	Labour	St. Albans	10.9%	3rd
P. Boateng	Labour	Hertfordshire West	22.3%	3rd
B. Bousquet	Labour	Kensington	29.5%	2nd
D. Colin-Thorne	Labour	Warrington South	30.0%	2nd

J. Thakoordin	Labour	Milton Keynes	22.2%	3rd
K. Vaz	Labour	Richmond and Barnes	7.1%	3rd
A. Alagappa	Liberal	Feltham and Heston	15.9%	3rd
Z. Gifford	Liberal	Hertsmere	25.6%	2nd
M. Nadeem	Liberal	Ealing Southall	15.8%	3rd
C. Williams	Liberal	Birmingham Perry Barr	9.3%	3rd
A. Ahmed	SDP	Manchester Central	11.8%	3rd
S. Fernando	SDP	Leicester West	12.8%	3rd
T. Mann	SDP	Brent North	20.6%	3rd
O. Parmar	SDP	Birmingham Sparkbrook	10.4%	3rd

Appendix 4: BAME Candidates at UK General Elections 1987-2010

General Election, June 1987

R. Chandran	Conservative	Preston	28.6%	2nd
N. Deva	Conservative	Hammersmith	38.1%	2nd
N. Khan	Conservative	Birmingham Sparkbrook	25.7%	2nd
J. Sayeed	Conservative	Bristol East	43.6%	1st
D. Abbott	Labour	Hackney North and Stoke Newington	48.7%	1st
V. Anand	Labour	Folkestone and Hythe	7.4%	3rd
M. Aslam	Labour	Nottingham East	42.0%	2nd
P. Boateng	Labour	Brent South	51.9%	1st
N. Hafeez	Labour	Stafford	21.2%	3rd
A. Patel	Labour	Eastbourne	8.8%	3rd
P. Patel	Labour	Brent North	24.8%	2nd
K. Vaz	Labour	Leicester East	48.2%	1st
V. Vaz	Labour	Twickenham	8.4%	3rd
Z. Gifford	Liberal	Harrow East	22.1%	3rd
P. Verma	Liberal	Merthyr Tydfil and Rhymney	8.1%	3rd
M. Ali	SDP	Blackburn	10.0%	3rd
M. Ali	SDP	Carrick, Cumnock, and Doon Valley	9.6%	3rd
S. Fernando	SDP	Nottingham North	11.7%	3rd
L. Kamal	SDP	Wakefield	12.1%	3rd
M. Moghal	SDP	Bradford West	11.4%	3rd
C. Sangha	SDP	Birmingham Ladywood	9.3%	3rd
B. Chahal	SDP	Liverpool Riverside	11.2%	3rd

General Election, April 1992

L. Champagnie	Conservative	Islington North	23.7%	2nd
A. Chaudhary	Conservative	Birmingham Small Heath	25.0%	2nd
N. Deva	Conservative	Brentford and Isleworth	45.8%	1st
M. Khamisa	Conservative	Birmingham Sparkbrook	24.8%	2nd

A. Popat	Conservative	Bradford South	38.4%	2nd
M. Rezvi	Conservative	Edinburgh Leith	21.1%	3rd
M. Riaz	Conservative	Bradford North	32.2%	2nd
J. Sayeed	Conservative	Bristol East	39.2%	2nd
J. Taylor	Conservative	Cheltenham	44.7%	2nd
D. Abbott	Labour	Hackney North and Stoke Newington	57.8%	1st
K. Abrams	Labour	Wimbledon	23.3%	2nd
P. Boateng	Labour	Brent South	57.5%	1st
D. Cameron	Labour	Ashford	20.0%	3rd
B. Grant	Labour	Tottenham	56.5%	1st
P. Khabra	Labour	Ealing Southall	47.4%	1st
A. Kumar	Labour	Langbaurgh	43.1%	2nd
C. Moraes	Labour	Harrow West	22.5%	2nd
K. Vaz	Labour	Leicester East	56.3%	1st
M. Ali	Lib Dem	Liverpool Riverside	9.2%	3rd
P. Nandra	Lib Dem	Ealing South	7.7%	4th
V. Sharma	Lib Dem	Halesowen and Stourbridge	12.4%	3rd
Z. Gifford	Lib Dem	Hertsmere	18.9%	3rd

General Election, May 1997

J. Arain	Conservative	Derby South	25.2%	2nd
K. Choudhury	Conservative	Bethnal Green and Bow	21.1%	2nd
N. Deva	Conservative	Brentford and Isleworth	31.8%	2nd
B. Khanbhai	Conservative	Norwich South	23.7%	2nd
M. Kotecha	Conservative	Liverpool Walton	6.3%	3rd
M. Riaz	Conservative	Bradford West	33.0%	2nd
J. Sayeed	Conservative	Mid Bedfordshire	46.0%	1st
G. Sidhu	Conservative	Blackburn	24.6%	2nd
S. Vara	Conservative	Birmingham Ladywood	13.3%	2nd
N. Zahawi	Conservative	Erith and Thamesmead	20.2%	2nd
D. Abbott	Labour	Hackney North and Stoke Newington	65.2%	1st
P. Boateng	Labour	Brent South	73.0%	1st

B. Grant	Labour	Tottenham	69.3%	1st
P. Khabra	Labour	Ealing Southall	60.0%	1st
Q. Khan	Labour	Aberdeenshire West and Kincardine	9.1%	4th
O. King	Labour	Bethnal Green and Bow	46.3%	1st
A. Kumar	Labour	Middlesbrough S. and Cleveland East	54.7%	1st
J. Lehal	Labour	Bedfordshire North East	32.6%	1st
C. Mannan	Labour	Christchurch	6.9%	1st
M. Sarwar	Labour	Glasgow Govan	44.1%	1st
A. Sayed	Labour	Argyll and Bute	15.7%	4th
M. Singh	Labour	Bradford West	41.6%	1st
K. Vaz	Labour	Leicester East	65.5%	1st
C. Anglin	Lib Dem	Leyton and Wanstead	15.1%	3rd
K. Appiah	Lib Dem	Lewisham Deptford	8.9%	3rd
A. de Freitas	Lib Dem	Great Grimsby	18.1%	3rd
A. Gupta	Lib Dem	Ealing North	7.0%	3rd
S. Islam	Lib Dem	Bethnal Green and Bow	12.0%	3rd
K. Kerr	Lib Dem	Vauxhall	16.0%	3rd
A. Khan	Lib Dem	Ilford South	6.3%	3rd
K. Lee	Lib Dem	Rutland and Melton	19.2%	3rd
R. Martins	Lib Dem	Hornchurch	7.8%	3rd
S. Marwa	Lib Dem	Birmingham Ladywood	8.0%	3rd
J. Motabudul	Lib Dem	Leicester East	7.0%	3rd
P. Munisamy	Lib Dem	Gloucester	10.5%	3rd
P. Nandra	Lib Dem	Harrow West	15.5%	3rd
A. Qadar	Lib Dem	Sheffield Central	17.2%	2nd
B. Sharma	Lib Dem	Harrow East	8.2%	3rd
E. Waller	Lib Dem	Halifax	12.0%	3rd
Y. Zalzala	Lib Dem	Manchester Withington	13.6%	3rd

General Election, June 2001

| S. Faruk | Conservative | Bethnal Green and Bow | 24.2% | 2nd |
| U. Fernandes | Conservative | Tottenham | 13.9% | 2nd |

I. Hussain	Conservative	B'ham Sparkbrook & Small Heath	10.8%	3rd
Z. Iqbal	Conservative	Bradford North	24.1%	2nd
S. Kamal	Conservative	West Ham	16.4%	2nd
A. Kapoor	Conservative	Doncaster North	14.7%	2nd
S. Kumar	Conservative	Ilford South	25.7%	2nd
A. Miraj	Conservative	Aberavon	7.6%	4th
H. Rashid	Conservative	Bolton South East	24.2%	2nd
M. Riaz	Conservative	Bradford West	37.1%	2nd
J. Sayeed	Conservative	Mid Bedfordshire	47.4%	1st
C. Selverajah	Conservative	Brent East	12.6%	2nd
S. Vara	Conservative	Northampton South	41.1%	2nd
S. Verma	Conservative	Hull East	13.8%	3rd
D. Abbott	Labour	Hackney North and Stoke Newington	61.0%	1st
H. Adeel	Labour	Rushcliffe	34.0%	2nd
W. Azmi	Labour	Worcestershire West	14.0%	3rd
P. Boateng	Labour	Brent South	73.3%	1st
P. Dhanda	Labour	Gloucester	45.8%	1st
M. Hussain	Labour	Stratford-on-Avon	16.7%	3rd
S. Hussain	Labour	Woking	20.3%	3rd
O. King	Labour	Bethnal Green and Bow	50.4%	1st
A. Kumar	Labour	Middlesbrough South & Cleveland	55.3%	1st
D. Lammy	Labour	Tottenham	67.5%	1st
K. Mahmood	Labour	Birmingham Perry Bar	46.5%	1st
C. Onuegbu	Labour	New Forest West	14.7%	3rd
C. Shafique	Labour	Wycombe	35.3%	2nd
M. Singh	Labour	Bradford West	48.0%	1st
T. Sulaiman	Labour	Huntingdon	22.8%	3rd
K. Vaz	Labour	Leicester East	57.6%	1st
Q. Afzal	Lib Dem	B'ham Sparkbrook & Small Heath	13.2%	2nd
H. Athwal	Lib Dem	Leicester East	12.3%	3rd
N. Batti	Lib Dem	Brent East	10.6%	3rd

M. Chaudhry	Lib Dem	Birmingham Ladywood	8.2%	3rd
M. Ece	Lib Dem	Hackney North and Stoke Newington	14.1%	3rd
K. Falkner	Lib Dem	Kensington and Chelsea	15.8%	3rd
A. de Freitas	Lib Dem	Great Grimsby	19.0%	3rd
P. Singh Gill	Lib Dem	Leicester South	17.2%	3rd
M. Khan	Lib Dem	Tottenham	9.5%	3rd
R. Khan	Lib Dem	Bradford West	6.4%	3rd
A. Keppitipola	Lib Dem	Barking	9.8%	3rd
N. Mohammed	Lib Dem	Milton Keynes South West	10.6%	3rd
I. Patel	Lib Dem	Blackburn	8.1%	3rd
A. Qadar	Lib Dem	Sheffield Central	19.7%	2nd
P. Singh	Lib Dem	Birmingham Hall Green	8.8%	3rd
H. de Souza	Lib Dem	Hove	9.1%	3rd
Y. Zalzala	Lib Dem	Manchester Withington	22.0%	3rd

General Election, May 2010

A. Abercorn	Conservative	Hazel Grove	33.6%	2nd
K. Adegoke	Conservative	Dulwich and West Norwood	22.2%	3rd
A. Afriyie	Conservative	Windsor	60.9%	1st
I. Ali	Conservative	Makerfield	18.8%	2nd
K. Ali	Conservative	Oldham East and Saddleworth	26.4%	3rd
R. Ali	Conservative	Burnley	16.6%	3rd
S. Awan	Conservative	Leigh	20.9%	2nd
S. Bailey	Conservative	Hammersmith	36.0%	2nd
R. Bhansali	Conservative	Streatham	18.3%	3rd
N. Bhatti	Conservative	Stoke on Trent Central	21.0%	3rd
R. Chishti	Conservative	Gillingham and Rainham	46.2%	1st
M. Clarke	Conservative	Tooting	39.0%	2nd
M. Dean	Conservative	Rochdale	18.1%	3rd
W. Emmanuel-Jones	Conservative	Chippenham	41.0%	2nd
K. Ghafoor	Conservative	Oldham West and	23.7%	2nd

		Royton		
H. Grant	Conservative	Maidstone and The Weald	48.0%	1st
Z. Iqbal	Conservative	Bradford West	31.0%	2nd
S. Kennedy	Conservative	Ashton-under-Lyme	25.0%	2nd
K. Kwarteng	Conservative	Spelthorne	46.0%	1st
G. Lee	Conservative	Holborn and St. Pancras	20.0%	3rd
N. Mahapatra	Conservative	Sedgefield	23.5%	2nd
G. Mohindra	Conservative	North Tyneside	18.4%	3rd
L. Morrison	Conservative	Bermondsey and Old Southwark	17.1%	3rd
S. Nayyar	Conservative	Hackney South	13.5%	3rd
S. Parekh	Conservative	Birmingham Hodge Hill	12.0%	3rd
J. Parmar	Conservative	Warley	24.8%	2nd
P. Patel	Conservative	Witham	52.2%	1st
S. Qureshi	Conservative	Bootle	8.9%	3rd
S. Rahuja	Conservative	Manchester Central	11.8%	3rd
S. Rajput	Conservative	Brent Central	11.2%	3rd
M. Riaz	Conservative	Bradford East	27.0%	2nd
A. Shafi	Conservative	Bristol East	28.3%	2nd
A. Sharma	Conservative	Reading West	43.2%	1st
G. Singh	Conservative	Ealing Southall	29.8%	2nd
D. Thomas	Conservative	Twickenham	34.0%	2nd
P. Uppal	Conservative	Wolverhampton South West	41.0%	1st
S. Vara	Conservative	North West Cambridgeshire	50.0%	1st
K. Wu	Conservative	Liverpool Riverside	11.0%	3rd
D. Abbott	Labour	Hackney North and Stoke Newington	55.0%	1st
A. Ahmed	Labour	West Suffolk	15.0%	3rd
R. Ali	Labour	Bethnal Green and Bow	43.0%	1st
A. Beg	Labour	Romsey and	6.4%	3rd

Southampton North

D. Butler	Labour	Brent Central	41.2%	2nd
B. Charalambous	Labour	Enfield Southgate	29.9%	2nd
P. Dhanda	Labour	Gloucester	35.2%	2nd
H. Dhindsa	Labour	Derbyshire Mid	24.5%	2nd
S. Garg	Labour	Uxbridge and South Ruislip	23.4%	2nd
M. Hendrick	Labour	Preston	48.2%	1st
A. Hussain	Labour	Aldridge Brownhills	20.0%	2nd
B. Joshi	Labour	Central Suffolk and North Ipswich	16.2%	3rd
M. Khan	Labour	Bury North	35.2%	2nd
S. Khan	Labour	Tooting	43.5%	1st
S. Khan	Labour	Carshalton and Wallington	9.0%	3rd
S. Klein	Labour	Ilford North	34.0%	2nd
H. Koundarjian	Labour	Lewes	5.0%	3rd
D. Lammy	Labour	Tottenham	59.3%	1st
B. Mahfouz	Labour	Ealing Central and Acton	30.0%	2nd
K. Mahmood	Labour	Birmingham Perry Barr	50.3%	1st
S. Malik	Labour	Dewsbury	32.0%	2nd
S. Mahmood	Labour	Birmingham Ladywood	55.7%	1st
S. Nandanwar	Labour	Maldon	12.7%	3rd
C. Onwurah	Labour	Newcastle Upon Tyne Central	45.9%	1st
A. Orhan	Labour	Hemel Hempstead	20.8%	3rd
F. Pepperell	Labour	Basingstoke	20.4%	3rd
Y. Qureshi	Labour	Bolton South East	47.0%	1st
A. Rehal	Labour	Faversham and Mid Kent	16.6%	3rd
T. Sadiq	Labour	South Cambridgeshire	10.2%	3rd
N. Sarkar	Labour	Reading West	31.0%	2nd
A. Sarwar	Labour	Glasgow Central	52.0%	1st
R. Seeruthun	Labour	Maidstone and	10.0%	3rd

The Weald

V. Sharma	Labour	Ealing Southall	51.5%	1st
M. Singh	Labour	Bradford West	45.4%	1st
M. Sood	Labour	North West Norfolk	13.3%	3rd
C. Umunna	Labour	Streatham	42.8%	1st
K. Vaz	Labour	Leicester East	53.8%	1st
V. Vaz	Labour	Walsall South	40.0%	1st
F. Ahmed	Lib Dem	Walthamstow	28.7%	2nd
Z. Ali	Lib Dem	Stoke on Trent South	15.9%	3rd
J. Allie	Lib Dem	Brent North	17.0%	3rd
A. Anwar	Lib Dem	Pendle	20.2%	3rd
A. Ayesh	Lib Dem	Leicestershire South	21.0%	2nd
N. Bakhai	Lib Dem	Ealing Southall	14.9%	3rd
H. Bisnauthsing	Lib Dem	Grantham and Stamford	22.0%	2nd
C. Blango	Lib Dem	Camberwell and Peckham	22.0%	2nd
A. Choudhry	Lib Dem	Leeds North East	19.6%	3rd
A. Diouf	Lib Dem	Derbyshire South	16.0%	3rd
M. Emerson	Lib Dem	Hammersmith	16.0%	3rd
N. Fekri	Lib Dem	Keighley	14.8%	3rd
A. de Freitas	Lib Dem	Great Grimsby	22.4%	3rd
K. Hamilton	Lib Dem	Birmingham Perry Barr	22.0%	2nd
Z. Haq	Lib Dem	Harborough	31.1%	2nd
Q. Hussain	Lib Dem	Luton South	23.0%	3rd
G. Jerome	Lib Dem	Croydon North	14.0%	3rd
A. Khan	Lib Dem	Birmingham Ladywood	27.0%	2nd
K. Khan	Lib Dem	Rushcliffe	21.7%	2nd
T. Khan	Lib Dem	Birmingham Hodge Hill	27.7%	2nd
J. Lee	Lib Dem	Greenwich and Woolwich	18.2%	3rd
P. Ling	Lib Dem	Bromsgrove	19.6%	3rd
R. Martins	Lib Dem	Luton North	11.1%	3rd
A. Masroor	Lib Dem	Bethnal Green and Bow	20.1%	2nd

S. Mustapha	Lib Dem	Glasgow South	11.8%	3rd
F. Qureshi	Lib Dem	Leyton and Wanstead	27.6%	2nd
D. Raval	Lib Dem	Hackney South and Shoreditch	22.4%	2nd
S. Samani	Lib Dem	Angus	10.8%	4th
S. Sheehan	Lib Dem	Wimbledon	25.0%	2nd
P. Singh Gill	Lib Dem	Leicester South	26.9%	2nd
M. Wilson	Lib Dem	Feltham and Heston	13.7%	3rd

Appendix 5: BAME Candidates and Successful MPs at UK General Elections in The Post-War Period, 1945-2010: An Overview

Year	Conservative	Labour	Liberal/Lib Dem	Total
1945	0 -	0 -	0 -	0 -
1950	0 -	0 -	1 -	1 -
1951	0 -	0 -	0 -	0 -
1955	0 -	0 -	0 -	0 -
1959	0 -	1 -	0 -	1 -
1964	0 -	0 -	0 -	0 -
1966	0 -	0 -	0 -	0 -
1970	0 -	1 -	2 -	3 -
1974F	0 -	1 -	1 -	2 -
1974O	0 -	0 -	0 -	0 -
1979	2 -	1 -	2 -	5 -
1983	4 -	6 -	8 -	18 -
1987	6 -	14 (4)	9 -	29 (4)
1992	8 (1)	9 (5)	5 -	22 (6)
1997	9 -	13 (9)	17 -	39 (9)
2001	16 -	21 (12)	29 -	66 (12)
2005	41 (2)	32 (13)	40 -	113 (15)
2010	47 (11)	51 (16)	43 -	141 (27)

Bibliography

Adolino, J. (1998) *Ethnic minorities, electoral politics, and political integration in Britain*, Pinter

Ali, R., and O'Cinneide, C. (2002) *Our House? Race and Representation in British Politics*, (IPPR)

Ansari, H. (2004) *The Infidel Within: The History of Muslims in Britain, 1800 to the Present*, C. Hurst & Co.

Anwar, M. (2001) 'The participation of ethnic minorities in British politics', in *Journal of Ethnic and Migration Studies*, 27(3), pp.533–539.

Anwar, M. (2010) *Ethnic Minorities and Politics*, Lambert Academic.

Anwar, M. (1998) *Ethnic Minorities and the British Electoral System*, CRER and OBV.

Anwar, M. (1994) *Race and Elections: The Participation of Ethnic Minorities in Politics*, (CRER, 1994)

Anwar, M. (1986) *Race and politics: ethnic minorities and the British political system*, Routledge.

Bald, S. R. (1989) 'The South Asian presence in British electoral politics', in *Journal of Ethnic and Migration Studies*, 15(4), pp.537-548.

Crewe, I. (1983) 'Representation and ethnic minorities in Britain', in K. Young and N. Glazer, (eds.), *Ethnic Pluralism and Public Policy*, pp.258-284, Heinemann.

Fieldhouse, E., and Purdam, K. (2002) *Voter engagement among black and minority ethnic communities*, The Electoral Commission.

Fielding, S. and A. Geddes. (1998) 'The British Labour Party and 'ethnic entryism': participation, integration, and the party context', in *Journal of Ethnic and Migration Studies*, 24(1), pp.57-72.

File, N., and Power, C. (1981) *Black Settlers in Britain 1555-1958*, Heinemann Educational.

FitzGerald, M. (1990) 'The emergence of black councillors and MPs in Britain: some underlying questions', in H. Goulbourne, (ed.), *Black Politics in Britain*, Avebury.

FitzGerald, M. (1987) *Black People and Party Politics in Britain*, Runnymede Trust.

Geddes, A. (1995) 'The logic of positive action? Ethnic minority representation in Britain after the 1992 General Election', in *Party Politics*, 1(2), pp.43-57.

Geddes, A. (2001) 'Explaining Ethnic Minority Representation: Contemporary Trends in the Shadow of the Past', in *Journal of Elections, Public Opinion and Parties*, 11(1), pp.119–135.

Geddes, A., Tonge, J. (2010) (eds.), *Britain Votes 2010*, Hansard Society.

Jeffers, S. (1991) 'Black Sections in the Labour Party: the end of ethnicity and 'godfather' politics?' in Werbner, P., and Anwar, M., (eds.), *Black and Ethnic Leaderships*, Routledge.

Le Lohé, M. J. (1993) 'Ethnic minority candidates in general elections', in *The*

Political Quarterly, 64(1), pp.107–117.

Le Lohé, M. J. (1998) 'Ethnic minority participation and representation in the British electoral system', in Saggar, S., (ed.) Race and British Electoral Politics, UCL Press.

LIFE (1950), (Magazine), 28(8), 20 February 1950, pp.29-36.

Messina, A. (1998) 'Ethnic minorities and the British party system in the 1990s and beyond', in Saggar, S. (1998) (ed.) *Race and British Electoral Politics*, UCL Press.

Miles, R. (1990) 'The racialisation of British politics', in *Political Studies*, 38(2), pp.491-485.

Modood, T. (2005) *Multicultural Politics: Racism, Ethnicity, and Muslims in Britain*, Edinburgh UP.

Mukherjee, S. (2004) "Narrow-majority' and 'Bow-and-agree': Public Attitudes towards the Elections of the First Asian MPs in Britain, Dadabhai Naoroji and Mancherjee Merwanjee Bhownaggree, 1885-1906', in *Journal of the Oxford University History Society*, 2.

Norris, P. (2001) *Britain votes, 2001*, OUP & Hansard Society.

Norris, P., Gavin, N. T. (1998) (eds.) *Britain Votes, 1997*, Hansard Society.

Norris, P., Wlezien, C. (2005) (eds.) *Britain votes, 2005*, Hansard Society.

Rich, P. (1998) 'Ethnic politics and the Conservatives in the post-Thatcher era', in Saggar, S., (ed.), *Race and British Electoral Politics*, UCL Press.

Saggar, S. (1997) 'Racial politics', in Norris, P., and Gavin, N. T., (eds.), *Britain Votes 1997*, OUP.

Saggar, S. (1998) *Ethnic Minorities and Electoral Politics, The General Election 1997*, CRE.

Saggar, S. (2000) *Race and Representation*, Manchester UP.

Saggar, S. (1998) *The General Election 1997: Ethnic Minorities and Electoral Politics*, CRE, 1998.

Scobie, E. (1972) *Black Britannia: A History of Blacks in Britain*, Johnson Publishing.

Squires, J. (2010) 'Gender and Minority Representation in Parliament, Political Insight', in *Political Insight*, 1(3), December, pp.82–84.

Visram, R. (2002) *Asians in Britain: 400 Years of History*, Pluto Press.

Werbner, P. (1991) 'The fiction of unity in ethnic politics' in Werbner, P., and Anwar, M., (eds.), *Black and Ethnic Leaderships in Britain: The Cultural Dimensions of Political Action*, Routledge.

Advancing Multiculturalism:
Learning Lessons From Scholarly Advocacy

Karim Murji[95]

Introduction

Is multiculturalism dead? It is certainly assailed on almost all sides. In Britain in 2011 the Prime Minister David Cameron's disavowed it in the spring but then backtracked somewhat on the importance of diversity and inequality after the riots in parts of England in August 2011. In between those events, on what is being called '22/7' in Norway, Anders Breivik launched a murderous assault in the name of cleansing Europe against the spread of Islam. Multiculturalism has other opponents. Radical anti-racists see it as an inadequate, shallow response to discrimination, indeed even as a cloak for liberal assimilationism. Alongside that, there are people on the right and the left who see it as too concerned with cultural separateness rather than national identity or community cohesion, or class inequality. From these points of view, the end of multiculturalism is due to the various and prolonged attacks on it, and/or the excesses and claims to cultural difference and separateness that are claimed in its name. Some scholars argue for another term – interculturalism – instead of multiculturalism. For Rattansi (2011) for instance, this entails a stress upon encounters and dialogues between faith and ethnic groups; a rejection of ideas that any group has strictly definable boundaries that demarcate it from others; and a refusal of the view that non-Western cultures have little in common with the west, along with a recognition of their long and shared histories (though see Meer and Modood 2012 for a view that the interculturalism is not as distinct from multiculturalism as is claimed).

Such debates and events indicate that multiculturalism – its meaning, extent and existence – is still a subject of lively debate, in political and academic circles. There are also active campaigns calling for the defence of multiculturalism, alongside an opposition to Islamophobia and racism. Such debates and dialogue are clearly important in defining what multiculturalism is and what is being argued for and

95 Dr Karim Murji is based in the Sociology department at The Open University, Milton Keynes, UK. He has written distance-learning materials for courses in Sociology, Social Policy, Politics, Geography and social research methods. His research interests are culture, ethnicity and racism and these are applied to fields such as race equality, policing, public sociology, and diaspora and identity. Recent publications on these themes appear in the Journal of Transatlantic Studies (2009), the Journal of Social Policy (2010) and Policy Studies (2011). With John Solomos, he is the co-editor of Racialization: Studies in theory and practice (Oxford University Press, 2005).

against. However, the purpose of this paper is not about meanings as such. Rather, concerning itself mainly with scholarly advocacy of multiculturalism, it sets out to offer some observations on what such debates entail beyond the scholarly environment or a seminar event. Instead of offering a hypothetical or a normative discussion, the observations in this paper are based on two case studies from the past decade.

The two cases – the Macpherson inquiry (1999) and the Parekh report (2000) – are well known and significant in the UK. Though very different in their purpose and scope, both concern issues of race, racism, culture, multiculturalism and the nation. They provide insights into what happens when scholarly interventions are taken into a public domain. While the nature of academic or scholarly advocacy or input into these two inquiries is of very different sort, it is the impact and afterlife of those inputs that I want to shed some light on here – and to use those as a template to reflect on academic advocacy of multiculturalism and/or interculturalism. Advocacy is being used as the key term to draw attention to intended or directed words and deeds, aimed at influencing a report and at impacting on policy, politics and public debate. To set this term apart from expertise is somewhat artificial, though it does draw a distinction between that and academic scholarship which is aimed largely at academic audiences. However, I use the word scholarship in relation to advocacy because it indicates that the views advanced are based on principles of good evidence-based research as well as a systematic approach to construct or present an argument.

The main thematic connection between the Macpherson and Parekh reports is about tackling ethnic and race and inequalities in the criminal justice system and in society. Macpherson is best known for its finding that the actions and failures of the Metropolitan police were due to institutional racism – a term and a view that continues to resonate and be argued over many years later. This is one of the key points on which academic inputs to the inquiry were significant. Ten years on from Macpherson, a review of research (Runnymede Trust 2009) found a mixed picture in terms of implementation, but there is no doubt that Macpherson has been a highly significant touchstone for public policy since it came out in 1999. In contrast, the Parekh report was an initiative to look in to the future of multi-ethnic Britain. Run by the Runnymede Trust it had at least two significant academic theorists among its membership. Its media reception was notable mainly for focussing one small part of the report, the view of the inquiry that 'English' and 'British' were racially coded terms.

Race and Racism

I have set out elsewhere the nature of the input that some scholars made to Macpherson – and the value the inquiry placed on those contributions – on institutional racism (Murji 2007, 2010). In brief, scholars attempted to reconcile the problems that had been evident in the idea since its inception in the 1960s. In particular, those were the confusion between individual and institutional forms of racism, and between racism as an outcome and as an intention. Although a number of different approaches were offered to the inquiry, the main connection between them was the recourse to some idea of 'culture' as a mediating level between the structural or societal forms of racism (institutional), and the individual ways in which some people acted on their prejudices. Alongside that view of institutional racism, it was also explained as a normal or routine aspect of police practice or policy, such as stop and search which – internationally or not – bears most heavily on particular populations including racial minorities. While scholarly advocacy was important to the way Macpherson formulated his inquiry, the issue here is the 'black box' between those submissions and the ways they appeared in public.

Three points are important to note. First, whatever the merits of the words and formulations that scholars put to Macpherson, the widely cited and influential derivation that the inquiry came out with was the result of some 'horse trading' within the inquiry panel. Thus, the form of words is shaped, but only in a loose way, by scholarly inputs. But there are competing scholarly views and approaches. And with a term like institutional racism there are many non-academic contributors who lay claim to defining the term. A multiplicity of views and perspectives exist – as there are on multiculturalism.

Second, the gap between scholarly contributions and policy and practice implementation is a large one. Few scholars are closely involved in policy formulation. My own experience here is informative. As a member for two years of one of the post Stephen Lawrence Inquiry groups – the one dealing with Black and Minority Ethnic groups' Trust and Confidence – I saw how difficult this group found it to engage senior people in the police and the Home Office. Its chair, Mrs Lawrence, resorted to going around them by meeting ministers directly; this did produce expressions of support but little follow up beyond that. Underlying that difficulty is that the Home Office and other parts of government were shifting away from race and institutional racism. It was not that these were not regarded as important, but in an environment of many and competing political priorities and voices, they did not possess the importance they did after Macpherson first came out. Third, and as a continuation of the previous point, various significant voices said more or less explicitly that it was time to move on from institutional racism. These include the Chairman of the UK Equality and Human Rights Commission (EHRC), senior politicians and a Commissioner of the Metropolitan police. The sense of limited movement in the past decade seems to be confirmed by the speech made by Trevor Phillips, the head of the EHRC in that organisation's commemoration of the ten years after Macpherson. Phillips (2009) said that it was time to move on from institutional racism. One of the reasons he gave – that it led to an assumption that all individuals become racists once they put on the police uniform – harks back beyond Macpherson to the debate as it was in the 1980s (cf. Neal 2003). It suggests that attempts by social scientists to provide nuanced explanations of institutional racism have made little impact on the head of the UK equalities body. There was a critical reaction to his intervention, which shows the extent to which the term is still fought over, although the most prominent critic was Duwayne Brooks, the friend of Stephen Lawrence who witnessed his murder.

Nevertheless, Phillips' speech seems to have been a harbinger for the political shift that became evident at the major official conference to mark the tenth anniversary of Macpherson, held in London on 24th February 2009. Jack Straw – who set up the Macpherson Inquiry when he was the Home Secretary – said that the charge of institutional racism against the police was 'no longer' applicable and that 'by and large the police service has purged itself of the systemic racism Macpherson identified'. If the acceptance of institutional racism a decade ago marked an era of action in both policy and rhetoric, these powerful voices made it obvious that a consensus among highly placed people had emerged that it is was time to draw the curtain on that issue. In this sense, the 'refining' value of academic research in revealing complexity and clarifying problems is out of step with a political moment in which the support for institutional racism was in decline, or largely absent.

The 10th anniversary of the Macpherson report in 2009 led pressure groups to restate the case for addressing institutional racism; however, the ears and minds of powerful people were not receptive to that message. Again, the gap between academic inputs – as well as much subsequent research on institutional racism – and policy and practice is a large one. Even where scholarly inputs come from think tanks such as the Runnymede Trust (2009) their impact and reception is muted. Where, when and how 'political spaces' become open – and maybe the issue of how spaces can be created and widened – needs as much thought as the ideas and arguments in the first place. Yet, the unexpected and conjectural can be just as significant. So the riots in part of England in 2011 and the conviction of two men for the murder of Stephen Lawrence in January 2012 both provided spaces where debates about racism and institutional racism – as well as multiculturalism – became live ones again at least in the media. Whether there is any political impetus or social movement able to drive that forward is more doubtful.

Culture and Nation

The second main example I review briefly is the Parekh Commission on the future of multi-ethnic Britain (2000). Discussions about the value of this document are commonplace and, once again, my purpose is not to review its contents. It is clear from what is known about the formulation of the report that two academics with a significant track record of writing on race and culture in Britain were instrumental in framing some of its key arguments. Its Chairman, Bhikhu Parekh, is a well known political theorist who has written about the place of multiculturalism in liberal societies, while the renowned sociologist Stuart Hall was a prominent member, and is commonly regarded as having written – or at least drafted – one of the key sections of the report. Thus, in this case the advocacy comes not in the form of evidence submitted (as with Macpherson) but directly from inside the inquiry panel. However, it is notable that the fact that both these men are of 'colonial' and 'non white origins' was, it was implied in media coverage, part of the lack of attachment to the British nation the report was said to contain (see McLaughlin and Neal 2007).

The report argued that the idea of a multi-cultural 'post-nation' would remain 'an empty promise', unless 'deep-rooted antagonisms to racial and cultural difference can be defeated in practice, as well as symbolically written out of the national story' (Parekh 2000 pp.38-39). On the day of the publication of the report, at least two national newspapers seized on this to denounce the report as stating that British was a term with racist connotations. The very hostile media reaction led the Home Secretary of the day, Jack Straw (who had set up the Macpherson inquiry only two years earlier) to distance himself from the report, which was greeted by the news media as a (welcome) retreat. Like with Macpherson, some of the people who contributed to the report were denounced as a metropolitan elite, out of touch with the sensibilities of ordinary British people. Curiously, leading parts of the black media also joined in this attack (McLaughlin and Neal 2004, 2007). Thus, to all extents and purposes the report was being buried on the day and in the week of its publication. Although it was greeted with extensive acclaim in academic circles for its vision, the arguments made in the report contribute significantly to intra-academic or scholarly discourse, but have a very limited life beyond that.

This is a story I relate at second hand, rather than through any direct involvement so let me move on to some observations of this episode and the politics of scholarly advocacy. The first one is obviously that whatever the contents and nuances of an argument, the ways in which these may be 'read' and received are far beyond the control of the producers of the arguments. Appeals to 'misrepresentation' are of limited value, since there is, without extensive resources, limited scope to 'balance' hostile media coverage. The Parekh commission may have been able to tackle this if it had a sustained set of engagements with the media planned, but it soon became apparent that the members of the inquiry were positioned on the defensive from the outset and did not have the time or resources to counter that. Having lost the political support of the government, they were further marginalised as part of the 'chattering classes' who failed to recognise how out of touch they were with ordinary Britons. The inquiry had lost control of the agenda – now framed by the Britishness theme in the media. Nothing else came close to dominating the coverage of the report as that point.

A further problem is that the advocacy contained in the report failed to consider that alternative forms of multiculturalism would be articulated in opposition to the report. So the argument was not about multiculturalism against non-multiculturalism. Rather the views mobilised in the media articulated a rather conservative kind of multiculturalism, or a 'nationalist multiculturalism' (Fortier 2008) in which the well-known trope of Britain as a tolerant, open nation was repeated. Adding to this was resort to various leading black figures from the world of sports who received extensive media coverage as they expressed how proud they were to be British. The narrowing of the Parekh report to one key theme – and the use of that to denounce the report as a whole and to focus attention on why it should be rejected – provides a powerful case of how scholarly advocacy can be derailed.

The power of the mainstream media can be overstated and there are alternative and 'counter' public spheres that the producers of the report could have sought to develop. However this seems never to have occurred. Despite having been produced under the auspices of the leading race equality think tank, that body itself became defensive in complaining about media misrepresentation. This is a valid point. But the number of people reached by the corrective message is far smaller than those who have heard of the report as the one that says 'British is a racist term'. (A similar point applies to the wide coverage given to the claim by Trevor Phillips about 'sleepwalking to segregation', and the important corrective research by Finney and Simpson (2009) A further difficulty is that the inquiry attempted its own news management with the mainstream media prior to publication and, unwittingly, got 'stung' by newspapers who found something newsworthy in the report; this took inquiry members – some even saw it as an inconsequential point - by surprise (McLaughlin and Neal 2004).

Conclusion

The purpose of this paper is not to decry scholarly engagement and advocacy, or to recommend a disconnection between academic and policy/political worlds. Both are vital for public engagement and discourse (see also British Academy

2008). The issue at hand is what sometimes happens when scholarly advocacy meets what is sometimes, and misleadingly, called the 'real world'. My aim has been to present, briefly, a couple of examples that have a bearing on debates about inter-multiculturalism. The lessons of Macpherson and Parekh are that scholarly contributions are important in the formulation and clarification of ideas, and in providing empirical evidence for ideas and examples of multiculture as a lived practice rather than a set of ideas.

However, in both the small and big senses of the word, there are politics involved that the scholarly engagement finds itself outside of, in the main. At one level, political support is a double-edged sword and what happens on the surface may not be the same as what happens in public policy. Thus, Macpherson was strongly welcomed by the then Prime Minster and led to many policy initiatives over the next decade. Yet evaluations of that (Runnymede Trust 2009) find a mixed picture of how much has changed; and in the wake of the riots in England in August 2011, many of the same issues and complaints about policing persist (Murji and Neal 2011). In contrast, Parekh was rejected by the politicians, but in some ways its underlying message about a multicultural nation has become part of the common consensus across mainstream politics, albeit there are more or less progressive and conservative varieties of multiculturalism. So, while building political coalitions is important, success can never be guaranteed, not least due to changing circumstances and priorities.

At another level, the lessons of the two reports and inquires are about 'unintended consequences' that, by their nature, cannot be predicted. Thus, not all the things that could happen when advocacy is practised can be controlled. However, the point of this paper is to pose questions about, first, what it would mean to consider politics (in its widest sense) of what is being advocated alongside, and not as an afterthought; and second, what it could mean to think about practice or policy considerations alongside – or even before – ideas (this would be the 'politics of the possible'). Putting political considerations before scholarly debate about ideas is challenging because it runs against the grain of academic independence and autonomy from government. (It could be argued that some think tanks have prospered in recent years because they have prioritised making political connections; however there are few case studies of how such advocacy works.) But politics does not need to be equated with government - or with political parties. A wider conception of public and political engagement – and of multiple 'publics' – is needed. My purpose here is to prompt thinking about what forms that could take in the present environment. Academic and scholarly research and advocacy on contentious issues is needed. But the substantial challenge to the formulation, development and advocacy of ideas and models will remain stuck when seeking to make a transition from ideas to practice – and with politics mediating between those things.

Bibliography

British Academy (2008) *Punching our weight: the humanities and social sciences in public policy making.* London: British Academy

Finney, N and Simpson, L. (2009) *'Sleepwalking to segregation'? Challenging myths about race and migration.* Bristol: Policy Press

Fortier, A. (2008) *Multicultural Horizons,* London: Routledge.

McLaughlin, E and Murji, K. (1999) 'After the Stephen Lawrence Inquiry', in *Critical Social Policy,* 60, pp.371-85.

McLaughlin, E and Neal, S. (2007) 'The public sphere and public interventions on race and nation', in *Cultural Studies,* 21(6), pp.911-933

McLaughlin, E and Neal, S. (2004) 'Misrepresenting the multicultural nation: the policy process, news media management and the Parekh Report', in *Policy Studies,* 25(3), pp.155-173.

Macpherson, W. (1999) *The Stephen Lawrence Inquiry,* London: TSO

Meer, N and Modood, T. (2012) 'How does interculturalism contrast with multiculturalism?', in *Journal of Intercultural Studies.*

Murji, K. (2007) 'Sociological engagements: institutional racism and beyond', in *Sociology,* 41(5), pp.843-855.

Murji, K. (2010) 'Applied social science? Academic contributions to the Stephen Lawrence Inquiry and their consequences', in *Journal of Social Policy,* 39(3), pp.343-357.

Murji, K and Neal, S. (2011) 'Riot: Race and Politics in the 2011 Disorders' in *Sociological*
Research On-line, 16 (4).

Neal, S. (2003) 'Scarman, Macpherson and the media: how newspapers respond to race centred policy interventions', in *Journal of Social Policy,* 32(1), pp.55–74.

Parekh, B. (2000) *The future of multi-ethnic Britain,* London: Profile books.

Phillips, T. (2009) 'Institutions must catch up with public on race issues', [online] 19 January, available at: http://www.equalityhumanrights.com/en/newsandcomment/speeches/Pages/Macphersonspeech190109.aspx

Rattansi, A. (2011) *Multiculturalism: A Very Short Introduction,* Oxford University Press

Runnymede Trust (2009) *Stephen Lawrence Inquiry 10 years on, a review of the literature.* London: Runnymede Trust

Part 4

MULTICULTURALISM IN THE UK - II

Multiculturalism and the Impacts on Education Policy in England

Richard Race[96]

Introduction

This workshop paper is part of an on-going debate relating to multiculturalism (Eade et al 2008; Parekh 2008; Modood 2011; Race 2011a; 2011b 2012a; 2012b) and the possibilities of 'new directions' (Vertovec and Wessendorf 2010). In an age of austerity, the need to continue to promote the concept of multiculturalism when it is under attack from politicians (Mahamdallie 2011; Murphy 2012) is paramount when reflecting on specific impacts on education practice and policy-making. This counters a more general 'backlash' against multiculturalism which re-introduces integration themes (Phillips 2005; Hasan, 2009; Miera in Triandafyllidou et al 2012).

This workshop paper draws upon research from two recent and current research projects relating to Multiculturalism and Education (Race 2011a) and Integration and education policy-making (Race 2011c; 2011d). The paper begins with an opening section, putting multiculturalism into context by not only examining the speeches of Angela Merkel, David Cameroon and Nick Clegg (November 2010 – March 2011) but by looking at international perspectives and attempts to define

---

96 Dr Richard Race is Senior Lecturer in Education in the Department of Education at Roehampton University, London. He is Programme Convenor of the Department's MA in Education which is delivered on site, off site and internationally in Athens, Greece at ASPETE University. He is author of Multiculturalism and Education (2011) with Continuum International Publishing which is part of the Series Contemporary Issues in Education which he also co-edits with Simon Pratt-Adams. He is also co-editor of the forthcoming volume, Precarious International Multicultural Education: hegemony, dissent and rising alternatives, which is published by Sense with Handel Wright and Michael Singh. His current research is based on Integration and Education Policy-Making which will be the title of his next monograph, in a second book series he is co-editing with Alaster Douglas and Barbara Read with Palgrave Macmillan. His is also co-editor of Advancing Race, Ethnicity and Education with Vini Lander which will also be published with Palgrave Macmillan.

the multiculturalism concept, using evidence from Canada, the USA and England. This then allows an examination of multiculturalism and education which will focus on English education policies from the 1980s (DES 1985) and the 2000s (DfES 2007) which both attempted to focus on the promotion of increased cultural diversity and citizenship within education. The paper ends by attempting to show the continuing influences of both multicultural and integrationist processes on education policy and highlights why one concept (integration) seems to be continually more influential than the other (multiculturalism) within state making education policy making processes.

Contemporary Multiculturalism

The contemporary issue of multiculturalism and its importance within current education debates is discussed within this paper. The aim of this paper is to continue to increase understandings of how multiculturalism has conceptually developed over time and how applications of the term have shaped specific education debates (Banks 2009; Race 2011a). The political speeches by German Chancellor Angela Merkel, Prime Minister of the United Kingdom, David Cameroon and the Deputy Prime Minister, Nick Clegg provide recent political contexts to the wider multiculturalism debate. The three speeches were delivered between November 2010 and March 2011. Part of Merkel's speech focused on a movement from multiculturalism back into integration policy but within the English-speaking world has been misquoted as Merkel actually focused on German multiculturalism and both its benefits and failings. It also has to be considered that all three of these speeches, were political and were theoretically appealing to differing electorates. Cameroon's speech, delivered in Munich in Germany (February 2011), talked about 'muscular liberalism' and the 'state multiculturalism' which produced a predictable but important response (Mahamdallie, in Mahamdallie 2011). But the third speech which is often forgotten was Nick Clegg's speech in Luton (England) in March 2011 where the Deputy Prime Minister praised cultural diversity and the importance and influence of multiculturalism in the United Kingdom. The paper will underline multiculturalism is far from dead – how after all can a concept or idea die? – But needs continual promotion in local, national and international contexts. And in all subject areas, not just within Education. As Murphy has recently persuasively argued:

> Perhaps the single most important message … is that there never has been anything like a single overarching multicultural experiment or a grand unified political philosophy of multiculturalism. There are in fact many ongoing multicultural experiments, a great deal of *ad hoc* multicultural policy, and a multiplicity of distinctive contributions to the political philosophy of multiculturalism. To understand contemporary multicultural political

philosophy (and practice) one must therefore examine it in all of its rich, if inconvenient diversity. (Murphy 2012 p.5)

And this paper is a contribution to the ongoing multiculturalism conceptual debate with the specific subject focus being on multiculturalism and education. As Race (in Eade et al 2008 p.1) wrote, 'Multiculturalism *still* matters and is even more important after 7/7 [and 9/11 than it was before.' That quote suggests that multiculturalism conceptual debates not only allow us to test our ideas and theories about society, but also allow us to focus on contemporary issues that surround us in potentially all subject areas, including education.

Multiculturalism as a concept has different histories and origins in different countries. Canada was the first country in the world to adopt multiculturalism as an official policy in 1971. It is interesting to look at how the contemporary Canadian government defines the concept:

> 'Canadian multiculturalism is fundamental to our belief that all citizens are equal. Multiculturalism ensures that all citizens can keep their identities, can take pride in their ancestry and have a sense of belonging. Acceptance gives Canadian's a feeling of security and self-confidence, making them more open to, and accepting of, diverse cultures. The Canadian experience has shown that multiculturalism encourages racial and ethnic harmony and cross-cultural understanding, and discourages ghettoisation, hatred, discrimination and violence'. (CIC 2009)

It is an impressive definition and theoretically has a wide-ranging cultural and social significance. Recognition and acceptance of differences in law and the discouragement of discrimination and racism is fundamental in any country that believes all citizens are equal. Conceptual debates within the Canadian state concerning multiculturalism have promoted the issues of equality and human rights alongside debates which address issues of ghettoisation and violence (CDSoS 1987; CMoSMC 1991). On the other hand, Day (2002 p.1) argues that, '...while Canadian multiculturalism presents itself as a new solution to an ancient problem of diversity, it is better seen as the most recent mode of *reproduction* and *proliferation* of that problem' (Johnson and Enomoto 2007; Biles et al 2008). Despite universal cultural fluidity, it seems that Canada, as a state, has come closest to not only defining but also trying to implement multicultural policies based on equal rights. As Day (2002) points out, these processes have not been perfect and the debates continue as Canada, like other countries, continues to culturally change and become more diverse.

Multiculturalism is defined in the Unites States of America by Banks and Banks (2007:474) as: 'A philosophical position and movement that assumes that the gender, ethnic, racial, and cultural diversity of a pluralistic society should be reflected in all of the institutionalised structures of educational institutions, including the staff, the norms and values, the curriculum and the students body.' Multiculturalism, in England, is seen by Parekh as a perspective on human life and contains central insights into how we socially construct our lives:

- First, human beings are culturally embedded in the sense that they grow up and live within a culturally structured world, organise their lives and social relations in terms of its system of meaning and significance, and place considerable value on their cultural identity

- Second, different cultures represent different systems of meaning and visions of the good life. Since each realises a limited range of human capacities and emotions and grasps only a part of the totality of human existence, it needs others to understand itself better [and] expand its intellectual and moral horizon …

- Third, all but the most primitive cultures are … plural and represent a continuing conversation between their different traditions and strands of thought. This does not mean that they are devoid of internal coherence and identity but that their identity is plural and fluid. (Parekh 2000 pp.336-337)

What Parekh calls a multicultural perspective is, '…composed of the creative interplay of these three complementary insights, namely the cultural embeddedness of human beings, the inescapability and desirability of cultural diversity and intercultural dialogue, and the internal plurality of each culture … From a multicultural perspective, no political doctrine or ideology can represent the full truth of human life' (Parekh 2000 p.338).

Acknowledging the above definitions from Banks and Banks (2007) as well as Parekh (2000) of multiculturalism which highlight different social constructions and educational structures, the aim of taking forward the notion of cultural diversity within a pluralistic society is useful. This multicultural perspective underlines the recognition of gender, ethnicity and race., alongside the desirability of cultural diversity and the internal plurality of cultures. Baber (2008 p.9) offers an interesting critique of multiculturalism claiming that, '…most people do not want to live in a plural monoculturalist "salad bowl"'. That salad bowl metaphor was created to produce a multicultural image but had a monocultural impact which did not aim to focus on different cultures. Multiculturalism, at the very least, is a desirable acknowledgement of cultural diversity within a pluralistic society.

One of the major issues that this paper seeks to address is whether the concept of multiculturalism does or can go further than this. Baber (2008 pp.14-19) suggests that the alternative in the United States to multiculturalism is integration and assimilation within schools, neighbourhoods and offers a potential solution to economic inequality. It would be disagreeable to support Baber's suggestion that by returning to the past and revising assimilation or integration educational and social policies, we can provide the solutions to pubic issues. In relation to a working definition of multiculturalism within this paper, let us reassert the Canadian state position (CIC 2009) of a multiculturalism that promotes equal rights and discourages discrimination, agree with Banks and Banks (2007) that multiculturalism cannot be thought of as a single concept which is socially on its own, and also agree with Parekh (2000) and his claim that multiculturalism is both plural and fluid which recognises how cultural diversity is constantly changing. Educational structures and agents – meaning e.g. the state, schools, colleges, universities, teachers, children and parents – all need to acknowledge this. However, changing educational structures and agents perspectives can be difficult when considering economic issues alongside the fluid nature of culture diversity when considering an issue i.e. the promotion of equal educational rights.

Multiculturalism and Education

Having introduced key general debates concerning multiculturalism we now move to the more specific debates concerning multicultural education. Banks (2004; 2007; 2009) and Parekh (2000; 2008) have played a crucial part in the development and promotion of multicultural education all over the world. For Banks (in Modgil et al 1986 p.222), multicultural education, '… is an inclusive concept used to describe a wide variety of school practices, programs and materials designed to help children from diverse groups to experience educational equality …' It's interesting to reflect on the date of the above quote as it is over twenty-five years old at the time of writing which shows to the reader how long these ongoing issues have been debated. Banks (ibid) mentions how multicultural education deals, or attempts to deal with 'serious problems in society' but can 'evoke strong emotions, feelings and highly polarise opinions'.

Parekh (in Taylor 1988 pp.14-16) suggests multicultural education is, '… a way of avoiding … mistakes … and cultivating such capacities as mutual respect, intellectual curiosity, dialogue, self-criticism and quest for critical self-knowledge.' The education system contains many sites e.g. primary or secondary schools, where these personal capacities can be developed or blocked. As Parekh shows (ibid) '… the school is part of society which is … characterised by specific ways of thought and life that is a specific historically evolved culture …', then to this extent, education is indeed monocultural. As Parekh continues:

- First, no culture, at least not in such a developed and self-critical society as Britain, is a monolithic and undifferentiated unit …

- Second, common culture is not a static entity. It is constantly exposed to new needs and influences, and evolves, acquires new sensibilities and makes appropriate internal adjustments in response to them …

- The third dimension of multicultural education relates to what we teach, and how. There is no good reason why our syllabus should not be made more broad-based than at present …

(ibid)

Parekh suggests within the plural, fluid nature of British cultural diversity and society, the important education issue concerning multiculturalism is what we teach in the curriculum and how we teach it. Parekh wrote these ideas down after the publication of the Swann Report (DES 1985) having been a member of the committee set up to report on these very multicultural issues. This education policy document is significant as I will suggest later in this paper that these three points above still apply to education policy today in England (Race 2011a). The implication from Parekh's evidence is that the recommendations from the Swann Report (DES 1985) do not apply or incorporate multicultural ideas within education. Developing Parekh's ideas, as well as focusing on what we teach and how we teach it, we need to focus more on the plurality of languages and the expressions of multi-cultures (Pathak 2008). Educational challenges need to be addressed so that all educational professionals can increase understandings of cultural difference student diversity (Cornbleth 2008) and student experiences within both domestic and international environments for majority and minority communities. This not only applies in England but globally if multicultural education is going to evolve into the twenty-first century.

The Evolution of Multiculturalism Within Education in England: Diversity and Citizenship

There is an interesting education link between the Swann (DES 1985) and the Ajegbo (DfES 2007) Reports which both recommended greater diversity was needed within English education. The Ajegbo Report (DfES 2007) carried out a review of diversity and citizenship education in the National Curriculum in England. The review took place two years after the 7/7 London Bombings, which refocused social and cultural debates on integration rather than multiculturalism and citizenship (Eade et al 2008; Osler 2008). The report underlined an essential lack of cultural diversity being taught in schools which draws uncomfortable parallels with Swann reported on in England and Wales, twenty two years before. As Ajegbo (DfES 2007 pp.4-5) himself wrote in the foreword to the Report: 'I believe issues around race, identity, citizenship and living together in the UK today are serious matters ... I believe that schools, through their ethos, through their curriculum and through their work with their communities, can make a difference to those perceptions.' Citizenship, because of events like 7/7 had become more politically visible within education during the first decade of the twenty-first century (Eade et al 2008; Race 2011a).

The first key finding of the Ajegbo Report (DfES 2007 p.6) was that, 'the quality and quantity of education for diversity are uneven across England.' Therefore, issues such as cultural diversity were not being taught universally in state-maintained schools across the country. In relation to Citizenship, the report found:

- Many teachers are unsure of the standard expected in Citizenship.

- Our Research Review found consensus among secondary head teachers and school staff that one of the biggest challenges to delivering Citizenship education was being taught by non-specialists.

- Issues of identity and diversity are more often than not neglected in Citizenship education.

- Much Citizenship education in secondary schools is not sufficiently contextualised for pupils to become interested and engaged with the local, national and international questions of the day and how politicians deal with them.

- Currently in Citizenship, issues of identity and diversity do not tend to be linked explicitly enough to political understanding (of legal and political systems) and active participation.

- The term 'British' means different things to different people. In addition, identities are typically constructed as multiple and plural. Throughout our consultations, concerns were expressed, however, about defining 'Britishness', about the term's divisiveness and how it can be used to exclude others.

(DfES 2007 pp.7-8)

Analysing the above points, many pre 2002 (the year citizenship was introduced into the national curriculum of England and Wales) qualified teachers are 'unsure' of citizenship because they have not been taught how to teach the subject. That in itself is an important observation because with the non-statutory nature of citizenship education in primary schools, the number of citizenship teachers who would have had the training or continuing professional development would have been minimal (Murphy and Hall 2008; Galton and MacBeath 2008). More teachers and specialists in citizenship were required. As the report acknowledges, coverage, meaning who and how the subject is taught, lacks not only conceptual depth but also teachers and students need to be engaged with relevant subject material. This lack of coverage also relates to issues like racism, segregation and the need to understand the changing nature of cultural diversity. Recommendations, to address these issues, from the Ajegbo Report (DfES 2007) are highlighted below:

- Pupils Voice – All schools have mechanisms in place to ensure that the pupil voice is heard and acted upon. Schools should consider the use of forums, school councils, pupil questionnaires or other mechanisms for discussions around identity, values and belonging.

- Education for Diversity in the Curriculum – All schools should be encouraged to audit their curriculum to establish what they currently teach that is meaningful for all pupils in relation to diversity and multiple identities. The Qualifications and Curriculum Authority (QCA) 'Respect for all' is a useful audit tool. In the light of this audit, all schools should map provision across years and subjects and ensure that coverage is coherent.

- Harnessing local context – Schools should build active links between and across communities, with education for diversity as a focus:

a. This might range from electronic links (local, national and global to relationships through other schools (for example as part of a federation), links with businesses, community groups and parents.

b. These links should be encouraged particularly between predominately monocultural and multicultural schools.

c. Such links need to be developed in such a way as to ensure they are sustainable.

d. Such work between schools must have significant curriculum objectives and be incorporated into courses that pupils are studying. This will help avoid stereotyping and tokenism. (DfES 2007 pp. 9-11)

Listening to what pupils and students have to say especially in relation to identity or identities in the classroom is important because it raises the issue of relevant curricula in relation to cultural diversity and multiculturalism. The issue of increasing student voice(s) is significant when considering promoting multicultural education as it gives education spaces for all students from different cultural backgrounds to express themselves. Changing the curriculum to make it 'meaningful' for all students highlights the previous point of promoting multicultural education in the sense that what is taught has to have contemporary relevance to the student. How citizenship is taught is also significant because this relates to teaching method and learning i.e. pedagogy. Links with the local community are significant and builds on existing legislation within the Education and Inspections Act (DfES 2006) which called for more involvement by parents in schools and the joining of schools into federations. The introduction of Beacon schools therefore theoretically offered subject centres of excellence and expertise in curriculum subjects. But there are also warnings about the promotion and recent opening of Academy and Free Schools in England with increased commercialisation and marketisation of primary and secondary schooling (Gunter 2011; Hoskins 2012) which continues to have detrimental consequences for both majority and minority communities in England (Gillborn 2008; 2011).

However, even within Free and Academy Schools, multicultural links 'should be encouraged' because it implies that multicultural education should be promoted within the classroom (Banks 2009). This yet again implies that the concept of multiculturalism is still very much alive if not being practically applied, as it is being mentioned and debated in the Ajegbo Report (DfES 2007). There is an agenda for a revised citizenship education which encompassed more diversity and a revised focus on the concept of multiculturalism was promoted (Osler 2009). The need for greater understanding of contemporary cultural diversity through citizenship education has also been promoted within international contexts (Banks 2004). Interestingly, Alred et al (2006) suggest that the concept of citizenship and citizenship education does not go far enough, focusing on the nation state and national identity, with a call for intercultural education with the focus being on a global or cosmopolitan citizenship (Jackson 2006; Gillborn 2008; Osler 2008). Hewitt (2005) addresses the development of citizenship education which should promote the capacity for autonomous thinking. Hewitt suggests that:

> Citizenship education not only involves promoting a certain sort of critical attitude towards authority, it also involved developing habits of civility and the capacity for public reasonableness. Both of these indirectly promote autonomy, since they encourage children to interact with the members of other groups, to understand the reasonableness of other ways of life, and to distance themselves from their own cultural traditions. (Hewitt 2005 p.308)

Interaction is crucial within citizenship education as majority and minority groups are encouraged to mix and learn from each other. However, autonomy suggests something a lot more individual and powerful then a respect for civil values. It should go beyond the notions of an integrationist, two-way relationship that is part of the community cohesion policy (Cantle 2008). Hewitt continues:

> … citizenship education typically has a dual function – it promotes a national identity within each constituent national group, defined by a common language and history, but it also seeks to promote some sort of transnational identity which can bind together the various national groups within the

state. Unfortunately, recent developments ... in states e.g. the breakdown of Yugoslavia and Czechoslovakia, the constitutional crises in Belgium and Canada – suggest that is very difficult to construct and maintain this transnational identity. (Hewitt 2005 p.214)

The promotion of a transnational identity, which Hewitt describes above as being difficult to teach, is in constant flux and continues to move with every migratory movement, has to be addressed to avoid what Hewitt (2005) describes in his research as a 'white backlash'. At the very least, the Ajegbo Report (DfES 2007) has offered recommendations that can attempt through student voice, community involvement; and continuing professional development, a culturally diverse agenda which can be theoretically addressed through citizenship, to produce and provide a more multicultural education curriculum in England.

Conclusions - Multicultural and Integrationist Impacts Shaping Education Policy

It remains debateable whether Ajegbo's (DfES 2007) recommendations were fully applied into the English education curricula as Citizenship still remains non-statutory in English and Welsh primary schools (for children aged 5-11) and statutory in secondary schools (for children aged 11-16). The uncomfortable similarity with the Swann Report (DES, 1985) and the failure of the recommendations to be fully implemented in both cases has to be noted. Recognition of cultural diversity is simply not enough within education policy making and practice. Indeed, as Race (2011a) has underlined, there are other education policy examples of where multiculturalism and cultural diversity has been promoted but has not been visible in consequent education legislation which therefore does not permeate down into classrooms, staffrooms and lecture theatres. However, it is reassuringly important to highlight that claims of multiculturalism's death are much exaggerated (Thomas, 2011). Indeed, Merkel and Cameron's speeches ironically underlined that the concept of multiculturalism was far from dead. If it was dead, why would politicians of all political persuasions be talking about it? Significantly, it produced a passionate response (Mahamdallie in Mahamdallie 2011) with the need for multiculturalism as both a paradigm and an institutional framework needing to move on to cope with new and varied social and political situations (Rattansi 2011). Education within multiculturalist frameworks continues to have an important role to play ... 'in challenging stereotypes, prejudices and ethnocentric perspectives of both individuals and groups in national and international settings' (Verma, in Verma et al 2007 p.21). Education systems need to continue to not only acknowledge but teach at all levels changing cultural diversity which in itself is complicated but by no means impossible as Spencer (2011) and Cesar (2012) highlight with the need to underline and teach migration narratives within not only citizenship but all curricula subjects (Bishop 2010).

How multiculturalist inspired debates and impacts evolve within education and in all areas remains to be seen. The benefits of multicultural education have been underlined in this paper but its failings also need to be recognised (Youdell 2012). We should be moving the debate forwards within culturally diverse education curricula and looking in 'new directions' (Vertovec and Wessendorf 2010) by examining subjects like Anti-Racism (Race 2009), Critical Race Theory (Chakrabaty et al 2012) and Anti-discrimination (Joppe 2010) within a broader Human Rights framework. Other commentators underline the importance of citizenship curricula (Fass and Street 2011; Race 2011a) or an evolutionary movement from citizenship to intercultural education (Gundara 2011). However, there is also a movement chronologically backwards, which in itself is an interesting application of Vertovec and Wessendorf's (2010) idea of 'new directions', towards integrationist, assimilationist and separatist ideas. As Spencer (2011:201) suggests ... we find a lack of coherence on policy across government... In part, I shall argue, this is because of a lack of clarity on what is mean by 'integration' and hence the aims of policy intervention; and in part because the policy paradigm had its origins in the post-war era and has not adjusted to the migration patterns of modern times.' The politics of integration, like multiculturalism has long domestic and international histories (Drissen and Merry 2011; Race 2011a).

We need to continue to increase our understandings, in particular how integration as a concept has impacted upon policy in the past (Taber et al 2010; Miera, in Triandafyllidou et al 2012) so that we have more of an idea of how integration shapes policy and politics today (Lentin and Titley 2011). Within education policy in England, it is true that both the Swann (DES: 1985) and Ajegbo (DfES 2007) Reports recommended increased cultural diversity in England but the education system continued to promote a more integrationist approach with the state having a conditional relationship over the individual enshrined within education policy making (Race 2011a; 2011b). My continuing research aims to explore and increase understandings of these integrationist processes e.g. the recognition rather than celebration of cultural diversity and how an idea like recognition within a wider integrationist framework has influenced and continues to shape present education policy (Race 2011c; 2011d; 2012a; 2012b; Wright et al forthcoming).

Bibliography

Alred, G., Byram, M., Fleming, M. (2006) *Education for Intercultural Citizenship. Concepts and Comparisons*, Clevedon: Multilingual Matters.

Baber, H.E. (2008) *The Multicultural Mystique. The Liberal Case against Diversity*, New York: Prometheus Books.

Banks, J.A. (1986) 'Multicultural Education and Its Critics: Britain and the United States', in Modgil, S., Verma, G.K., Mallick, K., Modgil, C. (Eds.) *Multicultural Education. The Interminable Debate*, Lewes: The Falmer Press, pp.221-232.

Banks, J.A. (Ed.) (2004) *Diversity and Citizenship Education*, San Francisco: Jossey-Bass.

Banks, J.A. (2nd Ed.) (2007) *Educating Citizens in a Multicultural Society*, New York: Teachers College Press.

Banks, J.A. (Ed.) (2009) *The Routledge International Companion to Multicultural Education*, Abingdon: Routledge.

Banks. J.A., Banks, C.A.M. (Eds.) (6th Ed.) (2007) *Multicultural Education: issues and perspectives*, Wiley: New Jersey.

Biles, J., Burstein, M., Frideres, J. (Eds.) (2008) *Immigration and Integration in Canada*, Montreal: McGill-Queen's University Press.

Bishop, R. (2010) 'Addressing Diversity: race, ethnicity and culture in the classroom', in Steinburg, S.R. (Ed.) *Diversity and Multiculturalism: a reader*, New York: Peter Lang pp.111-122.

Cantle, T. (2008) *Community Cohesion: A New Framework for Race and Diversity*, Houndsmills: Palgrave Macmillan.

Cassar. J. (2012) 'Living in Different Worlds and Learning All About It: Migration Narratives in Perspective', in Bekerman, Z., Geisen, T. (Eds.) *International Handbook of Migration, Minorities and Education: understanding cultural and social differences in processes of learning*, Dordrecht: Springer, pp.153-168.

Canadian Department of the Secretary of State (CDSoS) (1987) *Multiculturalism: Being Canadian*, Ottawa: Supply and Services Canada.

Chakrabarty, N., Roberts, L., Preston, J. (2012) 'Critical Race Theory in England', in *Race, Ethnicity and Education*, 15(1), pp.1-4.

Citizenship and Immigration Canada (CIC) (2009) 'What is Multiculturalism?' http://www.cic.gc.ca/multi/multi-eng.asp, last accessed 24th August 2009.

Canadian Ministry of State for Multiculturalism and Citizenship (CMoSMC) (1991) *Multiculturalism: What Is It Really About?* Ottawa: Supply and Services Canada.

Cornbleth, C. (2008) *Diversity and the New Teacher: learning from experience in urban schools*, New York: Teachers College Press.

Day, R.J.F. (2002) *Multiculturalism and the History of Canadian Diversity*, Toronto: University of Toronto Press.

Department of Education and Science (DES) (1985) 'Education for All' (The

Swann Report), London: HMSO.

Department for Education and Skills (DfES) (2006) *The Education and Inspections Act*, Chapter 40, London, HMSO: Full text available at: http://www.opsi.gov.uk/acts/acts2006/pdf/ukpga_20060040_en.pdf, (last accessed 17th August 2009).

DfES (2007) *Diversity and Citizenship Curriculum Review*, London, DfES. Full text available at: http://publications.teachernet.gov.uk/eOrderingDownload/DfES_Diversity_&_Citizenship.pdf, (last accessed 15th August 2009).

Driessen, G., Merry, M.S. (2011) 'The effects of integration and generation of immigrants on language and numeracy achievement', *Educational Studies*, 37, 5, pp.581-594.

Eade, J., Barrett, M., Flood, C., Race, R. (Eds.) (2008) *Advancing Multiculturalism, Post 7/7*, Newcastle-Upon-Tyne: Cambridge Scholars Publishing.

Fass, D., Street, A. (2011) 'Schooling the new generation of German Citizens: a comparison of citizenship curricula in Berlin and Baden-Wuttemberg', in *Educational Studies*, 37(4), pp.469-480.

Galton, M., MacBeath, J. (2008) *Teachers Under Pressure*, London: National Union of Teachers and Sage.

Gillborn, D. (2008) *Racism and Education. Coincidence or conspiracy?* London: Routledge.

Gillborn (2011) 'Fine Words and Foul Deeds: why coalition education policy will make things worse for Black students and the White working Class', in *Race Equality Teaching*, 29, 2, pp.9-14.

Gundara, J.S. (2011) 'Citizenship and Intercultural Education in an International and Comparative Context', in Grant, C.A., Portera, A. (Eds.) *Intercultural and Multicultural Education: enhancing global Interconnectedness*, New York: Routledge, pp. 294-315.

Gunter, H (Ed.) (2011) *The State and Education Policy. The Academies Programme*, London: Continuum.

Hasan, R. (2009) *Multiculturalism. Some Inconvenient Truths*, London: Politico.

Hewitt, R. (2005) *White Blacklash and the Politics of Multiculturalism*, Cambridge: Cambridge University Press.

Hoskins, K. (2012) 'Raising Standards 1988 to the Present: a new performance policy era? in *Journal of Educational Administration and History*, 44, 1, pp.5-20.

Jackson, R. (2006) 'Intercultural education and religious education: a changing relationship' in Bates, D., Durka, G., Schweitzer, F. (Eds.) *Education, Religion and Society. Essays in honour of John M. Hull*, London: Routledge, pp. 49-61.

Johnson, G.F., Enomoto, R. (Eds.) (2007) *Race, Racialization, and Antiracism in Canada and Beyond*, Toronto: University of Toronto Press.

Joppe, C. (2010) *Citizenship and Immigration*, Cambridge: Polity Press.

Lentin, A., Titley, G. (2011) *The Crises of Multiculturalism. Racism in a Neoliberal Age*, London: Zed Books.

Mahamdallie, H. (2011) 'Introduction: Defending multiculturalism', in Mahamdallie, H. (Ed.) *Defending Multiculturalism*, London: Bookmark Publications, pp.15-25.

Miera, F. (2012) 'Not a One-Way Road? Integration as a Concept and a Policy', in Triandafyllidou, A., Modood, T., Meer, N (Eds.) *European Multiculturalisms. Cultural, Religious and Ethnic Challenges,* Edinburgh: Edinburgh University Press, pp. 192-212.

Modood, T. (2011) 'Multiculturalism and Integration: struggling with confusions', in Mahamdallie, H. (Ed.) *Defending Multiculturalism*, London: Bookmark Publications, pp.61-76.

Murphy, P., Hall, K. (2008) *Learning and Practice. Agency and Identities*. London: The Open University and Sage.

Osler, A. (2008) 'Citizenship education and the Ajegbo Report: re-imaging a cosmopolitan nation', in *London Review of Education,* 6(1), pp.11-25.

Osler, A. (2009) 'Patriotism, multiculturalism and belonging: political discourse and the teaching of history', in *Educational Review*, 6(1), pp.85-100.

Parekh, B. (1988) 'Some Thoughts on Multicultural Education', in Taylor B. (Ed.) *Better To Light A Candle..." More Multicultural Education*, (Perspectives 39), School of Education, University of Exeter, pp.10-18.

Parekh, B. (2000) *Rethinking Multiculturalism. Cultural Diversity and Political Theory*, Harvard: Harvard University Press.

Parekh (2008) *A New Politics of Identity. Political Principles for an Interdependent World*, Houndsmills: Palgrave Macmillan.

Parekh, B., Jahanbegloo, R. (2011) *Talking Politics. Bhikhu Parekh in conversation with Ramin Jahanbegloo*, Oxford: Oxford University Press.

Pathak, P. (2008) *The Future of Multicultural Britain*, Edinburgh: Edinburgh University Press.

Philips, T. (2005) 'After 7/7: Sleepwalking to Segregation', Speech given by the CRE Chari, Trevor Phillips at the Manchester Council for Community Relations, available at: www.cre.gov.uk/default.aspx?textonly=0&LocID=0hgnew07s@RefLocID=ohg00900c002@Lang+EM&htm, 9last accessed 27th August 20090.

Race, R. (2008) 'Introduction', in Eade, J., Barrett, M, Flood, C., Race, R. (Eds.) Advancing Multiculturalism, Post 7/7, Newcastle-Upon-Tyne: Cambridge Scholars Publishing, pp.1-8.

Race, R. (2009) 'Troyna Revisited: conceptually examining anti-racism and multiculturalism in education', in Pilkington, A., Housee, S., Hylton, K. (Eds.) Rac(ing) Forward: Transitions in theorising 'race' in education, Birmingham: The Higher Education Academy / Sociology, Anthropology, Politics (C-Sap), pp.167-183.

Race, R. (2011a) *Multiculturalism and Education*, London: Continuum.

Race, R. (2011b) 'Integrationist to Citizenship education policy in England', Book chapter in Barrett, M., Flood, C., Eade, J (Eds.) 'Nationalism, Ethnicity' in *Citizenship: multidisciplinary perspectives*, Newcastle-Upon-Tyne: Cambridge Scholars Press, pp.181-194.

Race, R. (2011c) 'Integration, Choice and Tolerance: contemporary applications to social justice within education', Invited paper presented to the Social Justice within Education Research Group, University of East London, May 2011.

Race, R. (2011d) 'Multiculturalism and Education Policy-Making in England', Invited paper to the International Symposium, 'Rethinking Multiculturalism: Reassessing Multicultural Education', University of Western Sydney, Australia, August 2011.

Race, R. (2012a) 'Defending and advancing multiculturalism within education', Invited Keynote Presentation to be given at The European University, Nicosia, Cyprus, March 2012.

Race, R. (2012b) 'Multiculturalism, community cohesion and integration in London education', Paper for the conference *London – City of Paradox*, University of East London, April 2012.

Rattansi, A. (2011) *Multiculturalism. A Very Short Introduction*, Oxford: Oxford University Press.

Spencer, S. (2011) *The Migration Debate*, Bristol: The Policy Press.

Taber, P., Noble, G., Poynting, S. (2010) *On Being Lebanese in Australia. Identity, Racism and the Ethnic Field*, Beirut: Lebanese American University Press.

Thomas, P. (2011) *Youth, Multiculturalism and Community Cohesion*, Houndsmills: Palgrave Macmillan.

Verma, G. K. (2007) 'Diversity and multicultural education', in Verma, G.K., Bagley, C.R., Mohan Jha, M. (Eds.) International Perspectives on Educational Diversity and Inclusion, London: Routledge, pp.21-30.

Vertovec, S. Wessendorf, S. (Eds.) (2010) *The Multiculturalism Backlash. European discourses, policies and practices*, New York: Routledge.

Wright, H., Singh, M., Race, R. (Eds.) (forthcoming) *Precarious International Multicultural Education: hegemony, dissent and rising alternatives*, Rotterdam: Sense Publishers.

Youdell, D. (2012) 'Fabricating 'Pacific Islander; a pedagogies of expropriation, return and resistance and other lessons from a 'Multicultural Day', in *Race, Ethnicity and Education*, 15(2), pp.141-156.

Multi-ethnic Schooling and the Future of Multiculturalism in the UK

Helen F. Wilson[97]

Introduction

In the UK, schools are key to the realisation of multicultural cities and relations (Burgess et. al 2005; Wood and Landry 2008). Under the last government, schools had a statutory duty to promote community cohesion, tolerance and good relations between families and children from different backgrounds (DCSF 2007). The value of multicultural schooling in particular, has been extensively debated in the context of discussions on the role of faith schools, with key proponents of multicultural schooling arguing that the opportunity for contact with difference is central to learning about the breadth of cultures and religions that characterise contemporary society – and far more so than curriculum alone (Flint 2007). Indeed, one only needs to look as far as Northern Ireland to appreciate the value given to mixed or 'desegregated' schools for their ability to foster 'a culture of tolerance' and more open attitudes to difference (Stringer et. al 2009). This paper feeds into such debates to argue that the opportunity for encounters with difference can be significant to the preparation of children and families for a multicultural future.

Whilst there is clearly much to be said about schools as sites of state pedagogy and citizenship education, where moral values are learned and further conditioned (Pykett 2010), there is also much to be said about the school as a site of everyday multicultural encounter. A growing body of work attentive to urban encounter (Wise and Velayutham 2009), recognises that whilst the politics and policies of multiculturalism might be in decline – or even 'dead', (Mitchell 2004; Vertovec and Wessendorf 2009), the reality of multiculturalism is still very much alive (Clayton 2009). A renewed concern with the geographies of encounter (Valentine 2008, Wilson 2011) thus documents the importance of understanding how cultural difference is negotiated on the ground. Such a concern is not separate from wider debates on the structures and discourses of multiculturalism, but rather recognises

---

97 Helen F. Wilson is a teaching fellow in urban and social geographies, Durham University. Her work is broadly concerned with the challenges and accomplishments of living with diversity in contemporary societies. She has published work on urban multiculture in Britain, multicultural schooling, the politics of tolerance, intercultural relations and conflict management, with a specific focus on the city of Birmingham. She is currently working on a book project on urban encounters that will explore the role of encounter as a constitutive element of urban experience, urban politics and urban futures.

that macro-theoretical accounts are not enough alone.

Given that living with difference has always been a central feature of urban life (Amin 2008, Watson 2006) and is not only inevitable but increasingly central to growing questions of urban resilience and social sustainability, it is not surprising that a concern with spaces of encounter has risen up the political and policy agenda - particularly within the UK. In light of recent urban unrest, growing economic uncertainty and global concerns over the emergence of varied forms of cultural and territorial fundamentalism, it is entirely fitting that attention should move away from the 'space of the nation' as the key arena for the development of diverse and cohesive societies (Collins and Friesen 2011p.1), to focus instead upon configurations of the 'urban' in order to address the future challenges and possibilities of living with difference in multicultural societies (see also Amin 2006; Sandercock 2003, Uitermark 2005).

Wood and Landry (2008), in their work on planning for intercultural cities, have outlined the significance of urban 'zones of encounter' and urban schools in particular, to the future development and sustainability of multiculturalism. Of course, it goes without saying that this would rely upon a mixed school demographic that was able to provide the opportunity for encounters with difference. Nevertheless, despite the potential significance of urban schools to debates on multiculturalism, much current work tends to limit its focus to the development and learning of children, rather than extending it to the community more widely. Yet in Australia, work has recognised how significant encounters between parents might be in developing cosmopolitan sensibilities (Noble 2009), whilst back in the UK, concerns that the 'good work' of schools might be undermined by prejudiced home environments has seen a rise in policies promoting parental involvement in school programmes and a raft of policy interventions that have sought to inculcate new attitudes to the role of parenting (Holloway et. al 2011). What such increased participation in school life might do for community and what this says about the future of multiculturalism is not addressed. Indeed, elsewhere in the UK, scholars have noted the relative absence of work focused upon the mundane spaces of school *encounter* despite the significance of such spaces to the future development of multicultural societies (Hemming 2011), with current debates predominantly concerned with the institutional framework of schools or the demographic and academic achievements of pupils.

Primary schools in particular are unique in that they demand sustained parental participation, whether it is in curricular activities and assemblies, or with the less formal activities of school life – collection times, play dates and so on. They are thus part of the daily routine of parents, where they gather perhaps twice daily, five days a week for seven or more years. Whilst it has been argued that such sites bring together a set of common life-stage experiences (Witten et al 2000), multicultural schools also have the potential to bring together people from a variety of different backgrounds, a potential that is recognised in work attending to the class conflicts, racial segregations and religious divisions that permeate school environments (see Collins and Coleman 2008). Thus, if schools are key sites for understanding how multicultural relations might be developed and further encouraged; they are also sites for examining multiple segregations. Ongoing conflicts over faith, class, religious dress and competing interpretations of morality, are played out and reinforced in the school grounds. In the UK, arguments over the religious dress of teachers and pupils have seen disagreements in the classroom played out in the media and courts of justice, whilst further disagreements over the adoption of multicultural curricula, the celebration of religious festivals, the use of critical race approaches and the provision of language support, are all testimony to the enormous challenges faced by multicultural schools.

It is precisely for this reason that multicultural schools are crucial to questions concerning the future of multiculturalism in the UK, not least because of their role in facilitating new forms of learning (Amin 2002) and tackling urban segregation and disadvantage (Raffo and Dyson 2007). The remainder of this paper thus focuses upon research conducted in a multicultural primary school in Birmingham, UK, a city that has long featured in debates around the future of multicultural societies (Sandercock 2003). The paper focuses upon the experiences and actions of a group of British White parents in order to better understand how the attributes necessary for a more cohesive multicultural society are developed. Focusing first upon some of the challenges that the school has encountered and the anxieties around cultural difference that threaten the stability of the school community, the paper considers the ways in which parents discuss the future of the UK in relation to their experiences of multicultural schooling. Having recognised the importance of learning to live with difference, the paper details the ways in which parents' existing knowledges and ways of living are called into question by the formation of a community group, set up to provide a space of learning that would address and strengthen relations across cultural difference. At a time when the capacity to live with difference is under increased strain, I argue that it is vital to understand how these groups work towards a more positive multicultural future if we are to understand how the motivations for social change arise.

The School

The school upon which this paper is based is a state-funded primary school in Birmingham, UK, a city regularly positioned as a model 'city of difference' where conventional notions of identity, citizenship and belonging are challenged, and yet one that is paradoxically characterised by multiple segregations (Sandercock 2003).

It has also been the focus for debates concerning the future (un)governability of plural cities and concerns about the challenges that majority-minority cities might pose for future planning and social cohesion (Finney and Simpson 2009). Situated at the heart of the UK, it has over one million residents and is at the centre of a conurbation of 2.5 million people (Masboungi et. al 2007 p.20) with a long history of migration and the youngest population in Europe. According to the last census, 70% of residents described themselves as white (20% below the national and regional averages and exceeded only in areas of inner city London) (Birmingham City Council 2010). Approximately 70% of the school in question was majority British Asian of predominantly Pakistani and origin, whilst the majority of pupils in attendance spoke English as their second language. This is a figure that has changed rapidly over the past decade.

According to Ofsted[98], the school excels in both attainment records and its ability to develop good links and foster understanding across difference within the local community. It studies a different language each term, has set up a twinning scheme with a school in South East Asia, has special meal days and assemblies, dance events and a 'Values Education' programme which adopts a universal value each month -tolerance, respect, hope, honesty, courage and so on- as a key organising principle for personal development, collective worship and social education. Parents are encouraged to participate in key festivals and religious celebrations such as Harvest, Diwali, Eid, Christmas, Easter and Vaisakhi and the curriculum and pedagogical responses to government-led projects of diversity are clearly embodied in the visual cultures of the school and its classrooms (see Jewitt and Jones 2005). Visitors are welcomed in five different languages and a further thirty are displayed in the reception area along with the current language and value of the month. The breadth of different cultures, religions, languages, festivals and abilities on display attest to an inclusive school at ease with its diversity and gives the general sense of a happy pupil-body and community. On the surface the school would thus appear to be an exemplar of cultural tolerance, respect and acceptance and is precisely the kind of civic site through which core societal values are increasingly mobilised and pedagogically achieved (Brown 2006 and Kundani 2007).

Whilst a variety of authors have cautioned against assumptions that the ethos of a school necessarily translates into the desired practices on the ground (Donnelly 2000), the school's success in celebrating its diversity and promoting intercultural learning was consistently confirmed by parents, who detailed how the school

---

98 Ofsted is the Office for Standards in Education, Children's Services and Skills. Set up following the Education and Inspections Act, it regulates and inspects the care of children and young people, and education and skills for learners of all ages to provide annual reports for Parliament (Ofsted 2010).

activities, curriculum and ethos were enriching their children's lives as well as their own. Sandra's response is typical of such an account:

> Sandra: "I'd say that I was happy with the society that my children are growing up with and I've been happy with all the racial – and ethnic, and you know, all the different cultures and representations. I think it's making my children much more tolerant – or is that the right word here?! Nothing is different. I think it really enriches the lives of my daughters, ... and I think we get a lot of that from the school." (Focus Group 2009)

What is presented here is a celebrated multiculture that is valued on a number of levels but most specifically in relation to the advantages that it may bring for Christine's children. Yet despite such a 'happy multiculture' (Ahmed 2008) on the surface and despite the glowing reports from Ofsted, the school's future was considered to be far from secure. At drop-off and collection times, the playground was segregated along lines of religion and race at drop off and staff at the school repeatedly described the 'white anxieties' that threatened to disrupt or even destroy the school's multicultural community. 'White flight' to local faith schools was considered to be one of its biggest problems alongside disagreements amongst the parents about the place of Christianity in the school's curriculum and a persistent complaint that the needs of the South Asian community were prioritised.

The accounts were typical of many contemporary writings on multicultural societies, which have focused on the conditional acceptance of difference (Hage 1998 2001). As Jenkins argues in relation to Australian multiculturalism, the limited and conditioned nature of so-called generosity towards otherness, can be described as being 'tempered' by a concern for maintaining one's own well-being, which would predict the withdrawal of such generosity to be the point at which the benefits for the majority are compromised or they are required to 'adjust their ways' (Jenkins 2002 and Scanlon 2003). Such sentiments were apparent across a variety of discussions and are perhaps best articulated by Claire, a young mother with two daughters at the school:

> Claire: "The fact that Britain is so multicultural, so welcoming and so accepting and promoting of culture is brilliant, but why then should it mean that the actual culture of this country actually gets side-lined and it is beginning to feel like that." (Focus Group 2009)

The tensions between the celebration of a multicultural society on the one hand and the concerns over the maintenance of a nostalgic English culture on the other outline a 'domestic space that is not to be sacrificed' (Lewis 2005 p.544). Tensions thus appeared around a number of points; around the apparent loss of Christian values; the 'watering down' of Christian festivals such as Easter and Christmas; the food provided for special school events; and the lack of English spoken by some f the parents; all of which amounted to what the parents considered to be the erosion of English culture. The uncertainty of position that multicultural schooling created, was thus often located in a rhetoric of victimhood – a fear of cultural annihilation – for in embracing multicultural schooling, the parents felt that their own religious beliefs and identities were made somehow vulnerable as a result.

Anxieties about the loss of identity were discussed alongside more persistent concerns about the lack of common ground that existed between some of the parents. This was a concern that was made most apparent in discussions around some of the Muslim families at the school, with a focus in particular upon Muslim mothers. This particular group of women were regularly considered to be self-segregated, beyond integration and unable to communicate, as Angela suggested:

> Angela: One of the children's jackets was left so I said I'd take it round to the house and have a chat and all… and she opened the door and it was like guarded, she was covered, and sort of quickly took the jacket in. And that's you know, they're still so very very traditional and I have to say that sometimes, that does really quite grate on me. (Focus Group 2009)

In many of these accounts, Muslim women were considered to be unwilling to participate in the school community and the social interactions that are considered essential to the mundane routines of school life. Whilst this may reveal, as Wise (2010 p.925) suggests, a 'breakdown of everyday rituals of recognition', the assumptions that are made here about Muslim families and their contribution to the school threatens the stability of its community and the celebratory ethos that the school prioritises.

Taken together these multiple accounts reveal a rather unstable picture of multicultural schooling and emphasise the negative undercurrents that exist beneath the outward acceptance and apparently open appreciation of cultural diversity. The continued sense of entitlement and segregation that the British White parents communicated highlights some of the challenges that multicultural societies face whilst questioning the extent to which mixed schools can affect positive change beyond the classroom. As a Cabinet Office report suggested in 2007, 'publically, Britain is a country in which few people now express negative feelings towards someone else, [yet] privately [it is] a very different country' (p.91).

Perhaps the key concern is whether the embracement of multicultural schooling by the parents relies solely on the benefits that it brings for the development of their children – which would produce a rather cynical account of celebrated multiculture. Yet whilst the hierarchies of belonging outlined here are clearly problematic these positions are not necessarily fixed. Indeed as a space of encounter, the school is a space of potential transformation and one where many established assumptions are drawn into question precisely because of the sustained contact that they demand over a number of years. Parents talked for example about the learning curves that they had undergone, the difficulties of catering for birthday parties, negotiating play dates with other parents, helping their children with their homework and participating in religious celebrations, assemblies and cultural events that were regularly held by the school, all of which became opportunities to learn, not only for the children but for them as well.

In the second part of the paper I want to focus on a parents group which was established to address precisely the issues that I have outlined to this point. In doing so, I want to highlight the value of community work to rethinking the future of multiculturalism and its challenges and possibilities.

The Parents Group

The Parents Group upon which this discussion is based, was set up in 2008 by two working mothers. Both had children in attendance at the school in question and had noticed that whilst the children were mixing well, the opposite was true of the parents. Their overriding concern was thus with providing a space within which parents could learn about each other from each other in order to develop 'good links between the diverse cultural, religious and racial groups that [made] up the local community' (anon). The group holds regular events such as coffee mornings, picnics, dance classes, cookery evenings and daytrips – all of which are run by parents for parents – in order to bring parents together on a regular basis beyond the school gates. Whilst associated with the school, the group was established as an independent group with the intention of reaching out to other schools within the local community as a means to extend their influence.

The initial desire for action was driven by their observations of the school playground (see Wilson 2012), which was often characterised by segregations along lines of race and religion. For Christine this presented a number of problems:

> Christine: "The parents weren't mixing, the mothers were sitting or standing, or chatting in their groups – which were apparently along racial lines – but were not really mixing or talking to each other. And we thought that was a bit odd. I want my child to grow up getting on with people of other races and backgrounds and not to have a shock and not know how to deal with people from other races or religions. [I]t was quite disappointing (...) that there was a lack of communication.[...]

"What we thought was that erm, that if you try to identify ... something that we all have in common, regardless of race, religion, and then if we try to build on that and see if we can do anything and what we chose is that we all want our children to succeed when our child goes out into the big world. Everyone wants that and because of the fact that we live in a very multicultural city and it is becoming an increasingly multicultural city, it's very important for children to have the life-skill of being able to get on with children of different background from theirs." (Interview 2009)

This not only says a lot here about Christine's expectations of multicultural schooling, and the opportunity for multicultural engagement and learning that it should present, but also highlights how the need to act now is directly related to her visions and hopes for the future. This is further confirmed by her concern with identifying a point of commonality around which parents could organise and establish new relations.

There are two concerns here that I want to highlight. The first concern is directly related to the future demographic of Birmingham and the much-cited prediction that it will become a majority-minority city within the next decade (Finney and Simpson 2009 p.142). For the parents, growing fears about the city's future social stability highlight how important the capacity to live with difference will be for their children when they finally leave school, positioning the ability to live with difference to be both a necessary and valuable 'life-skill'. It thus becomes a crucial part of their education, which, as Christine suggests, is jeopardised by the current segregations, and lack of interaction amongst the school's parents. According to Noble (2009 p.57), in wanting their children to 'survive in a culturally complex world' these parents might be considered pragmatists who perceive such negotiations of 'pervasive difference' to be strategic for the purpose of co-habitation. It might thus be considered that the 'trade-off' for the more 'worldly' and tolerant experience that their children get, is considered to be more than worth it in the longer term (ibid).

The second concern focuses upon the parents' own experience of shock as mentioned by Christine -of the inability to adequately respond to differences within the school community- which revealed a lack of knowledge about others that was in urgent need of address. This is something that was recognised by many of the parents involved in the research. Of particular note was the way in which parents' evaluation of the future was often formed through their own past experiences and assessment of their own 'practical competence' in matters of diversity (van Leeuwen 2011). This was outlined by Deb who had moved to the area from the North of England in her late teens and now had two children at the school:

Deb: "When I went to school it was white all the way through education before I came [to Birmingham] for university and for me, I had never had that kind of experience, it was absolutely a shock. My children won't ever have that and that is absolutely fantastic. And now we have chosen to live in this area, and I want to stay in this area, but it is something that I have had to learn and hopefully they won't have to learn that." (Interview 2009)

Deb's hopes for the future of her children are touched by the memory of past encounters. She recounts the shock that came when encountering difference for the first time and talks of the learning process that she has had to undergo as a result. This not only hints at the often overlooked 'intercultural labour' demanded in such spaces of close contact (Noble 2009), but highlights the desire for new ways of living that the fear of shock can develop (Stewart 2000 p.409).

In an assessment of multicultural dialogue across Europe, Gressgard (2010) has acknowledged just how productive such cultural shock might be for social dialogue. In an encounter with something or someone that 'escapes our classificatory categories, [or] is beyond the horizon of our experience' (p.126), the resultant sense of shock she argues, reveals a lack of knowledge that demands a better *understanding* of the other before a judgement can be possible. It is precisely here where the possibility for dialogue across difference emerges and the desire to learn about each other *from each other* gains currency. What both of these concerns demonstrate are the ways in which geographies of multiculture are lived and further organised around a concern 'for acting in advance of the future' (Anderson 2010 p.777). Parents were very conscious of the future needs of their children and their responsibility as parents to set a good example and provide a good environment to learn in.

Given that there has been much interest in the UK regarding what 'works in enabling cross-community interaction' (DCLG 2009) and an increased focus upon the spaces, activities and networks that might lay the grounds for the development of mutuality, solidarity and tolerance (Andersson et. al 2011), examining the successes or failures of such voluntary community groups is crucial. Understanding the motivations and circumstances that give rise to their development alongside the shared commitments and commonalities from which they draw strength is vital to the facilitation of such encounter in the future.

At the time of the research, the group was still in its early days, but early feedback suggested that a wide variety of parents were regularly attending events. What was important for this group was the focus upon activities. Askins and Pain (2011) have recently highlighted the value of participatory activities for enabling positive interaction. Through an attention to the materialities of encounter, the tactile and sensuous engagements with things, and the communications demanded by activities such as cooking, cricketing and dance lessons, it is possible to see how a variety of activity-based encounters between parents can open up a space for conversation and a shared sense of investment:

> Deb: "The coffee morning that I came to (...) was lovely and they put a board up around taking different languages and I actually got there a bit late you know, but when I got there they'd got about twenty languages of hello and goodbye on the board and that worked really really well"

Whilst the group and parent involvement in it might be considered strategic, I suggest that it has a value that far exceeds the relatively narrow ambitions of some of the parents. When reflecting upon the opportunities that had opened up, many parents talked about the new sense of familiarity that it had developed between them and expressed surprise when they realised that other parents wanted to learn about their own backgrounds and religious beliefs. For Gemma, a new sense of familiarity made it easier to ask what she considered to be potentially 'difficult questions' about the religious practice of others and their family life and beliefs, allowing her to learn a bit more about the background of others and to dispel some of her assumptions. She thus heralded it a fantastic *opportunity*. Such connections were further noticeable in the playground when Gemma reflected upon her movements following a day trip with the parents group:

> Gemma: I don't know whether you've noticed, but there is the group by the picket fence. Yeah? Yeah, now I know them, because they are the people that came on the coach trip and I will happily go up and say hello and how are your children? And that's fine, erm, so, but so, there are now crossovers and people are now starting to talk to people. So I think we're doing okay (...) I feel that overall it has been beneficial and you know the one thing that it has done is start an awful lot of dialogue.

Whilst this might be only a very small gesture in the context of a segregated playground, the key emphasis here is on the 'dialogue' that the parents group has opened up and it is this beginning that I suggest is most valuable.

Conclusion

To conclude, it is clear that multicultural primary schools provide a crucial site of investigation for work concerned with the ways in which cultural hybridity is negotiated. Of course, different schools face very different challenges and these relate to local demographics, school policy and funding, but also to the wider school ethos and the relative commitment of teachers, parents and governors. Despite such caveats there is clearly some indication here that mixed schools can provide a form of learning that faith schools alone perhaps cannot, and this can be found first and foremost in the opportunity such schools provide for regular encounter. This very ordinary space of contact provides a crucial account of the ways in which existing knowledges and ways of living are brought into question. It documents the personal labour that is demanded of individuals by contemporary societies – work that is often overlooked in favour of celebratory accounts of 'convivial culture'. Interculturalism is thus learnt and negotiated, as limits and boundaries are challenged, further adjusted or sometimes hardened.

As I have made clear, a positive space cannot be achieved through institutional frameworks and multicultural curricula alone. Whilst on the surface the school is an excellent example of an institution that has embraced and further celebrated diversity, whilst maintaining excellent achievement records and rolling out a multicultural curriculum and programme, the school ethos and commitment is clearly not enough to tackle the many anxieties and misunderstandings that segregate the school community along various lines. The anxieties around national identity and the loss of traditions alongside concerns about the lack of commonalities amongst some of the parents mirror some of the wider anxieties that have led to the denouncement of multiculturalism in the political mainstream, and for the school amounted to concerns about its social stability and multicultural future.

Given these concerns, whilst the school space is clearly a vital site of learning and development for children, it is the experiences and practices of parents that can tell us a lot about the ways in which schools might foster multiculturalism beyond the classroom. It is for this reason I argue, that it is paramount that we better understand the parental motivations that underpin the prosaic negotiations that take place within and beyond the school grounds. There are two key points that I have suggested are of import here, both of which concern the ways in which multicultural futures are envisioned and then utilised to demand action in the present. The first focuses upon the predictions made regarding the future demographic of Birmingham. The anxieties linked to the unknowable effects of 'super-diversity' have placed emphasis on the necessary ability to live with difference. Understanding how these fears for the future directly relate to action in the present provides new ethico-political accounts of the ways in which interculturalism is developed and assembled. For the most part this provides a very pragmatic account of a group of individuals, who not only recognise the inevitability of a super-diverse future, but the value of learning to live with it. The second focuses on the past experiences of parents and their experience of shock in particular – an experience that they did not wish upon their children and one that highlighted their lack of knowledge about others. Alongside their hopes for the future, these two concerns when taken together provide a much clearer sense of what motivates community action and provides the foundations for multicultural dialogue.

Bibliography

Ahmed, S. (2008) 'Multiculturalism and the Promise of Happiness', in *New Formations*, 63, pp.121-137.

Amin, A. (2002) 'Ethnicity and the multicultural city: living with diversity', in *Environment and Planning A*, 34, pp.959-980.

Amin, A. (2006) 'The good city', in *Urban Studies*, 43, pp.1009-1023.

Amin, A. (2008) 'Collective Culture and Urban Public Space', in *City*, 12, pp.5-24.

Anderson, B. (2010) 'Preemption, precaution, preparedness: Anticipatory action and future geographies', in *Progress in Human Geography*, 34, pp.777-798.

Andersson, J., Vanderbeck, R. M., Valentine, G., Ward, K., Sadgrove, J. (2011) 'New York encounters: religion, sexuality, and the city' in *Environment and Planning A,* 43, pp.618-633.

Askins, K. and Pain, R. (2011), 'Contact zones: participation, materiality, and the messiness of interaction', in *Environment and Planning D-Society & Space*, 29, pp.803-821.

Birmingham City Council (BCC) (2010) Census and Population Data. Available at: http://www.birmingham.gov.uk/cs/Satellite/census?packedargs=website%3D4&rendermode=live [Accessed 30/10/10]

Brown, W. (2006) *Regulating Aversion: Tolerance in the Age of Identity and Empire* (Princeton University Press, New Jersey)

Burgess, S., Wilson, D., Lupton, R., (2005) 'Parallel lives? Ethnic segregation in schools and neighbourhoods', in *Urban Studies,* 42, pp.1027-1056.

Clayton, J. (2009) 'Thinking spatially: towards an everyday understanding of inter-ethnic relations' in *Social & Cultural Geography*, 10, pp.481-498.

Collins, D. and Coleman, T. (2008), 'Social geographies of education: looking within and beyond, school boundaries', in *Geography Compass*, 2, pp.281-299.

Collins, F. L. and Friesen, W. (2011) 'Making the Most of Diversity? The Intercultural City Project and a Rescaled Version of Diversity in Auckland, New Zealand', in *Urban Studies*, 48, pp.3067-3085.

Crozier, G., Reay, D., James, D., Jamieson, F., Beedell, P., Hollingworth, S. and Williams, K. (2008) 'White middle-class parents, identities, educational choice and the urban comprehensive school: dilemmas, ambivalence and moral ambiguity', in *British Journal of Sociology of Education,* 29, pp.261-272.

Department for Communities and Local Government (DCLG) (2009) *What Works in Enabling Cross-Community Interactions? Perspectives on good policy and practice.* Wetherby: Communities and Local Government.

Department for Children Schools and Families (DCSF) (2007) *Guidance on Duty to Promote Community Cohesion.* London: DCSF.

Finney, N., Simpson, L. (2009) *Sleepwalking to segregation? Challenging myths about race and migration*, Policy Press: Bristol.

Flint, J. (2007) 'Faith schools, multiculturalism and community cohesion: Muslim and Roman Catholic state schools in England and Scotland', in *Policy and Politics*, 35, pp.251-268

Gressgard, R. (2010) *Multicultural Dialogue: Dilemmas, Paradoxes, Conflicts*, Berghahn Books: Oxford.

Hemming, P. J. (2011) 'Meaningful encounters? Religion and social cohesion in the English primary school', in *Social & Cultural Geography*, 12, pp.63-81.

Holloway, S. L. and Pimlott-Wilson, H. (2011) 'The politics of aspiration: neo-liberal education policy, 'low' parental aspirations, and primary school Extended Services in disadvantaged communities', in *Childrens Geographies*, 9, pp.79-94.

Jewitt, C. and Jones, K. (2005) 'Managing Time and Space in the New English Classroom', in *Materialities of Schooling Eds M Lawn, I Grosvenor* (Symposium, Oxford) pp.201-214.

Kundnani, A. (2007) *The End of Tolerance. Racism in 21st Century Britain*, Pluto Press: London.

Lewis, G. (2005) 'Welcome to the margins: Diversity, tolerance, and policies of exclusion', in *Ethnic and Racial Studies*, 28, pp.536-558.

Masboungi, A., de Gravelaine, F. and Isherwood, B. (2007) Birmingham: City Renewal Through Partnership Editions de la Villette: Paris.

Mitchell, K. (2004) 'Geographies of identity: multiculturalism unplugged', in *Progress in Human Geography*, 28 pp.641-651.

Noble, G. (2009) 'Everyday Cosmopolitanism', in *Everyday Multiculturalism* Eds A Wise, S Velayutham Palgrave Macmillan: Basingstoke pp. 46-65.

Okin, S. M. and Reich, R. (1999) 'Families and Schools as Compensating Agents in Moral Development for a Multicultural Society', in *Journal of Moral Education*, 28, pp.283-298

Pykett, J. (2010) 'Citizenship Education and narratives of pedagogy', in *Citizenship Studies*, 14, pp.621-635.

Raffo, C. and Dyson, A. (2007) 'Full service extended schools and educational inequality in urban contexts - new opportunities for progress?', in *Journal of Education Policy*, 22, pp.263-282.

Sandercock, L. (2003) *Cosmopolis II: Mongrel Cities of the 21st Century*, Continuum International Publishing Group: London.

Stewart, K. (2000) 'Still Life' in *Intimacy* (Edt.), L Berlant Chicago Press: Chicago, pp.405-420.

Uitermark, J., Rossi, U. and Van Houtum, H. (2005) 'Reinventing multiculturalism: Urban citizenship and the negotiation of ethnic diversity in Amsterdam', in *International Journal of Urban and Regional Research*, 29, p.622.

Valentine, G. (2008) 'Living with difference: reflections on geographies of encounters', in *Progress in Human Geography*, 32 (3) pp.323-337.

van Leeuwen, B. (2010) 'Dealing with Urban Diversity: Promises and Challenges of City Life for Intercultural Citizenship', in *Political Theory*, 38, pp.631-657.

Vertovec, S. and Wessendorf, S. (2009) *The Multiculturalism backlash: European discourses policies and practices,* Routledge: London.

Watson, S. (2006) *City Publics: The (Dis)enchantments of Urban Encounters,* Routledge: London.

Wilson, H. F. (2011) 'Passing Propinquities in the Multicultural City: The Everyday Encounters of Bus Passengering', in *Environment and Planning A.*

Wise, A. (2010) 'Sensuous Multiculturalism: Emotional Landscapes of Inter-Ethnic Living in

Australian Suburbia', *in Journal of Ethnic and Migration Studies,* 36, pp.917-937.

Wise, A. and Velayutham, S. (2009) *Everyday Multiculturalism,* Palgrave: Macmillan: Basingstoke.

Witten, K., McCreanor, T. Kearns, R. and Ramasubramanian, L. (2001) 'The impacts of a school closure on neighbourhood social cohesion: narratives from Invercargill, New Zealand', in *Health & Place,* 7, pp.307-317.

Wood, P. and Landry, C. (2008) *The Intercultural City: Planning for diversity advantage* Earthscan: London.

Multiculturalism and Faith Traditions in the UK: Education, Ethnography, Empiricism and Everyday Lives

Ian G. Williams[99]

Introduction

The period from 1950-1970 is a period of great significance for the Muslim community in Britain. It witnessed the arrival of large numbers of Muslims into the country and ever since a number of issues have arisen concerning the British Muslim community. Some of these relate to concrete matters, such as the provision of voluntary-aided status schools, or planning permission for building mosques. However, there are other and perhaps more subtle substantive issues which face the "community" as well.

One of these is the question of identity, specifically, religious identity among the younger generations in official government sponsored multicultural policies especially in the field of education. The parents and grandparents of the third and fourth generations of British Muslims have enduring concerns about the place of Islam in the lives of their young. They look around at the wider society and face the reality that Muslims are but one faith community among others, and realise that they must find a place for themselves amid a number of other religious and ethnic groups within the larger plural religious and cultural society. Additionally, they find that this society often fails to support an Islamic worldview. In fact, the plurality of competing secular ideologies has the potential to relativise the absolutes of Islam, and draw young Muslims away from the values and traditions their parents have nurtured into them.

From the point of view of the younger generation, their identity concerns are bound up with questions of belonging, and the extent to which others will accept their participation in the wider society. In view of the multicultural and religiously

99 Prof Dr Ian G. Williams teaches, supervises and researches in Islamic and Religious Studies at the Markfield Institute of Higher Education, Leicester / University of Gloucestershire, UK. Prior to this he has taught at the Universities of Chester, Derby and Birmingham City University. Ian's research interests include the Fethullah Gulen Movement, Faith Sector education, and Material Religion especially the 19th century pre-Raphaelite School. Ian and his fiancée Patricia, who is a Primary School head teacher, are marrying in August 2012. They share passions for music (classical and jazz), theatre, and travel. They are both members of Birmingham Cathedral.

diverse society in which they live, how are young Muslims affirming, altering, or abandoning their identity? What is the effect on their identity of living in a society such as Britain where they constitute a minority group? It is this specific question of identity and social diversity in relation to young British Muslims of and in themselves a plural "Islam" that is the focus of this paper.

Identity Defined

Among the early psychologists who studied identity, often in conjunction with other disciplines such as philosophy, 'identity' was a term referring to a sense of sameness and continuity as a person: 'either as a subjective phenomenon or as an objective deliverance, as a feeling, or as a truth. This sense of personal identity is the sense of sameness "perceived by thought and predicated of things thought-about" (James 1977 p.315). For them it was an awareness of the flow of subjective feelings that goes some way toward making up the sense of identity. In the period between the turn of the century and the mid-1950s, elucidation of the concept of identity had progressed and had become intrinsically bound up with continuity of existential feeling as well as with the "ego quality of this existence" (Erikson 1980 pp.20-21). Erikson defines identity as an essentially psychosocial phenomenon where the sense of 'me' or 'myself' is formed in relation to others and their responses. This process is thus perceived as an on-going one, but with particular stages of the lifecycle, such as adolescence, as especially critical points of development.

In religious studies, few scholars have given considered attention to the notion of identity. However, Mol has written extensively on the subject. In his book Identity and the Sacred Mol suggests that religious myth, rituals, commitment, and the sense of the transcendent "sacralise" identity (Mol 1976). By this he means that "on the level of symbol-systems certain patterns acquire a stable, eternal, taken-for-granted quality." (Mol 1976 p.5). Furthermore, he adds, "religious practices give special underpinning to particular conceptions of order and views of reality within a culture making the security of the individual less precarious." (ibid p.5). A religion has the potential to justify and legitimate norms and values, as well as social institutions and the interpretation of reality that lies behind religious customs. Mol suggests that "the family constructs identity, and religion sacralises it." (ibid 137). Through the influence and example of parents, the child learns a worldview and norms for social interaction, while sacred codes safeguard the family and the threats to identity that changes in the family structure and society may initiate. Therefore, such things as rites of passage serve as techniques to strip away an old identity at key points in the lifecycle, while at the same time ushering in and building the foundations for a new one. Thus, identity is rarely a static phenomenon, but is constantly being shaped and evolved in an on-going process of self-definition.

The Marginality of Identity

In Mol's terms Muslims in Britain's multi-religious and culturally diverse environment are in a 'situation of marginality'. This he asserts is largely due to their being a minority. Given the universality of the minority condition in multicultural societies, Mol identifies and proposes the particular consequences of this status for identity formation. "Marginality refers to persons or groups who stand on the boundary of larger groups or societies, neither completely belonging nor suffering outright rejection. Migrants are often marginal people...Being treated as alien has an adverse effect on the sense of belonging" (ibid 31-32).

Thus, for minorities in multicultural situations, community boundaries become important markers of group identity. Boundaries define and focus the community itself, while making clear to outsiders the character of the neighbourhood. Religious buildings, street decorations, ethnic shops may become important symbols of community identity. For many of the early Muslim migrants to Britain after the 1950's the development of "institutional completeness" in many ways cemented the boundaries within which communities lived. With the arrival of women and children from home countries to join their husbands and fathers already living in Britain before the implementation of entry restrictions from 1964, the uniting of families further strengthened community identity and religious life.

The period of family migration became a significant phase in the history of Muslims in Britain. It witnessed a replacement of temporary male residence for immigrants with permanent family settlement. From this point on, the well-documented "myth of return" began to dissipate (Anwar 1979). The attention of the community was focused on more than just the basic facilities for religious observance, but also on the development of institutions that would enable future generations to live as Muslims in Britain. The 1970's thus saw the proliferation of Islamic organisations committed to the welfare of the community. It is perhaps at this point in British Muslim experience that the question of identity becomes pertinent and extends across many of the linguistic, ethnic and theological divisions of the community.

Defined numbers of the current Muslim communities in the UK today await publication of the 2011 National Census data. The 2001 National Census, which included for the first time in England, Wales and Scotland a question on religious affiliation revealed 1.6 million Muslims resident in the UK. The community continues to grow in size as members of the next generations themselves become parents. However, there is little dispute among scholars that the Pakistani community currently makes up the largest proportion of Muslims in Britain (Anwar 1993; Beckford, Gale, Owen, Peach, Weller, P. 2006; Gilliat-Ray 2010).

Minority Status and Identity: the Theoretical Issue

Before considering in detail how Muslims in Britain appear to have been affected by multiculturalism and religious diversity, some attention must be given to the theoretical problems that minority status poses to identity. Berger points out that for the purposes of identity construction there is a massive difference between situations in which an entire society serves as the plausibility structure as for example in as Pakistan or Saudi Arabia, for a religious world and situations in which only a sub society serves as such. In other words, the "social engineering" problem differs as between religious monopolies and religious groups seeking to maintain themselves in a situation of pluralistic competition. It is not difficult to see that the problem of world maintenance is less difficult of solution in the former instance. When an entire society serves as the plausibility structure for a religiously legitimated world, all the important social processes within it serve to confirm and reconfirm the reality of this world (Berger 1969 p.49).

In an environment of social diversity, identity may be "sacralised" by any number of sources besides the religious. The absolute, 'taken-for-granted' quality of a religious identity may be relativised and thrown into question by the plurality around which its construction has taken place or by which it finds itself surrounded. In such situations, boundaries around the community come into their own as in 'pluralistic situations, the religious group must organise itself to support its meaning system' in view of the lack of a single "comprehensive world view" (McGuire 1987 p.33). There is an implicit relationship between the cohesion of social institutions and the individual's subjective cohesiveness of values, *weltanschauung*, and beliefs.

For example, in a social situation in which everyone with whom the individual has significant ties is a soldier, it is not surprising that the soldier's view of the world, with all that this implies, will be massively plausible. Conversely, it is very difficult to be a soldier in a social situation where this makes little or no sense to everyone else (Berger 1980 p.12). Substitution of the word "believer" for "soldier" makes the same point for religion in multicultural and religiously diverse societies. In an environment where most of the population is likely to have limited and often distorted impressions of a foreign religion, and where its norms and practices have no overarching plausibility, it is not surprising that the followers of minority faiths undergo crises of identity and belonging. Therefore, in Britain, where there is much antipathy towards Islam from many quarters, the racism many Muslims face mitigates against a sense of being British. This is compounded by the fact that many of the cultural values and customs of the home country may mean little to the third and fourth generations of British Muslims.

In the minority situation boundaries are important mechanisms for communal preservation. Sometimes the pressures to create and maintain boundaries mean that the essential issues of identity preservation are ignored. Unlike religious communities in a majority situation where there is often a continuity between the past history of the faith and current development, the experience of migration to a minority situation severs the on-going narrative bound up with locality. Under such circumstances attention may fall upon secondary dimensions of faith and "more with the instruments and symbols of identity and security than with questions of primary religious importance" (Askari 1991 p.6). Evidence for this in the British situation can be seen in some of the peripheral issues and struggles with which some Muslims have been caught up, and to which they devote much time. Mosque debates and disagreements focussed around such matters as the constitution of the mosque committee can distract attention away from issues of more general importance for the community. But seen in a wider perspective, some of these conflicts and tensions are as much a question of internal politics as they are about attempts to formalize the community's relationship with the larger society. By constructing clear norms about internal matters a potential consequence is that group identity is cemented vis-a-vis the other ethnic communities and the population at large. Where attitudes of prejudice towards others are part of this process, identity may be further reinforced: "…preaching against prejudice is relatively useless when specific forms of prejudice and scapegoating fulfil basic functions for personality and group integration, and when national, social, group, or personal identities are fragile" (Mol 1976 p.91).

The Response of the Third Generation

Many of the younger generations of Muslims have become dissatisfied with the example and preoccupations of some elder members of the community upon what they see as secondary issues. For all this, however, many do not wish to surrender their religious identity, and indeed for many it is a central part of their lives. Despite the multiplicity of ideologies, other faiths, and cultural groups in society, many young Muslims in the UK are looking to their faith as a means of identifying themselves and as a tradition in which they hope to find a sense of belonging (Nielsen 1987 p.393; Lewis 1994/2003 and 2007; Gilliat-Ray 2010).

Young Muslims who are fervently committed to their faith defy the secular, materialistic ideologies that seem to pervade Western society. Though it may appear that they are unaffected by them, it is likely that they are conscious of the relativising effect that the social and ideological diversity may have. Those who oppose secularism by unswerving adherence to their faith hold on to "a system of beliefs and practices which treat scriptural absolutism as the way to counter the pluralism and relativism engendered by modernity" (Gill 1989 p.23). Their convictions support those foundations for religious identity outlined by Mol while they foster "cognitive uniformity" at least among themselves (ibid 35). Islam for them is at the nucleus of their personal identity. It is seen as having a "stronger basis than mere ethnic identity" (Rex 1993 p.8). Regarding basic Islamic beliefs, they differ from other Muslims not so much in *what* they believe, but *how* they believe. In the first instance, in a society that has no single legitimation system, for some members of a minority group the clear answers provided by rigid adherence to particular religious beliefs can help to avoid the cognitive dissonance of plurality. Secondly, the knowledge many young Muslims now have is based less on superstition and more on the Qur'an and other Islamic sources. Religious identity can be sacralised more effectively through the rituals and theology of Islam, rather than by the cultural traditions of their ethnic community.

"Three-quarters of Muslims in Great Britain live in 24 cities or authorities in the five major conurbations of Greater London, the West and East Midlands, West Yorkshire and Greater Manchester. In absolute terms, Birmingham is the local authority with the highest *number* of Muslims, while the five local authorities with the highest *proportions* of Muslims are Tower Hamlets, Newham, Blackburn, Bradford and Waltham Forest (Hussain and Choudhury 2007). Within these local authority areas, Muslims are disproportionately represented in the most deprived urban communities. One-third of the Muslim population live in the 10 per cent most deprived neighbourhoods." (Beckford *et al.*, 2006 p.39) (Jayaweera & Choudhury 2008 p.2)

As a religious minority in Britain, many British Muslims are also members of different racial and ethnic minority groups. Unlike earlier generations who often accepted racial intolerance as part and parcel of their situation in Britain, the younger generations have begun to challenge the racism directed towards them. The formation of groups such as the 'Guardian Asians' indicate that in some areas constructive initiatives have been undertaken to counter racist attacks. The revival of religious identity among British Muslims has been one of the direct outcomes of racism in Britain. This phenomenon is especially visible among British Muslim youth. The late Zaki Badawi, director of the Muslim College in London, referred to this trend over twenty years ago in an article "Ingrained Racism Brings Muslim Youth Back to Islam" (Badawi 1988 p.25). He suggested that while at school, many young Muslims may identify with the youth culture and are influenced by their white, non-Muslim peers. However, after leaving school and when it comes to finding a job or career, many members of the community find themselves facing barriers of exclusion. But it is at this point, suggested Badawi that "they start to identify more closely with Islam" (ibid). Where the practices of multiculturalism fail to meet the aspirations of some young Muslims they may turn to their faith tradition in order to find a social group to which they can identify and belong.

Furthermore, they may be unprepared to use majority yardsticks to measure their self-worth:

> ...many previous empirical studies on minority identity have revealed an unjustified assumption about minority dependence on, and conformity to, the ongoing majority definitions. The studies in this volume make it quite clear that there is no general validity in the proposition that discriminatory views about one's group result in self-devaluation? (Liebkind 1989 p.237)

This evaluation may go some way towards explaining the self-confidence that some young Muslims have derived from a religious identity based upon Islam.

Racist attacks have increased dramatically...and tension has grown following the British National Party's success in local elections last year. But far from fearful of standing out as targets of violence, many of the devout Muslim girls regard the hijab as a gesture of defiance. The Islamic groups have been quick to take action in the anti-racist struggle, offering not only self-defence classes but also a new and powerful sense of identity to members.

A number of imams, youth workers, community leaders and Muslim academics were interviewed for an earlier study by the author in which they were questioned about their perceptions of Islam in Britain, the development of the community over the past decades, their religious identity in a secular, pluralistic society, and the relationship of Muslims to other faiths and ethnic groups (Gilliat-Ray 2011). Many respondents pointed out that Islam emerged in a multicultural environment, and that there are many insights in the Qur'an and in Islamic history from which Muslims in Britain today may find guidance. Among other things, such sources clearly indicate that Islam and multiculturalism in terms of peoples and beliefs are not alien to each other. However, many young Muslims face the questions that multiculturalism poses when it comes to making practical decisions about lifestyle choices, friendships, marriage partners, and so on. They need answers to dilemmas such as "Can I go to a Hindu temple to join wedding celebrations?" or "Will I compromise my faith by marrying a Christian?" It is on the level of grassroots that the relationship of Islam to other faiths and cultures is most pertinent. As Edward Said notes in his penultimate Reith Lecture:

> The fundamental problem is therefore how to reconcile one's identity and the actualities of one's own culture, society and history to the reality of other identities, cultures, peoples. This can never be done simply by asserting one's preference for what is already one's own: tub-thumping about the glories of 'our' culture or the triumphs of 'our' history...especially not today when so many societies are composed of different races and backgrounds as to beggar any reductive formulas. (Said 1993)

And as Archbishop Rowan Williams asked rhetorically in his Zaki Badawi lecture:

> Is the pragmatic goal for a Muslim always going to be a universal political order of Muslim character? That may be the hope and prayer, but is it actually what Muslims ought to be working for today and tomorrow? And even if it is a long-term goal, what are the means towards it? Does the very fact of living in a non-Muslim jurisdiction undermine Muslim integrity? (Williams 2007 p.17)

The current Chief Rabbi of Great Britain also makes salutary comments:

> Britain is the nation – perhaps the only one in the world – where the leaders of all the major faiths know each other as personal friends, where Christians, Jews, Muslims, Sikhs and Hindus caught up in conflicts elsewhere in the world, meet in warmth and mutual respect. It is where I, as a rabbi, am encouraged to speak to people of all faiths and none, not just to my fellow believers. I do not know of anywhere else where this happens to quite the same degree...............this is what Britain means to me. (Sacks 2007 pp.167-168)

The third and fourth generations are in a key position to tackle such issues. They are twice removed from the migration experience of their grandparents, and their relationship to a cultural past has been broken enabling fresh understandings. Islam in Britain seems to have reached an interesting and innovative point in its history. It is as if the multicultural situation of modem Britain is pushing British Muslims towards a crossroads. The future religious identity of individuals and communities now rests on the direction taken by the third generation of British Muslims who are trying to live in a multicultural society while subscribing to their own faith traditions.

The expressions of religious identity of young Muslims in Britain reflect a number of factors including: the legacy of the migration experience of their parents and grandparents, the minority status of their community, Western ideologies surrounding them, and their religion, Islam. However, from a whole range of identities, which exist in the community at present, some universal aspects of religious expression, which transcend particular contexts, are being revived among the youth. Some 'core' elements of Islam are being reaffirmed while diminishing attention is being paid to the minutiae of boundaries separating the different linguistic and ethnic traditions of the community. The cultural baggage with which Islam in Britain was packaged some thirty or forty years ago appears to be losing its hold for many young Muslims. They are eager to discover a particular 'British Islam' in consonance with their situation in Britain. Often this means 'joining forces' with other young Muslims who share their religious identity, but who may come from different linguistic or ethnic backgrounds. This seems to be part of a process identified by a former president of the 'Young Muslims' who is quoted as saying in a popular British Muslim weekly newspaper:

> We want to create a British Islamic culture. By doing this we will be carrying on what our great forefathers achieved, who developed Islamic cultures wherever they went. It is our job to be innovative, creative, adventurous, bold, chivalrous and create a new British Islamic culture. (Q-News 27 August 1993)

Conclusion

The experience of Islam in Britain in a wider context is still a relatively short narrative. However, there are already a number of young adults in the community who are beginning to provide leadership in terms of ideas, and role models for being "British and Muslim" in contemporary Britain.

Despite the complexity of issues bound up with the development of this new British Muslim identity, the difficulties and confusions faced by young Muslims cannot be considered apart from the dilemmas of identity, which are being confronted by the society at large. Muslims are not the only people in Britain who are faced with questions posed by modernity, social diversity, and the decline of time-honoured traditions. A concern with matters of identity appears to be a universal and a particularly twentieth and twenty-first century preoccupation. Why should this be, and what is the nature of this self-absorption? Some of the answers may be found in the fact that modern life imposes specific challenges upon many people. Through the constant flow of information, persuasion, fashions, and messages, humanity is being pushed and pulled in many conflicting directions at once.

Thus, any understanding of religious identity for Muslims in Britain must take into consideration the trends and characteristics of the wider society in which the communities are based. Though many of the younger generation are still living within tight-knit community neighbourhoods, compared to their parents and grandparents, they are more influenced by the larger society around them and are moving towards the lifestyle of the majority in many significant ways (Anwar 1994 p.25). There have also arisen marked differences in the conceptions of selfhood between the first generation of Muslim immigrants to Britain and the third generation born and raised in Britain. To deal with their situation positively, a growing number of young Muslims are drawing upon Islamic sources to find a religious identity centred on their faith, and based upon a fine balance between what is old and new, combining innovation and tradition. Seeking this balance is not new to Islam, however, for the faith is based upon was at or balance, particularly when it comes to human social relationships.

The next generations of British Muslims, living in a multicultural, pluralistic society, have found strength in the basic tenets of Islam as a source for their identity.

Bibliography

Anwar, M. (1993) *The Myth of Return*, London: Heinemann, 1979 *Muslims in Britain: 1991 Census and Other Statistical Sources*, Research Paper 9 (Europe), Birmingham: Centre for the Study of Islam and Christian Muslim Relations

Anwar, M. (1994) *Young Muslims in Britain: Attitudes, Educational Needs and Policy Implications*, Leicester: The Islamic Foundation.

Askari, H. (1991) *Spiritual Quest: An Inter-religious Dimension*, Leeds: Seven Mirrors.

Badawi, Z. (1988) 'Ingrained Racism Brings Muslim Youth back to Islam', in *New Horizon*, London, April-May.

Beckford, J.A., Gale, R., Owen, D., Peach, C. and Weller, P. (2006) *Review of the Evidence Base on Faith Communities*. London: Office of the Deputy Prime Minister.

Berger, P. (1969) *The Social Reality of Religion*, London: Faber & Faber.

Berger, P. (1980) *Heretical Imperative: Contemporary Possibilities of Religious Affirmation*, London: Collins.

Erikson, E. (1980) *Identity and the Lifecycle*, London: W.W. Norton.

Gillat-Ray, S. (2010) *Muslims in Britain: An Introduction*, Cambridge: CUP.

Gill, R. (1989) *Competing Convictions*, London: SCM Press.

Jayaweera, H. & Choudhury, T. (2008) *Immigration, faith and cohesion. Evidence from local areas with significant Muslim populations*, York & Oxford: Rowntree Foundation.

Liebkind, K. (1989) (ed.), *New Identities in Europe: Immigrant Ancestry and the Ethnic Identity of Youth*, Aldershot, Hants: Gower.

Lewis, P. (2003) Islamic *Britain: Religion, Politics and Identity among British Muslims*. London: Tauris Press.

Lewis, P. (2007) *Young, British and Muslim*, London: Continuum Press.

McGuire, M. (1987) *Religion: The Social Context*, Belmont, CA: Wadsworth.

Mol, H. (1976) *Identity and the Sacred*, Oxford: Blackwell.

Nielson, J. (1987) 'Muslims in Britain: Searching for an Identity', in *New Community*, Spring, 13(3).

Rex, J. (1993) 'Religion and Ethnicity in the Metropolis', in *Religion and Ethnicity: Minorities and Social Change in the Metropolis*, ed. Rohit Barot, The Netherlands: Kok Pharos.

Sacks, J. (2007) *The Home We Build Together*, London: Continuum

Said, E. (1993) Reith Lecture reproduced and edited in The Independent, 22 July 1993.

Williams, R. (2007) *Islam, Christianity and Pluralism: Zaki Badawi Memorial Lecture*, London: AMSS.

London: How Successful a Multicultural Model?

Jonathan Fryer[100]

London prides itself on being the most cosmopolitan city on earth. Though data from the 2011 ten-yearly Census are not yet available, it is acknowledged that more than one third of London's inhabitants were born outside the United Kingdom. In at least two of the city's 32 boroughs (administrative districts) – Brent and Newham – ethnic minorities comprise more than 50 per cent of the population. Though inner city areas have a higher level of ethnic and religious diversity than most of the outer boroughs, all the capital's local councils, as well as the regional Great London Authority (GLA) and the national government, officially acknowledge and celebrate London's diversity. Indeed, the richness of London's ethnic mix and its cultural expression was a major element in the city's successful bid to host the 2012 Olympics and Paralympics. Yet the nature of London's normative multiculturalism, as promoted and developed by all three main political parties – Conservative, Labour and Liberal Democrat – since the 1960s has increasingly come under critical scrutiny. The core question that this paper will address is: Has London's multicultural model brought Londoners together or driven them apart?

Like other diverse English cities such as Bradford and Leicester, London became multicultural mainly as a result of immigration (Modood 2007). As the metropolis of an Empire that was one of the dominant world powers for at least 400 years, London attracted incomers from all parts of the globe. This was often as a by-product of international trade, though it was also sometimes a result of active solicitation, a good example being the arrival in the 14th and 15th centuries of Flemish weavers, whose skills were appreciated by the royal court and London guilds. As

---

100 The writer, lecturer and broadcaster. Jonathan Fryer teaches part-time at London University School of Oriental and African Studies (SOAS) and contributes to a wide range of publications in Britain and abroad. After graduating in Oriental Studies from Oxford University, Jonathan joined Reuters news agency before going freelance, working mainly for BBC Radio 4 and BBC World Service, as well as writing for the Guardian and a wide range of magazines including Diplomat, the Economist and Turkish Review. During his career he has reported from more than 150 countries around the world and is a frequent guest lecturer on cruise ships. Since 1993 he has taught a Humanities course at SOAS which includes a unit on Multiculturalism. He has written 14 books, the last two being a history of Kuwait and a study of (Iraqi) Kurdistan. He is a member of the Advisory Board of the London-based Centre for Turkey Studies and Development.

London grew as a major manufacturing and financial centre, the British authorities encouraged the importation of specialised foreign labour, as well as offering asylum to those fleeing religious or political persecution on the continent of Europe. A boost to the City of London's role as an international financial centre was received with the arrival of refugee bankers leaving Amsterdam to escape various wars in the 17th and 18th centuries. Some of these were Jews whose ancestors had previously been expelled from Portugal. Similarly, Protestant Huguenots suffering persecution in France were offered sanctuary in England by King Charles II. Between 1670 and 1710, up to 50,000 Huguenots sought refuge in England, about half of them in London.

Initially, the Huguenots kept their own identity and beliefs, speaking French and living in tight communities, notably in and around Spitalfields in the modern borough of Tower Hamlets, though eventually they assimilated, anglicised their names and many joined the Anglican Church, the established Church of England. In time, the East End of London would be settled by a new wave of refugees: Jews who were fleeing the pogroms of Russia and Poland, and later the threat of genocide from Nazi Germany (Thomas 2004). The East End was the obvious place for them to settle, as it was near London's docks, which were bustling until the 1940s. Accommodation in the area was cheap, though often people there lived in dreadful conditions; life expectancy was at least 10 years less in London's East End than in the elegant streets of the West End. It was also near the docks, at Limehouse, again in Tower Hamlets, that a Chinese community first established itself, with Chinese sailors who had come in on ships deciding to stay on shore and set up businesses such as laundries and restaurants.

However, the most dramatic influx of newcomers occurred after the Second World War, when Britain needed a fit and willing workforce to help rebuild bomb-shattered cities including London and to get the country's industry back on its feet. The Age of Empire was coming to an end, beginning with the independence and partition of India in 1947 and the gradual accession to statehood of former British colonies in Africa, South East Asia, the Caribbean and the Pacific (dubbed the New Commonwealth, as opposed to the predominantly white dominions of Australia, Canada and New Zealand). Hundreds of thousands of these colonial peoples had fought on the Allied side during the War and had been encouraged to think of Britain as the Mother Country. The curricula in their schools usually contained a great deal of British history, as well as English literature and British concepts such as individual liberty and democracy. Indeed, many former colonies and dominions initially established parliaments that were based on the Westminster model. King George VI, and after 1952 Queen Elizabeth, was the monarch not only of Britain but of many of the colonies too. Indeed, Queen Elizabeth remains the official Head of State of nearly a score of former colonies and dominions as diverse as Australia and Jamaica. So when the call went out for workers to come to Britain to help in its reconstruction, many young men and women – who had been given a type of British citizenship as residents of the colonies – got on ships and later planes to come to England, a high percentage of them arriving initially in London.

Among the first of this new wave of incomers was a boatload of 493 Jamaicans who arrived on board the MV Empire Windrush at Tilbury, on the outskirts of London, on 22 June 1948.Most of these new immigrants were dressed in their Sunday best clothes, as if going to church, as they wished to make a good impression. But they did not all receive the warm welcome they had expected. As they sought lodgings in cheaper areas of the capital such as Notting Hill (Kensington & Chelsea) and Soho (Westminster), they were often greeted by signs in the windows of landladies who had rooms to rent, saying: *'no blacks'*. It was an experience many Irish labourers, who had come over to England in their hundreds of thousands after the potato famine of the 1840s, could identify with, as they had similarly often encountered signs reading: *'no dogs or Irish'*. Racial tensions flared in The West Indian riots in Notting Hill in 1958, leading the then Conservative government led by Harold Macmillan to address the question of racial equality and to promote community cohesion (though that term was not yet in common usage). Macmillan even took that message to apartheid South Africa, declaring in Cape Town in 1960 that the 'winds of change' were sweeping across Africa. Despite the place of its delivery, this was a message also targeted at a more traditional audience back in London.

The shame liberal Londoners felt about such overt racism would later lead to the passing and implementation of some of Europe's first and strictest anti-racial discrimination laws. By the time the Race Relations Act outlawed such discrimination, in 1976, the number of immigrants had swelled exponentially, with large numbers arriving from Africa and South Asia in particular. Britain was irrevocably on the road to being a multi-racial nation and nowhere was that more obvious than in London (Philipps 1998). Gradually, immigration curbs were introduced, to try to limit the numbers of newcomers, but when there was a crisis in any far-flung part of the ex-Empire, as for example when President Idi Amin of Uganda expelled Asians from his country in 1972, British governments tended to react compassionately and let them in. In the case of the East African Asians, many of whom arrived with nothing except the clothes they were wearing, they quickly set themselves in business, notably in newsagents and 'corner shops' which they turned into convenience stores that have become a feature of the new London.

Unlike Germany, which invited Turkish and Yugoslav workers to the Federal Republic as *Gastarbeiter* in the 1960s and 1970s, in the expectation that after some years they would return home, Britain generally assumed that the New Commonwealth immigrants would settle, raise families and become truly British. That assumption originally implied that they should assimilate and adopt a British way of life, but it soon became clear that many wished to retain their distinctive beliefs, customs and practices, while filling essential jobs for which there were insufficient or unwilling native British workers, in such sectors as public transport, the National Health Service and manufacturing industries. Some right-wing politicians, most famously the Conservative MP Enoch Powell, warned that attempting to integrate large numbers of people of different cultural backgrounds would inevitably lead to conflict – 'rivers of blood', as he memorably said in one notorious speech in Birmingham in 1968. That was not a message that the Labour Prime Minister of the time, Harold Wilson, wanted to hear. His Home Secretary (Interior Minister), Roy Jenkins, advocated a liberal type of multiculturalism that would focus on cultural diversity and celebrate ethnic variety – a normative approach that was largely maintained when a Conservative government led by Edward Heath came to power in 1970. Mutual tolerance and understanding became the mantra of the government in London.

Enoch Powell noted that immigrant communities tended to congregate in specific areas, as early arrivals later invited relatives and friends from their home country to come and join them. This phenomenon was particularly noticeable in London in the 1970s and 1980s, by which time Bengalis from Bangladesh were replacing the Jews in Tower Hamlets, Africans had largely settled in the south London boroughs of Southwark and Lambeth (notably around Brixton) Turks and Cypriots were establishing themselves in the north London boroughs of Hackney, Haringey and Enfield, Indians had settled in Ealing Southall and so on.

At first sight that might seem like ghettoisation, a phenomenon experienced in several US cities, including New York. But government at the local, regional and national levels in London was determined that communities should remain mixed and harmonious, even when one particular ethnic or religious minority predominated. NGOs were encouraged to help the process of community cohesion, with the Christian churches often taking an important lead, many of them entering into inter-faith relationships with synagogues, mosques and temples. It was accepted that education would have a vital role to play in raising a new generation of Londoners who would be at ease living side-by-side with others of different ethnicities and faiths. Whereas the Law had long stipulated that all schools must organise a daily act of Christian worship or assembly for their pupils, increasingly schools in London shifted their focus to 'comparative religion', which meant that all children studied the basic tenets of the world's major faiths and even celebrated related festivities, such as Hindu Diwali or Jewish Hannukah. The liberal ideological motivation behind this was the belief that ignorance creates fear and prejudice, therefore all the different communities in London (and to a lesser extent elsewhere in Britain) should learn about each other and all be encouraged to feel that they were an integral part of this kaleidoscopic whole.

Though one can trace the origins of normative multiculturalism in Britain back to the policies of Home Secretary Roy Jenkins, as mentioned earlier, it was really only when the Labour maverick Ken Livingstone became leader of the then regional government, the Great London Council (GLC), in 1981 that London was first championed officially as a multicultural city. Considerable financial resources were devoted to the funding of black and Asian community groups of various kinds and numerous community-specific events, such as St Patrick's Day for the Irish and the Notting Hill Carnival for West Indians, received generous sponsorship. During the five years that Livingstone was in office in the old City Hall located opposite the Houses of Parliament, the GLC became the main promoter of championing diversity. While this was greatly welcomed by many of the capital's various communities, it led to a clash with the Conservative government of Margaret Thatcher, who successfully engineered the abolition of the GLC in 1986. Livingstone himself was subsequently elected to Parliament for one of the ethnically diverse Brent constituencies and later he won election as Mayor of London in both 2000 and 2004 following the creation of that new office. His championing of multiculturalism while Mayor, interestingly, put him on a collision course with Trevor Philipps, a black Labour member of the London (regional) Assembly who went on to become Chairman of the Commission for Racial Equality. While Livingstone continued to trumpet the benefits of celebration of diversity, as indeed he has done in his campaign to win back the Mayoralty in May 2012, Philipps became a strong voice arguing for a political focus on what unites people rather than on what differentiates them.

The London boroughs with the highest level of ethnic minority population were and remain nearly all controlled by Labour or Liberal/Liberal Democrat administrations which accepted the thesis that it is the responsibility of local government to meet the needs of diverse communities rather than expecting everyone to conform to a white Anglo-Saxon norm. These local authorities therefore gave large grants to community-specific organisations and institutions such as sheltered housing for South Asian elderly, black women's self-defence groups, women-only swimming sessions for Muslim girls and so on. Moreover, although English remained and still remains the official language of government in London, service provision in other languages became the norm. Thus in a borough such as Hackney, local government information leaflets were made available in a wide range of languages such as Turkish and Vietnamese, while in Tower Hamlets even some of the street signs are in Bengali as well as in English. A key principle – reinforced in some cases by legislation – adopted by local, regional and national government became accepted that it is the authorities' responsibility to provide services in a wide variety of languages, including interpreters in law courts and hospitals, at public expense. Similarly, schools and other institutions in which a significant proportion of pupils or users were from one particular ethnic or religious minority have been expected to provide appropriate catering, such as kosher or halal meat for Jewish or Muslim children or clients. The deliberate implication of this policy was that all cultures are of equal value and deserve equal respect.

Within a period of 50 years, from 1950 to 2000, the face of London had changed dramatically. Even if most of the historic monuments were still in place, the high streets and markets of the capital had been transformed. Even the lifestyle of indigenous white Londoners was no longer the same. Their eating habits were unrecognisable, not just as a result of a more affluent society spending its growing disposable income in restaurants offering every imaginable element of global cuisine but even in what they ate at home. Chicken *tikka massala* (originating in India) was declared to be Britons' favourite food. Moreover, countless cultural events including theatre, cinema, dance and music introduced Londoners to sights and sounds from all continents. Opinion polls consistently showed that this type of consumer multiculturalism – sometimes derided by Modood and others as 'salsa, samosas and steel-bands' – was hugely popular right across the city's population and indeed was cited by many residents of London as a reason they wanted to live in London, despite the high costs, overcrowded public transport, traffic congestion and so forth.

However, in the first decade of the new millennium the picture became less rosy. Whereas most Londoners were fairly relaxed about Sikh men being given an exemption from having to wear motorcycle helmets because of the religious significance of their long hair and turban, for example, and those schools with a significant number of Muslim girl pupils happily provided an alternative school uniform which was more akin to Islamic concepts of modest dress, there was widespread concern when the late Ayatollah Khomeini issued a *fatwa* against the London-based Indian-born novelist Salman Rushdie, who had to go into prolonged hiding in real fear for his life. Voices began to be raised saying that tolerance should not be a one-way phenomenon. Moreover, the increasingly liberal social consensus amongst white Londoners on moral issues such as LGBT rights – which will culminate in the recognition of gay marriage during the lifetime of the current parliament – was finding itself at odds with the more traditional values espoused by various minority ethnic and religious communities in the capital.

The biggest challenge to the notion of London as a happy rainbow city in which everyone can pursue his or her lifestyle within the diverse patchwork of a multicultural whole came about as a result of the 9/11 attacks in New York and Washington in 2001 and London's own smaller scale but still shocking 7/7 tube and bus bombings in 2005 (Modood 2007). The latter, carried out by British-born Muslims from the north of England, caused considerable soul-searching amongst lawmakers and the media in London. Why would British Asians feel so alienated from British mainstream society that they were prepared to carry out suicide attacks in which the victims would be ordinary members of the public going about their daily business? And did this mean that the American academic Samuel P Huntington was right when he argued that there was going to be an inevitable 'clash of civilisations' between the Islamic world and the West? It was striking how after the 7/7 bombings, the public debate about multiculturalism shifted almost entirely to a discussion about the compatibility of Islamic and 'British' lifestyles, with strong attempts being made by the then Labour Prime Minister Gordon Brown to try to redefine Britishness (summed up by a Conservative predecessor, John Major, in the 1990s as being a love of cricket and warm beer). The senior cleric in the Church of England, the Archbishop of Canterbury, Rowan Williams, unwittingly stoked the fires of the multicultural controversy in 2008 by suggesting that some elements of *shariah* might be unavoidably incorporated into aspects of the Law of Personal Status within Muslim communities in Britain – a statement that was misrepresented in some of the tabloid Press to suggest he had said it was inevitable that Britain would one day be subject to *shariah*. This unfortunately fed into the narrative of some on the right wing of London politics who were arguing that multiculturalism had been a disaster and that far from bringing people together, it was driving them apart.

Such criticisms did not only come from the right. Trevor Philipps's misgivings about normative multiculturalism have already been mentioned. But even before 9/11, a liberal commentator such as the East African Asian journalist Yasmin Alibhai-Brown, who had settled in London 25 years previously, was writing in the Daily Telegraph newspaper in May 2000 that 'multiculturalism is pitting all communities against each other. People who used to think of themselves as black are now retreating into tribal identities – demanding attention and resources for their particular patch. White people have no stake in multiculturalism, either. It is seen as something that black people do. The English are understandably disgruntled that their ethnicity is denied while all other identities – Welsh, Scottish, Hindu, Caribbean and the rest – are celebrated.' (Alibhai-Brown 2000b).

This refrain has been heard at a growing volume within British political discourse. Lentin and Titley (2011) have analysed the rise of racism in our neo-liberal age and London has seen its share of associated conflict. In the 2006 local elections, the British National Party (which amongst other things favours assisted voluntary 'repatriation' of immigrants) won a dozen seats on the local council in the East London borough of Barking and Dagenham, which paradoxically has one of the lowest percentages of non-white residents in the capital. Similarly, a BNP representative was elected to the London Assembly (the current forum of regional government) in 2008. The rise of the BNP in predominantly white working class areas of the city led to the organisation of anti-racist campaigns by a broad coalition of political groups – though spearheaded by the anti-Nazi League – and in the 2008 local elections, the BNP lost almost all its seats. That did not mean the end of overt political campaigning against multiculturalism in London, however. In 2011, there were attempts by a relatively new organisation, the English Defence League (EDL), to hold marches or rallies in areas with a high level of ethnic diversity, notably in Tower Hamlets. Echoing the tactics of far-right groups in countries such as Germany and Belgium, the EDL has particularly highlighted what it sees as the threat of the Islamisation of Britain. It declares Islam to be incompatible with British values and has attempted to stoke Islamophobia, thereby prompting a strong reaction among some Muslim youth.

The current Coalition government of Conservatives and Liberal Democrats at a national level is divided in its views about what should be done. The (Conservative) Prime Minister, David Cameron, speaking at a security conference in Munich in February 2011, stated that he believed multiculturalism had failed in Britain and had actually enabled the radicalisation of young Muslims and the growth of extremism of various kinds. That view was flatly contradicted by the (Liberal Democrat) Deputy Prime Minister Nick Clegg in a speech in Luton shortly afterwards. Not surprisingly, this leaves some government officials somewhat confused. Nonetheless, it is not only politicians who are having second thoughts about multiculturalism, or have concerns about the effects of its implementation. These worries are an increasing feature of related academic discourse as well, as illustrated in the work of Rumy Hasan. One of Dr Hasan's inconvenient truths' (as he calls them) about multiculturalism in Britain is that, in his view, many of the beliefs and cultural/religious practices of religious ethnic minorities are oppressive, especially those affecting women and children and that they are profoundly damaging the lives of many of those now trapped within 'mono-religious, mono-cultural' segregated communities (Hasan 2010). He argues that multiculturalism is in fact a demand for separate rights, exemptions and provisions which, according to Baroness Frances D'Souza, Convenor of the Independent Crossbench Peers in the House of Lords, in her appraisal of his book, 'discourages and even prevents the mixing of peoples; the corollary of which is a high degree of isolation.' (Methuen publicity)

So where does that leave us, in our consideration of the question as to the success or failure of London's model of multiculturalism? Without a doubt, at the national level, Britain is undergoing a serious rethink of how multiculturalism should be implemented, in which greater emphasis will be put on stressing similarities rather than differences. More emphasis will in future be put on ensuring that people living in Britain do learn English. Similarly, immigrants and asylum seekers who wish to apply for British citizenship (which is granted more easily in the UK than in most European states) now have to pass an examination in British history and society. Yet empirical evidence suggests that such changes will be less profound in London than in the rest of the country.

That is partly because the ethnic and religious diversity in London is so much more marked than almost anywhere else in Britain. But there are other factors at play. One is the transience of a significant proportion of London's population, particularly relating to the substantial numbers of other EU nationals, from countries as varied as France, Portugal, Poland and Lithuania, who are able to settle in the UK under EU rules of freedom of movement. A very high percentage of EU migrants base themselves in London, but after a few years go back home, which means that they have less incentive to 'integrate'. Moreover, in London the pressure to integrate – in the sense of speaking English and adopting a British way of life – is far less than in other areas of the country. People living in London on the whole accept that it is a polyglot society and truly cosmopolitan. Indeed, one could maintain that London is now *sui generis*, unlike any other city in the UK. One thing the main party candidates in the Ma 2012 London Mayoral elections agree on is that London is not just the capital of England or the United Kingdom. It is a global city, by definition multicultural, and whoever wins the Mayoralty is determined to build on that. In that sense, it is not far-fetched to conclude that London cannot be a model for other British cities, but it can be a model for other global cities that are developing in different parts of the world. And even if not everyone in London feels multiculturalism has been a success, most have chosen to live or remain there because it is a place to celebrate diversity and enjoy an unparalleled degree of choice.

Bibliography

Alibhai-brown, Y. (2000a) *After Multiculturalism*, London: The Foreign Policy Centre.

Alibhai-brown, Y. (2000b) *Why Multiculturalism Has Failed*, Daily Telegraph, 23 May 2000

Baumann, G. (1999) *The Multicultural Riddle*, London: Routledge.

Crick, B. (2000) *Essays on Citizenship*, London: Continuum.

Hasan, R. (2010) *Multiculturalism: Some Inconvenient Truths*, London: Methuen.

Keith, M. (2005) *After the Cosmopolitan: Multicultural Cities and the Future of Racism*, London: Routledge.

Kymlicka, W. (1995) *Multicultural Citizenship*, Oxford: Oxford University Press.

Lentin, A. & Titley, G. (2011) *The Crises of Multiculturalism*, London: Zed Books.

Mahamdllie, H. [ed.] (2011) *Defending Multiculturalism*, London: Bookmarks.

Modood, T. (2007) *Multiculturalism*, Cambridge: Polity Press.

Modood, T. (2012) *Post-Immigration 'Difference' and Integration*, London: The British Academy.

Oakland, J. (2011) *British Civilization: An Introduction*, London: Routledge

Parekh, B. (2000) *Rethinking Multiculturalism: Cultural Diversity and Political Theory*, Basingstoke, Macmillan

Philipps M. & T. (1998) *Windrush: The Irresistible Rise of Multi-Racial Britain*, London: HarperCollins.

Sardar, Z. (2004) *Beyond Difference: Cultural Relations in the New Century*, London: British Council.

Taylor, C. (1994) *Multiculturalism*, Princeton: Princeton University Press.

Thomas, C. (2004) *Life and Death in London's East End: 2000 Years of Spitalfields*, London: Molas.

Unity and Diversity in a London Mosque

Judy Shuttleworth[101]

Introduction

I will draw on material from an ethnographic study of a mosque whose congregation is made up of worshippers from different ethnic and cultural communities with different conceptions of being Muslim. From the outside such congregations can appear homogeneous. Indeed Muslims may sometimes seek to convey an image of homogeneity. I want to look at the internal differences in this mosque, they way in which they are lived out and the implications this has for engagement with others within the wider society.

The mosque in question is a small community-based organisation, entirely funded by its membership but open to all local Muslims. The mosque is the product of the 50 year long post-migration experience of a group of Muslims who came to the UK from Guyana while the congregation it attracts now includes worshippers from a number of other groups who differ culturally and ethnically and who migrated to the UK more recently. The official mosque imams and those that preach on Fridays are also from a range of ethnic and cultural backgrounds while English is the common language of the mosque.

Layers of Difference

The group that built the mosque think of themselves as coming to the UK from a religiously, culturally and ethnically diverse society to which their grandparents and great grandparents originally migrated from the Indian sub-continent in the 19th century. In the second half of the 20th century there was a second migration to the UK where they have maintained contact with fellow migrants from their community, not only Muslims but also Christian and Hindu Guyanese, retaining

---

101 Judy Shuttleworth is a Consultant Child and Adolescent Psychotherapist at the Tavistock and Portman NHS Trust (a higher education institute) and the Whittington Health NHS Trust. Her first degree was in Social Anthropology. She trained as a child and adolescent psychotherapist and her career has been as a clinician and clinical teacher within child and family mental health services in the National Health Service. In order to pursue an interest in the social and cultural context of the families she were seeing within her clinical practice she took a MSc in Medical Anthropology in 2005 at University College London. She subsequently registered for a PhD at the London School of Economics. Her fieldwork was in local mosque and her focus is on the communal life of the congregation. She continues to work as a child psychotherapist in the paediatric department of a general hospital and as clinical teacher in a mental health training and research centre.

what they describe as a multi-cultural identity and a conscious espousal of the value of having, within their shared memory, a society of origin that contained within itself a measure of diversity. The congregation were later joined by Mauritian Muslims whose pattern of migration has some similarity with that of the Guyanese. By contrast some groups who attend this mosque are from the more homogeneously Muslim societies of Pakistan, Bangladesh, North Africa and Somalia. There are two distinct dimensions in which ethnic and cultural difference is operating here – firstly, the complexity of Guyanese society as part of the life experience of older Guyanese that remains active as a unifying idea within their community in the present and secondly, the ethnic, cultural and religious complexity of the congregation, with the twist that many of these groups have within *their* life experience a more homogeneous idea of a Muslim society.

Another source of difference within the congregation is that between traditional ways of living a Muslim life handed on as implicit knowledge within family and community and those for whom religion has become as an object of more explicit knowledge. It is argued in a volume edited by Salvatore and Eickelman (2004) and by Bowen (2004) that one of the consequences of large scale migration and globalised communication has been a greater awareness of the reality of Muslim diversity and with it the emergence of a self-conscious perspective and the desire for a renewed grounding in the text of religious revelation. These implicit and explicit forms of religious knowledge may exist side by side within a congregation, or within an individual's experience, as part of an internally complex whole, but there is a potential conflict between these two currents, between traditional and text-based Islam. Within the mosque there are classes in which some individuals seek to learn about Islam but this creates tensions within them and their families around traditional forms of religious practice that may now be seen as man made, cultural elaborations of divine revelation.

For those who use the mosque, it is potentially both a physical place of prayer and a social and emotional resource. However, this latter, involves accepting the reality of ethnic, cultural and religious diversity within the congregation with all its impingements – the mosque as it really is. While the sermons at the mosque often address the external difficulties of living alongside others in the wider non-Muslim society, the diversity within the congregation is rarely acknowledged. That such experiences are inherently difficult is referred to in an ayah in the Qur'an (49:13) on the purposive creation of a diverse humanity, as translated by Abdullah Yusuf Ali, 'that ye may know each other (and not despise each other)'. This idea of knowing implies a measure of anxiety and risk, if only to our preconceived ideas about ourselves, and the need for a strong enough context in which knowing each other can grow over time. The mosque I am describing may be seen as providing such a context, a container in which different ways of being Muslim can come into sustained contact, despite the upset this may cause.

The Mosque as a Context for 'Knowing' About Difference, Internally and Externally

This relatively new, purpose built mosque stands in a busy street at the point where 19th century residential housing gives way to small shops and light industrial buildings. Nearby are churches and small cultural centres that reflect the diverse ethnic composition of the local community. As well as a place for collective prayer, the mosque also functions partly as a community centre for the Guyanese, both those living locally and the more geographically dispersed. A more diverse group of individuals drawn from the different cultures and ethnicities within the wider congregation have since joined them, feeling they share something of the same vision. Celebrations of life events and gatherings to pray for the sick and those who have died take place here. There are links with two local hospitals so that the needs of Muslim patients can be appropriately met and there are thoughts about building a centre for Muslim elderly. A number of different Muslim groups use the mosque for religious classes for both adults and children. There are collections from time to time at the mosque in support of Islamic educational institutions both in the UK and abroad and to raise funds for the Palestinians.

As well as meeting the needs of its congregation and making links with a wider Muslim world, the Trustees of the mosque also see themselves as part of UK society through participation in the local borough, through community open days at the mosque, events at which the Police, local authority services and voluntary groups speak or have stalls. Local schools make educational visits and their pictures and thank you letters are on the wall. The mosque is represented, along with other community and religious groups, at the local ceremony to mark Remembrance Sunday, a day when the dead of the armed forces are publicly remembered. The mosque has been active over many years, through different styles of community participation, but keeping such events and networks going, even when attendance is disappointing, means doggedly pursuing the aim of wider community engagement.

The current mosque started with the use of a room in a private house. The energy and imagination that has sustained this endeavour over half a century has its roots in Guyana and the experience of successful mosque building that took place there among earlier generations but the development hasn't always been smooth. In the past a number of internal rifts took place driven by personal differences and the attraction of a charismatic form of Islam within another community in the UK. The challenges around different conceptions of Islam continue. When the group first acquired a non-residential building in the 1980's (an industrial building that had been used as a synagogue) and established a mosque open to all rather than remaining a private organisation open only to their own community, some members of the original community resisted this development fearing that it would deprive them of a place in which they felt comfortable. Creating a space open to all Muslims has indeed meant that many who use the mosque for the collective ritual of Friday prayer would not share the same perspective on a range of religious and social matters. Simply at the level of dress there are indications of difference with respect to ethnicity, styles of engagement in UK society and the debates about Islamic renewal. While these differences can appear to be submerged within the collective practice of prayer, some do mount explicit challenges to the mosque leadership.

This raises questions as to how far these different perspectives can co-exist. The issue is partly sidestepped because, outside of the main rituals, there are several parallel user groups that do not necessarily mix. There is a distinction between those who attend the mosque on Fridays, Ramadan and major festivals and those who join in other mosque events, religious practices which are associated with the Islamic traditions of those who built the mosque, fund-raising activities, open days, study circles and lectures. The mosque is open during the week for collective and private prayer but those who use it are for the most part male. While older women and women with young children attend Friday prayers in quite large numbers, for those in work or full time education attendance is limited to major festivals, evening and weekend events. Despite this, Friday prayer overflows with male worshippers who work locally are not in employment or who are retired. This causes some conflict over the division of the space between men and women. The women have a large prayer balcony that is integrated into the main design and looks down on the male prayer space so that they can directly hear the imam and, from some points on the balcony, can see what is happening, which is not the case in other mosques I have visited nearby. While prayer is gender segregated, other areas and other activities are not. This reflects the culture of the group who built and continue to run the mosque, among whom women are active and visible but this does not go unchallenged by more conservatively religious men and women.

Since opening the doors to others, the mosque leadership have had to work hard to protect the mosque as a place where their community would feel comfortable to pray and to socialise. They are conscious of coming from the periphery of the Islamic world and have at times felt judged insufficiently Muslim by those who saw themselves as nearer the centre of Arabic speaking Islam. Yet over the years the mosque has attracted a large and diverse congregation as well as the long-standing commitment of individuals from other groups living locally precisely because, despite their very different home cultures, they, as individuals, share the sensibilities of the Guyanese, particularly with respect to gender mixing and their involvement with the wider non-Muslim society. However the impression now is of a group whose communal and religious identity is squeezed between the religious traditions of recent migrant groups living in the immediate area of the mosque and the theological currents of Islamic renewal. So far these tensions have been contained within the structures of the mosque and a commitment to multiculturalism, rooted as much in their home society as in any ideas within wider UK society, yet they remain deeply serious and contested matters.

Encounters with Difference

Though few women at the mosque wear the *nikaab* those that do stand out and I am aware that some of these women were previously wearing less strict forms of dress. This transformation is indicative of a particular kind of religious development that is inherently difficult to maintain contact with from the outside. Thus for example I first met one young women as a stylishly, colourfully dressed Muslim woman working in the media and was somewhat surprised to learn that she had only given up Western clothes a few weeks earlier. When I met her again following a gap during which she married and had a child, she was dressed entirely in black and with her face covered, even on the prayer balcony. We had spoken freely in the past as I used to give her a lift in my car to a gender-mixed Muslim study group we both attended. I felt she was interested then in what I thought and I, in turn, felt able to ask her questions. Now these sorts of conversations were impossible as she felt that this openness to different kinds of thinking was not helpful in finding the correct path that would lead her to paradise. As she put it to me, 'You have to understand there is only one right way'. Although it coincided with her marriage and her leaving the world of work, I don't have any reason to doubt that it was her own choice or rather one that her view of God's will imposed on her but it was a choice that radically restricted a more fluid and reciprocal contact with difference in others, both Muslim and non-Muslim. She now attended a women only group in another mosque.

A more public and on-going encounter between different ways of being Muslim emerges at the mosque particularly during those events that are religious, attracting a gathering from across the congregation, but are not part of the main ritual of prayer. Such events take place in the hall adjoining the mosque that is now used as an all-purpose space for semi-religious and social events. The communal meal served during weekends in Ramadan combines the ordinary evening prayers, the additional prayers and recitations of Ramadan with a social event – the meal. Here the food is cooked and served by a gender - mixed gathering drawn from the Guyanese and Mauritian community and some individuals, male and female, from other ethnic groups, who have joined them in these events over the years. When

I first arrived the meal was served in the hall with men and women separated but visible to one another. For prayer the men departed to the main mosque and the women mostly stayed in the hall with younger and female children. In recent years, partly because of the increased numbers it has been necessary to draw screens across the hall during prayer to allow some of the men to pray there. The screens are then drawn back for the meal. However there have started to be demands, mostly from men but occasionally from women, for the screens to remain *in situ* during the meal. How far this is because the ethnic/cultural composition of the congregation is changing and how far it is part of an increased concern with issues of religious orthodoxy is unclear but it is strongly resisted by those who run the mosque. Thus one of the Guyanese women on the Board of Trustees asked if I had noticed the argument she had just had to deal with. It arose from the demand from one man for complete segregation during the meal - that the curtain drawn during prayer should remain drawn. She was shaking and clearly very upset. She said that he had threatened that if this didn't happen he would lead others in a walk out from the mosque. She had apparently insisted that the curtains remain drawn back for the meal explaining to me that if they gave in over this it would be another demand next time. The mosque caretaker who, just to add to the complexity, belongs to the same ethnic group as the complainer, came and asked if she was alright. She said she was but went on to explain to me that if he, and those who thought like he did, had their way she would not be in the mosque at all, none of the women would. They would all be at home.

The mosque is a physical space in which men and women with different cultural expectations and religious outlooks feel impinged on by the perceptions and needs of one another. For the conservatively religious male the mosque is their space and women can and should prayer at home. One might ask why they do not seek out a mosque more aligned to their views and no doubt this is partly to do with location but the congregation continues to expand though there are other mosques within a short bus ride. For the women the situation is clearer. They come to the mosque in large numbers, not only those from the main ethnic group, but also from groups who have come to the UK from societies where women were excluded from the mosque. Those women who would not come to a gender mixed event appreciate the women's prayer balcony and the facilities offered for young children. The mosque is to be expanded soon and some of the tension generated simply by the pressure of numbers may then decrease but serious differences of view are present within the congregation and it is a matter of uncertainty as to how far this can be contained as part of a continuing communal experience with the potential for mutual 'knowing' of one another.

The Space Created by an Awareness of Different Perspectives

There would certainly be a view within the mosque, expressed not only by sections of the congregation but also by some of the imams and teachers, that this dispute over the place of women is a cultural tradition for which there is no basis in the Qur'an and the practice of the Prophet. However such a view is not easily assimilated into a Muslim identity based in tradition rather than text. While a proper understanding of the text is the aspiration of some individuals within the congregation it would mean either a dependence on translations, and therefore a pre-interpreted text, or knowledge of Qur'anic Arabic among groups who do not at present know the language. Moreover if you have grown up with an implicit interpretation of your faith handed on through family life, it is not easy to adopt a different perspective and any change of practice that comes through study groups may be felt by those close to you as a criticism or a rejection.

Although in the early centuries of Islam different traditions of scholarship grew up in relation to one another, presuming a space for legitimate difference between them, over time it has become the norm for different ethnic groups to follow only one tradition of interpretation and often without awareness that this is the case, thus removing the original dynamic relationship between different scholarly opinions. As one woman in a class said, 'I just thought I was Muslim. I didn't realise I was Hanbali'. While reinstating the internal dynamic between schools of interpretation, as one Guyanese teacher in the mosque seeks to do, might allow a more complex internal debate that can't be equated with the image of different cultural traditions living alongside one another tolerating and enjoying each other's way of life. What is at stake in a religious perspective is a particular understanding of God's plan for mankind and how it is to be followed. This poses a challenge to the view that there is value in an engagement from different perspectives so that the fact that my presence was tolerated at all within the mosque was itself part of its internal diversity.

Although both sides in the dispute about the Ramadan meal would invoke the Qur'an in a general way, the disagreement is more rooted in the taken for granted nature of habitual life experiences, what Bourdieu called the *habitus* (1972). Being held out of awareness, we are not only shaped but limited in our capacity to understand by these same experiences. The point was used by a Guyanese man to produce a sympathetic understanding of others who had challenged him about attending a church funeral..

> As you know we have a lot of friends...not only Muslim. And not only friends but family. In their belief (those with whom he was in dispute) if a

non-Muslim passed away you can go to the home and pay your respects but
you can't go to the burial ground or to the church…its *haraam*, forbidden.
…. But I have been to several churches and cremations and so on and I cannot
see for the love of God what I would be doing wrong…this is a dear friend
who has passed away. ……. Probably they don't have non-Muslim friends
or family so maybe it's straightforward for them but for us it is different.…
Apart from that I grew up with people of different faiths…in fact for me
with neighbours of different faiths… it's helped me tremendously in my life.

For this man the diversity within his social group and the human commitments
such relationships entail may make his situation complicated but also has the
potential to deepen his knowledge of others.

Collective Experiences and Images of Unity

Though there are minor differences which get discussed in the classes, the
overwhelming sense during congregational prayer is of a group attuned together
to the 'music' of the Qur'an and the choreography of the movements of prayer
established by the Prophet. The architecture and decoration of the prayer space in
this mosque undoubtedly increases the sense of the beauty of prayer as the sounds
rise up through the darkness of a winter evening into the domed space with its
chandelier. Here the experience for the individual, both participant and observer, is
of a direct bodily and emotional phenomena rather than one mediated by language
and concepts from within a particular tradition of thought or part of a conscious
attempt to convey a particular point of view. Charles Hirschkind has written about
this direct, psychosomatic, level of religious experience in his study of the impact of
listening to tape sermons (Hirschkind 2006 pp.67-104). However the experience
of Friday prayers creates not only a direct bodily experience of sharing a sense of
focused coherence but also, through transformation into language, an explicit ***idea***
of a united Muslim community stretching across national and ethnic boundaries,
the *umma*.

The idea of unity invoked in the sermons is often detached from its grounding in
religious practice and re-presented as an idealised image, at odds with the complexity
of lived experience and the mundane human realities that surround ritual. Like the
jostling on the stairs to get a place to pray in the mosque, all such religious rituals
have, of necessity, a material and emotional human context that has to be managed.
The conflicts that arose regularly around the issue of health and safety with some
people feeling that their right to pray overrode the fact that the mosque was now
completely full, left those responsible for the mosque to cope as best they could
by eventually closing the doors and accepting the opprobrium. This is about more
than mere domestic arrangements. Even in sermons that seek to use experiences of
the *umma* at prayer or on the hajj for religious inspiration, the surrounding realities

may be recognised and found a place or disallowed and exported. For instance, some sermons would direct the attention of the congregation to failures within the *umma* and the need for God's forgiveness and help but others locate the problem in the outside world of governments who divide the hajj pilgrims by nationality, or seek to generate a sense of unity by describing all Muslims as the same and in contrast to all non-Muslims. One sermon at the mosque acknowledged that the wording of the Qur'an's injunction to modest dress meant that its current manifestations were subject to different scholarly interpretations. However the preacher went on to insist that, as no woman wore the *niqaab* except in seeking to follow her religion, Muslims should not voice their differences but rather support her. One can well understand the sense of external threat that might drive this impulse to close ranks but in fostering an idealised illusion of unity among believers, it denies space for the obvious and legitimate reality of differences between Muslims and the need to *know* these differences.

Developing a Space for Difference Within the Individual

One class I attended was led by a teacher who had been born in rural Guyana. After a long struggle to teach himself Arabic he went to study in Saudi Arabia but left to move to the UK where he now works in the health service and, on a voluntary basis, as a freelance imam. His theological position is at odds with most of the Guyanese in that he draws a clear distinction between what has grown up as part of culture and that which is revealed in the Qur'an and the practice of the Prophet. At the same time he maintains a commitment to gender equality and an active engagement with non-Muslims. His class attracts women from across the whole spectrum of ethnic groupings within the congregation and, within context of commitment built up by attendance over time, the problematic nature of our response to difference could sometimes be explored as a common human failing. While Islam promotes an idea of unity across ethnic divisions it was recognised that in reality individuals identified primarily with their own ethnic group and that moreover there was a sense of ethnic hierarchy in the minds of some Muslims, in which the Guyanese felt themselves to be at the bottom. In reply to a comment that 'people say there are 72 forms of Islam and only one is correct' the Guyanese teacher said 'I don't like talking about "the one" because everyone thinks they are "the one" (that is correct)'. Although this teacher had a particularly clear sense of how one should use a knowledge of Qur'anic Arabic to understand what God wants, he also spoke of the need to develop 'a thinking mind' that could reflect on the sources of difficulty as lying within our own need to follow others, whether parents or new spiritual leaders, and our impulse to abrogate the difficult responsibility of thinking for oneself. From his perspective only knowledge gained through active personal study, rather than passed on by parents, absorbed as hearsay or through TV, could offer an appropriate foundation for being Muslim. Rather than a primarily emotional response to the image of a united *umma,* there was an attempt to acknowledge and struggle with the gap between the form of life revealed through the Qur'an and embodied in the life the Prophet and the reality of one's own life.

A paradox was often voiced in the class by those who felt it was easier to practice Islam in the UK than in their home countries. While I sometimes thought this might be a friendly gesture towards me, I came to feel it was expressing a particular, if puzzling, reality. Those who had migrated as adults, and who only started to practice and learn about their religion after they had come to the UK, might be saying that they experienced a greater need for their religion in the midst of all the losses associated with migration and that they valued this need to think more deeply. However some cited problems in practising their religion while visiting Muslim majority societies where the religious practice differed or where the general level of religious observance had declined. In these latter situations it seemed they were saying that they felt it was more difficult to practice in the presence of less observant Muslims than among non-Muslim colleagues at work or college in the UK.

The idea of religious knowledge and practice as a private and individual responsibility for which account would have to be given on the Last Day, though more consonant with the position of religion in the West, is not without its difficulties for the religiously committed in a pluralistic society. While some people may feel this gives them the space to make a private accommodation with the exacting demands of religious practice, for others it increases the aspiration to piety as well an anxiety about personal failure. Thus, at her parents' suggestion, one young woman sought advice during a class about a formal event at her work at which alcohol would be served. She had spoken to her manager who suggested she just avoid the alcohol but participate in the event and the teacher and others in the group seemed inclined to agree with this solution. However the young woman herself felt that her understanding of the Qur'an and the life of the Prophet led her to feel she must not attend the event at all. Later she was troubled that the matter had created a bit of an atmosphere at work. This was in marked contrast to a similar account I heard in another group from a young man who felt that his presence, but conspicuous abstinence from alcohol, during such occasions was a source of serious interest to others.

Despite the apparent contrast, both these individuals were actively engaged in thinking about the complications of their own positions within the workforce and wider society and were involved with groups that encouraged this. The real contrast is between the desire to withdraw from contact with difference and the struggle to build a context that is sufficiently robust and enduring over time for differences and disagreements to be contained and managed within it. For some this mosque provides such a context but to different degrees and in different ways. For the Guyanese, the Mauritians and others who feel at home there, it provides a place for prayer, education, sociability and wider community involvement. Others within the same congregation, while continuing to attend, nonetheless seek to re-create something more culturally familiar to them or to create, with like-minded others, new exacting standards of religious observance.

Bibliography

Bourdieu, P. (1979) *Outline of a Theory of Practice,* New York: Cambridge University Press.

Bowen, J. (2004) 'Does French Islam Have Borders? Dilemmas of Domestication in a Global Religious Field', in *American Anthropologist,* 106(1), pp.43-55.

Hirschkind, C. (2006) *Ethical Soundscapes,* New York: Columbia University Press

Salvatore, A. and Eickelman, D. (eds) (2004*) Public Islam and the Common Good.* Leiden: Brill.